EXTINCTION
OR
SURVIVAL?

The Dilemmas of Our Technological Existence

M.J. TURNER

ARDMORE PUBLISHING
Sidney, British Columbia

Copyright 1996 by M.J. Turner
First Printing

Published in 1996 by
Ardmore Publishing
875 Ardmore Drive, RR2
Sidney BC, Canada, V8L 5G2

Canadian Cataloguing in Publication Data
Turner, M.J. (Margaret Janice), 1935-
 Extinction or survival?

Includes bibliographical references and index
 ISBN 0-9680850-0-8

1. Overpopulation. 2. Technology and civilization 3.
Environmental degradation I.Title.
HB871.T87 1996   363.9'1   C96-910406-5

Printed in Canada on recycled paper

ACKNOWLEDGEMENTS

This book is dedicated to my mother and my aunt who asked all the right questions which needed answering. Their questions led me to this rather wide-ranging analysis of the environmental and technological complexities threatening our existence. It is not the typical in-depth study of modern environmental degradation, followed by pages of physical solutions. Nor does it tell the reader how to get involved locally in cleaning up the environment. That has been done many times. Instead I chose to try for a broader understanding of the many political, economic and cultural dilemmas so ingrained in our evolution through constant destructive exploitation of the environment. A growing sense of pessimism has led me to believe that we must prepare ourselves for a very chaotic, dangerous future.

I am very grateful to Heather Carlini who led me through the tangled route of self-publishing and marketing. Many thanks must go to Lynne Wright for her hours of generous help and her computer expertise in making the manuscript camera-ready for the printer. To Dr. Cy Hampson, who always believed in my ideas and told me so often that this is a book that must be read by everyone, my deepest gratitude for encouraging me to see the project through to the end. Above all thanks to my husband who constantly kept me supplied with pertinent articles and news item and who so graciously accepted the many hours I spent researching and writing over the years.

TABLE OF CONTENTS

FOREWORD

We all face death whether we die in small numbers or in the masses. Death is present daily in many guises from gentle collapse to violent death by torture or starvation. We have faced it in its worst forms in the past and continue to meet its widening horrors in the present. The natural forces of species' annihilation could not bring us physical suffering more difficult than what we have already experienced through self-imposed atrocities or through the natural catastrophes we have endured throughout our tenure on earth.

Yet our will to survive as a species and our belief that we will not be denied the future remains strong within us. These are the human forces of mind and body that draw us back from the abyss and give us the hope and faith that move us on into the future. Therefore, we do not fear the loss of our individual lives, for death is the natural conclusion to all life; but we do fear the extinction of our entire species. We fear the loss of our immortality through the loss of future generations; we fear the loss of humanity as thinking, creative beings with vast accumulations of knowledge and technology; we fear the loss of all that our civilizations have recorded and all the future dreams we hold of even greater accomplishments. Our emotions are stirred by thoughts of what heights humanity has yet to reach. It is our will to live, to dominate and to conquer which promotes the fears we have of our own extinction.

But such fears exist within our minds only; our survival has no meaning beyond its value to ourselves. In the scheme of the universe, our disappearance would be of no consequence. We have come to realize in very recent times that the earth is not the center of the universe, but one small floating object in an eternity of space, time and matter.

In the 21st Century we will have reached a crossroads in our evolutionary existence that gives us only two choices: Extinction or Survival. In making the purview of our survival our own in the belief that we can "manage" this earth to fulfil even the most destructive aspects of our dreams, we may have taken over full responsibility for our extinction...

INTRODUCTION

Hypothesis: Having Taken Over Our Survival, We May Have Set In Motion Our Own Timetable for Extinction

INTRODUCTION

Hypothesis: Having Taken Over Our Survival, We May Have Set In Motion Our Own Timetable for Extinction

Easter Island, a small volcanic island lost in midPacific, is a desolate place, without trees, streams or lakes and covered with rough, parched grasses. Only a few planted shrubs and trees dot the coastal fringe. Looking out to sea, great monolithic statues stand guard over the ghosts of a vanished civilization.

Recently the island gave up its secrets as scientific and archaeological studies traced the rise and decline of the people who carved those statues. Through the examination of hundreds of skeletons and the stories and DNA of the few surviving descendants, it was possible to piece together the major events of 500-600 years of a progressive "Stone Age" civilization.[1]

In 980 A.D., a band of people on rafts or in canoes reached Easter Island and chose to settle it. Sediments and pollens found in a small dry lake bed disclosed that when they first arrived, the island was covered with a rich, tropical forest of 20 different species of trees. Birds, animals, nuts and fruits had flourished in abundance for over 30,000 years. Further examination of the pollens proved that many of the species had been useful to the new settlers. In the beginning it was a paradise.

Over the centuries the Easter Islanders cut down large patches of trees, then burned over the areas to remove the natural vegetation and plant crops. They consumed the trees as fuel to cook their foods, logs to build their houses and lumber to manufacture their canoes. For clothing "the bark of the paper mulberry was used to make tapa cloth"[2] and the fibers of coconut palm were woven into ropes and fish nets. Eventually trees were cut to move the heavy stone statues which the people had carved to honer their gods and protect their island.

Food supplies consisted of crops grown from the plants and seeds they had brought with them. Nuts and wild fruits harvested from the forest and fish caught from large schools which once inhabited the coastal waters of the island rounded out their diets. Survival was relatively easy. Over the next few centuries their numbers multiplied dramatically, peaking at about 8000, and all totally dependent on the carrying capacity of an island only 35 miles in circumference.

The appearance of the giant monoliths which dot the island, carved between the 14th and 17th Centuries, parallel the destruction of the forests when the population was at its highest. Perhaps the lack of work for so many on this tiny, overcrowded land base may have been reason enough to conceive of such a momentous task as moving these huge monuments, requiring much labour and many long wooden poles to move the stones. Without metal tools or wheels to aid them in the work, "a crew of 20 men would take almost a year to create each one. The manpower required to move one of these statues is estimated to have taken another crew of about the same size many months"[3] Was it a ruse by the leaders to keep the "unemployed" busy and docile? We may soon find our modern nations putting their people to work building useless monoliths as tens of millions roam the earth in search of work and a sense of purpose.

But the bounties of the island, once so prolific, were only sufficient to sustain a relatively small population indefinitely. As their numbers grew, they cut down more and more of the trees. Within a few centuries wood for building houses, constructing fishing canoes and moving statues were in short supply. As in tropical areas, it is the trees which produce the soil, carry the nutrients and store the moisture among their roots. Removing the forest bared the thin layer of volcanic soil to the elements. Exposed to an annual rainfall of 56 inches, the scanty layer of soil was easily leached in heavy downpours through the porous volcanic rock and into the sea. The cleared farmland began to suffer chronic drought, caused by the sweeping winds which dried the land quickly after every rainfall. The soil and fresh water flowing into the sea contaminated the shore waters and drove away the fish. Rough grasses replaced the natural vegetation.

Eroded, exhausted and infertile, the remaining soil produced smaller and smaller crops. Fish, forced away from shore by polluted water and eroding soil, were disappearing and no longer an available supply of protein. The few remaining wild nuts and fruits were eaten in desperation, leaving none to regenerate new growth. Poor diets debilitated health, strength and endurance. Hunger stalked the islanders.

A once flourishing civilization was rapidly declining into warfare and anarchy. The "rich" or small privileged class of the island, known as the Long Ears for the heavy ornaments they wore which stretched their ears almost to their shoulders, decided to test the weakening endurance of the Short Ears who comprised the bulk of the population. In demanding the Short Ears clear the land by throwing the many scattered volcanic rocks into the sea, the Long Ears found themselves in a war with the "masses". To protect themselves they built trenches, then filled them with logs and brush which they would set afire should the Short Ears attack them. Betrayed by a servant's signal to the Short Ears that they were asleep, the Long Ears were attacked during the night. All but one were killed. Anarchy followed. The Short Ears broke up into tribes, warring against each other and destroying the remaining resources and croplands with fire.

Working in the fields became both dangerous and degrading once the class system was destroyed. The ruling elite were no longer present to give order and purpose to the society. Shrinking food supplies dwindled even further as the tribes wrecked vengeance on each other's property, burning crops and houses. For nearly two hundred years the conflicts raged. Spurred on by warrior religions in which the gods were militaristic and blood thirsty, the survivors fought battles over the few remaining resources and food supplies. Famine, religious anarchy and cannibalism emerged. Sacred objects were desecrated. Earthquakes aided in toppling several of the great statues.

The Islanders turned their anger on their original gods, blaming them for their situation, believing the gods had deserted them, and in turn, unleashing that anger on each other in battles to the death. They could no longer survive; nor could they escape from the island.

They had ignored the realities of what was happening to their environment. Centuries of living well at the expense of the island's natural resources had blinded them to the growing threats overpopulation and environmental destruction were to their continued survival. They had failed to protect and conserve their resources. Most of all they had let their populations grow far beyond the carrying capacity of the island. Their water and food resources had all but run out, forcing them to seek new sources. But they had failed to prepare for this eventuality in that they had destroyed their only means of escape, --the trees with which they might have built seaworthy canoes. Trapped by their own undoing and shortsightedness, they perished from a collapsed environment and an unwinnable struggle to survive.

In their final tragic stage, Peruvian ships visited the island about 1860 A.D., seizing and carrying off into slavery the remaining leaders and strong, young men of the community. Only fifteen returned years later, sick with smallpox and tuberculosis. The epidemics they brought with them decimated the already dwindling population, leaving only a few hundred survivors on the island out of the thousands that once lived there.

The years of anarchy and conflict had taken their toll. When the Europeans came to offer help to replant the vegetation of the island with trees and new seeds, those islanders who had survived proved unwilling to work at replacing the trees or growing food. They chose instead to eat the imported animals, seeds and tubers rather than build walls to protect the seedlings and creatures from the winds. A few emigrated to other islands on foreign vessels. Today, only 36 families in the world can claim they are descended from Easter Islanders.

This story has repeated itself many times in the disappearance of former civilizations: overpopulation, destruction of the soils, forests and water reserves, warfare over deteriorating food and water supplies, all leading to religious and racial genocide for possession of remaining resources. The one crucial difference is that the people of most other disappearing civilizations could walk away from their destroyed environments and begin again. But the Easter Islanders had no means of crossing the ocean to find new land to begin again. Are we, like they, trapped on this small "island" planet without sufficient means of survival and afloat in an uninhabitable universe from which there is no escape?

The experience of the Easter Islanders sets the stage for the major hypothesis of this book: When human populations grow beyond nature's limited abilities to nurture them, they establish their own parameters for survival. By doing so, humanity also assumes responsibility for its own timetable of extinction. The Easter Islanders took control of their expansion and extinction when they settled the island and began to dismantle it, just as Homo sapiens initiated the extinction process of our species when they began settling the land to domesticate crops and animals 10,000 years ago. In relinquishing nature's evolutionary parameters for our own, the timetable for human survival is now forfeit to the speed at which our populations and technologies overwhelm and destroy the earth's carrying capacity.

At this point in our evolution, we are struggling to see whether or not we have the ability to manage those parameters wisely, for along the way we have treated nature more as an "enemy" to be conquered and exploited without redress, when we should have made her our guide and teacher. The length of our "stay" is now dependent on the speed with which we overwhelm and destroy our "enemy". In so doing we have forgotten that there can be no rectifying our destruction of a "defeated" nature. Ultimately, we are still subject to natural laws and the environmental forces which control survival and extinction.

By natural law species always reproduce to the maximum, their numbers rising and falling with the quantity of available food supply. To ensure survival of species in nature, limiting factors must be present that will maintain a balance between fertility rates and death rates and allow a species to continue in a healthy, viable state within the carrying capacity of a given territory. Many built in controls, --infertility, gene superiority and reproductive seniority within a social group, a lack of "nesting" space, disease, physical injury, disabilities, starvation and predation-- also help maintain a balance between species' populations and territorial carrying capacity. Our human species is no exception to the law of maximum reproduction as our exploding populations show; but through our technologies we have reduced nature's built in controls and lowered the natural attrition rates that would normally maintain a viable balance between the death rates and the fertility rates appropriate to environmental carrying capacity as experienced by all other species.

Although natural laws of survival and death still control human existence to some degree, our technologies have aided in sustaining far larger numbers of humans in any given territory, regardless of its natural carrying capacity. Domesticating and distributing crops and animal protein in quantities much beyond the needs of the individual producer has not only fed more people per acre of land, but it has gradually freed the majority of people to use their energies in tasks other than food production.

As a consequence over the past 10,000 years populations have grown from a basically two-tiered society of landed aristocracy and peasant farmers and craftsmen to evolve into a many-tiered society whose populations are concentrated in urban areas. This change has occurred or is occurring almost without exception worldwide. The efficiency and production of technologies have made farm labour almost totally redundant in the major crop producing countries, while ensuring a constant flow of food to the cities. The result is unprecedented urban industrial growth and the displacement of millions of rural people forced to migrate to the urban areas in search of work.

With the aid of a large brain, an upright body and the universal use of language which facilitated our technological development, we must credit our survival and expansion as a species to the constantly evolving benefits and improvements our technologies have given us. They continue to move us forward in great leaps over smaller and smaller periods of time. The last 10,000 years multiplied our development manyfold over the previous 100,000 and the last 100,000 brought developments that far outpace and outweigh the progress of the previous 5 million years. Even more spectacular have been the technological advances of the last thousand years, only to be outdone many times by the progress of the 20th Century, ending with the unprecedented leaps of knowledge and invention of the last 30 years. Present changes and technological developments are now coming so rapidly, they are outpacing our global ability to cope with the quantity and abundance of new materials, new technologies for collecting and dispensing information and the chemical and industrial output which raise our living standards, not from century to century, but from month to month, or even day to day.

The extent of our technological progress has had wide impact, above all, permitting the "explosion" of populations around the world. Technologies have enabled us to eliminate or bring under control most fatal diseases and have aided in medical advances which now repair the majority of physical deformities and damage to the body that are the result of disease or accident.

Natural aggression has been largely contained and redirected into productive activities through imposed laws of civilizations. Religions have given an excessively large dose of sanctity to the value of human life, preventing most acts of neglect or violence against the individual. Of course, there are many exceptions to these conditions within democratic as well as oppressive political states as the history of human violence and warfare attests. The evolution of highly sophisticated transportation technologies has enabled civilizations to find their commodities in every part of the world, unfortunately creating its own dangerous phenomenon. The more access we have gained to every part of the world, the more we have degraded the environment to sate our bodies with every kind of edible food and physical convenience we could invent. The practice continues and expands as technologies improve and populations grow.

Television and transportation are building a desire for "luxury" commodities among the "have nots" throughout the poor and developing countries of the world. More and more nations are industrializing to supply this demand, while the entrepreneurs fulfil their desire for more profits and nations create jobs. This is a precedent in technological development whose inherent dangers are spurned by governments and business interests alike. They refuse to let the destruction of the environment and its eco-systems stop them from increasing their exploitation of the earth's resources.

The ever-expanding abundance of scientific knowledge and its technological application to our lives has had a direct influence on the evolution of our minds and bodies. The result is an inexorable intellectual drive. The human mind has become insatiable in its need to understand, explore, control, define, explain and impose its own interpretations on the physical world, a need which has imbued us with an ingrained passion for both creativity and destruction. The pattern of our activities which has evolved, as a result, is one of invent, construct, overuse and destroy. To date, nature has accommodated the human species in its exorbitant consumption of natural resources and ecological destruction throughout its evolution. But we continue to ignore nature's warning signs and are now surpassing the earth's sustainable limits.

If we are to survive into the distant future, we must learn immediately how to live in harmony with nature. Herein rises our major dilemma. Only the most primitive life styles of the nomadic hunter-gatherer can qualify for such an existence as primitive societies do not utilize the variety of toxic chemicals, mineral ores, irrigation and pumping systems, cement and steels, fossil fuels and entire ecosystems which are the essentials of industrial civilizations. Rather, nomadic peoples are relatively benign inhabitants of the planet like all other species, retaining a pristine environment, in which wastes from food gathering, housing and human sewage are minimal and decay back into the wilderness. But they remain so only until their numbers overwhelm the carrying capacity of their land bases or civilization moves in and reduces the size of their territory and introduces them to technologies of destruction. Presently, ninety nine percent of the world's people have living standards or basic survival needs which are aligned with settlement of the land and exploitation of the natural resources. The pressure of increasing numbers of people expands this dependency daily. We are now the prisoners of our own genius. Our megacities are the ultimate manifestation of that genius; but they are technological prisons from which we cannot escape in our overwhelming numbers.

In attempting to prove the theory of self-imposed extinction through technology, PART ONE sets the stage through the cataloguing of the historical technological progress and the parallel survival and expansion of the human species through five million years of evolution. It inventories those technologies which have not only been the vehicle of our survival and instrumental in building the character of our societies, but shows how they have been the underlying cause for civilizations disappearing.

The success of our technological progress in facilitating human survival and expansion has led to unmanageable demographics as well as a consequential degradation and overwhelming of the natural environment. PART TWO analyzes the universal crisis building as high fertility rates explode on this finite planet.

PART THREE takes a surface look at the economic, political and social dilemmas inherent in our dependency on technologies, dilemmas which will haunt human survival throughout the 21st Century. These chapters examine both sides of the equation of exploitation and conservation.

To justify the conclusion that we alone are responsible for our present course of self-destruction is to evaluate the degree of environmental deterioration our technological exploitation has done to the earth during our tenure and to speculate from hindsight whether we can successfully "manage" the earth in the future to ensure our survival.

PART FOUR makes this evaluation by summarizing some of the many unsolvable problems threatening us with environmental collapse as we continue on our present course of industrialization, overpopulation and "sustainable management" programs. By failing to curb our populations, reduce our consumption of resources and prevent our destruction of arable lands and clean water reserves are we setting in place the forces of our own extinction: starvation, disease, wars over land and food, climatic changes, an unstoppable industrial and agricultural expansion, a polluted and deadly biosphere and an unsustainable birth rate? Our time of extinction is programmed into the rate at which we destroy the environment so that we alone may exist; for in doing so, we destroy ourselves.

PART FIVE presents several philosophical conclusions evaluating our chances of undoing our dilemmas or even reducing them. The chapters speculate as to what our future will be if we continue to parade our hubris through continued expansion and exploitation of the earth as present indicators of greater and greater industrial expansion suggest.

In setting ourselves up as the master species and ignoring the ecological laws that govern the workings of the earth's biological systems, we have, in the metaphor of the Ancient Greeks, "behaved like gods" in our arrogant, defiant treatment of the natural world. Such "hubris", they believed, could only bring grief and calamity to all involved. The "nemesis" or punishment for human beings when they rose above their place in the natural devolution of men and gods was retribution equal to or greater than the offense. To complete the analogy with Greek tragedy, humankind, in destroying the earth's natural order, has risen above the gods and now faces retribution: Death by EXTINCTION.

The major conditions which will bring on retribution and determine the time of its arrival might be summed up in the following equation: UNLIMITED HUMAN REPRODUCTION AND RISING CONSUMPTION EQUAL IMMINENT EXTINCTION; CONTROLLED REPRODUCTION AND DIMINISHING CONSUMPTION; EQUAL EXTENDED SURVIVAL.

PART ONE

Human Evolution and Survival: The Product of Our Technologies and Environmental Exploitation

Human Evolution and Survival:
The Product of Our Technologies and Environmental Exploitation

The emergence of Homo sapiens after five million years of evolution as the dominant species on earth is directly related to the physical construction of the human body and the increasing capacity of its brain to invent, manufacture and implement tools and weapons. The more developed our minds and bodies became as a result of our growing technologically-determined existence, the greater was our ability to provide food, shelter and clothing to ensure our survival and population growth.

The most definitive event in human development came when our ancestors gave up the communal, nomadic life of the hunter-gatherer and settled the land to cultivate crops and domesticate wild animals. In so doing we began to usurp nature's control over our evolutionary development while setting in place the forces of our own self-destruction.

This dramatic change known as the Neolithic Agricultural Revolution had not only established human control over our survival as a dominant species on the planet, it brought the first major increase in population as food supply stabilized relative to the uncertainty of life as a nomadic hunter-gatherer. No longer constantly on the move, women were able to manage the care and raising of additional children. Significant spurts in population growth also forced frequent mass migrations in search of new arable lands to colonize, which highly stimulated population growth in newly settled areas.

Just as periods of colonization brought rapid expansions in human numbers in the past, so have the many wondrous technological innovations of modern times caused population "explosions". Birth rates in the last half of the 20th Century, for instance, have continued to double over shorter and shorter periods of time. The trend promises to continue throughout the

21st Century. Technologies which have permitted us to overcome most natural causes of death and limit our populations to territorial carrying capacity have given us power to keep far more people alive than the planet's resources can sustain indefinitely.

What may loosely be described as an "exponential" growth rate in population and technological development has begun to plague humanity. An "exponential" growth rate means the existing population will double in predictable time intervals. For example, a one percent annual population rise will double in 70 years, a two percent rate will double in 35 years, a 3 percent in 23 years and so on. At present most nations' fertility rates are over 2 percent, with the industrial nations varying from 1.2 to a high of 2.2 in the United States.[1]

According to United Nations' estimates this exponential growth of population carried into the 21st Century will eventually double the earth's present numbers to 10 billion between the years 2030 and 2050.[2] It is predicted that population expansion will level out somewhere between 10 and 14 billion by the year 2100 if they continue to grow at present rates. At the same time exponential birth rates may be curbed somewhat from an exponential growth by a drop in environmental carrying capacity that will raise the death rate through increasing starvation, malnutrition, epidemic diseases, pollution, natural catastrophes, civil violence and wars. In 1995, for example, the increase in population dropped from the expected 90 million to 87 million, 80 million of them added in the developing countries. It will also be inhibited by a wider use of contraception, sterilization and abortion. Despite setbacks populations are estimated to expand and double at least once in the 21st Century.

Analyzing the present physical state of the planet as a result of overpopulation and environmental destruction, it is clear that the same technologies which have nurtured our expansion in the past are now the major threat to our survival as soon as the next century.

CHAPTER ONE

Prehistorical Evolution of Homo Sapiens Through Technology

Human origins actually predate our earliest use of technologies by some two to three million years; whereas, the parallel growth of populations with their technologies has its beginnings in evolutionary changes our earliest ancestors underwent approximately one and a half million years ago.

Through fossil identification and carbon dating, we can trace our evolutionary beginnings to the hominid, Australopithecus, which appeared on earth about five million years ago, surviving, as did all other hominids, on the largesse of warm, moist jungles, eating fruit, soft leaves and vegetation while making its home in the trees. Evidence now exists that these early ancestors of ours walked erect and were largely human in form, although their brains were still relatively small as long ago as three million years. Then about two and a half million years ago, the earth's climates changed dramatically; temperatures cooled and the air above much of the land became drier. Glaciers formed over vast areas of the Northern Hemisphere and jungles shrank in southern lands, leaving behind open woodlands and large savannas. The loss of jungle habitation in much of Africa forced Australopithecus to move out into the open grasslands where traveling on the ground rather than in the trees was more dangerous and food supplies more elusive. Survival depended on adapting to a diet of coarser vegetation and the flesh of small animals; it also entailed traveling long distances and ultimately, the use of weapons to kill prey.[3]

Paleontologist Steven M. Stanley believes this exodus from the forests enabled the development in these hominids of a larger brain that grew to 400 and 500 cubic centimeters in volume, a capacity that equals that of the great apes. By natural selection those hominids with the largest brains survived more easily. "The smarter ones would have done better," he claims. "That is, the pressures of natural selection would have favored Australopithecines with bigger brains, for they could develop the tools, weapons, speech and the high reasoning they needed to survive in the open country."[4]

Stanley also believes that, once out of the trees, the brains of the baby hominids kept growing just as human brains do for a full year after birth, while an ape's stops at birth. This would have allowed the size of the brain to increase and improve the intellectual capacity of the hominid, but it also increased the period of helpless infancy in the young. This was offset by the changes in social structure as the male hominids learned to travel and hunt in groups, leaving the females at a "home base" to care for the young.

The cooler, drier climates two and a half million years ago catastrophically affected most of the early hominids, bringing on their extinction while at the same time promoting the evolution of the Australopithecines. Once these ancestors of ours had left the trees permanently and settled on the ground, they continued to evolve physically through natural selection. Their brain capacity continued to grow, their bodies made the necessary adaptations to an upright stance and their digestive systems adapted to an ever widening variety of foods. Walking on two feet, with their hands free to hunt, gather and carry food supplies, their survival techniques slowly improved.[5]

For the next million years they lived primarily on scavenged carrion, ate small animals caught by hand and learned to use sticks and animal bones as clubs to fend off predators and to kill prey. They made their homes in caves where they lived without fire or tools, gradually working towards the more sophisticated ways of the hunter-gatherer. Their life span was short, uncertain and difficult, but their constantly increasing intellectual capacity made survival possible in circumstances that would have killed off any other species with the same physical limitations without the intelligence.[6]

Nearly one and a half million years ago Australopithecus disappeared and was gradually replaced by "Homo erectus", the first real ancestor of Modern Man. The brain capacity of this hominid had almost doubled in size, averaging 900 cubic centimeters in volume. Homo erectus was taller, stronger and had a growing array of technologies that made him a formidable hunter of larger and larger animals. He learned to manufacture weapons and tools with which to kill and prepare animals for his consumption. Among his catches he included wild horses, camels, bears and elephants. Primitive forms of social organization within his family or tribal units were beginning as he learned to share the responsibilities for the growing numbers which comprised his social groups. This period of development is known as the Early Stone Age, reflecting the technological and cultural advances in stone tools and weapons. A million years ago this earliest human ancestor of ours peopled the lands of the Mediterranean.

Homo erectus invented stone tools for cutting and cleaning animal hides as well as for honing weapons and killing prey. In colder climatic areas they learned to use animal skins for warmth. Primitive speech aided them in their social and cultural development.[7]

Surviving until 300,000 years ago, Homo erectus made many technological improvements in their survival techniques which allowed their expanding populations to spread into Europe and Asia. Sites dating their existence are plentiful, many of them ranging from as early as 700,000 to 125,000 years ago.

The tools of these Stone Age hominids reveal much about the mental development and abilities of their evolving brains and intellectual capacity. The shapes of their tools suggest they were produced by stone workers who knew the processes they must follow to manufacture the specific tools suited to the numerous tasks for which they were made, all of which aided in the procuring and preparing of foods, clothing and shelters. Among their major advances in tool making was the handaxe whose use 200,000 years ago had spread throughout Africa, the Middle East, most of Europe, much of the Indian subcontinent and most of the Asian mainland.[8]

Learning to produce and control fire was a major technological advancement. Fires provided needed warmth in the northern climates, offered protection from predators and enabled the cooking of foods, which by modern experience, improves the digestive qualities of foods and kills harmful bacteria that often prove fatal to humans. Fire also aided in the manufacturing of wooden objects which could be shaped with heat and heated flint flaked more easily. The ability to control and use fire brought many advantages to the struggle to survive, but most importantly, it increased the technology of tool and weapon making.[9]

The use of fire was the first major technological discovery which set mankind apart from all other species. Its powers were so significant that fire became basic to spiritual rites, beliefs and cultural developments. Evidence turned up in recent centuries has shown the use and knowledge of fire was universal among ancient peoples as early as one and a half million years ago. In later palaeolithic sights from 300,000 to 200,000 years ago, much evidence of its use remains in hearths left at many "camp sites". The brain capacity of these hominids during their last half million years of development increased to 1400 cubic centimeters by the time Homo sapiens arrived on the scene over 250,000 years ago. Such capacity gave this evolutionary creature an intelligence level that closely approached that of modern humans. Their technological abilities were demonstrated in the engineering skills they applied constructing primitive buildings for shelter, using trees and animal hides. A structure measuring 60 by 20 feet, held up with tree trunks as columns and the added feature of two hearths, has been discovered near the Mediterranean coast of France. Carbon dating estimates it was built 250,000 years ago.

The emergence of the earliest form of Homo sapiens at this time initiated the final evolutionary stages which produced Modern Man. Approximately 200,000 years ago the first subspecies, Neanderthal Man, appeared. It was the Neanderthals who peopled Europe during and between the great Ice Ages of the last 300,000 years, living at the southern edge of the continental ice sheets and moving northward during interglacial periods. The winters were very cold for life forms and vegetation, forcing most varieties of birds and animals to move south during the winters, then to migrate north during the warmer summers, establishing migrating patterns in many bird species that continue to this day. The extreme cold and short summers restricted the vegetation to tundra plants such as tough grasses and sedges and a few dwarfed tree varieties until interglacial periods allowed the forest to reclaim the continent.

In spite of the difficulties they had to face in such cold weather conditions, the Neanderthals increased their numbers. Both their physical characteristics and improving technologies enabled their survival. They were relatively squat in structure with thick bones, heavy muscles, short forearms and shinbones and possessed great strength. They manufactured knives for skinning and cleaning animal hides, awls and needles for sewing clothes and tents of animal furs. They developed the skills to build relatively warm, effective shelters for protection against the icy winters. However, survival was obviously difficult for them in spite of the advantages of new technologies. Bone specimens show evidence that more than half of them died in their teens.

Their weapons and tools grew increasingly more sophisticated and varied. Radio carbon dating reveals that as early as 44,000 years ago, amputations of infected limbs were performed. Furthermore, daggers, shaped and honed for killing other Neanderthals were prevalent. Stone weapons, fire for a multitude of purposes and improved hunting skills permitted the Neanderthals to increase their living standards and skills enough to initiate the painting of decorations on cave walls which recorded their hunts and activities. Indications in their art works and their bone deformities suggest they indulged in intertribal conflicts over territories and catches of prey animals.

By the time handaxes were in common use 200,000 years ago, organized patterns of hunting and gathering had been established. These early humans had learned to work within relatively defined territories. They knew their environments very well and operated efficiently, getting the most from their lands.[10]

Over the thousands of years of evolution, tribal life of the early hominids must have required some degree of social organization, a division of the work and a sharing of responsibilities between the men and the women. Hunting was obviously the realm of men while the gathering of seeds, roots and berries was left to the women who remained in or near "home bases" with their children. These roles have their parallels in the territorial habits of most animals as well as in their rank and file roles established to protect their young and their territories. There is much in these early social patterns of individual and community responsibility which is still ingrained in our cultures and remain basic to the order and efficiency of modern civilizations.

Using the research studies of Richard Lee on the !Kung tribe of the Kalahari, one of the few remaining tribes of hunter-gatherers, Richard Leakey in THE MAKING OF MANKIND suggests these early humans found they lived and worked best in bands of about thirty people. Only when settled and working the land could more than thirty survive successfully. To facilitate the exchange of goods and ideas, gathering of small tribes, especially during the wet seasons, would take place at water holes for the exchange of gifts, for marriage brokering and for the trade of tools and weapons. The tribes would share in ritual customs for short periods of time as food would soon run out when so many more people were concentrated in one area. Large communities always meant more work to be done, hunting distances were increased and communal living problems were exacerbated. While concentrations of people led to an interchange of tribal members, they also heightened personal conflicts.[11]

Overall populations of hunter-gatherers tended to remain small as droughts, disasters and food shortages severely curtailed the number of children a group could sustain. Numbers were also curbed by the physical limitations that moving from place to place put on women's child bearing abilities. Carrying and nursing two children at the same time while gathering food was too difficult. One child had to be able to move about on its own before the next one was born. This reduced the fertility rate of one child to each woman every four years. Only in a settled, sedentary life can women withstand the arduous task of caring for a growing infant while pregnant with another.[12]

During the coldest times of greatest glaciation, areas of Southern Europe were not covered by the ice. The Mediterranean lands stayed relatively warm as the sea itself did not freeze up.

However, in the formation of continental glaciers, huge quantities of sea water were stored in them, lowering sea levels several meters worldwide. This, in turn, exposed land bridges between continents such as those in the Mediterranean Sea, joining Corsica to Sardinia and linking up the Greek islands and facilitating the movement of peoples and large animals out of Africa. The movement of Homo sapiens north into Europe brought those humans who were to replace the Neanderthals and cause their disappearance about 35,000 years ago.

Evidence that Modern Man began to appear about 40,000 years ago was discovered by archaeologists in the Middle East, Africa and Australia. The first findings in Europe indicated their presence in South West France at Cro-Magnon, which gave its name to these latest of our ancestors.

With the appearance of Cro-Magnon, Neanderthal as a separate human species is believed to have disappeared, leaving Cro-Magnon as sole heir to the kingdom of Homo sapiens. Cro-Magnon were generally modern in physical appearance, perhaps taller, averaging over six feet in height, but still somewhat archaic in features. Their bodies were more finely structured than Neanderthals' and their heads were narrower, higher and rounder. Their physical strength was less but their intellectual capacity had increased through natural selection.

The cultural advances of Cro-Magnon were more sophisticated than Neanderthal's, producing a much wider variety of tools, weapons and artifacts over shorter periods of time. As Richard Foster Flint observed in THE EARTH & ITS HISTORY, "Human skills (had) improved with time, at first very slowly but later on at an increasing rate."[13] During the period from 40,000 to 10,000 years ago, there was a marked acceleration in cultural development. Specialized stone blade tools, bone harpoons, spears for throwing, bone needles, knife blades for all purposes, hammers, and flint arrows were in wide use. Between 16,000 and 9,000 B.C. metal tools such as burins and awls were manufactured for carving.

Dramatic ecological changes began with Cro-Magnon as their efficiency in hunting grew rapidly. They were so skilled in killing prey that their abilities may have been the major cause for the extinction of many large mammals across Europe whose existence did not depend on the Ice Age. Vast herds of wild animals disappeared: the great wild bulls, the woolly mammoth, the woolly rhinoceros, the ibex, the elephant and the bison. By 12,000 years ago only horses, deer, goats, cattle, sheep and other smaller mammals were still in existence on the European continent. Food prey for these meat eating hunters diminished as rapidly as their technologies improved and their populations expanded.

Until the arrival of Cro-Magnon, all previous human ancestors had been predators, but they had not been so numerous that they endangered the survival of the herd animal populations. Neither did they destroy the environments in which they lived to the same extent. This newest mutational species of Homo sapiens with their increasing intellect and physical dexterity was to change the world extensively and very rapidly by comparison with all their predecessors.

From the earliest appearance of the hominid, Australopithecus, some five million years ago up to the Neolithic Age, 10,000 years ago, populations world wide reached somewhere between four to ten million in total. Estimates put population increases between 30,000 years and 6,000 years ago at 28 times the previous number of humans in existence.[14] These numbers have, in turn, multiplied a factor of 55 over the last 6,000 years.

Technology and the Neolithic Agricultural Revolution

For the hunter-gatherer mobility permits no capacity for food storage nor the accumulation of goods other than a few basic tools, weapons and in recent times, the addition of cooking pots. This fact was basic in prehistoric times in preventing the over harvesting of naturally grown foods on which the people lived. The variety of foods gleaned through gathering of seeds, roots, berries, leaves and the killing of edible wild animals was generally sufficient to ensure a nutritious diet of proteins, carbohydrates and minerals. Both mobility and small populations ensured the regeneration and balance of ecological systems. Life was integrated with the seasons and the availability of food.

Populations were controlled by infanticide through accepted social customs which involved killing of twins as they imperilled the health and mobility of the mother, or of handicapped, deformed babies which hindered mobility and safety of the tribe and to rid the group of any excess females.[15] The Inuit of Northern Canada in the 20th Century killed up to 40 percent of their female babies as recently as the 1930s. The sick, mortally injured, dying and old were also killed or abandoned to the elements.

By 10,000 years ago hunter-gatherers had settled nearly all parts of the globe. Some of these groups had developed primitive forms of agriculture in which they cleared land and burned off vegetation to allow the natural growth of the more usable or edible plants and vegetation that encouraged the grazing of wild herds. At the same time the hunter-gatherers were increasing their proficiency of killing species and preserving the meat. This led to the massive killing of single species to extinction, a practice that has remained with us to this day as our fisherman destroy all species of food fish. The impact was always life threatening to the people as one species after another disappeared in rapid succession. In Australia, for instance, over the last 100,000 years aboriginals in their expanding numbers were responsible for the extinction of 86 percent of all large animals that once roamed the continent. What hunting did not make extinct, disturbing the natural eco-systems of the land did.

The greatest die-out of food species came in the Northern Hemisphere with the gradual warming that followed the retreat of the continental glaciers and the extinction of so many Ice Age mammals between 16,000 and 10,000 years ago. Survival for the hunter-gatherers deteriorated, forcing them to find new sources of food to sustain their growing numbers. Their reliance on certain of the plants and the remaining animals, --wild horses, cattle, sheep and goats,-- began the slow process of taming the wild animals and sowing and harvesting crops. The collection of seeds and their accidental germination near campsites must have long predated the actual process of "farming" crops, but the knowledge would have been partly responsible for the decision to settle the land and become dependent on domesticated crops and stock. Signs of successful domestication appear in many excavated archaeological sites dating back 10,000 years.[16]

This time period saw the end of the Ice Age. As the continental ice sheets retreated northward, warming climatic conditions in both the Northern and Southern Hemispheres encouraged the growth of vast forests. The Sahara, very dry during the Ice Age, now received heavy rainfalls and was drained by many rivers whose banks and hinterlands were lush with vegetation and forests which remained for several thousand years. Much the same happened throughout Asia where increased rainfall caused extensive vegetation changes.

Unable to sustain their growing numbers on the scarce population of prey animals that changing climates and over hunting had caused, the hunter-gatherers were forced to find other means to provide for themselves or they would die out. Using modern hunter-gatherers as a paradigm of survival in nature, it is estimated that the hunter-gatherer needs about 200 square miles per 100 people to survive; whereas the settled "farmer" can provide for the same number on the farm production of a square mile of arable land.[17] Need plus temperate climatic conditions and the knowledge that was accumulating in the taming and raising of wild baby animals and the regeneration of food crops at campsites were incentive enough for Homo sapiens to begin domesticating their own food supplies. In this way the most unprecedented period of human change and development in human evolution began.

For the first time, humans exchanged a life of hunting and gathering for settlement on the land and the domestication of plants and animals. Although this change evolved over several thousand years, it was a very short time period compared with the previous four to five million years of evolution that had brought them this far in their development. It was also a remarkably fast technological adaptation in evolutionary terms, indicating that human intellect and cultural innovation were improving at a rapid pace. Above all, human superiority as a species both in population numbers and in the mastery of the environment were an established fact.

Life as a hunter-gatherer had been entirely dependent on nature to provide sustenance where survival was linked to following the wild herds and to good seasonal conditions which nurtured the growth of wild cereal grains, roots, berries, and fruits. Droughts, floods and permanent climatic changes as well as the disappearance of food species were a constant threat to the nomadic life; whereas life as a farmer brought immeasurable changes in life styles and a much greater security of food supply. Above all, farming brought a massive leap forward in collected knowledge, intellectual capacity and technological innovation. Successful settlement demanded adaptability and social organization.

The change from nomad to settler can be dated quite accurately, beginning in the Middle East during the eighth millennium B.C., followed by settlements in Europe during the sixth millennium, then in the fourth in East Asia and the third in Africa. The last areas to turn to farming were in North and South America during the second millennium, B.C.[18]

Modern day archaeological excavating continues to unearth earlier and earlier village sites. Among the oldest found settlements in the Middle East were those along the Nile River. Villages that have been uncovered reveal farming technologies dating back as early as 14,500 years ago in the Aswan Dam area where grindstones and sickle blades were dug up. Between 7000 and 6000 B.C. the climate changed so dramatically with the end of the Ice Age that the area we call Egypt today then occupied a wide, lushly vegetated flood plain along the Nile that was drained by many tributaries, receiving high rainfall where presently only a narrow, irrigated strip remains to support life.[19]

One of the earliest settlements found in the Middle East was Catal Huyuk in central Turkey, inhabited over 8400 years ago by about 6000 people living on thirty acres of land. They occupied homes that were built of tightly packed mud brick with flat roofs through which they entered the house by way of a ladder. Many shrines and clay models as well as horns and skulls of bulls were found built into the walls of the houses, indicating a growing ritualized form of worship.[20]

Other early sites in the Middle East are found predominantly located in the Fertile Crescent of Iraq. Among them is the famous village of Jarmo which dates back to about 6000 B.C.. Archaeological findings show that the inhabitants raised sheep and goats as well as pigs. As excavating continues in this area, many other villages are being discovered along the Euphrates which predate Jarmo.[21]

Information gathered on sites of these early villages have led to conclusions that people had learned to live in one place the year around by about 9,000 to 8,000 B.C., depending on one or two reliable food sources.[22] Had populations remained small, early settlement of the land would have provided a stable, sustainable existence for a long time. But the growing populations demanded a constant increase in food supply which could only be satisfied by opening up more lands for crop production and establishing larger and larger herds of grazing animals, especially goat herds which could live on very sparse vegetation.

It can be assumed that expanding populations, disappearing food prey and declining ecologies had been the motivating force that moved these early peoples to settle the land in order to cultivate their own food supplies. But this change in life style forced an equally if not greater increase in populations, which, in turn, meant that cultivation had to be maintained year after year or people starved to death. Cultivation and husbanding of a perennial food supply soon came to require large families to share in the work. Such were the beginnings and underlying causes of a spiralling population growth.[23]

Successful settlement of the land precluded many new technologies and social skills of the people. To be effective the art of farming requires tools for sowing, weeding and harvesting as well as containers for collecting and storage. Consequently, the arrival of an agricultural society heralded a dramatic increase in technologies: grinding stones, sickles, storage bins, permanent farm buildings and homes, and the introduction of pottery. Agriculture provided a food surplus, requiring techniques to store the excess for use during periods when the crops failed. Excess crop production also freed the farmer from the daily hunt for food and led to the concept of commercial trading.

Assurance of food supply now permitted the social organization needed for life in larger and larger groups. The earliest farming settlements, occupied by a few families and the buildings they required to live in, house their animals and store their grains, formed the first villages which soon expanded to include others who were not farmers. People were now able to diversify their employment and production, initiating the sharing of labour and the pooling of knowledge. The formation of complex social structures with hierarchies developed and expanded rapidly from these early beginnings.[24]

Cultural change has always been much more rapid than genetic change, but when survival depended on expansive innovation and technologies, humanity evolved a greater intellectual capacity and ingenuity which promoted the faster evolution of its societies than at any previous time in human existence.[25] All of these human activities of survival have been transmitted from generation to generation and still prevail to this day, along with the need for spiritual and fertility rites that have remained basic to agricultural societies ever since.[26]

Substantial villages, large enough to be classified as towns, appeared in some Middle East areas as early as 8,000 B.C. The building and rebuilding of mud brick structures on the same sites suggests permanent settlements over thousands of years. One of the best archaeological sites of an early town is Jericho, a few kilometres north west of the Dead Sea. It is the oldest known town to be excavated. Located near an oasis, it was first used by seasonal occupants. In its next phase it became a town populated by about 2,000 people who lived in a cluster of closely grouped houses, round in shape and encircled by a protective wall with a massive solid tower some 10 meters in diameter and 8.5 meters high.

A major upheaval about 7,000 B.C. brought total destruction to the original town of Jericho, but it was rebuilt. The technologies used in the first rebuilding were quite different from the first walled settlement in that the houses were square instead of round and they had plaster floors. Jericho was to be rebuilt many times over the next thousands of years.[27]

By 7000 B.C. people in the Middle East settlements had learned to tame and domesticate wild goats, sheep, cattle and horses so that they could raise them to supply the food and clothing that previously wild animals had provided. They had devised new technologies for use on the land and in the villages that included those of farming, carpentry, fishing, tool making and weapon manufacturing. The cultivation of crops extended to irrigation, storing grains, saving and sowing seeds, milling grains and exchanging food and tools through trade and barter. The first architectural concepts were appearing in the building of mud brick houses and other structures. Forests were cut down and land cleared. The art of using charcoal to manufacture plasters, metals and tools ushered in the Age of Metals.

The Old Stone Age that had begun over 100,000 years ago came to a gradual end beginning between 7000 and 3000 B.C. It was not known how to use the first discovered metals some 10,000 years ago, but by 3000 B.C. fine detailed jewellery and eventually iron weapons and bronze tools replaced the flint arrowheads and knives, the weapons, tools and ornaments of bone.

The Age of Metals began with the discovery of copper which could be hammered into shape to make usable objects. The earliest known implementation of it was in Southern Turkey where artifacts using it were found at sites dating back to 7000 B.C. By 4000 B.C. copper was in wide use throughout the Middle East for bracelets and pins. The greatest technological advancement in metallurgy came with the melting of copper and tin together, heralding the arrival of the Bronze Age about 3000 B.C. This first metal alloy, bronze, could be used to make better weapons and tools. Its advantage lie in its ability to flow at lower temperatures and could be used more readily in casting. The use of gold came into wide use about 2,500 B.C. because of its appeal and its malleability. It could be worked into intricate shapes and designs that glorified royal tombs and jewellery.[28]

The discovery and use of iron occurred in a few isolated areas during the third millennium, but its true value was not realized until smelting and forging techniques were developed about 1200 B.C. Harder than bronze, iron could be used in the manufacturing of more deadly, effective weapons such as swords, enhancing the offensive and defensive capabilities of armies.[29]

These technological advances in metallurgy were remarkable innovations that raised the living standards of early human settlements and contributed to the growing concepts of civilization. Evidence of settlements built behind fortified, protective walls by the sixth and fifth millennium B.C., are signs that the overall population was growing fast. Villages were forced to protect themselves from roaming warrior bands looking for plunder. Biblical stories in the Old Testament tell of peaceful settlements overrun, all their people massacred and their structures and farms utterly ruined.[30]

As early as 5000 years ago, farming was widespread. Concentrations of growing populations built many villages scattered throughout the Fertile Crescent of the Tigris-Euphrates, where primitive irrigation systems were dug to permit crop production on a year-round basis. The degree of economic development and civilization that emerged in these settlements was determined not only by the size and surplus production of their arable farmlands, but by the permanent availability of fresh water supplies. The greater the carrying capacity of the farmlands, the greater the number of people living in the area.

But the technological advances in mining and farming the land also heralded the beginning of mass environmental destruction. As is natural in the course of human events, too many people cultivating crops rapidly depleted the nutrients in the soil and opened the lands to erosion, turning inhabited areas into deserts as human society unwittingly took more from nature than she could replace. Extensive forest areas were destroyed to provide cooking and heating fuels and to make the charcoal necessary in the manufacturing of plaster and usable metal products. The hunter-gatherer had brought extinction to the large wild animals of Mediterranean Europe and North Africa, but the settled farmer and the civilizations to come destroyed the forests and the land.

Settlements disappeared and their occupants either died off or moved elsewhere to repeat the process again and again throughout the prehistoric world. Evidence of their disappearance because of degraded environmental conditions lies in most archaeological sites discovered today in that the majority of the sites have been found in what can only be described as deserts.

The Neolithic Agricultural
Revolution and Human Development

The Agricultural Revolution of the Neolithic Age turned Homo Sapiens from a totally communal existence dependent on group "sharing", which is "central to the hunter-gatherer way of life, (to) one of "saving" or husbanding of resources, which is equally central to the farming and herding way of life."[31] In the process, human social behaviours and attitudes experienced several basic changes which have had serious repercussions for human existence ever since.

The greatest impact of our new status as a "self-sufficient" species showed up in the rapid rise in fertility rates that came with security of food supply through "artificial" production. Where customarily a woman gave birth to one child on average every four years while living a nomadic life, settling down to farm enabled a woman to give birth every two years, until finally the average was one born every year during recent centuries.

However, the birth rate throughout human existence has always exceeded the death rate over the long term, maintaining a constant if irregular, expansion in world populations, "exploding" somewhat during the first centuries of the Neolithic Revolution and then again in the period of industrial and agricultural growth of the 18th, 19th and 20th Centuries. These last three centuries have experienced the largest increase in population expansion, as the survival rate of births over deaths soared with improved diets and medical care throughout infancy and childhood and into old age.

Populations at the turn of the 21st Century have reached such horrific numbers that even minimal growth in the future will still be more than enough to exceed the carrying capacity of the planet.

Next in importance to population growth were the fundamental changes in human character that rose out of commitment to owning and defending one's own land and property. A nomad could run away from his enemies, but a farmer had to stay to defend his property and crops. Neither could a farmer afford to share his total production freely with others if he intended to save a food supply for himself and his family until the next harvest and also have seed to plant the next crop. The "sharing" traditions of the hunter-gatherer had to be sacrificed by the farmer for the "saving" or husbanding of resources, otherwise he would be out of business.[32]

Life on the land in a farming society not only brought many changes to the way in which humans survived but it influenced the development of human character as we have come to know it today. Farming dispersed people and made them more self-reliant and independent within the group. Successful productivity depended more on selfishness and the trading of goods than on sharing them freely as nomadic societies demand of their members. Using Richard Lee's studies of life among the !Kung tribe of the Kalahari, as the modern example of a hunter-gatherer society and its final submission to settling down on the land, Richard Leakey concludes that the concept of property ownership and accumulated material wealth developed a "flow of emotions and feelings" that promoted attitudes and behaviours that were "anticommunal".[33]

Using social behaviours of these modern hunter-gatherers turned farmer as a paradigm, one can conclude that owning property aroused latent aggressive instincts in the ancient settlers as they learned to guard their holdings with force against "outsiders" or neighbours who coveted their land and material wealth. Artifacts discovered in a cemetery at Jebel Safaba, north of Wadi Halfa in Egypt, dating back 12,000 to 10,000 B.C., tell of extensive violence, perhaps the result of territorial battles in which fighting and killing are suggested by the number of skeletons of men, women and children with embedded fragments of flint in their bones.[34]

In the evolution from nomad to settler, human aggression, whether acquired genetically as Darwin would have it, or instilled by social tradition as the Behaviourists wish us to believe, evoked greed, acquisitiveness and aggressive covetousness in our ancestors. They sought illicit gains from others in violent ways, ingraining attitudes and desires which came into full force within the character of the individual as people moved from the interdependence of communal life within the wandering tribe to the self-dependence of the property owner in defence of his land and its production. A natural result was the measurement of success and self-esteem gained in terms of the amount of wealth and economic independence the individual and his family gained within the tribal group, yet separate. The aggressiveness that arose in defense of one's lands and wealth has remained a powerful influence in human societies ever since. Not only the wealth but the power represented by ownership of large land tracts has constantly driven the search for better, more efficient technologies to raise crop output while promoting the invention of more effective, powerful weaponry to defend the gains. Being able to accumulate enough wealth translated into the ability to purchase and maintain an army with which to plunder neighbouring lands, steal their lands and reduce the inhabitants to slavery.

The Classical empires of Greece and Rome were built on the size and armaments of their military. Their physical domination of the Ancient World and its tribes is credited to the power and mobility of the Roman legions, paid for and commanded by an elite of wealthy landowners. Roman military strength conquered the Mediterranean lands and enslaved the indigenous people who then provided the manual labour of the Empire. The ruling elite and the wealthy landowners enjoyed a freedom to indulge themselves in riches and military conquests for 500 years. "Greek liberty was for the people who had the military means to express it -- those who could afford it."[35] The declining wealth and corruption of both the ruling elite and the military played a major role in Rome's decline and fall. It could not defend itself against the superior numbers, nor the relentless infiltration and eventual military conquest by the barbarian invaders.

Ownership of land, whether by the individual, the city state, the nation or the empire, has largely determined the various political and military forms of government that evolved over the millennia, most of which were autocratic, military dictatorships, gained either by force, landed influence or inheritance. Only during the last two centuries has democracy come into its own in Europe and North America. The ruling elites in most Third World countries remain aristocratic dictatorships today, receiving their authority through democratic elections or self-appointed military leadership. Ruling bodies of most Asian, African and South American nations hold political power through their influence as landed aristocracy who own the largest share of their nations' arable lands. Still others have gained their wealth and power through control of processing and distributing agricultural products.

The majority of the nations in Central and South America are governed by members of the landed aristocracy who derive their wealth and power from commercial agriculture. Few of these nations have built a successful industrial base as industrialization was discouraged until recent years by the landed aristocracy who refused to allow a powerful industrial and middle class to rise in opposition to them and eventually usurp their power as had occurred in Britain, Europe and America throughout the 19th Century.

The effect of this agrarian policy led to national impoverishment, indebtedness and wide foreign ownership of land, natural resources, agricultural production and any industry that was established. Argentina is an "a priori" case. For a short period of time, its dependency on one primary resource, cattle, with its many products of beef and leather goods, raised it to the sixth largest trading nation in the world. As happens with one-industry nations, Argentina soon failed to retain her world markets. Foreign competition in beef products and the decline in use of leather products, its replacement with more practical synthetic "leathers" and changing international fashions, landed Argentine cattle ranchers in deep debt and the country in a period of extreme inflation. Argentina sank rapidly to Third World status. The ruling aristocracy, determined not to lose its wealth and power, began to print money to pay their debts and maintain their living standards. The following years of high inflation and military control eventually gave way to democratic reforms, but a continued dependence on natural resources and foreign ownership of land and industry still dominates their economy.

The unequal distribution and ownership of land has always accompanied the development of civilizations. Historical uprisings and revolutions occurred with regularity in agrarian nations as displaced peasants, uprooted by the powerful, wealthy farmer or rancher, organized and fought to take back the land.

However, successful revolutions which attempted to redistribute the land more equitably are very few in number. In modern times the most dramatic attempts were those of the Communists in their take-over of Russia and the adjoining nations of Eastern Europe. They violently seized the farmlands from the aristocracy and the landed peasantry, giving ownership to the state. Control and production, if not ownership, remained with the political elite of the Communist states whose "management" profited those in power, allowing them to rule much as the former aristocracy had done.

Enforcement of the Socialist doctrines of human equality and state ownership of land and property permitted the ultimate tyranny. In Ukraine, taking the land from the kulaks or farmers, entailed the murdering of over 20 million people through starvation in a brutal program to erase their tendency to hide their production from government confiscation as well as their desire to own their land. The effect of this loss on the farmers of Ukraine was reflected in over 70 years of inefficient, declining production and a polluted, degraded environment. The total collapse of state owned enterprises and a highly indebted nation in 1989 revealed the horrendous chaos that had come with the loss of private ownership of land and property.

The degree of suffering and inhumanity inflicted by the Communist leadership on their people in the process of taking away their ownership of the land and its production was outdone only by China whose willingness to impose the death penalty on over 100 million Chinese in the name of state ownership of all property and wealth exemplifies the extremes to which human beings can go to expand their own personal power and accompanying wealth. The rise and fall of Communism in less than a hundred years presents a strong case for arguing the extent to which human character and aggression are molded by the desire to own property.

Occupation and cultivation of the land still dominate the economies of the most populated nations such as India and China where 70 to 80 percent of the people live in rural villages. As overcrowding reduces the carrying capacity of farmlands through increasing erosion, drought and soil loss, rural poverty deepens. An estimated 100 million Chinese farmers are combing the major industrial cities in search of work to supplement their income. By 1992 this was a yearly average of more than four million farmers leaving the land.[36]

The land base and physical resources which constitute a nation are bounded and identified by the land its people occupy and over which it claims sovereignty. Land has come to define race, culture, laws, traditions, economics and the living standards of its occupants. It has been the prime motivation for the majority of violent confrontations which have erupted in civil, international and world wars for the last 10,000 years. The human drive for wealth and dominance over land bases has led many leaders to challenge their neighbours since prehistoric times. The earliest civilizations and empires of Mesopotamia were built on conquered lands. The glory that was Rome was built on technologically superior military strength and cunning which enabled the Romans to conquer vast areas of the Mediterranean where less technically advanced peoples fell victim to the Roman lust for empire. History is a pageant of battles over land bases from the ancient Babylonians to the Romans, the Mongols, the Goths, the Moslems, on through to the many European peoples who built colonial empires and fought two world wars in the 20th Century to gain hegemony over all continents.

So much of human aggression over the millennia has come about over the unequal distribution of land, its wealth and the power it represents. Some lands have much to offer in resources, climate and arable lands. The greater a nation's land base, the greater its ability to build its strength to defend itself and to improve the living standard of its citizens.

Land or territory also defines racial and ethnic origins; it defines the human sense of who we are and what we are. We will build vast armies to conquer and defend those lands against intruders or foreign conquest, even sacrifice our lives to protect them from an enemy. Nothing in our entire evolution has had more effect on our behaviours and attitudes towards each other and to the environment than the ownership of land and property.

The possession of land, whether on a family, tribal, racial or national scale, while building identity, self-esteem, patriotism, social traditions and racial characteristics, has also provoked hatred, racism, inequality, widespread poverty, xenophobia and violent conflicts; all emotions and conditions which have become socially inherent in every human society. Violent aggressions associated with national racism are now the greatest barrier to human co-operation and peaceful co-existence world wide. As lands become overcrowded and incapable of sustaining the burgeoning populations, the drive to obtain land, fresh water reserves and food supplies will enhance each of these undesirable social qualities and evoke violent responses in the future.

CHAPTER TWO

BC: 3000 Years of Human Settlement and Technological Evolution

During the last 6000 years, many civilizations have risen and then disappeared in different parts of the world. Favourable climatic conditions following the end of the Ice Age made possible the domestication of increasing varieties and quantities of food crops which supported a steadily expanding population in the Northern Hemisphere. People generally settled near rivers and oceans where they were surrounded by arable lands and forests.

Among the first such civilizations was a group of self-supporting villages, known as Mesopotamia, which grew up between 4000 and 3000 B.C. on the Fertile Crescent of the Tigris-Euphrates River plains. Several of these villages were large enough to form the first known city states. However, the geography of the land still isolated them from each other which encouraged them to grow as autonomous political communities. Some covered several hectares of land, some formed settlements which by virtue of size and population qualify as cities. Human ability to design and invent building technologies enabled them to enclose several of these cities within protective walls.

The early city states of Mesopotamia initiated many advances in governing, specialized crafts and agricultural methods. Their pottery styles reflect a complex religious and caste system in which their kings were considered divine and each member of his court played symbolic ritual roles.[1] Society was becoming sophisticated at an ever increasing pace, as both governing and religious castes quickly learned to exploit technological progress.

The most successful early civilizations were those located in the Middle East and in Egypt where food crops could be cultivated the year round. Among the earliest of these ancient cities was the Sumerian city of Ur, carbon-dated to have existed between 2800 - 2000 B.C. Artifacts found buried with the city's kings included bowls, lamps and helmets of gold, weapons and daggers of gold and silver and bowls of copper. The tombs of these ancient kings contained the skeletons of large numbers of retainers, ranging from soldiers to servants and animals, all buried alive with the body of the king. This custom was indicative of the religious beliefs held by these peoples that a "socially manifest cosmic order (existed) to which every individual must uncritically submit if he is to be anything at all", so as to ritually "cast off their bodies to be born again".[2]

Civilization is generally considered to have officially arrived with the beginning of recorded information in symbols and hieroglyphs. The use of written language and the origin of mathematics and geometry was perhaps the next greatest advancement in social and technological development following the settlement of the land. The first full system of writing appears between 3100 and 3000 B.C. in the Sumerian sites of lower Mesopotamia (Southern Iraq) where wood or bone styluses were used on clay tablets to record numbers and quantities for the purpose of keeping accounts. The earliest forms of writing are pictographs or small pictures, each representing an object. A very complex set of symbols to reproduce, they gave way to cuneiform which is accomplished through the use of a series of wedges. But even these posed difficulty as they could only be read by trained scribes.[3]

Hieroglyphics was an Egyptian form of pictographs which arose about the same time as the pictographs in Mesopotamia. But they were primarily used to decorate Egyptian temples rather than to keep records. The similarity to the pictographs of the Mesopotamian symbols suggests this early writing form was transplanted to Egypt. With time the Egyptian pictographs evolved into a stylized form of script for various uses.

Between 1250 and 750 B.C. the Greeks and Phoenicians replaced the difficult and cumbersome system of pictographs with the phonetic signs of the first alphabetized system which was in common use from Egypt through to India and China within 500 years.[4]

Without writing human society may have come to a standstill and the compilation of scientific knowledge and the extraordinary architectural feats we have achieved would not have happened. Observing primitive societies today anywhere in the world who do not have a written history or even an alphabet suggests humanity as a whole would have remained at the hunter-gatherer or primitive farming level of technology had they not had the written word and number systems. We would still be living in small groups under very primitive conditions at the mercy of natural phenomena had we not been able to store ideas and turn structural problems into mathematical formulas which enabled the building of our city states and their technological cultures. This basic difference between civilizations and primitive tribes has come to define civilization and to yield ever unfolding technological dimensions. Throughout the millennia city states and urban centres have nurtured human intellect and ingenuity.

During the first 3000 years of civilization, progress was obviously accelerating, motivated by the demands of larger and larger populations as they crowded together in growing towns and cities. Analyses of excavated ancient cities reflect the advancing social and technological development through discovered artifacts, architecture, temples, tombs, monuments and written records. These findings indicate that primary organization and control required in any human situation began then as now with political leadership and the delegation of power to assistants to enact the policies of authority. Taking control and maintaining it required economic and military strength, often imposed by terror and backed by religious sanctions. The hierarchies included chieftains or kings, a military elite, a ruling class of advisors and priests and a public of servants, farmers, craftsmen, builders and traders. The people probably fell into their roles quite naturally as human nature is much like that of all other species which recognize a rank and file order within their social groups. We more or less instinctively accept our place in the order of society. Some lead and others follow, a delineation which has come to define social and economic classes throughout human history.

The same ingrained traits which recognize the need for social order and a hierarchy carry with them an aggressiveness that motivated regular wars of conquest and destruction of one tribe or city state by another. Battles for control over wealth and farmland led to the first empires such as the Kingdom of Ur described above. These early empires were built much as colonial empires have been in recent centuries, with large armies, outfitted with deadly weapons and trained to kill and conquer. The very name, battle-ax people, given to the Celts who were spreading across Northern Europe in these millennia B.C., describes both their natural instincts and their social/political direction.

Roles within the hierarchies were enhanced through religious rituals which formalized their powers. In many cases kings were given the "divine" right to rule. Menes, pharaoh of the ancient city of Memphis, a collection of villages and farmlands, bolstered his kingship by surrounding himself with priests and images of the gods. Some kings deified themselves and their descendants to gain obedience and to ensure the lineage to the thrones of their kingdoms. The pharaohs of Egypt had themselves immortalized and mummified in giant pyramidal tombs which would "last for all time". Ruling elites became priests, giving their authority religious weight and calling on the gods to provide charismatic power of enforcement. Battle feats were immortalized in religious myths and legends. The hubris gained through religious authority enabled leaders to redirect the natural aggression of their people into erecting huge monuments to the gods and the kings while uniting them in excursions of conquest or against invading enemies.

The architectural feats of the temples, sculptures, tombs and pyramids of ancient Egypt required huge leaps in mathematical concepts and geometry to design them, and great forward strides in social organization to erect them. The progress made in Ancient Egypt stands out in sharp contrast to the rest of sub-Saharan Africa where tribalism and hunting and gathering remained the major social framework until the 20th Century.

Early political, social and religious structures promoted technological advances in architecture, especially in Egypt where limestone was readily available. Imhotep, head of the Third Dynasty of Egypt sponsored the use of stone to build the first step pyramid at Saqqara, introducing masonry techniques and the use of large, limestone reliefs and statues. The technologies of pyramid building had advanced so well that between 2600 and 2500 the three pyramids at Gizeh were constructed.

By this time, a similar political dynasty had risen and taken control of lower Mesopotamia. Lacking stone, the technological developments in building and manufacturing of statues and artifacts were done in bronze and copper, advancing metallurgical processes.

The power of both these empires began to disintegrate by 2200 B.C. as incompetent leadership and corrupt ruling elites weakened their states.

While the Egyptian and Mesopotamian empires were in decline, neighbouring peoples were upgrading their trappings of civilization, improving their weaponry, increasing their numbers and preparing for conquest. The battles that ensued saw the city of Ur, for example, vanish beneath the destructive forces of the invaders. The land of Mesopotamia entered a 1000 years of invasions, conquests and changes of authority. In the 1700s, B.C., the suffering of its vanquished peoples forced them to migrate to new lands. Among them was Abraham who not only led his people out of the ravaged lands, but also away from worshipping animal gods and on to believing in one god whose image was essentially human.

As daily survival came to depend more and more on civilized technologies and urban existence and less on natural phenomenon, the total dependency on the whims of nature no longer predicated the need to worship the elements of nature. New methods of preserving and storing grains, berries, nuts and roots, the ability to replant crops from preserved seed, the development of primitive irrigation systems and the use of organic fertilizers eased the total dependency on nature to grow food supplies. The belief in human powers grew.

Emerging civilizations could move away from worshipping nature and create human gods in their place, gods they could more easily communicate with and endow with powers of reason as well as human character traits. The Ancient Greeks devised a pantheon of human gods, living on earth, whose purpose was to restrain the pride in this newly found sense of self-reliance. Their role was to dole out punishments to the offenders.

Favourable environmental conditions were paramount to the successful rise of these civilizations just as they are today. A habitable landbase requires ample fresh water resources, large tracts of relatively flat, arable land, extensive forests, large deposits of minerals, temperate climates, dependable seasonal rainfall and access to rivers and oceans which encourage development of economic and social structures. Without these attributes the growth of intellectual thought, the refinement of technologies, the availability of investment capital, the leadership and the collective ambitions are not present. Human life in environments lacking these assets is generally at a subsistence level; the inhabitants are few in number and are forced to scratch out a minimal living that is all consuming of human energy and time.

The destruction of good land bases while under human occupation was instrumental in the demise of many ancient civilizations as well as more recent disappearances of settled peoples. Once the settlers destroyed their immediate environment to accommodate growing populations, the civilization itself failed rapidly. The depletion of natural reserves of fresh water, the removal of forests and the erosion of arable soils brought climatic changes which led to chronic crop failures, famines and disease, depleting and scattering the populations.

The Colorado Plateau of South Western United States was the home of one such lost culture. Having graduated from being nomadic hunter-gatherers, the Anasazi of Arizona settled down to grow corn, squash and beans between 500 and 700 A.D., By 1200 A.D., only five to six hundred years later, they had dispersed and their land deserted. Through heavy cultivation they had destroyed the fertility of the soil. In cutting down their forests, the soil and water were lost to erosion. Without trees, extended periods of drought occurred, also contributing to crop failures. As always happens with settlement, their population had grown and their culture advanced. Improved farming techniques enabled them to build canals to carry water to their fields. However, solutions proved very short term. The Anasazi degraded their environment and its capacity to sustain human life beyond repair, forcing them to move on.[5]

Many ancient civilizations have been destroyed by even more dramatic causes: invasion, conquest and burning. Invasion and conquest in most cases meant the absorption of one race by another either through slavery or through forced marriages and the destruction of their "cities" by burning. Technologies and collected knowledge, designed to enhance living standards, were often lost in the struggle, setting back human progress for centuries, until newly discovered or revived. In some cases knowledge and technologies were taken hostage, absorbed by the conquerors and further refined. In this way the Romans benefitted by their conquest of Greece in their willingness to absorb Greek culture, then modifying it to suit their own particular beliefs and social needs. The conquest of the Roman Empire by the barbarian hordes of Europe during the 5th Century buried these technologies and recorded Classical knowledge for a thousand years until their reappearance in the 14th Century. With their rediscovery European civilization developed rapidly to establish Western technological and philosophical supremacy which has dominated the world for the last 500 years.

A number of smaller lost civilizations, the victims of environmental collapse, are now the sites of hundreds of archaeological digs throughout the Mediterranean area. North Africa, once the major source of food crops for the Roman empire, is primarily desert today. Mesopotamia (modern Iraq), the centre of the first human civilizations, declined into poverty and subsistence living conditions as irrigation waterlogged and salted most of the Fertile Crescent. The many towns and cities of the ancient Middle East have disappeared beneath the sand of the desert or to the powers of erosion and drought which followed ancient civilizations wherever they settled the land and destroyed the forests.

The story of ancient Ephesus in Western Turkey during the time of the Romans is one of the more outstanding examples of this human abuse of the landscape. The area of Ephesus when first settled by the Romans (B.C) was covered in forests of oak trees. At its height, the city was a thriving community of some 26,000 people.

The topography of the land comprised low hills and very small valleys, cut by a deep inland waterway, ideal for the passage and docking of ships in the heart of the city. As the hills and valleys were cleared of their trees, pasture lands gave way to farmed terraces, opening the soil on the slopes to regular periods of heavy erosion. The soil flowed off the land during the rainy seasons, silting up the inland sea channel and decreasing its use as a deep sea port.

The city itself had to be constantly relocated along the silt filled channel until its lands and seaport no longer provided a means of livelihood for its inhabitants and the city was abandoned to the elements. To this day the site of ancient Ephesus remains dry and desolate. Only sheep and goats trod the lands of the ancient city. Sadly, these animals, by eating any vegetation that takes hold, add to the degradation of the soil and prevent the regeneration of forests. Today, life on this land provides a very harsh existence for its few herdsmen.

The process of ecological and land destruction followed the Roman civilization wherever it settled in the Mediterranean area. When the trees and soils of the coastal lands were largely gone, the Romans moved their armies north into Europe in search of new lumber supplies, pastures and arable farmland, where they repeated the same process once again. To this day, much of Europe has no original forests and what trees do exist were largely planted by humans and are protected in national parks. Germany has the largest forested areas, but acid rain from burning fossil fuels during the last two decades has killed many of the trees.

In the final analysis it must be remembered that good land bases, rich in natural resources, have always been relatively scarce and have, therefore, always limited the number of concentrated settlements where people might develop successful civilizations. Such areas are very few in comparison with mountain areas, deserts, water bodies, dry plains and rocky plateaus. Past civilizations, as a result, tended to occur in isolated pockets of habitation in areas where they could be largely self-sufficient in food and fresh water reserves. They could not depend on large shipments of foods to come to them from distant lands, nor could they depend on dams and diverted rivers to ensure fresh water supplies. Those city-states with the greatest number of environmental assets such as extensive arable flatlands were usually those with the largest populations. Such assets helped them take power and extend their authority over neighbouring cities.

What we tend to ignore as we expand and develop every viable land base on the planet today is that ecological and environmental destruction have always followed in the wake of human occupation. No civilization has been exempt from this reality as the disappearance of so many early civilizations such as the Mayans and Aztecs in Central America attest to the effects of human abuse of their land bases. Hieroglyphic artifacts of these civilizations suggest deforestation and starvation. Finally wars of survival drove them off their land, bringing death to their ancient cities.

An anthropological researcher, Richard Hansen of UCLA, suggests that the Mayan civilization collapsed after centuries of successful development because "the elaborate architecture of this civilization required large amounts of lime stucco, produced by subjecting limestone to intense heat. Because as many as 20 large trees had to be burned to create a pile of stucco one metre high, whole forests were cleared. This led to soil erosion that filled in the seasonal swamps where the Maya got peat to fertilize their crops, possibly impairing their food supply."[6]

Ancient civilizations depended primarily on the amount and quality of the production of their arable lands. However, their cities and states were relatively small in size and population by today's standards which meant the ancients occupied few of the earth's fertile lands. This is in sharp contrast to our almost total occupation of global lands today. In our unsustainable numbers, not only are we forcing our presence onto all land areas from the marginal wetlands and drylands to the deserts, but much of the world's finest farm lands are disappearing beneath homes, buildings, concrete, asphalt roads and reservoirs.

Our cities are gobbling up the most accessible stretches of food growing lands. What is even more foolhardy is the universal use of farming technologies which lay waste our soils through chemical sterilization, salinization, overcropping, overgrazing and erosion.

It is worth noting that citizens of failed civilizations in the past were able to emigrate to virgin lands and begin again. But where can we go today? At present we seek solutions in one "global civilization" co-ordinated and functioning through "sustainable management" programs. Unfortunately, the present status of global development is riddled with signs of environmental collapse paralleling those of lost civilizations: deforestation, erosion, drought, salinization and desertification, accompanied by crop failures, hunger, malnutrition, disease and tribal wars. Survival for many nations today depends on importing excess food supplies produced in nations with large agricultural economies. At present over 60 nations rely almost entirely on food imports, whether through trade or aid programs.

CHAPTER THREE

AD: 2000 Years of Technology and Population Growth

Although human expansion and occupation of the earth for 4000 years B.C. grew manyfold, the last 2000 years of technological development and population growth have eclipsed that period many times.

Survival following the Neolithic Age was advanced through improved communal food production and an expanding trade in goods and ideas. Living standards rose immeasurably with developments in architecture, irrigation, water distribution, preservation and storage of food, long distance transportation and the introduction of writing. Society grew intricately more complex, requiring innovative social and political organizations to manage the production and distribution of goods as well as the administration of large numbers of people scattered over hundreds of miles of territory.

Patriarchal hierarchies, empowered by increasingly larger armies and improved weaponry, amalgamated villages into states. Maintaining and policing these early empires depended on the expanding military and political skills of their leaders to terrorize neighbouring tribes into subjugation.[1] A large, virile population of young men and women were basic to building armies, growing food and providing the goods and services which sustain a military or urban society. Consequently, emerging civilizations have always encouraged a high fertility rate among their people.

An estimated 300 million human beings populated the earth by the time of Christ. Homo sapiens had "mastered" the art of survival and was well established to meet the challenges of the next 2000 years. Although constantly increasing in numbers, populations were still relatively slow growing by modern standards. High infant mortality rates, whether from disease, hunger, neglect, abuse, accidents or intentional infanticides, dominated the causes of death, maintaining a low but expanding birth rate. The average life span for those who survived infancy and childhood averaged 20 to 30 years. Longevity was not common as poor nutrition, unsanitary practices, infections, diseases, accidents, wars, pollution and environmental degradation took their steady toll.

While human populations and cultures continued to expand over the last 2000 years in spite of so many adversities, progressive technologies and related knowledge of the physical world fuelled political and military ambitions. Civilizations and empires which proved most successful and enduring were those which rose to power on the shoulders of educated, skilled populations, trained in the arts of reasoning, mathematics and administration, supported by superiority of weapons, tools and modes of transportation. Simple technologies which we take for granted today, such as the wheel, the saddle and stirrup or the invention of gun powder, gave full advantage to those who first attained them. Populations and nations with increasingly sophisticated technologies have always been the leaders in changing the balance of political and military power.[2]

The Roman Empire dominated the Ancient World for the first 500 years of the last two millennia. Its power and size were made possible by the metal swords and armour they manufactured for their soldiers. Their increasingly sophisticated architecture enabled them to transport fresh water over hundreds of miles in aqueducts to thirsty populations and dry fields. The construction of roads paved with stones sped up the delivery of weapons and food supplies to their armies, and their chariots and wooden ships were designed to give mobility to their armies and traders.

With so much technology in their favor, the Romans were assured of superiority over the Mediterranean. Able to move both food supplies and well armed soldiers across Europe as well as provide laws, administrative organization and the general knowledge of a superior civilization, the once tiny city-state of Rome built an Empire which included the many lands and tribes of the Mediterranean and large areas of the European continent.

Populations continued to grow throughout the 500 years of Rome's imperious expansion until the Empire collapsed in 476 A.D. The fall of Rome came with the weakening and corruption of those same administrative and military skills which had so effectively built it. Barbarians from northern territories and bordering lands gradually infiltrated the outlying provinces and eventually Rome itself. The Empire could not defend itself against these growing barbarian armies nor could it hold together.

Corruption, debt, ruinous taxes and decaying cities sapped its energy and political-economic strength. Most of the classical knowledge and technologies which had enabled the Roman Empire to conquer the Ancient World and hold power for so long disappeared throughout Europe in the hands of the illiterate barbarian heathens, not resurfacing until the 14th Century, a thousand years later. In view of the present day aggressive ethnic behaviors worldwide and the migrations of millions of people from primitive to advanced cultures, one is struck by the similarity in social and economic problems cropping up in today's world with those that destroyed Rome. It is not unreasonable to wonder if the same fate is encroaching on Western Civilization.

During the 500 years which followed the invasion and collapse of the Roman Empire, the Dark Ages descended on Europe, bringing a period of chaos and isolation. Societies reverted to tribalism, political and civil order disappeared, trade died down and money went out of circulation. Only Christianity maintained ties with the tribes and preserved some of the knowledge of their civilized past. People survived in small, isolated communities whose only contact with other tribal enclaves was through the few traders, travelling missionaries and the marauders who came to kill and plunder, not to enlighten. Charlemagne, (742-814 A.D.) with the aid of the Christian Church, attempted to return some sense of civilization and progress to Europe, but his success was short lived. Barbarians continued to invade his empire as centuries of violence and primitive tribal organization produced widespread ignorance and xenophobia throughout Europe, dominated by massive migrations of barbarian hordes, seeking land and plundering whatever they found.

Wherever there were people trying to improve their lot, to gain land bases and to dominate or fend off their neighbours, rising fertility rates were promoted and populations expanded over shorter and shorter periods of time. The Catholic Church, once established as the major political force as well as the only religious power throughout a chaotic, unruly Europe after the fall of Rome, sought to promote its strength and universal power through doctrine which taught "Go forth and multiply... and subdue the earth." This decree has since been in practice and as recently as 1968 and 1995, been reinforced by papal encyclicals which forbid contraception and abortion with an eye to continued growth of Catholic populations the world over.

Technologies and refined knowledge accumulated by the Greeks and Romans had largely disappeared into the archives and libraries of Arab states and Eastern monasteries. It was as if life in Europe had returned to prehistoric times when farming and related crafts were all the technological knowhow in existence. Life came to be dominated by debilitating wars and religious dogmas. Those who escaped dying by the sword of invading tribal hordes often suffered punishments and sacrifices imposed by Church clerics.

Farming, done with the most primitive of tools and requiring many backbreaking hours of labour, generally produced only as much food as was needed to maintain the farmer's own family. Trade was limited to buying and selling locally handmade crafts at the village fair. If wealth existed, it was at the highest echelons of society among the emerging aristocracy and clergy. Travelling was arduous and dangerous, attempted only by traders, groups of religious pilgrims or adventurous pirating armies.

By the 11th Century, barbaric migrations and incursions ceased and the self-containment policy of feudalism brought a more socially organized but equally dangerous lifestyle to Europe. Although more socially organized, contact between members of feudal manors was generally in battle, as knights with their armies marauded over the countryside, destroying crops, killing serfs and villagers and storming castles. The same aggressive warfare for accumulating land and empires which had dominated life during the time of the Greeks and Romans and drove them to master the known world, now drove the knights of Medieval Europe as they fought to build themselves large, powerful domains.

Populations, having grown sparse during the Dark Ages, began once again to expand steadily throughout Medieval Europe until the 14th Century. Feudalism had reasserted a social setting for political/military power to re-establish social stability through the technologies of superior weaponry and a powerful hierarchy which demanded loyalty and obedience. Europe was preparing for the return of an interchange of goods, ideas and technologies.

In the Western nations the majority of people in Medieval times lived in rural areas where their survival needs fell under the full responsibility of the land owner, whose major purpose in life was to feed and house his tenant farmers and their families, his servants, labourers and craftsmen. At this point in time, he had little desire for riches and luxury goods, mainly because they did not exist. Life was localized and although relatively primitive, it was self-sufficient, remaining so for nearly 500 hundred years under the protective arms of feudalism. When nations began exploring other lands in the 15th and 16th Centuries, exotic goods from foreign countries were introduced for the first time, beginning a rush to explore and conquer the world beyond the European continent.

The accumulated knowledge of the ancient empires of Greece, Rome and Islam began to trickle back into Europe through Arab scholars migrating to Spain. They helped translate Arabic books into European languages. This new knowledge was then increased by the abundance of Classical knowledge which arrived with the monastic scholars who had fled Constantinople during the Turkish invasion of that city in 1453. The next 500 years became Europe's domain as science, philosophy, mathematics and rational thinking placed European scholars and leaders in the forefront of world technological and cultural development.

Technological advances included the compass and gun powder, opening the way to global colonization. The invention of the printing press in 1476 awakened Europe to accumulated knowledge, thrusting it into the Renaissance. However, by the year 1500 AD., the world's population is estimated to have reached only 500 million, an increase of 200 million in 1500 years.

The cause of the slow population growth was the high death rate which accompanied the technological progress and increasing international travel during this period. As cities became overcrowded and the sewage and filth accumulated, frequent virulent epidemics swept Europe. Bubonic plague transmitted by rats took millions of lives over several centuries. The Black Plague which began in Constantinople in 1347, spread throughout Europe and killed as many as one third of the continent's population in the 14th and 15th Centuries.

Over the millennia, epidemics have been symptomatic of crowded cities and travelling armies. Death rates rose dramatically during periods of territorial and colonial wars as conquering soldiers and colonists carried with them the many diseases of civilization to which the native peoples of other lands had no resistance. It is estimated that North and South America were inhabited by over 100 million indigenous natives at the time Columbus discovered America, a number quickly reduced to just tens of thousands following their conquest by European armies.

Large numbers of deaths also occurred throughout Europe and Asia from frequent famines and related diseases, the result of natural climatic cycles which brought drought, pestilence and floods while destroying crops. Overpopulating and overcropping farm land led to a decline in clean water supplies, depleted topsoils, erosion, crop diseases and low yields, all contributing to increasing periods of hunger and disease among humans and animals. While the death rate climbed during periods of war, famine and plague, fertility rates shot up dramatically during times of peace and good harvests, offsetting the negative birth rates of periods of scarcity and adversity, thus ensuring a slow, but steady increase in the population.

World populations remained relatively stable at 500 million for nearly 300 years. The first major increase in human numbers came in the 18th and 19th Centuries when world populations were estimated to have reached the first billion.

Impact of The Industrial Revolution
on Human Development

If settling the land has molded human nature, it has also been the catalyst for extraordinary developments in human technological innovation and intellectual evolution. It set the stage for the two most significant events to affect our social behaviours and attitudes as well as population expansion. These were the Industrial Revolution of the 19th Century and the colonization of the world by European nations.

The Industrial Revolution began in England in the latter half of the 18th Century with an agrarian revolution. Between 1730 and 1755 the country experienced an unusual number of bumper harvests that had a twofold effect: (1) the demand for labour to harvest these crops brought about a real rise in wages; and (2) the excess crop production caused a significant drop in food prices, alleviating hunger among most of the peasant population. Increased food supply improved their health and energy levels and lowered the infant mortality rate.[3]

Famines, epidemics and low wages in the past generally wiped out large population gains, but the revolution in farming in Britain that was under way offset normal patterns of attrition. New farming methods, new technologies and the enclosure of the common lands led to rapid advancements in crop production, creating a demand for labour to do the work of fencing, draining, ditching, animal tending, planting and harvesting on private lands for both small and large landowners. Having fenced their properties, farmers could now produce both better crops and animals as they were protected from the vagaries of raising herds on the commons where disease destroyed many animals and scattered landholding, rendering farming inefficient and time wasting.[4]

The ownership of solid blocks of land and the new technologies available to work it, --seed drills, crop rotation, improved seeds and grasses, animal breeding and winter fodder, light iron hoes, harrows and a new plough drawn by a single horse,-- required much less labour per acre and resulted in greater food production, more wages and higher profits. Most importantly, it gave incentive to the landowners to invest in the new farming techniques and become exporters of grains and meats.[5]

Mechanized farming of food production and good job opportunities in Western cities enabled people to leave the land to find employment and excitement in the cities. New opportunities in industry and manufacturing, as well as better distribution of farm ownership for those who remained behind, meant men could marry much younger and have larger families. Farmers no longer had to wait for a house and a strip of farm land to come open before they could wed as they had in the past. Able to provide food in excess quantities, farmers supplied those who lived in urban areas. The fertility rate of the Western World exploded.

The benefits of food surpluses for sale at lower prices in the towns and cities aided in an unprecedented drop in the nation's death rate and a corresponding rise in the birth rate. Having an excess of food grown at home, Britain, for instance, was able to feed her people while not spending her capital to buy imported foods to feed the growing populations. Instead, the money remained at home to fuel the industrial developments that would follow in rapid succession during the next few decades and throughout the 19th Century.[6]

The last 500 years of progress in technologies were instrumental in empowering the European nations to dominate the world's culture and development. The successful colonization of the world by European nations from the 16th to the 20th Century was accomplished through superiority of metal weapons and a vast improvement in ships. The Mayans of Central America and the Incas of Western South America, armed only with wooden clubs, succumbed easily to the power of guns and metal swords of the Spanish invaders. The civilizations of India, China and Japan also gave way to European guns, war ships and superiority of battle strategies.

After conquering the many nations of the world, European empires were built and administered on an impressive array of new inventions and industrial manufacturing. Steam powered machines, telegraph communications, large steamships, asphalt highways, the many technologies of the Industrial Revolution gave Europe superiority of food supply, military power, administrative skills, mass production of goods and the easy movement of commodities and people around the world.

Western nations had the advantage of wealth, educated workforces and political freedom until recent times, contributing the energy of their people and their vast pool of knowledge which established Western civilization as the standard and source of technological and economic development for the entire world until the late 20th Century.

However, the early stages of the Industrial Revolution were a period of gross exploitation and dehumanization of domestic workers. Their needs were subjected to extreme horrors of poverty, hunger and disease in the cities until government reforms in the latter half of the 19th Century in Britain and the early decades of the 20th Century in the United Sates forced the improvement of working conditions, reduced working hours and increased safety precautions. By the middle of the 20th Century, the most important change in relations between owners and workers in industry was the rise in wages, permitting good living standards and affluent purchasing power for the work forces. This change in direction on the part of the industrial owners created the mass domestic markets which brought great wealth to Britain in the first half of the 20th century and then brought super power status to the United States after World War II.

The greatest age of human innovation and technological development had begun. The industrial age which started in the textile industries swiftly opened the door to vast employment in iron and steel production. Newly created jobs and several innovative modes of transportation made life in the cities possible for hundreds of thousands who, formerly, would have been tied to the land, struggling to survive on food they had grown by hand. The Industrial Revolution in England had led the way in establishing a successful agricultural/industrial pattern for producing wealth and prosperity throughout the Western World.

Today Nations Are Defined
According to Their Technological Development

Since World War II successful levels of human survival in the modern world have been measured by the sophistication and variety of the technology a nation possesses to produce the array of goods and services now available. The more sophisticated a nation's "high" technologies, the better the quality of life and the higher the rate of survival experienced by the majority of its people.

Of the 180 or more nations presently in existence, few can be described as highly industrialized at this point in time. To categorize the various degrees of technological progress or the lack of it, the terms "developed" and "developing" were coined. The term "developing" is meant to give every poor nation or Third World nation a sense that it, too, can become fully industrialized and entitled to the name of "developed nation" with all the riches and privileges that entails.

In applying the criteria of industrialization, accepted terminology designates two large general categories: industrial or developed nations and Third World or developing nations. In actuality five can be more clearly defined.

(1) At the top of the scale are the highly industrialized "rich" nations located largely in the temperate climate zones and known as the Developed Nations. Able to support over 90 percent of their people at living standard above a subsistence level, they are the nations with the most advanced technological industries. Categorized as "rich", based on their Gross National Product (GNP) and income per capita, these economies generally have both an industrial and agricultural base which support affluent living standards for the majority. "Developed nation" implies industry and the widest use of computer and communication technologies whose utilization of technologies and their production determine a nation's measurement of economic success. Nations in this category include those of North America, Western Europe, Australia, New Zealand, South Africa and the Asian nations of Japan, Taiwan, South Korea, Hong Kong, and Singapore. Together their populations comprise 20 percent of the world's people today, but it is estimated they will make up only

12 percent by 2050,[7] as their populations stabilize relative to the poor nations which will maintain a fertility rate of 2 to 3 percent over the 21st Century.

Production of goods and services in developed nations far outweighs the consumption of their domestic markets, enabling them to enjoy the profits of billions of dollars worth of exports and foreign investments. The majority of their people are well fed, educated, employed and healthy. Surpluses of food and manufactured goods are exported and traded for oil, raw materials, foods not grown in their climate areas and a wide variety of "hi-tech" and luxury consumer goods.

(2) Next are the "Second World" countries which once had very active industrial bases, but are now in political and economic chaos after the fall of Communism. Their birth rates are generally falling or are relatively stable. Their nations face huge debts, stagnant industrial production, a decaying energy complex, and unprecedented environmental pollution and destruction. Sometimes referred to as the Second World, they lie somewhere between developed and developing.

They have a large industrial base but their productivity is low and of poor quality. Technologies are outdated. Living standards are rapidly dropping for the majority as production and competency remain poor. These nations are plagued with incompetent political leadership, a shortage of investment capital, a lack of financial and contractual systems, unskilled workforces for modern industrial output, disintegrating and under-financed infrastructures, impassable roads and a growing xenophobia between ethnic groups and races. A general shortage of food and consumer goods, poor, ill-equipped medical services, decaying, almost unusable transportation systems and inadequate communication and computer networks are all commonplace in the disintegrating former Eastern European and Russian bloc of Communist nations.

When and if these ex-Communist states are able to revitalize their economies and raise their living standards to the level of the industrial nations, they should regain their place as fully developed nations. The degree of success they reach will depend on how fast they rid themselves of centralized government ownership of land and industries, adapt to the entrepreneurial systems that will enable them to compete on the open markets of the world and overcome the growing powers of the criminal world which have grown out of political chaos and a lack of economic structure and law. For over forty five years their isolationist Communist policies relegated them to the designation of Second World. For purposes of argument here, they will be included generally under the heading of developed nations of the Industrial world.

(3) The third group comprises the "developing nations" of the "Third World" which have a relatively good industrial base, but any social progress and economic gains at present are offset by large, expanding populations, growing faster than the economy. These national economies are categorized as the newly emerging industrials (NEI's). They are nations in the Third World who are achieving a substantial industrial and agricultural base as well as infrastructures and are managed by relatively stable governments. They include the Central and South American nations and the Asian countries of China, India, Indonesia, Thailand, Vietnam and Malaysia.

At present much of their gains in productivity and development remain offset by large populations. Most have reduced their fertility rates, but longevity, higher infant survival rates and a smaller, but still definitive rise in the birth rate are causing an unsustainable increase in their populations. China's policy of one child per couple is severe, but will still see its present population of 1.2 billion reach 1.5 billion by 2025. India is predicted to reach 1 billion people by 2000 and 1.4 billion by the year 2025.[8]

The economies of the Asian nations in this group are booming, but the advantages remain with a relatively small sector of the population who are directly involved in industrial entrepreneurship or in manufacturing jobs. Industrial workers, most of whom receive "slave" labour wages and have no benefits such as medical care or holiday time, are able to raise themselves out of abject poverty and enjoy a slightly better standard of living. The economic advantages remain minimal, however, for the majority and will do so until the nations are fully industrialized, their workforces educated and trained in the skills of "hi-tech", and their populations stabilized and gradually reduced. Taiwan and South Korea were in this category until only a few decades ago, but now have skilled populations enjoying a relatively high standard of living and have moved into the industrially developed category. Birth rates are generally down, although population numbers are up.

Until fully industrialized, the majority of people in the NEI's will remain relatively poor, and either consume their agricultural and domestic output or go without so that production can be exported to gain foreign credits, purchase technologies and pay national debts.

In the past when their governments demanded increased production of agricultural output for purposes of export trade, a large percentage of the population suffered. In India and the Philippines during the 1980s, the expansion of commercial agriculture in place of domestic farming resulted in widespread malnutrition and dislocation among peasants who were forced to stop growing a variety of nutritional foods to feed their families so that the land could be given over to commercial monocultures of export value.

In this same category of "developing" Third World nations, struggling to establish a sound industrial base, but having suffered many setbacks are the nations of Central and South America. Most South American nations have ample natural resources and land area. During the 1970s they imported technology and foreign investment to develop their industrial base through the construction of large projects such as dams, roads and mines which left them with huge debts, millions of displaced people and on a binge to destroy the most precious environmental asset they have: the rain forests of the Amazon Basin. Fortunately, their inability to repay those debts brought an end to foreign investment in those large projects which did more damage to the environment and the people than they did good.

The elite in these nations remain wealthy through agricultural production as they own most of the land in Central and South America. Unfortunately, they have a history of dependency on one or two export commodities - beef and their byproducts or coffee and sugar cane, making their economies dependent on the whims of world market prices and sales. This dependency has helped keep them in debt and political turmoil while selling off their land and natural resources to multinational corporations. Consequently, the bulk of production and profit tends to migrate out of the country to the rich nations to pay Third World debts accrued through loans. What little profit returns to the nation is used largely by the elite to buy imported luxury goods for themselves.[9]

In Brazil almost all agricultural production in recent years has been grown for export to finance the nation's foreign debt. Many of the peasant farmers, forced off their land by commercial monocultures, have migrated to the cities. A large sector of the Brazilian population now lives unproductive lives in some of the largest, most dangerous overcrowded urban areas in the world.

Foreign investors continue to exploit the work forces of Central and South America's cities by paying very low wages and refusing to finance any social costs or benefits, including environmental regulations and conservation programs. As the demand for raw materials and commodities grows on world markets, these nations are re-establishing a minimal industrial base and communications infrastructure. But poverty, inflation, debt and corrupt leadership continue to hinder their development. Meanwhile, their human numbers expand. The total population in Latin America in 1990 was 450 millions. It is expected to reach 750 million by 2025, a 60 percent increase.

(4) At the bottom of the developing scale are the "poor", agriculturally-based nations of the Third World, located primarily in the tropical climate zones. The majority of their citizens are impoverished and their populations are exploding. In these poorest of nations, the most pervasive forms of production exhibit little if any industrial development and employ non-mechanized farming methods. Yet many are euphemistically referred to as "Developing Nations".

Their populations are far too large for the national land bases they occupy; all overwhelm the carrying capacity. Life for the majority is at a subsistence level where malnutrition, unemployment, a lack of purchasing power, disease and overcrowding cause debilitating stress on the vast majority. Wealth, if it exists, is in the hands of a small, ruling elite. Industrial output is very minimal at best. Most manufacturing must be described as labour intensive, often carried on under slave conditions.

Agricultural production is generally non-mechanized, carried out on small, individually owned or rented plots so that crops are produced through manual labour. Output is low, quality of production is poor, climatic conditions are generally unfavourable, and farming is often done on exhausted lands, crowded with subsistence farmers who depend on their large families to work the fields.

Plots of land are divided up to feed growing families, surpassing the carrying capacity of the land to sustain them all. The production diminishes as farmers are forced to live on smaller and smaller parcels of farm land until every one lives on the verge of starvation. The bulk of the people in Africa, India, Pakistan, Bangladesh, Egypt, the oil-poor nations of the Middle East and a myriad of small island nations around the world fall into this group.

Faced with the highest unsustainable fertility rates in the world, the cities in "poor" developing nations are large and very overcrowded, filled with the overflow populations of impoverished peasants who were forced off or could not survive on the land. The little wealth these nations produce remains in the hands of the small, rich elites who make up the only social class which is well fed, educated, healthy and productive.

(5) The final category is relatively new. It is a growing phenomenon emerging in both developed and developing nations: the overcrowded, impoverished populations of the inner city slums. They are the dispossessed refugees from the land, from civil wars, from collapsing environments, the unemployed and the unemployable, all seeking survival in the cities. They are the burgeoning, superfluous millions who have little or no contribution to make to the modern technological revolution and consequently lack purchasing power. They live in tenements or on the street, barely supported by public welfare and aid

programs. Their numbers are expanding at 2 to 4 percent a year, generally producing the majority of every nation's new births.

Their numbers are running into the tens of millions. By the year 2000, the twenty largest cities in the world will be home to 10 to 20 million people each. Two of them will even exceed 20 million. Mexico City is predicted to reach 25 million and Sao Paulo 22 million. Several more cities are expected to surpass 20 million in the early half of the 21st Century.[10] These are populations greater than the total populations of many nations and are creating social and economic problems for their governments worse than those of most nations in Asia and Africa.

Although five levels of development are described here, the general terms "Industrial Nations", Newly Emerging Industrials (NEI's) and "the Third world" are commonly used terms to differentiate among developed nations, developing nations and "poor" nations. However, categorizing nations according to their industrial development or lack of it cultivates an avarice among the less developed who desire their "fair share" of the myriad of commodities and services now enjoyed by the few.

Furthermore an honest assessment of today's technologies in the highly developed nations suggests they have arrived at the brink of technological usefulness. Every new technological invention from here on will be either superfluous to our survival, a manifestation of our hubris and a means to provide for our gross overpopulation; or it will be a necessity developed to undo the environmental damage we have done to the planet. Unfortunately, nothing in our present course of industrialization and population expansion suggests we will make rational choices and end the damage of our technological existence. A very dangerous dilemma now lies in our determination to advance our technological dependency. Policies which expand universal industrialization and general affluence can only guarantee human survival in the short term and threaten extinction in the not too distant future. The speed at which human existence will collapse now depends on the ultimate size our overall populations will reach and the extent of industrial development we attain worldwide to provide for those excessive numbers of consumers and polluters.

PART TWO

Unmanageable Demographics

Unmanageable Demographics

The past 250 years have brought unprecedented improvements in our standards of living. They are manifest in the various forms of transportation and communication, the amassed collection and dispersement of knowledge, the abundance of scientific and technological inventions, the ever increasing industrial output and the accruing medical capacity to keep so many sick and injured people alive. These have been the harbingers of human dominance, expansion and exploitation of the entire planet. They have permitted high fertility rates and reduced infant mortality, allowing the world's populations in every nation to grow exponentially.

The outcome of so much technological development over the last three centuries has forced a social, religious and ethical dilemma of unmanageable dimensions on the human species: the means to keep too many people alive through infancy into their reproductive years and on into old age, without universal institutional powers to control the number of children conceived by every woman.

Until the 18th Century population expansion was slow by 20th Century standards, with fertility rates remaining almost equal to death rates. Much depended on annual weather conditions, crop production, local wars and epidemics. With the technological innovations in farming, ensuring greater and more varied food supplies, populations grew from 500 million in the latter half of the 17th Century to reach one billion in 1804. Although infant mortality rates remained high throughout much of the 19th century, women were having a large number of pregnancies. With the discovery of antiseptics and anaesthetics in the latter half of the 19th Century, greater medical control over infection, medical operations and epidemic diseases achieved a far higher survival rate among infants and children in the Western nations than ever before. Women were averaging 12 to 16 pregnancies of which most were surviving into adulthood. This high survival rate also meant that the majority of children were living to reproductive age in the industrial nations, primarily because diseases were being controlled with vaccines and improved sanitation practices. Above all most people were living well into old age.

From 1850 on the annual birthrate began to exceed the death rate. Whereas human populations had previously taken over several million years to reach one billion, the second billion after 1804 was reached by 1927, just over 125 years after reaching the first billion.[1] The third billion was added by 1960, 33 years later, one quarter of the previous time. Birth rates exploded throughout the 20th Century as world populations reached 4 billion 14 years later in 1974, then 5 billion in 1987, only 13 years later, and an estimated 6 billion in 1997, less than 10 years after that.

Humanity everywhere is presently in trouble with the environmental destruction being done by its 6 billion inhabitants. The human race has spread over the entire planet and multiplied its numbers beyond all natural controls on a species' fertility rates. It is estimated that more people are alive in the world today than have lived and died since our Australopithecine ancestors first appeared. No human forces or cataclysmic natural events can be foreseen to reduce this equation of growth or even dramatically slow it down over the 21st Century.

The major cause of this population "explosion" (a term coined by Paul Ehrlich) during the 20th Century and continuing throughout the 21st Century has been the huge surge of birth rates over death rates world wide. Most recent statistics show that in 1988 the ratio of births to deaths was 120 million births to 40 million deaths, which means that the total population increased by over 80 million in 1988, an increase of 1.8 percent, 18 additional persons for every 1000 already here. This annual rate is complicated by the fact that the rate of 1.8 percent is added on top of the 1.8 percent added for the precious year and so on.[2]

During the 1970s ecologists and demographers, recognizing the impending threat to the planet posed by "explosive" birth rates in the world's populations, projected their findings onto the future. They realized that the birthrate over the death rate would add over 70 million people each year during the 1970s, increasing to 80 millions in the 1980s and reaching well over 90 millions annually in the 1990s. This forecasts a population of over 6.1

billion in the year 2000. The demographers' numbers were on
track in the 1990s as the population reached 5.5 billion by 1992
and steadily rose, but a decline in the yearly rise was measured in
1995 as populations grew at only 87 million, not at the predicted
90 million plus.

This exponential growth rate carried into the 21st Century
will certainly double to 10 billion between 2030 and 2050 at
present rates of growth. Whether it will level out somewhere
between 10 billion and 14 billion before the year 2100 will depend
on the carrying capacity of the planet. It is this equation of human
survival on a diminishing environmental scale that will determine
whether or not 10 to 14 billion people can exist at one time, let
alone live successfully.[3]

How will the planet cope with the needs and wastes of 10 to
14 billion people within the next 100 years? What quality of life
can any of us expect to have as our numbers rise steadily? Will it
be a world in which the majority suffers extremes of
overcrowding, deprivation and violence while the few wealthy
live within heavily protected "fortresses"? Can anyone, rich or
poor, survive the impact of the "green-house effect" and related
climatic changes, ozone depletion and ultra violet B rays,
destroyed food chains and increasingly scarce fresh water
resources, all caused either by changing natural forces or human
activities?

The time is upon us to total up and assess the threat five
million years of evolution and 10,000 years of civilization have
had upon our only territorial land base, the earth. Our survival as
a species has been successful by all criteria governing species'
evolution. But have we been too successful? Is the human species
now a destructive aberration of nature rather than a success story?

In the past human populations grew very slowly because food
supplies and natural attrition placed limits on their fertility
rates. Now that science and technology provide so many ways to
overcome territorial carrying capacity as well as offering mass
solutions to endemic disease, populations have soared. Improved
sanitation, better nutrition, knowledge and control of epidemic
diseases, medical cures and prevention of bacterial infections,
distribution of food aid, storage and preservation of food supplies,

sewage and garbage disposal, all have provided the means to overcome most causes of death among infants and children and to prolong life into old age in both rich and poor nations.

Modern moral attitudes have also brought a reduction in abortion and infanticide which was once common. Although a much smaller ratio of infants die in these ways today, the World Health Organization (WHO) estimates that over 13 million infants and children under the age of five still die annually from neglect, starvation, abuse and murder.[4] Furthermore, in 1994, WHO estimated that over 54 million pregnancies are terminated annually by abortion, the majority of them in the Third World.[5] Yet the number of pregnancies brought to term and surviving childhood annually outnumber the death rate by over 93 million per year and rising. The estimated number of live births in 1991 was 143,519,000; the numbers of deaths that year was 50,289,000, a difference of 93,230,000, indicating a world population increase of 1.7 percent in that year.[6]

Demographers and scientists had hoped for a noticeable decline in fertility rates which began in the 1960s and 1970s, but the trend lost momentum during the 1980s when the Reagan administration in the United States stopped all American support for the UN Population Fund and the International Planned Parenthood Federation. President Reagan disapproved of the UN's decision to send family planning aid to China where the Communist regime forced abortion on women who had more than one child. President Bush continued this policy until his defeat in 1992.[7] World populations soared.

During the 1980s existence became difficult and life threatening for families throughout the Third World. The inability to sustain large families gradually encouraged the wider use of contraceptives in the late 1980s and through the 1990s, reducing some of the need and desire for many children. National governments supported family planning programs as well as education and self-help projects which helped slow the birth rates some. To this day only half the women in the Third World have access to family planning services which might have prevented tens of millions of unwanted pregnancies.[8] Furthermore, the number of fertile women in the world who will have children, if only two or three, still means a rapid increase in overall population numbers.

In this way any decline in world fertility rates in the 1990s is offset by the increasing number of teenagers and young women reaching their reproductive years and giving birth. A United Nations report predicts that "...an actual decline in world population...is not expected for a century or more... Four decades of the fastest growth in human numbers in all history lie ahead."[9]

The United Nations' optimistic goal of a maximum 2.1 children per couple by the year 2000, a number they promote because it limits families to their replacement rate, is now seen as an impossibility. If family planning were in existence world wide, it is estimated it would reduce the birth rate to just under three children per family, but present medium fertility rates projected over the 21st Century still indicate a total world population of ten billion by 2030 and a possible 14 billion by 2100.[10] If the fertility rates remain above replacement rates of 2 children per family, the high fertility projection by 2100 is over 18 billion people.[11] Just the impact of an additional 90 million yearly and growing is staggering, let alone an additional 4 to 5 billion over the next forty years. But 14 to 18 billion is unfathomable.

The first repercussions of our attempts to sustain the existing 6 billion are with us now in the 1990s. The impact of so many human beings can be seen in our overcrowded cities and nations where racial tensions, poverty, violence, crime, murder, illegal refugees and internecine wars have become the norm. It is there in the growing number of nations unable to maintain or afford the urban infrastructures and industrial technologies vital to human health and social stability. Few national governments, including those in rich countries, can raise enough tax revenue to finance the bureaucracies needed to maintain social services, education, medical care, roads and bridges, water and sewer, electric power, police forces, welfare and the many other services which ensure city populations a life of law and order, employment and good health. Most importantly, human numbers are growing faster than the environments in which they live can regenerate themselves.

Of the 6 billion people who are alive today, it is estimated that only one billion live very well, that over 4.5 billion live at one fifteenth of the standard of the "rich" one billion, and of the remaining 4.5 billion, over one billion are too poor to buy enough food to sustain life.[12] Among these numbers over 1.2 billion lack access to safe supplies of drinking water.[13] United Nations' estimates say about 15 million die of hunger and disease-related causes each year. Of the 85 to 90 million added to the world's population annually, nearly 95 percent will be born in Third World countries of Africa, Asia and South America which can least support them.[14] The greatest threat to human survival in the 21st Century will be the impact on this planet's total environment of an estimated 10 to 14 billion people within the next 40 to 100 years.

The average yearly addition of 90 million people throughout the 1990s has already placed an unsupportable strain on existing food supplies, arable soils and fresh water reserves. A recent study published by the U.S. Worldwatch Institute showed populations in China are increasing at 13 millions a year, a rate based on the one child per couple rule. If China continues to raise the living standards of its people at its present rate through industrialization, by the year 2030, it will require quantities of food greater than the world's present total of grain exports as well as the entire fish harvest of 100 million tonnes. This is based on an equivalent level of consumption per capita as that of Japan today.[15]

Supplying the existing 6 billion people on earth has and is forcing occupation and cultivation of the few remaining natural habitats and dry lands still in existence. In Guatemala, for instance, immigrants pour into the rainforest, burn the trees and vegetation to farm the land. The thin, poor soil is soon exhausted from the demands of the corn and bean crops, forcing the farmer to move on and repeat the process or face starvation. In 40 years Guatemala's population grew from 3 million to 7 million by 1980. It is estimated to reach 12 million by the year 2000. As a primarily agrarian nation, nearly all will need land, fuel and grazing areas on which to live. Over 65 percent of the country's virgin forests have been cut to date and the land ruined by peasant farming to stave off starvation.

The amount of clean water, mineral resources, trees and energy needed to supply the world's additional 90 million human beings each year is beyond comprehension. They must be fed, clothed and housed. In advanced areas they must be educated, transported, employed and provided basic services of health care, police protection, energy and personal living space no matter how small or huge their demands on each. The strain of large population increases each year on national tax bases, infrastructures, judicial systems and land will soon grow beyond the ability of any city or state to finance and maintain. The quantity of sewage, garbage, toxic wastes, industrial damage, polluted air and water and diminished ecology the yearly increase of 90 million will add to the environment must be calculated into the annual production of present emissions of pollutants and the costs of disposing of them into an already overpolluted environment. Any technological advances made to reduce present pollutants both into the air and onto the land will further diminish the remaining resources of energy and raw materials, while adding to the pollution of the biosphere.

What is critical in immediate terms of coping with our survival as a species is that we have increased the burden of our daily existence on this earth threefold in only 50 years and will triple it again in the next 100 years. Never before have the planet and our technologies had to meet the exponential expansion and destruction of so many people. Human numbers are outrunning our capacity to provide sustainable technologies which will increase food and water production or provide liveable social space on the scale required by the increasing rate of consumption that six, soon to be 10 billion, people will require in just the next few decades, well within the lifetime of many of us.

Even more critical, all resources exploited to fulfil these insatiable needs must be extracted from a planet already unable to provide a productive existence for two thirds of those now alive. As Llwewellyn-Jones expressed it, "Not only is the rate of population growth exponential, but so is the production of consumer goods, so is the production of waste, so is pollution and so is land occupancy."[16]

CHAPTER FOUR

Overpopulation or Sustainability?

To determine at what point populations are sustainable or must be considered overpopulated, some scale of living standards and productivity such as the following is needed.

For a population to be sustainable and productive, it must have a land base which offers a relative degree of arable soils for farming, good water reserves, variations in vegetation from grasslands to forests, and if possible, some mineral resources which can be used either to advance the local industrial development or used in trade with other nations to obtain those goods needed for survival. If a nation lacks any or several of these elements, it must have a population sufficiently energetic, educated and skilled to produce either agricultural products in excess of its domestic needs or manufactured goods and raw materials for export to be traded for products it cannot produce. The many land and resource assets of North America have made both the United States and Canada productive and relatively self-sustaining industrial nations; whereas Japan's great success has come with developing a highly educated, energetic and skilled workforce able to manufacture the technologies needed by the rest of the world in exchange for raw materials and food supplies.

Overpopulation must then be defined by the opposite set of conditions. An overpopulated nation can no longer provide sufficient amounts of the basic needs of fresh water, farm land, forests, seed, food, fuels, mineral resources, housing, tools, clothing and employment necessary to sustain the bulk of its people at a healthy, productive level. The overpopulated nation must be considered as having grown beyond the carrying capacity of its land base, either through overcrowding or by destroying the natural environment, or both.

Nepal and Bangladesh form a definitive example. The barren mountain slopes of Nepal have turned the monsoons from a natural blessing to an annual event of ecological disaster. The forests, which once offset the eroding forces of the seasonal monsoons, have been cut down and the terraced lands which replaced them are plagued with torrential floods which sweep down the steep mountain slopes each year, taking with them large quantities of arable soils. The runoff water then floods the river deltas of neighbouring Bangladesh where the majority of Bangladeshis are congregated on temporary river flood plains. These plains are annually washed away in the floods which then reform. Once again, they are settled by the millions of annually displaced people. Life under such circumstances is lived from one flood to the next, with the hope that enough land will remain to grow sufficient food crops to prevent starvation before the next monsoon arrives. Life is extremely precarious and poverty ridden. Bangladesh has a population over 110 million and growing at 3 percent a year which at present averages out at more than 800 people per square kilometre and growing.[17]

Carrying capacity is calculated as the "numbers of people in an area relative to its resources and the capacity of the environment to sustain human activities" on an indefinite basis[18] This ratio gets out of balance when the population rapidly depletes the nonrenewable resources or "converts renewable resources into nonrenewable ones".[19] This conversion to nonrenewable resources occurs when the land is stripped of all its forests and grasslands and its hillsides are overgrazed while its arable soils are exhausted by the year round growing of crops. The land's resources are further degraded through the constant use of chemicals to replace nutrients and kill weeds and pests. Vast quantities of soil disappear through erosion and salinization. Water reserves are depleted both on the surface and underground at rates beyond nature's ability to replace them. Eco-systems are rapidly destroyed and permanently lost. Paul Ehrlich claims that measured "by this standard, the entire planet and virtually every nation is already overpopulated.[20]

Once overwhelmed, insufficient carrying capacity leads to numerous endemic economic problems and deficiencies.

Overpopulation is then equated with extensive poverty, overcrowded cities and farmlands, unemployment of the majority, mass migrations and widespread hunger. Social chaos and political instability follow in the footsteps of poverty and displacement. This is the case in so many West African countries which suffer frequent famines and chronic civil disorder.

In many nations overpopulation exists where the total economic output and wealth derived from its production enrich a small elite but are insufficient to ensure the majority access to employment and to the basic needs of survival. It exists where the majority must live at a subsistence level generally in conditions so poor that the people are malnourished, unhealthy, uneducated, unskilled and unemployed. Many poor, overpopulated nations of the Third World, especially where populations continue to grow at 3 percent and higher, are facing a future of fresh water shortages, polluted and degraded environments and a constant threat of ethnic and tribal wars over occupational control of the land and ownership of resources. African famines and civil wars have been motivated by these causes for years, turning much of the continent into a land of chaos and civil wars.

Ambitious warlords, seeking power through tribal wars, steal the land, kill members of opposing tribes and debilitate environments and people. "Ethnic cleansing" has turned wars inward, replacing traditional territorial wars between neighbouring countries. The rise to power of one "ethnic tribe" within a multicultural society or multi-tribal nation is indicative of one social group attempting to find self-esteem and identity through destroying and overpowering another social group. Diminishing land and social space, a shortage of work, food, housing and purchasing power motivate aggressive social behaviours and a desire to gain property, wealth and political power through terrorism and warfare. This was basic to the civil war among the nations of the former Yugoslavia during the first half of the 1990s or the massive acts of genocide in Rwanda during the summer of 1994 and the continuing genocide which spilled over into neighboring Burundi where the same tribes continued to kill each other.

Overpopulation creates a loss in individual earning power, reducing per capita buying power to a very low level. This, in turn, forces governments to subsidize basic consumer foods to prevent hunger riots. Poor nations dependent on foreign infusions of aid and capital often use the money to pay these subsidies. Many developing nations during the 1970s in Latin American, Africa and Asia went deeply into debt to finance large scale resource projects and industrial programs financed by the World Bank and the International Monetary Fund. The aim was to raise earning power and living standards through industrialization and improved infra-structures. However, the realities were increased poverty and unemployment for the people, while forcing open the door to the arrival of large scale agri-business throughout the Third World nations and the displacement of millions of peasant farmers. Either to offset national debts or having been convinced by foreign investors of the gains to be made through commercial agriculture of specialized commodities that could be sold in the "rich" nations, national leadership in many Third World countries stole the land from their peasant farmers and consolidated millions of acres into vast estates.

Asian and Latin American countries turned their farm land along with its care and production over to foreign corporations to grow single, often nonedible, crops which are exported to the rich nations. A fraction of the dispossessed farmers found jobs on these new estates, setting adrift millions of men and their impoverished families to migrate to the urban areas. Once they became refugees from the land they were forced to migrate to already overcrowded cities where poverty and life is far more dangerous, stressful and likely to kill them. In the cities many cannot find employment or housing. Their overwhelming numbers and extremes of poverty only add to the pollution and the horrors of the overwhelmed cities. The deprivation they suffer has put in place the major elements which initiate a population explosion: little or no contraception, nothing much to do, low self-esteem and a dominantly male attitude which cares nothing for women's rights, only for their own marital and sexual privileges. The consequence is an exploding birth rate in the Third World.

When poor people in a nation far outnumber those with substantial incomes, social and political instability grows. At present over one million people a week are moving into the world's cities. Displaced by bankruptcy or a lack of arable land, farming families migrate to urban centres in search of work. Here they experience even greater extremes of poverty. As their presence overcrowds cities, unemployment and homelessness begin to destroy their lives. Abject poverty, pollution, insecurity, disease and hunger spread among them. Dissatisfaction, restlessness and poverty motivate many of the dispossessed to enter a life of crime and drug use. Gangs and mafias rule the streets through violence.

Human suffering will be widely acute by the turn of the century as an estimated 391 cities in the world are inundated with over one million people each. Of these, 26 will be megacities with more than 10 million. Future estimates of urban growth put their total populations at 3.8 billion by the year 2020, nearly three times their present numbers.[21]

Providing better living conditions and preservation of natural resources in and around megacities may soon prove impossible to accomplish. The sheer weight of unemployed, homeless, disease-ridden people living in slum conditions, barely existing from day to day, will far exceed the earth's carrying capacity, let alone the industrial output envisaged as the way of the future. When a nation cannot ensure its people access to nutritious food, sufficient employment and adequate housing, almost any size of population is too much for the land base. Present day extremes of weather patterns and civil wars are proving sufficient to diminish crops and cause widespread famine. African nations such as Sudan, Nigeria, Somalia, Ethiopia, Mozambique, among many others, face frequent periods of drought, famine and tribal wars which diminish food production and overburden their economies with ravaged, starving refugees.

Overpopulation carries with it the stigma of mass unemployment. When less than 50 percent of a nation's work force can find work and maintain a satisfactory standard of living, the bulk of its citizens end up in large slum areas, living in squatters huts which encircle many Third World cities today, outnumbering proper housing. These people overwhelm public and social infrastructures, forming communities where there is little if any access to clean water supplies, sanitation facilities and sewage disposal, security of job and home or access to health care, police protection and social justice. The overcrowded cities of South America encompass slum areas larger than their prosperous areas. Poverty, epidemics, begging, filth, crime and personal fear dominate life for the majority.

Overcrowded landbases exhibit many social signs of overpopulation when they cannot guarantee their people police protection because there is not enough public money or political will to provide communities with stability and lawful order. When infrastructures become overburdened, laws tend to be ignored and chaos reigns. Cities in both rich and poor nations are plagued with increasing violent crimes, gang wars and public fear for personal safety. The inner cities of North America are overpopulated with impoverished, unemployed inhabitants whose existence is the equivalent of Third World nations.

Overpopulation takes its heaviest toll on children. Where poverty reigns, children suffer from diseases of malnutrition and contamination such as diarrhoea and dysentery. Tens of thousands die annually from dehydration and starvation. Millions are born unwanted to parents who lack access to contraception and abortion. Unable to care for them, parents throughout the world have abandoned millions of unwanted children to the streets, into slavery or to prostitution. In Brazil 7 million such children, many as young as four and five years of age, must survive on their own on city streets.

Throughout the Third World parents sell their children into slavery for small amounts of cash. Overburdened with childbearing, indebtedness and poverty, the families try to get out of debt by indenturing their children to slave traders. The children become the property of factory owners who not only overwork them at manual jobs, but house and feed them in conditions which destroy their health or kill them through exposure to toxic chemicals and machine accidents. Children have been observed literally chained to their jobs for years at a time.

Overpopulation contaminates the landbase where children are forced to live and play in filth and polluted waters. Many are sold into prostitution and to criminal gangs only to die of AIDS and other sexual diseases or be killed in gang wars. Still others are forced to become soldiers as young as eight to ten years of age in chronic civil wars. According to United Nations' statistics, children die on the average of 30,000 to 40,000 daily around the world from neglect and the horrors of a life in abject poverty.

Even in nations where the majority have all the food they can eat and live very well, overpopulation exists. In these circumstances it stems from a lack of personal living space in urban areas where stress from overcrowding, unemployment and noise pollution add to the anxiety caused by too much competition to hold onto a job. Fear grows for one's physical safety as increasingly violent and aggressive social behaviours cause a high rate of unnatural deaths and murders. These are the overall effects of a growing disregard for human life where land bases are overcrowded. Inner cities throughout the United States have become boiling cauldrons of xenophobic, overcrowded ethnic groups. Here crime, violence, teenage murder, the sale and consumption of drugs and street gangs are the general rule. The personal safety of both rich and poor is threatened by the growing lawlessness of this underculture.

Overcrowding also has its effects on highly industrialized nations. The small colony of Hong Kong with its bustling economy and affluent living standards is overpopulated in that it has all the problems of extensive environmental degradation. Its harbors are contaminated with huge quantities of unmanageable garbage and sewage that must be disposed of and constantly high smog content pollutes the air. Hong Kong depends almost entirely on the importation of all its basic needs of food, energy and raw materials, a dependency which denies it any possibility of living within the carrying capacity of its land base. Should its manufacturing base fail through a lack of imported food and resources, its people would be forced to move away.

Nations whose unlimited industrial expansion and production are rapidly depleting their resources of fresh water, forests and arable lands must also be categorized as overpopulated. In overconsuming these resources in the process of industrializing, nations deplete their water supplies, pollute their air, alter local climatic conditions and destroy ecosystems. Often the result is more long term damage to environments than that done by populations living in relatively primitive agrarian conditions. However, recent conditions resulting from overpopulation of rural lands is proving as devastating to the environment as is Industrialization.

By definition nations throughout the world are now overpopulated. Farmlands and cities have become so densely occupied that many citizens are unable to acquire housing within city limits, even if they can afford it. Consequently, the shortage of building space is forcing development onto precious farmland. Much of the finest farmlands in the United States and Canada, (river valleys and coastal plains), are now covered with asphalt, cement and buildings. The Niagara Peninsula in Southern Ontario and the San Fernando Valley in California, once both outstanding farming areas, are now megalopolises. Demand has priced land and homes beyond the financial capacity of millions of people. The impoverished homeless of the industrial West are a very recent phenomenon. People living in boxes, cars, underground stations, eking out an existence through begging are obvious indications that a nation is overpopulated.

Our world must be overpopulated. There is no room, no employment, no food, no housing, no purpose and no joy for a billion people, 20 percent of the entire population. At the same time nearly 80 percent of the remaining 5 billion live at or near a subsistence level of nourishment and housing.

Our environments cannot withstand the stress our exponential population growth is causing. The carrying capacity of the entire planet is rapidly approaching its finite ends with the 6 billion people already exploiting it. If we are to survive, we must decrease our total populations by several billions, not increase them.

CHAPTER FIVE

Forces Against Rapid Population Reduction

The earth's population in 1994 increased by 275,000 people each day. Yet the Cairo Conference on International Population and Development in September, 1994, showed that few of our political and religious leaders were openly willing to tackle the problems of high fertility rates and to cooperate universally in implementing the many technological solutions available.

As this example indicates, international attempts to slow population growth over the last 20 years has been relatively ineffectual. The first conference held to discuss population control was held in 1974 in Bucharest, Rumania. It did succeed in initiating Family Planning programs in all nations willing to cooperate, but its success rate was minimal because it was debunked by attitudes that held universal use of contraceptives could not be implemented until the economic and social life in the Third World was improved and people could afford them.[1]

A notable decline in the infant mortality rate followed as did a drop in abject poverty worldwide with the improvement of the diet of millions of people through the Green Revolution. But population figures continued to explode. At the time of the Bucharest Conference, world population was 3.9 billion. When the Cairo Conference was held in 1994, only 20 years later, it had grown to 5.7 billion, an increase of 1.8 billion.

Negativism towards birth control worsened with each conference following the first in Bucharest. The next was held in 1984 in Mexico where the issue of overpopulation was lost in the general view promoted by the United States that population growth was a "neutral factor in development"[2] which could be helpful to a booming economy and harmful to an impoverished one. The next failed attempt was the Conference held in Rio in

June, 1992, which lost its impetus in the squabble between industrial nations and developing nations. The former claimed the global environmental problems were caused by overpopulation in the Third World, and the latter fought back saying that consumption in the industrial nations was more damaging than population growth.

The International Conference on Population and Development held in Cairo, Egypt, in September of 1994, once again attempted to cover an agenda on population control and industrial development, aimed at reaching some international consensus for future reduction of both. Leaders of the Catholic Church, including the Pope, and political and cleric leaders of Islam filibustered against the agenda until the conference ended. The weak-kneed outcome was to allow each nation to decide its own policy on birth control.

The Cairo Conference reflected the traditional conflict which political and religious authorities have with popular preference. The agenda bogged down over the contentious right to abortion and the empowering of women through Family Planning programs. Reactionary religious attitudes of the Vatican and the Islamic Fundamentalists, particularly among their priests and political leaders, prevailed against the United Nations' efforts to provide every woman and teenage girl with sex education and birth control. They derailed the entire conference with archaic arguments that such knowledge contributes to immorality and to the murdering of the unborn, using their traditional religious powers to obstruct consensus.

Although political and religious authorities remained deaf to the world, the voices of warning were much louder in Cairo than at any of the three previous conferences. People in every nation were admitting they are in trouble with their exploding populations. Political and religious leaders were fighting what will soon be little more than a surface battle to retain traditional archaic dogmas and practices of our religious past. For in spite of them, statistics given at the Cairo conference relayed that universal family planning had reached nearly 50 percent of the world's women, and if they permitted access to contraception and could afford it, most of the remaining 50 percent would practice birth control.

Italy is the best example where popular preference is given priority. Ironically, it is the home of the Vatican, but it has the highest rate of contraceptive use and abortion in the world, along with the lowest birth rate of 1.3. While Catholic religious leaders continue to prohibit contraception and abortion, the majority of Italian women choose birth control to keep their families to a manageable minimum.

Unfortunately, the social forces against women's right to control their own reproduction rates are powerful and many. What should be a simple matter of rational logic in the struggle to reduce world fertility rates and ensure the survival of future generations is strangled by the patriarchal powers which govern so many of our societies. Men control the legislative powers, the religious dogmas, the economic structures and the cultural traditions. They have the final say in how many children their women will produce. Their power is especially strong in Third World nations ruled by patriarchal practices which treat women as inferior and as chattels. These are the nations in which 95 percent of the babies will be born during the next century.

Unyielding Causes of High Fertility Rates
1. Traditions of High Birth Rates and the Sanctity of Human Life

Fertility rates in the 20th Century increased at unprecedented rates for many reasons. Their continuing to do so will be the major dilemma of human existence in the 21st Century. In the wake of antiseptics, antibiotics, vaccinations, inoculations and all other medical advances in the 20th Century, widespread death rates from plagues, starvation, indigenous diseases, infections and accidents no longer take the horrendous toll of lives they once did. Instead, medical advances, working hand in hand with social forces, have fostered an explosion in fertility rates and placed the onus for control of reproduction onto the very sectors of society which promote high birth rates: political, religious, economic and cultural institutions.

Social and economic pressures favouring high birth rates have their roots in human evolution and the history of our civilizations

Ancient fertility rites which originated in prehistoric times and the psychological attitudes they nurtured through the millennia are still with us in various cultural practices. Their basic purpose has always been to promote fertility of crops, domestic animals and especially of people. Communities then as now need youthful populations to sustain them, protect them against invaders, work in the fields and factories, tend the animals and share in the tasks of the community.

Sexual freedom where practised in early and primitive civilizations was a natural part of social and religious ceremonies promoting fertility. However, restrictions and sexual taboos were inculcated to prevent inbreeding. As populations grew, religious doctrine was invoked to control promiscuity and restore some safety for women and children from rape and incest. The Christian Church and Islam still frown on sexual freedom while promoting large families. In past centuries this religious principle combined with a high infant mortality rate caused by disease, infection, accident and infanticide yielded a slow increase in fertility rates. Populations frequently declined from extremes of starvation or epidemics; many populations remained static over extended periods of time.

In the 20th Century world wide social and religious controls over sexuality waned dramatically. Media and global economics now determine the direction our social behaviours take and have initiated a universal sexual revolution. Overpopulation, sexual promiscuity and rape, now so widespread, show that the influences of media and technological progress are proving more destructive than socially advantageous.

The loss of religious and cultural mores have removed the social stigma illegitimacy once carried with it and has brought a plethora of social problems as well as overpopulation to the majority of nations. With few countries exhibiting prejudices against large families, teenage motherhood and illegitimacy, the taboos against premarital sex have all but disappeared, causing fertility rates to soar. Although AIDS and other sexually transmitted diseases are having some impact on promiscuity, overpopulation of this planet is already with us and will continue to be throughout much of the 21st Century.

The sexual revolution of the last few decades, aided by the mobility transportation technologies have brought us, released the bulk of people from the economic and cultural restraints on large families that rural life once imposed. In past centuries couples were not likely to marry and have families until a plot of land, a home and a trade were available to them. Today urban living, industrial employment and social welfare have eliminated this restriction on reproduction. Early marriages now add many years to a woman's reproductive period.

Combined with this new sexual freedom is the added problem that few industrial nations have population policies which support family planning or encourage legitimate abortion. Most nations of Europe and North America permit contraception and abortion with reservations, but remain openly negative in their acceptance of abortion as it countermands major religious doctrines and moral values dominating Western societies. Consequently, few Western nations encourage and permit abortion on demand. Several still criminalize abortion except under circumstances dangerous to the mother's health and others condemn its use outright, leaving women to the risks of illegal or self-inflicted abortions. This stand is detrimental to Western interests, if they expect Third World countries to control their birth rates. The offshoot of this attitude is the death of thousands of women annually who undergo unsafe abortions in both the industrial nations and the Third World.

Some countries have economic and political forces which, by their very nature, restrict family size. Japan had a negative fertility rate of 1.53 in 1991, a drop from 5.1 children per woman in 1925.[3] The birth rate is low because all Japanese women have access to and knowledge of contraception and abortion. They are also motivated to have small families because they must live in small apartments or in very expensive homes where good living standards, education and social expectations are very costly. Highly educated and able to find satisfying employment outside the home, Japanese women no longer see themselves as mere baby producers. However, cultural attitudes in Japan remain strongly against this liberation of women so that they are the first to lose their jobs in periods of recession or downsizing of industry. The male population of this very economically advanced nation still prefer to see women as bearers of children first and women holding industrial jobs as a sign of cultural degradation.

Poverty and overpopulation in China, on the other hand, have made China the most outstanding example of political repression of birth rates in the world with its imposed limitation of one child per couple and severe economic penalties for abusers.

Russia, under the horrors of Communism and in its present state of chaos, has a negative fertility rate among its white races at present. Abortion throughout the Communist and Post Communist countries has been readily available to the women; whereas contraception is expensive and highly suspect among the Russian people. On the other hand, a high birth rate still exists among former Russian republics of non-white and Muslim peoples nurtured by Islamic religious dogma. They believe large families give prestige to both men and women and will eventually give political and military strength to the Muslims who are presently reawakening in search of sovereignty for their people and revenge for their long suffering existence under white Russian domination.

The variety of positions taken by political and religious authorities makes a universal agreement to reduce populations impossible to implement. The poorer classes, --those most vulnerable to social and religious forces, those unable to take advantage of family planning and those least able to produce healthy, productive progeny,-- will continue to have the greatest number of children. Women with the opportunity to raise intelligent, well educated, healthy offspring and wisely choose to limit their families to one or two children will remain a small, privileged elite well into the future. This is borne out by UN statistics in 1994 which estimate that 95 percent of surviving infants over the next century will be in Third World nations.

Consequently, populations will grow far beyond the ability of the earth to sustain them productively, promoted by social attitudes as well as political policies against extremes of population control which are deeply embedded in our cultural and moral fabric. Moreover, the majority will acknowledge the additional numbers. Authorities will attempt to feed them all;

larger populations will motivate industrial expansion and the growth of consumer markets; religious sects and pro-life groups will lobby to have abortion abolished. The criminalizing of any form of infanticide from the time of conception through infancy is internationally condemned. This creates a moral, humanitarian dilemma at odds with the consequences of watching the living deteriorate in the horrors of overcrowding, poverty, hunger, war and ethnic cleansing.

The moral value and sanctity given to human life that is in question here stem from Western civilization and its past colonial implementation of Christian moral laws on all conquered races. It is difficult to argue against the morality that sees human life as a gift from God, to be protected above all other life forms in spite of the threat overpopulation is to the existence of all.

But the morality and ethics of preserving human life at conception tend to fade in light of natural human aggression which nullifies the value of any human life. As land bases are becoming overcrowded and populations are fighting to retain some sense of identity and purpose, human aggression turns from being a constructive, civilizing energy into a violent, destructive force. It is manifest in the loss of civilized behaviour showing up everywhere. Murder has become the most common means to procure what you want, if you cannot pay for it. Witness the number of murders in North American cities where children carry guns to school and kill each other over a pair of shoes or a jacket.

Historical records show how common it has been for humans to kill each other, especially where lands became too crowded and no longer could sustain the indigenous population. Records of tyrannical leadership seeking power over neighboring lands, of civil wars for racial or tribal dominance of one group over another occupying the same land base and of wars between nations where genocide has been practised to reduce populations flood the pages of our history books. Both Lenin and Stalin thought the implementation of the Communist state more important than the 50 million lives they destroyed in the process.

Obviously doctrines sanctifying human life have been needed over the millennium to curb human tendencies to kill their own species. Such doctrines have also been needed to nurture population expansion. It is unlikely humanity would have expanded as rapidly and as successfully as it has were it not for the civilizing influence of religious and political forces throughout much of our settled existence.

Unfortunately, the cultural, moral principles imposed by world religions and political powers on their populations are now amplifying an unsolvable dilemma. As they promote the sanctity of life to the extremes of disallowing contraception, sterilization and abortion, they threaten our entire existence as a species through the overpopulating and degrading of our fragile planet.

2. Religions and Birth Control

As fertility rites in ancient times and in primitive societies tended to be very licentious in nature and in practice, Christianity chose to purge pleasurable sex from life, declaring it a sin. Attempts were made in the past to enforce reproduction, not as an accident of pleasurable sex but as a God given duty. The Church taught that sex was strictly an act of procreation to be kept for that purpose alone and conception of life was seen as a gift from God that cannot be intercepted. A hangover of this attitude continues today among Catholic doctrines in that the Catholic Church continues to associate sex with procreation, not pleasure, and forbids all forms of contraception and abortion.

Unfortunately, sexual pleasure is often the only enjoyment a large portion of the world's people experience, and not one they willing give up. At the same time conception may be a detriment to their existence. In such cases all forms of birth control should be available to those who need the comfort of sexual contact. Only then can they reduce their unwanted pregnancies and have smaller, more sustainable families.

Historically, having large families has been encouraged by ethnic self-seeking interests. Large racial or religious groups have used their followers as the means to power and prestige in both the primitive and civilized worlds. The Catholic Church, in controlling the personal lives of its people, held sway over the ruling dynasties of Europe and its colonies, especially in North and South America for many centuries. They still do. The Catholic Church today boasts of a following that numbers nearly one billion members worldwide. To hold sway over its flock, the

Church hierarchy continues to promote high birth rates and sanctifies human life above all other earthly matters. To ensure the continued growth of their flocks, Catholic authorities fly in the face of human survival by preventing technologically safe practices of birth control and abortion. Outdated ecclesiastical law, enforced by a reactionary pope prevents rational change, a stand that is a contributing force to the many elements shaping humanity's nemesis of extinction by way of overwhelming the planet's carrying capacity.

Islam holds much the same position against controlling fertility rates, but adds a further motivation for large families. The majority of Muslims live in the Middle East where customs and political systems have meaning only within the family. Power is enhanced by the strength and wealth of the leader's extended family. This tradition is tribal, fostering hatred and xenophobia of outsiders. It has been the basis of internecine wars throughout the Arab world for centuries. Therefore, Islamic laws promote large families for security, identity and religious authority embodied in the jurisdiction of the family patriarch.[4] In return for his protection, he demands large families so as to have sufficient men to fill his military ranks.

No better example illustrates this than that of Saddam Hussein of Iraq. He is a Sunni Muslim who, as head of a large family, fills his government and his military with family members. He cares nothing for other tribes or religious groups which have known his wrath since the Gulf War in 1990. The general populace of Iraq must endure hunger under the sanctions the world imposes on them until they rid the nation of Saddam; yet he continues in power through the support of his extended family and is safely able to purge his nation of those who oppose him or are of different religions. The Kurds and the Shiites have withstood several of his attempts to massacre them in recent years.

Exchanging social traditions for stringent birth control measures may prove next to impossible in nations such as those of the Middle East and Latin America where having large families is deeply ingrained and extolled by their religious dogma.

3. Racial and Ethnic Chauvinism

Another endemic force against fertility control is racial and ethnic chauvinism. Many nations, both in the developed and developing worlds, have within them racial or religious groups who are seeking political control of their countries through ethnic majorities. To build their power base, the various races or ethnic groups encourage their own people to have large families so that the group can survive and increase its political strength. The late Communist regime of Ceaucescu in Rumania forbade contraception and abortion, demanding each couple have a minimum of four children. Through strength in human numbers alone, Ceaucescu believed he could rule much of Europe. Unable to cope with raising so many children under the extremes of poverty and oppressive Communist leadership, Romanian parents deserted their infants to state orphanages, where the health and well-being of the babies were almost totally neglected and they were cruelly abused. When the truth was learned of the horrors these children had experienced under state care, the world was shocked at the barbarity of the regime in its use of human lives to gain its racial and militaristic goals.

In some Third World countries, the sheer weight of numbers of one race over another is a threat to political stability. The exploding populations of Jews and Palestinians in Israel and The West Bank are both attempts to overwhelm each other by racial chauvinism. The Israelis import large numbers of Jewish immigrants while the Arabs keep pace through a high birth rate. In Sri Lanka, the demand for political sovereignty of the Tamils in a state of their own is indicative of racial and religious struggles for dominance of one "tribe" over the other by weight of numbers, just as are the terrorist acts for political independence of the Sikhs in Northern India and the war of ethnic cleansing in Rwanda in 1994 and Burundi in 1995-96.

4. Military Advantage:

Promoting large families became national policy in European nations in past centuries so as to build large conquering armies capable of colonizing empires. The imperialism of Europe depended on a surplus of healthy young men, willing to fight for the empire and rule the barbaric world to the advantage of the motherland.

It is still one of the modern day myths that a nation's military strength and power lies in the size of its armies. Civil wars throughout much of the world are wars between tribes or racial enclaves whose purpose is to establish the dominance of one tribe over another or several others. Historically as now, this power is thought to exist through superiority of numbers. Women have long been expected to produce boys for fighting tribal wars. Foolishly this expectation has forced women to have children until they provide enough boys to fulfil military needs, but an expectation which carries with it a surplus of girls.

In reality, overpopulation in a technologically-determined world tends to weaken a nation's military strength. The costs of materiel, transportation and physical maintenance of large armies soon deplete a nation's wealth. The experience of the United States and the USSR during the Cold War of the latter part of the 20th Century revealed the debilitating expense of maintaining standing armies. In both countries their military forces were the first line of defense to be dismantled when the Iron Curtain came down.

International wars are no longer designed to be fought on battle fields with lightly armed, standing armies. In fact, highly sophisticated weapons and their transportation, both requiring a minimum of man power and doing a maximum of environmental damage, have made international wars obsolete. They exist largely in the minds of generals and their strategists.

Wars today are almost exclusively racial, tribal conflicts fought over diminishing resources of land and overcrowded social space. They are a struggle for survival of the gene pools, not for building empires. Civil wars are increasingly ethnic wars, motivated to reduce populations through "ethnic cleansing" to gain land cleared of other human beings so that the winner can occupy it. Armies are not targeted. Civilians - men, women and children -are!

5. *Special Interest Groups:*

With modern communication technologies, even the most isolated peoples receive knowledge of universal cultures and living standards through television, cellular phones, global commodities and world travellers. As information, ideas and new forms of employment become global, once strongly defined cultural boundaries are disappearing. Special interest groups, fearing assimilation and loss of their ethnicity within larger, more dominant cultures sponsor high fertility rates to offset the imbalance.

To protect or establish racial dominance in the face of present day mass migrations and civil wars, ethnic minorities are encouraged by their leaders to have large families. In this way they hope to fill any local labor shortages themselves and maintain their racial gene pools. Japan, for instance, imports a significant number of migrant workers but refuses any of them citizenship. At the same time the nation stimulates the desire in women to produce Japanese babies. Quebec, recording negative birth rates among French Canadians in recent years, offers baby bonuses and tax incentives to families to have extra children. Each additional child brings a higher bonus. France also follows this policy.

Special interest groups such as businesses, industries and governments foster population growth because they provide large pools of workers who can be fully exploited while becoming consumers of mass products. To governments growing populations represent an expanding source of capital, taxes, pensions and insurance funds. Consequently, political and economic forces promote increased populations by encouraging higher fertility rates and global migration policies. Governments and businesses seek out and offer extended benefits and often citizenship to immigrants who have money to invest or are highly skilled technicians and engineers of modern industry. While this aids the nation's industrial competence, it expands national populations.

Increased population numbers and rising fertility rates are also elevated by Western governments for humanitarian reasons. They permit continuous influxes of refugees out of concern for the millions of people forced to flee oppressive governments, overpopulated land bases, impoverished nations, civil wars and destroyed environments. Fearing they might become the victims of racial cleansing, these refugees endure a reawakening of violent; universal racism and xenophobia.

Philanthropy and humanitarian policies have led Western governments to pass legislation permitting easy entrance of immigrant refugees escaping life threatening circumstances in their native lands. At the same time they contribute to a rise in local populations. The highest birth rates in developed nations are now among these newcomers, especially those from Third World nations who, finding themselves better off than ever before, tend to have large families.

Another government policy of several Western governments which encourages higher fertility rates rather than decreasing them is the unconditional right of illegal aliens to take up residence on the strength of having had a baby born in the country. This has encouraged the entrance of thousands of alien women into Canada and the United States during the last month of their pregnancies so that the child is born a legal Canadian or American citizen. The parents can then claim legal immigrant status. Canada has been particularly vulnerable to this immigration scam in the 1980s and 1990s as hundreds of Chinese women arrived in Canada from Hong Kong to have their babies. They then left with their infants birth certificates in hand, ensuring that the whole family could return to Canada before 1997 when China takes over Hong Kong.

Special interest groups extend to the large minorities who stand against birth controls. At present they represent a strong lobbying power in the highly developed nations of North America and Europe. In Canada and the United States pro-life groups refuse to see their countries as already overpopulated by definition and fight to protect every unwanted pregnancy. Governments even rise and fall on their position for or against abortions. To appease the pro-life power groups, international agreements reflect this influence in letting every nation set its own fertility goals. The United Nations, able to remain somewhat aloof from political and religious pressures, has condescended to support a replacement rate of 2.1 child per woman with the hopes of a long term reduction and stabilization of populations however it is accomplished.

6. *Self Interest, Illegitimacy and Science*

Perhaps the greatest barrier remaining to reduced fertility rates is emotional: the concept of "motherhood" and the universal love of babies and children. A picture of a mother and her cute, smiling baby appeals to all and arouses almost everyone's procreative desires. Images of women and children soften the human heart whether they are of a happy gurgling baby in a mother's arms or of a sick, emaciated child at a mother's empty breast. During the summer of 1992, television commercials showing beautiful children were used by pro-life organizations against abortion in the United States, manipulating public opinion with the image of human love and the right to life for every conceived child.

More recent technological innovations have offered many avenues to infertile "would be mothers" through abnormal methods of fertilization: artificial insemination, invitro-fertilization, transfer of eggs from one woman to another, surrogate mothers, implanting fertilized eggs into women long past child bearing years. The forces of nature which strive to curb reproduction rates are falling to the battalions of medical technologies which grant every parent wanting children with the means to have them.

The social traditions of adoring motherhood, rising infertility among middle and upper class women and a more open, less morally conscious society in Western nations has led to the social acceptance of promiscuity and illegitimacy. Former traditions and social taboos of behaviour once frowned on promiscuity and unwed mothers. Today our cultural mores encourage the unwed mother and our governments to subsidize their roles through welfare. Public support has accordingly promoted teenage promiscuity and teenage parenthood, commonly referred to as "babies having babies." Such social principles negate parental obligations and sanction unwanted pregnancies, especially among unmarried women.

Such behaviours were widely condemned during much of the 19th Century and the first half of the 20th Century when sexual mores remained prudish. The increasing number of babies surviving infancy because of improved medical treatments produced an overabundance of surviving children, many of whom could not be properly cared for by their mothers. Infanticide became the number one cause of murder in many Western nations as late as the 1890s, just as it is in many Third World countries today. Curbing sexuality came to be seen as a social necessity.

The stringent sexual mores imposed on Victorian society in England were also a religious backlash against Darwin's theory of evolution. The idea that man had evolved from the apes was seen as a threat to the established role of God and the Church in maintaining social order. Prudery against overt sexuality was also an attempt to repress the popular theory of Freud who taught that sexual repression was the cause of insanity.

However, sexual moral codes injected into social behaviors could not succeed for long in curbing the rise in promiscuity. Contraception, introduced in the 1920s, dramatically changed the entire Western view of sexuality once the number of pregnancies a woman had could be controlled. The revolution against taboos and illegitimacy continued to expand with each successive generation, until today when sexual freedom has become the social norm.

What this trend tells us is that our societies must preach and practise birth control. In removing all cultural restrictions and stigmas on our reproductive activities, we have returned to nature's plan that all species will reproduce to the fullest extent. As technologies have given us the power to overcome the majority of nature's controls on fertility, and because we have removed most social and cultural taboos, we must accept what is left to us: birth control which prevents conception, unless consciously and intentionally planned.

7. *Teenage Pregnancies*

Teenagers having babies are an outgrowth of the diminishing sexual taboos and the failure of society to help them deal with their sexuality. More than 15 million girls between 15 and 19 years of age become pregnant each year; one-third of them have abortions.[5] "Of all 14 year olds alive today, 40 percent will be pregnant by the time they are 20. In some Asian and African countries, teenagers below the age of 18 account for half of all pregnancies", according to a UN report.[6] In general they are young girls who are ignorant of the sexual reproductive process, have little or no access to contraceptives and are ignored by family planning agencies. Yet they account for an increasing proportion of the live births each year throughout the world. A reluctance to recognize teenage sexuality and provide them education and contraception pervades most societies, especially the strongly religious communities of Christianity and Islam. The Catholic and Islamic representatives see aid to teenagers as promoting promiscuity, rather than a step in the battle to reduce universal birth rates.

8.   Poverty Promotes High Fertility Rates

The 20th Century has seen a world wide phenomenon evolve in which every continent is now overpopulated for numerous reasons. Unfortunately, the greatest consequence has been to entrench poverty for increasing majorities which, in itself, is a major cause of high fertility rates. Poverty holds the bulk of its victims captive to generations of impoverished living standards, human decline and social disarray.

Large populations overwhelm employment opportunities. The majority soon come to depend on state welfare and food subsidies. Education and medical care are beyond their purchasing power. Ignorance, lawlessness, malnutrition and all their incumbent problems expand. Trying to provide employment as well as social programs for growing populations increases national debts. The entire nation declines under the weight of unmanageable numbers. Dispensing law and order, apportioning living space and financing infra-structures of an overpopulated nation rapidly overburdens the relatively small, economically productive sector of entrepreneurs. Taxing this small earning constituency forces them to take their money out of the country. The nation is left with a tax base too small to maintain the public infrastructure. The final blow comes when the middle class is so overtaxed that it is driven to cheating governments or gives up working or investing its money within the nation.

Both rich and poor nations of the world are presently encumbered with this set of problems. Poverty and high birth rates are physically, economically and socially interwoven. Together they are draining the health of every nation. The poverty that has descended universally has created its own fertility rates. A lack of purchasing power, unemployment, poor health, ignorance, a lack of birth control technologies and archaic social and religious traditions, --all contribute to high birth rates or necessitate large families.

Those caught in the web of poverty are the men and women with children and elderly parents who must live on very small incomes which buy insufficient food, largely of poor quality and low in nutritional value. Consequently, the poor are generally undernourished and low in immunity to disease and infection. With little or no medical care, recuperation is often lengthy and death common. Underfed and often chronically ill, such people have a low physical capacity and little energy to work. When they do find work, their productivity is low, which exacerbates their poverty, hunger and malnutrition. A vicious cycle results from which few escape and more are entrapped as their populations grow.

The inability to get out of this cycle is deepened by the increasing number of dependents a family must care for, especially the number of offspring. For example, a man in a Third World nation may only earn a $1000 a year which he spends on himself. But once he marries he must divide his income between two people. He is then reduced to $500 a year to meet his own needs. When his first child arrives, the division of income is by three, or $333 per family member. If he has more children, the amount allotted per person diminishes proportionally.

As this man's income per person diminishes, the amount of food and basic survival needs each family member receives decreases until the health of all is debilitated and the energy levels so low that there are few ways left in which he can improve his lot. He and his children become mired in abject poverty, poor health and hopelessness.

While having large families deepens their own poverty, it is not uncommon, however, for such people to believe that large families are the only means to their survival. What little joy and entertainment are experienced usually come from family gatherings. The strongest incentive arises when family members have only each other to depend on for earning money or caring for the children, the sick and the elderly. Consequently, custom has nurtured large families for their own protection. Every additional child is seen as a money earner who must contribute to the upkeep of the entire family. This forces the children to become earners at a very young age, denying them a childhood and an education that might have brought them a better future. It is not unusual to see eight year olds working at tasks in India that men should be doing or ten year old boys fighting alongside men in a civil war in Africa.

Unemployed or sick parents generally depend on their children to earn money in many unsavoury ways to support the family. They work as "slaves" in factories at very low wages and are often indentured for years; or they are employed in demeaning service jobs in the community, while many are sent to the streets to beg or are sold into prostitution. In Asian nations such as the Philippines and Thailand, children of the poor, sold into slavery and prostitution, must withstand the horrors of physical and moral abuse. Every industrial nation in the world now has its street kids who left home to escape physical or sexual abuse or were abandoned by parents unable to care for them. Life for the poor is in rapid decline.

The only increasing factor in this social trend is the number of children born to most couples in the Third World. The average woman has between 3 to 8 live births, the bulk of which will grow to the age of fertility and reproduce, increasing the population exponentially.

Why then do parents in abject poverty have any children at all if their existence means deeper and deeper poverty and suffering? At the lowest, most personal level of human existence are a few simple but prevalent causes for these high birth rates in the Third World. The most basic reasons are a lack of birth control technologies, family planning and even an understanding of how conception occurs. Sex is often a moment of pleasure and comfort in a life of misery where there is little else to do for entertainment on a regular basis. Having no electricity, therefore no lights, families retire very early for the night and spend upwards of ten to twelve hours in bed which is the average length of a night in tropical zones.

Furthering virility has become the mark of manhood in poverty. A man's self-esteem is often measured by his ability to father children. In North American city ghettos, the young man who can father the most children among the local girls receives the admiration of all his friends. His stature lies in being able to seduce and impregnate more girls than his buddies. Fathering is a mark of social success in a society bereft of employment and possessions.

Even a woman may have no other means of gaining self esteem, except through the number of children she can bring into the world, especially if those babies are boys. In some societies a barren woman is treated as a pariah. She is said to be bewitched or is being punished by the gods if she is infertile. A man in Islamic countries is free to desert a barren woman, leaving her to be shunned by a cruel society for her failure.

Fortunately, harsh extremes induced by abject poverty may reverse these unmanageable trends. Perhaps the desire for smaller families and no illegitimate pregnancies will have preference. Deprivation and continued pregnancies rapidly destroy a woman's health so that she cannot care for her children. Weakened and unable to get medical attention, women in poverty make up the majority of the estimated 600,000 who die annually in childbirth in unsafe attempts to abort their unwanted pregnancies.[7]

The Influences of Technological Determinism on Fertility

Beyond the inflexibility of established authorities, cultural traditions and human self interests, technologies have exerted recalcitrant influences on reproduction. Not only have the plethora of medical, industrial and agricultural technologies enabled billions of people to survive through birth, infancy, adulthood and into old age, they have created social conditions which foster population explosions. Modern technologies of transportation, television, global economics and multiculturalism have broken down restrictive sexual barriers and opened up global travel and migration of the young. They move away from their homes, their families and their national land base, leaving behind the moral practices of the family or tribe, as well as traditional and repressive social taboos and mores.

Some taboos and repressive sexual practices still remain culturally strong among primitive tribes such as the removal of the clitoris among North African tribes, which makes intercourse so painful for women, they are unlikely to be promiscuous. Repressive religious practices in Islamic nations still isolate women in harems and treat them as baby producers. Such practices are intended to prevent inbreeding in lands where the gene pools are small or contact with outsiders is infrequent so as to keep racial lines pure.

However, isolation and inbreeding are rare in this world of rapid, cheap transportation. Today gene pools are continental; for many they are global. Millions of people are able to move ever outward from their birth places to take up residence, find employment and mingle their cultures with those of other nations. In most cases, social traditions and conventions are soon shed in the anonymity of urban society far from the frowns and disapproval of family and neighbours. The breakdown of family, tribal and ethnic codes of sexual behaviour in every society has resulted in the universal phenomenon of unprecedented numbers of illegitimate births, especially among teenage girls.

In a global context sexual contact is unlikely to produce deformed inbred children, so the taboos have all but disappeared. Without ethnic tensions controlling their reproductive lives, both men and women in free societies are turning to sex as a major source of pleasure. Unfortunately, it is a pleasure which is producing high fertility rates in both rich and poor nations. Sexual freedom and promiscuity are now rampant in much of the world. The price is the epidemic magnitude of sexual diseases such as HIV, AIDS, and Hepatitis C. These diseases have become lethal plagues, killing off parents and leaving orphaned and sick children in the thousands abandoned on every continent. These plagues now leave no society untouched.

Uphill Battle against Population Growth

Life sustaining technologies are rapidly becoming a self imposed curse on humanity as our numbers proliferate beyond the earth's carrying capacity. Estimated conceptions throughout the world are a million a day. That would be an increase of 356 million a year if all pregnancies came to full term. Miscarriages, abortions, fetal deaths, disease and accidents reduce the number of babies born to less than a third of the number conceived. Yet in almost every country the birth rate still exceeds the death rate.

With 60 percent of the world's people soon to be children under 16 years of age, the bulk of them living in poverty, even the fittest among us may be in jeopardy from the impact on food and water supplies and human health this horrific number of children will have. Excessive reproduction within this sector, where an increasing number are sick and malnourished, is weakening genetic physical and mental capacities. Medications do not cure the agonies of permanently lost energy and intelligence nor the lack of immunity to crippling diseases which accompany severe malnutrition or exposure to environmental contamination. The incidence of mental deficiency among deprived children is skyrocketing in poor nations. Genetic deformities are already multiplying among those who must live in the shadow of industrial toxic wastes and emissions or depend on polluted water to drink. A research team at the Harvard School of Public Health reports that children living in "more polluted communities are lagging behind in the development of their lungs.[8] This reduced lung capacity may be responsible for the rise in deaths from asthma in every industrial nation.

Hunger constantly initiates human aggression as the poor struggle to survive at the cost of others; often the victims are children. In Somalia in 1993, a year of civil war and mass starvation, adults were noticed to eat first, then children were fed if anything was left.[9] An immoral behaviour pattern to the well fed Western mind, but one which explains why so many more children die in Africa than adults during times of famine, a situation which also affects the health of future generations in these nations.

Human survival as a species has become complicated by humanitarian and religious beliefs which decree that all human life must be protected and nurtured no matter how poor the quality. Scientists and sociologists are working towards the day when medical technologies can keep all children alive who suffer from malaria, diarrhoea and other viral or bacterial diseases and infections which often prove fatal if untreated. They have promised the discovery of a super vaccine which will permanently protect children against diseases which cause well over tens of thousands of infant deaths daily around the world.

What we are creating through our excessive sanctifying of human life is quantity, not quality, which is anathema to nature. All life forms have natural instinctual controls on their breeding and reproduction whether it is an inability to reproduce because there is no territory or food supply with which to raise young or whether it is through natural order and seniority of breeding rights, through the eating of the excess young when too many are born, or through infertility under population stress. All species in nature are controlled by laws of survival of the fittest which pare their numbers to conform to the territorial carrying capacity and the social space beyond which survival of the entire social group is at risk.

With the aid of technology, survival of the fittest among humans is giving way to overproduction of the unfit. The consequences are more unhealthy, nonproductive, violent and excessively destructive human beings. Species Homo sapiens has overcome natural selection and replaced it with an overweening sense of self-importance and a refusal to practise population controls which promote strong, healthy gene pools.

As harsh and calculating as it may sound, scientific altruism to save every life may soon threaten us all. Having overcome nature's carrying capacity, we endure debilitating physical health in a deteriorating environment producing shortages of clean air, fresh water and food supplies while increasing the annual deaths from starvation, drought, pollution and disease. As our individual living space grows smaller, there are too many of us to share the riches of the earth. Reactions to this increasingly competitive existence are displayed in outbursts of violent behavior among people living in industrial cities, displaying a callous disregard for human life. Teenagers and young men shoot each other over insults, possessions and urban territory, an aggression which escalates from gang warfare into civil violence and often ends in civil wars and outbreaks of ethnic cleansing.

Ethnic cleansing has become synonymous with civil wars. It is the ultimate manifestation of violent racial aggression indicative of overcrowded gene pools where the members are struggling to retain their share of social space on the planet.

A life plagued with tribal warfare, frequent periods of drought and starvation and nations collapsing into violent civil chaos is symptomatic of existence in much of West Africa today. Suffering from encroaching deserts, rapidly diminishing food production, insufficient water reserves, overpopulation and human dissolution are the horrors of their daily lives. Such conditions may be the harbinger of what survival on this planet will become for all of us in the near future.

The catastrophe that is West Africa is the first truly visible, large scale experience of human suffering resulting from overpopulation and collapsing environments. A revelation of what the future for all humanity may come to be was witnessed in 1990 in the television coverage of an army of 1500 young boys who walked out of the bush in the Sudan, totally naked, starving and all without parents. Following the massacre of their families in their villages, the boys had moved as a group about the countryside, evading Muslim authorities who sought them out to enslave them or to force them to become soldiers in Arab armies.

Living in overcrowded, impoverished conditions arouses our survival instincts and puts them at war with our 20th Century philanthropic aspirations. The individual's identity and "social space" within the group becomes distorted or lost as his territorial parameters shrink. Over five million years of evolution as hunter-gathers ingrained in our minds the concept of vast open land bases from which the social group gleaned sustenance and derived identity. There is a point at which social and individual space becomes overcrowded beyond our psychological ability to function. Apprehension grows as individual social space shrinks. The need for more territorial space manifests itself in a desire to seek out new land bases. But there are no more!

What remains is only relatively less overcrowded land to which tens of millions are trying to migrate. With few exceptions, landbases no longer exist which are not already occupied by a mixture of racial/ethnic groups, crowded together in urban areas, separated only by the self-imposed segregation of city blocks. Industrial nations which have provided an exceptionally high standard of living for the majority of their citizens, now have their living space filled to capacity, many to overflowing not only with human bodies but with cars, houses, building complexes, factories, industrial plants, transportation systems and millions of square miles of asphalt roads and concrete megalopolises. The consequential loss of individual and social space exerts a stress on the occupants which fires up xenophobia and racial conflicts.

In reviewing these omnipresent threats to human existence at this stage in our intellectual and technological development, it is difficult to understand how the Catholic Pope in 1995 justified his banning of all contraceptives and family planning for all members of the Catholic Church in perpetuity. It is even harder to comprehend the weak-kneed stance of Western leadership which continues to deny abortion and euthanasia. But it is even more incredible that the rich nations of the world should deny the United Nations the cooperation and the $17 billion needed annually to fund family planning programs and abortions around the world. That the bulk of nations choose political expediency and cave in to religious coercion over controlling fertility rates through contraception, sterilization and abortion, and choose poverty and environmental collapse instead is human folly of the worst sort.

CHAPTER SIX

Why Most Solutions to Population Control Aren't Working

The truths of our human population dilemma have become self-evident. The price of unlimited fertility threatens the existence of the human species as soon as the 21st Century. Not only are our numbers overwhelming the planet's carrying capacity, they are forcing an irreversible environmental collapse. United Nations' studies released in 1992 offered three conditional future projections: If fertility rates fall to the replacement level of 2.0, then populations just might stabilize at 10 billion by the end of the 21st Century. If fertility rates should drop below replacement level, they could reach a plateau between 7 and 8 billion. But, if the world's birth rates remain above the replacement level as all indications suggest, the earth's population could approach 20 billions by the year 2100.[1]

Knowing the possibilities, a majority among us, ranging from political and religious leaders to the general populace, still refuse to admit that humanity as a whole is in crisis and a reduction in our numbers must be forced on us. Heads of state and religions continue to capitulate into accepting the myth that population is not the problem, but poverty and underdevelopment are. The general belief remains that if everyone has a living standard which will ensure their wellbeing, overpopulation will not be a problem and birth rates will decline.

Security of their jobs makes leaders politic. It is more tactful to blame the lack of fair distribution of resources and industrial development than to admit that a policy of birth control must be enforced in every country. The rich nations blame the poor for overpopulating the world and the poor nations blame the rich for polluting the planet and making it uninhabitable. As long as the differences between rich and poor remain so emotionally and economically entrenched, practical solutions will continue to elude organized conferences and world authorities in their search to reduce populations and industrial development to environmentally sustainable levels.

The remedies exist, but they require draconian changes in traditional practices, religious dogmas, military and racial egoism, cultural attitudes and world poverty. Ingrained social and economic forces stand in the way of implementing these changes and a widespread tendency exists to dismiss warnings of imminent environmental collapse, while promoting an overwhelming desire to believe in human goodness to "do the right thing". Such wishful thinking culminates in the foolhardy belief that all couples will realize their responsibility to the earth and limit their families to one or two children. The problem is that the bulk of the world's people do not have enough control over their reproductive output to "do the right thing" nor do they have the appropriate education to know what is right.

Historically, humans have practised birth control, ranging from contraception to infanticide. Many past practices were harsh and physically cruel, certainly shocking by modern ethical standards. They included primitive forms of abortion, exposure of newborns, death through neglect and untreated disease, the sale of children into slavery and various forms of infanticide. All helped keep the fertility rates growing at a very slow pace.[2]

Babies were easily conceived. But the costs of raising them exceeded the ability of the majority of parents to provide for them. Surplus or unwanted children of poverty were a threat to the entire family's survival; consequently, desertion and infanticide were common in the past, especially if they were a hindrance to women who worked long hours in the fields or at other physical jobs while still caring for siblings.

Similar living conditions today are compelling parents to chose infanticide once again. Killing of children is re-emerging in many different ways where human life has become so prolific that it has little value. They range from murder of infants in several Asian countries to the horror of life on the streets of the industrial nations where children so easily murder each other. It may be universally immoral and illegal to expose one's babies to the elements or even abandon them to the streets, but there are increasing numbers of mothers in the Third World who do so while their governments ignore the offense. The murder of newborn girls in India is not uncommon where boys are preferred by custom and poverty cannot support large families. Female infants are seen as a greater financial burden to parents who must pay out large dowries to get their girls married off.

In China, where a couple is allowed to have only one child in the urban centres and two in rural areas, an estimated 1.5 million baby girls disappear each year. Many cases of infant deaths have been well documented world wide. Over 40,000 children die each day or more than l25 million a year through desertion, exposure, infanticide, neglect, hunger, disease and poverty.[3]

As children will soon comprise 60 percent of the earth's populations, their lot will be ever greater suffering and exploitation. Abused, driven from their homes, sold into slavery or prostitution and abandoned by parents, they are already haunting the streets throughout the Third World, where many of them die, unable to sustain themselves or fall victim to nightly killings by police patrols.

Another growing threat to the children of the world is the number forced to accept employment working with toxic chemicals and physically dangerous manufacturing processes. Such children are treated as "slaves", receiving starvation wages or paid nothing because they were sold to manufacturers by impoverished and indebted parents for the equivalent of one or two hundred dollars. South and Central America, China, Thailand, India, Malaysia, the Philippines, even the United States where migrant workers are guilty of using their children to pick crops for less than minimum wage, depend on child labour to produce goods and services cheaply, enabling traders to sell them on world markets at cutthroat prices. Death from hunger, physical abuse, beatings, disease and murder stalks the lives of tens of millions of unwanted children worldwide. Their numbers will rise dramatically as 95 percent of the additional population born now and throughout the 21st Century will be in poor, overpopulated countries, pushing the ratio of children to adults to 60 percent of the world's population.

One has to wonder at the human values of religious and political leaders who place life of such poor and horrific quality above the rights of all women to have free access to birth control technologies or to abort unwanted pregnancies without threatening their own lives, especially mothers with aids or genetic problems. It is cruel and unnecessary that so many women in this age of wonder drugs and medical technologies are forced to use barbaric methods to reduce their fertility or shed themselves of unwanted pregnancies. Yet the majority hold to emotional and religious biases which are less committed to the survival of those already born than to the billions of human seed which pass through the bodies of women annually, an unmanageable portion of which may become fertilized and permitted to be born when they should be stopped before conception or in the early months of pregnancy.

Solutions must begin with the recognition that any population growth, however small, will only speed up the time left before we have destroyed the earth's carrying capacity for our species. Immediate universal goals must reach a negative fertility rate that will stabilize the world's population at or below two billion, an estimate considered sustainable by demographic experts.[4]

UN studies argue this could be accomplished through an annual global donation of $17 billion which would provide sufficient population control through sexual education and contraception. In comparison with the one to two trillion dollars traded daily on world currency markets by speculators, the $17 billion dollars a year requested by the United Nations' at the Cairo Conference towards world Family Planning programs[5] is a mere pittance. Unfortunately, our actions remain self-serving and our priorities topsy turvey!

But even then two billion people may be an extremely optimistic goal, if historical precedence of civilizations dying out as their environments collapsed are realistic paradigms. Therefore, any approach to population control or its reduction must include universal birth control and protective, regenerative measures for the environment. But who could be empowered to enforce such draconian measures of population control and how might they be carried out? What we may not overcome is that rational solutions are not compatible with human emotions and behavioral customs.

Empowerment of Governments

To empower governments with control over population numbers would entail giving them the right to set and enforce realistic universal fertility rates. Family Planning programs would have to be made available world wide and backed by all major political and religious institutions. A global agreement on fertility rates such as the one presented at the Cairo Conference would be reached among nations and their governments empowered to enforce it. This, in turn, would demand a willingness of all nations and religions to legalize and promote contraception, sterilization and abortion, expand health care and family planning programs, educate and empower women and foster economic opportunities for them.[6] Moreover, it would permit punitive measures to be imposed by governments on couples who have more children than they are allowed. To be truly effective, such a universal policy of negative birth rates would have to be imposed over several generations.

This empowerment of governments translates into giving their bureaucracies complete control over our sexual lives. Government regulation and interference in any aspect of our private lives is abhorrent to democracy. It raises a conflict of interest between the individual and the tyranny of the power elite, generally producing a constant struggle of the populace to break the rules. The policing necessary to enforce a national policy of one or two children per family would be so extensive, so invasive of our privacy that few nations could afford the costs nor would tax payers tolerate them. Furthermore, the universal reality of social corruption and government incompetence could place control of our personal lives in the hands of brutal, authoritarian governments. Communist China with its one-child policy and its totalitarian regime is an example in action.

Sadly, human nature is not so easily redirected. Giving governments control over our sexuality is "to make deals with the devil". The power to control human reproduction rates raises the spectre of privilege, the loss or disappearance of family lines, carte blanche to injustice, power to stifle opposition, racial discrimination and/or ethnic cleansing. Power leads to tyranny and repression leads to rebellion.

Even propaganda promoting contraception and family planning has many enemies within democracies. Governments in the Western nations have found passing legislation for or against abortion is so emotional an issue that whichever side a politician takes, it may mean the end of his political career. What remains is democratic governments protecting their citizens right to "choice" to ensure political and social stability.

Empowerment of Women

The most practical route to reduced fertility now popular among advocates for population control is the universal empowerment of women. Women must be released from male dominance over their reproductive lives, freeing them from patriarchal traditions which espouse that their sole purpose in life is to give birth to sons. Their emancipation can be accomplished through education about their own sexuality. This will enable them to control their reproduction and gain employment which will raise their living standards and improve their wellbeing. Studies have shown that women who received as few as four years of schooling have fewer children who are healthier and better cared for.

Many Third World women are already the family's major income earners, albeit those incomes generally maintain them at a subsistence level. Their earning power could be increased by giving them greater access to business loans and environmentally sound agricultural practices while releasing them from their dependency on large extended families to do the work. In those few situations where better advantages for women exist, a marked decline in birth rates has occurred. Economic opportunities to be beneficial must be accompanied by access to medical care, family planning services, education and skill training.

Kenya once had the fastest growing population in the world at 8 to 10 children per woman. This rate is now less than five because one third of the women have been given a sexual education, access to contraception and economic opportunities, while the other two thirds remain hidebound by taboos and tribal customs which decree a woman must have enough children to name each one for a living relative.

However, incontrovertible social forces are at work reducing the birth rates naturally. As Kenya's population grows, fewer and fewer parents have enough farmland, water reserves or employment to feed themselves, let alone divide their plots of land into smaller and smaller divisions to give to their offsprings' families. Increasingly more devastating is the AIDS virus which is taking the lives of women in their fertile years and infecting a growing portion of the children they bear.

Women throughout the world would gladly reduce their families and protect their lives if they had access to or could afford modern technologies of birth control. The majority of women spend over 25 years, twelve months a year, three weeks a month from the age of 14 to 40 in fear of becoming pregnant. This is a fear and a physical struggle no male expert for or against family planning, contraception and abortion can ever comprehend. Pregnancies and the ability to avoid them dictate the level of every woman's achievement in education, economic standards, industrial production, political power and family responsibilities during the most active, productive years of her existence. No job opportunity or living standard reduces this constant female struggle. What industrial employment offers is the money to buy contraceptives and abortions so that a woman can control her life by being able to control her reproductive capacity. Above all, controlling pregnancies is the key to population control.

South Korea is a present day paradigm of the effective empowerment of educated women in patriarchal societies. Until recently, Korean Family Law forbade women legal rights to custody of children or inheritance of money or property. Two out of three South Korean women could be legally beaten by husbands and fathers. Many still are, a regressive social contradiction in a "democratic" nation.[7] Male superiority in the nation had produced a violent society in which women were considered property without rights, just as they have been treated since ancient Egyptian times when warring, patriarchal societies first established male dominated civilizations, a cultural practice which remains throughout most of the world to this day.[8]

However, the present demand for their labour in South Korea's booming industrial economy has given women the opportunity to use contraception and abortion so they have an equal say in how many children they will have. The majority are now educated, many fill professional occupations and they have the right to vote. These assets have empowered South Korean women to unseat anti-feminine leaders and elect politicians who are willing to address women's rights and reduce the customary violence against them.[9]

Although the technology exists, statistics submitted to the Cairo Conference estimated that only 50 percent of women in their reproductive years have access to contraception or bother to use it. Many, especially teenage girls, have little or no understanding of how sexual reproduction works. This is particularly devastating in that 40 percent of the babies born each year around the world are born to unmarried teenage adolescents. This is of particular concern as 60 percent of the world's population will be children under the age of 16 by 2005.[10] This trend may be enough to offset any gains contraceptive technologies might make in reducing fertility rates, especially in those societies willing to support teenage pregnancies or those unable to prevent teenage promiscuity.

But even the assurance of birth control to reduce pregnancies has its risks. Many women experience health problems through the use of contraceptive pills and IUD implants. Many cannot tolerate the added oestrogen in their systems because of other illnesses or the presence of cancer. Some sterilization drugs such as quinacrine, an antimalarial drug when placed directly in the womb forms scar tissue which blocks the fallopian tubes, may produce cancer and other side effects.[11] Also, contraceptive devices are prone to failure. Diseases such as HIV, AIDS and Hepatitis C plague the lives of women on every continent without access to condoms. The death from sexual diseases of tens of thousands of mothers each year only adds to the growing social crisis of orphaned children abandoned into poverty and sickness.

In June, 1996, the World Health Organization of the United Nations released a report that estimated the yearly number of deaths at 600,000 world wide among women who undergo both legal and illegal abortions, and an average 15 million are injured during abortions or in child birth.[12]

For women living in nations where religious and patriarchal powers forbid birth control, the struggle is both physical and emotional. Most cultural improvements available to women fly in the face of tradition and religious practices. Until the males in a nation are educated and employed, educating and empowering women will not occur. To succeed in establishing a universal system to control population requires religious dogma be redesigned to favour Family Planning programs which offer sterilization and abortion. The chances of major religious sects taking this position in the foreseeable future is as unlikely as a revolution occurring in patriarchal societies to end the power men have to subjugate women.

The United Nations' Conference on Women's Rights held in Beijing, China in September, 1995, demonstrated the enormity of the roadblocks to empowering women. Every means to discourage the successful outcome of the conference was used by the Chinese authorities to interfere with the possible attendance of 50,000 women from around the world. Only enough conference facilities to handle 10,000 of the 35,000 women hoping to represent non-governmental organizations was provided, and those facilities were located in a city over an hour's drive from Beijing for which few transportation conveniences were provided. One conference building didn't have a roof. The excuse was without it the women would keep cool. Visas were denied to delegates who failed to get hotel accommodations, both of which were delayed by bureaucracy. Laws in China were strengthened against social demonstrations. Transportation, telephones, faxes, all forms of communication were in short supply. The accommodations were intended to make the stay of the women as uncomfortable as possible.[13]

How many of these inconveniences are the product of a backward Communist regime and a decaying infra-structure and how many reflect government censorship and disapproval of women's rights remain open to speculation and propaganda. Preferably, the Chinese authorities would have liked to see the women go shopping. In their patronizingly way they planned to make this happen by providing inadequate conference facilities. Does any demonstration of patriarchal/cultural traditions portray more clearly the Chinese attitudes towards women, especially as this event happened in the most overpopulated nation in the world where women are brutally coerced into having only one child.

Several events in the 1990s have indicated an actual backlash to political and economic gains women have made in recent years to improve their status and control their reproductive capacity. Former communist countries of Eastern Europe are experiencing a return to conservative, religious governments which do not tolerate abortions and cannot afford contraception and family planning programs. Poland, once again dominated by the Catholic Church, has all but outlawed abortion and contraception. This in a nation where poverty and chaos still cause extensive social suffering and economic want.

Conservative governments in Western nations are actually rolling back their abortion laws and the right of women to have abortions on demand. Abortion in Germany still remains illegal but not punishable if carried out during the first trimester. Republicans in the United States Congress would do away with all circumstances permitting abortion, from deformities to rape and incest.

As Muslim Fundamentalism gains political power throughout the Middle East, the leaders are forcing women to stay in their homes or hide behind the chaddor. Disobeying these religious laws risks persecution, even stoning, in the streets. In Algeria, Muslim guerrillas killed over 370 women in 1994-1995 alone. These were women holding jobs and living Western-style, emancipated lives.

The growing persecution of women is a backlash that comes with the fear of cultural change and any threat to patriarchal social structures throughout the world. According to UN reports in August, 1995, women's rights lagged behind those of men in over 130 nations.[14] Many of these nations view emancipated women as evil to be severely castigated, even physically punished.

Social Solutions

We can glimpse the future and the folly in our actions by observing much that is happening in the many battle-torn and impoverished nations today. Their suffering and disarray are the harbingers of future world struggles for land, food and water supplies as populations grow and landbases become overcrowded. In trying to improve living standards worldwide, Western governments through their development banks imposed impossible debt loads on the Third World during the 1960s and 1970s. By encouraging them to take on advanced technologies, large loans for industrialization, high priced foreign expertise, vast destructive dam and irrigation projects, the industrial nations caused massive dislocation and poverty on local and indigenous peoples. Once relatively stable, agrarian economies became the domain of unscrupulous dictators and foreign investors and developers. The same debt load now engulfs the industrial nations as the debts incurred through national social programs grow larger than their GNP's and sap their economies.

And their populations exploded! The realities of the future are that if nature doesn't reduce our numbers through climatic changes, starvation and thirst, we will certainly do it for her by the misuse of our technologies and our overwhelming presence. Overcrowding and human frailties will bring on increasing numbers of civil and international wars. The struggle to survive in a depleted environment will culminate in so much hatred and anger that we will unwittingly lease nuclear and biological weapons on our neighbors which will, in turn, destroy us all.

To curb population expansion, social, religious and political attitudes must be changed. Reason must replace sentiment and human hubris. Can we continue promoting the "joys of motherhood" and the "virility of manhood"? Should we encourage the scientific reproduction of babies through invitro-fertilization and surrogate motherhood? Can we continue to force life on all persons no matter the costs to their human dignity and suffering by preventing medical authorities from helping the terminally ill to die peacefully at their own choosing? Are we really such monsters that we have no faith in our own capacity to regulate and legally provide euthanasia? Are we dooming the human race when we try to overcome all of nature's limitations on our reproductive abilities by such things as imposing life sustaining drugs and machines on our sick and dying?

These are modern day ethical questions which attack thousands of years of social and technological evolution. They arouse emotional biases, religious prejudices and human extremes of action. Sadly, the evidence of our folly lies in keeping alive traditions which foster population growth while denying birth control. In Western nations and countries heavily influenced by Western values and Christianity, we are enchained by deeply held moral and social codes of the past which prevent us from meeting the realities of the present head on. Pope John Paul in his encyclical of April, 1995, strongly denounced both abortion and euthanasia as a "culture of death". He took his decree a step further by claiming there is no justification for executing criminals.[15] We all stand to be done in by the arrogance of our overweening sense of human importance and the sanctity of life, no matter how poor the quality of that life.

To date, sustaining our sick and dying at any cost remains the foremost policy of the Western industrial nations and world aid organizations. But, in trying to convince ourselves we must support the proliferation and maintenance of life at any cost, we are strangling our economies as we ignore the reality that "no society can afford to carry the heavy burden in resources of extending human life indefinitely for a substantial number of its members."[16]

CHAPTER SEVEN

The Industrialization Solution

The solution that remains universally palatable as the best means to control the population explosion is the myth that industrialization and a more equitable distribution of purchasing power and goods will reduce the desire for large families. This could be accomplished through more investment from the rich nations and aid to poor governments to finance social programs and public infra-structures. These economic policies would then offer the major solution to reducing birth rates throughout the developing world.

The concept is reminiscent of failed socialism in that it supports a more equitable distribution of jobs and wealth. However, the myth persists because it does not demand enforced cultural or religious changes.

According to the myth, industrial development should gradually reduce world poverty and promote small families through improved living standards. Industrialization dramatically reduced birth rates in both the West and in developed Asian nations in the past; therefore, it should do the same for poor nations where populations are exploding.

The general consensus is that technological-determinism and a marked improvement in living standards worldwide will gradually reduce the need for large support families who earn subsistence incomes, work on family farms or care for the sick and elderly. By utilizing technologies and investment capital, domestic industries, manufacturing and commercial agricultural projects could be established with the resulting wealth and purchasing power used to offset the present need for having many children. Most important, industrialization requires women in the workforces. Employment will give women a degree of domestic freedom, self-esteem and eventually an education. All three will then enable them to raise healthy children who will survive into adulthood, decreasing the birth rate to the minimum necessary to ensure the continuation of the family.

Although the fertility rate per woman may drop in an industrialized nation, social and economic forces to date have kept populations expanding within industrial nations, none have decreased. The advantages of industrial wealth cause many changes which actually promote population growth. For instance, entire populations have gained the capacity to live well into old age through better nutrition, medical care, higher sanitary standards, allowing as many as four generations to be alive at the same time. Furthermore, infant survival rates explode through medical improvements. Even the chronically sick remain alive well into adulthood as now their illnesses can be managed so that they live longer lives. Moreover, the genetically ill are reaching adulthood and successfully reproducing. Many from newborns to the very elderly who would die from natural health problems are kept alive by machines and medications. Euthanasia remains a punishable crime in the majority of industrial nations. The general consensus is that with the help of modern technologies, what cannot be cured, must be medically and financially supported.

Industrial Populations Expand Initially

Three major problems are inherent in the industrialization solution. First, populations initially increase dramatically with better employment opportunities, higher living standards and industrial production. Second, many cultural and economic factors directly related to industrialization work against population control. Third, all recent environmental studies prove industrialization on the present scale is destroying the planet.

If industrial technology is accepted as the route to improved living standards and population control, then we stand to populate and industrialize ourselves into oblivion in the interim. Only a billion of the six billion now alive enjoy the fruits of industrialization. With the predicted 10 to 14 billion living at the same time during the 21st Century, each increasingly dependent on agricultural and industrial production, will the planet's environment be able to sustain such numbers or will it fail us all?

During the 19th and 20th Centuries the rapid growth in technologies and industrial development in Western nations played a marked role both in the initial expansion of populations and then in their gradual reduction in fertility rates. Britain's population during the Industrial Revolution, for instance, climbed from 10 million in 1800 to 41 million in 1900 to its present day numbers of 58 million. These numbers would be much higher if not for massive emigrations to British colonies over the last 150 years. A similar increase in population occurred throughout Europe with industrial expansion in the 19th and 20th Centuries. The continent's population in 1750, estimated at 170 millions, is now well over 650 millions, despite the massive death tolls of two World Wars and heavy emigration to colonies. That is almost a fourfold increase following industrialization, a population increase that cannot be sustained or tolerated by any nation's environment today.

Population figures show that Western industrial countries have never experienced a zero or negative birth rate since the Industrial Revolution began in the mid-18th Century. They have always expanded and continue to do so, despite women working and eventually gaining control over their reproductive lives.

When Western nations fought two world wars in the 20th Century, labor shortages in factories turning out war equipment gave women their first major opportunity to enter the working world and prove they could handle industrial jobs as well as men. Once they enjoyed the wages of their labour, they could no longer be treated as baby producers alone. However, the return of men from war brought a baby boom in the late 1940s and 1950s, but women were never again excluded from industrial jobs in the West. The rise in living standards and the use of contraception after World War II gradually gave women the freedom to choose jobs or family. The result was a decline in the reproduction rate per women during the 1960s which has remained to this day.

Yet Western populations have not stopped growing. In truth, they have expanded dramatically since the 1960s. With improved health care, infant mortality rates plummeted and people began to live longer. After World War II Europe and North America opened their doors to tens of millions of immigrants. Canada's population, as did those of all Western nations, more than doubled, rising from 12 million to reach 30 millions in the 1990s.

European nations now average 1.6 to 1.8 percent growth per year. France, for example, is growing at 1.8 percent per year and Ireland at 2.4[1] North America averages 1.8 percent growth with Canada's rate at 1.7 and the United States at 1.9.[2] Attempts to reach a replacement or negative birth rate throughout Europe and North America is continuously offset by the influx of immigrants and refugees from many parts of the world whose reproductive rates actually rise when they migrate to industrialized countries. "Poor women in Mexico City should have more children than their counterparts in the U.S. who have better health care and a higher standard of living. But peasant families tend to have two or three children in Mexico City, while those who migrate to the U.S. average four or five children".[3]

Studies continue to show that populations rise rather than fall with improved employment opportunities and higher living standards. A drop in fertility rates usually follows a decline in the well-being of a populace, when prosperity and political stability fail or when any or all of The Four Horses of the Apocalypse, famine, pestilence, war and death, are rampant. "A study of Nigerian communities revealed that bad economic times in recent years caused young Yoruba families to turn to contraception even though infant (deaths) were rising...".[4]

India is one of the most recent examples of excessive population expansion during its period of industrial development. Since World War II, India's population doubled from 342 million in 1947 to 685 million in 1981. Then by 1994 it had surpassed 900 million. Its population is expected to reach 1 billion by the year 2000 and surpass China in 2035 at 1.6 billion.[5]

India began a strong upturn in industrial output and export trade between 1990 and 1995. For the first time, the GNP at 5 percent was greater than the birth rate of 3.9 percent.[6] And yet the population of India increased by over 17 million a year during that period. The global economy, which freed up trade in manufactured commodities between the Third World and the developed nations, encouraged India, like so many Third World nations, to build their production on cheap "slave" labour. Since the majority of the population are children, the majority of workers are mostly children and will continue to be as their numbers outrun the adult population and keep fertility rates high.

Births per women in India averaged 3.9 from 1990 to 1995. At the same time life expectancy jumped from 23 years of age in 1900 to 59 in 1994. Only 43 percent of the population were known to use contraception in 1994, but "the death rate (fell) faster than the birth rate" rose.[7] Of the more than 900 million alive today, 360 million live in absolute poverty. Living conditions are made more intolerable by diminishing urban viability of the overcrowded cities which have grown beyond all possible civil management and regulation.[8]

What must be calculated into the effects of these statistics is that growth in the GNP can be very misleading when compared with population growth. Expanding industrialization may register a definitive increase in GNP, but a very small percentage of the whole population is enriched by the increase in production in nations as overpopulated as India. At the same time, industrialization has attracted tens of millions to urban areas where populations are exploding, poverty is deepening and the health of city inhabitants is endangered and weakened by the industrial and vehicular pollution which inundates India's cities. The present burst in industrial growth may soon prove to be India's worst nightmare.

It is a persistent fact that large populations in Asia and Third World countries during the 20th Century continue to grow. Development of resources, higher living standards, education, improved medical care, pesticides and insecticides, more abundant and affordable nutritious foods, lower infant mortality rates and extended life expectancy all raise fertility rates in both developed and developing countries. The estimate that 95 percent of population growth in the 21st Century will be in Third World countries will not only be the product of spreading poverty, but also the result of expanding industrialization as Asia and South America become major industrial competitors on world markets.

This assumption is predicated on the experience of the most highly successful industrial nations of Asia, --Japan, South Korea, Taiwan and the cities of Hong Kong and Singapore. All have seen their populations expand. Japan is perhaps the most outstanding case because it has surpassed all other nations in industrial development and per capita wealth.

After World War II Japan's population was 70 millions. From 1945 to 1980 it grew to 125 millions. Japanese political and industrial leadership, bound by tradition, tried to keep women servile and at home, adding to the workforce through producing male offspring. However, the immediate need for a larger workforce in the mushrooming economy was desperate. Either increase the domestic workforce or go abroad to build plants in industrial nations where there were available workers. To avoid the monetary drain of either choice initially, women had to be allowed to enter the labor force in large numbers. The birth rate took a decided drop and the population stabilized.

In the 1990s Japan's annual birth rate is 1.7 percent, a small but continuing expansion primarily in the number of people living into old age. What must not be overlooked in these statistics is that many other reasons account for the continuing low birth rate other than industrial employment of women: an overcrowded land base, easy access to birth control and abortion, disciplined cultural/religious community traditions, an excessively high cost of living, very expensive, small housing units, overworked men and women, and a stressful national demand for full dedication to education and industrial production. Added to this list of factors discouraging women to have children has been the recession of the 1990s, the highly valued yen, glutted world markets and the expanded use of technologies in place of labor. Japan now has a low but rising unemployment rate and women are usually the first workers to be laid off.

At what point does industrialization mythically reduce fertility rates?. During the most expansive and productive years of industrial development, populations have always expanded, not decreased. It is also known that once a nation's economy has moved towards greater and greater technological capacity and output, the existing labor force is often in short supply and more demanding of higher wages. A large migrant labor force may then be imported to provide the labor for mass production tasks and do the menial jobs of an affluent society. Industrial expansion and high living standards in Japan during the 1970s and 1980s necessitated the importation of over a million workers from other countries. Japanese industrialists and governments pushed for a higher birth rate as a preferable ethnic solution, quite the opposite goal desired by supporters of the industrial myth of reducing population through industrial employment. While Japan does not allow foreign workers to stay very long nor to become citizens, most industrial countries do, absorbing millions of migrating workers into their nations on a permanent basis and raising population totals and fertility rates.

Now a fully mature industrial state, Japan has entered the age of industrial maturity, experiencing much slower growth rates. Huge national debts and a creeping unemployment rate are more influential in reducing the desire to have children than is putting women to work. These economic factors are common to all the old industrial nations throughout the West. Recessions, disappearing jobs, declining purchasing power, technology replacing workers, high personal debt, failing government social and welfare programs, loss of personal living space in which to enjoy one's affluence and financial problems trying to live well in old age, all are present Western conditions reducing the desire to have more than one or two children. Now that the initial upswing in living standards which increased fertility and longevity have levelled off, the fertility rates are finally below replacement levels.

Unquestionably, industrialization in several Asian nations has improved the living standards of their workforces over a shorter period of time than it took in Western nations. Several have already registered a marked decline in fertility rates, but at the same time they have experienced a sharp rise in imported migrant labour, longevity and infant survival rates. These factors must make us realize that the population growth innate in initial industrialization actually threatens us all as it will expand our numbers in the immediate future beyond the carrying capacity of the planet long before developing nations reduce their fertility rates and overall population numbers.

Another aspect of Asian industrialization is that populations in these nations are already too large for the carrying capacity of their landbases. Industrialization and fertility curbs have lessened the birth rates, but they have not solved the problem of overpopulation. China's one-child per couple policy should be the exemplary case. China has practised negative population expansion for several decades, yet estimates show her population will still grow to an unsupportable 1.5 billion by 2025. Based on previous experience and predicted population growth in all nations, the replacement or negative birth rates needed to prevent overpopulation will not happen within the next century; it may never happen in time to prevent environmental collapse.

High fertility rates will continue to hold sway throughout the 21st Century in Africa, Central and South America, India and much of Asia, especially in countries of Muslim and Catholic persuasion. Most of these areas share the same survival problems: too large a population to be sustained on the national land base, a growing dependency on imported food supplies, an insatiable need for foreign expertise and capital investment, overcrowded urban areas moving onto precious farm land, diminishing soil fertility, disappearing forests, fresh water shortages, air and water pollution, nonexistent or overburdened infra-structures, a shortage of natural resources and a large majority living in poverty.

While GNP rates are surpassing fertility rates for the first time in China, the residual supply of workers is so large it is unlikely the planet could sustain a nation of 1.5 billion employed within an industrial economy. We are already experiencing grave environmental degradation with the industrialization of less than one billion people worldwide. The addition of another billion industrial workers will far surpass the earth's carrying capacity.

Only the enforced "one child" policy of the Communist regime has kept China's numbers from exploding beyond environmental collapse. Even this attempt to control fertility rates is in jeopardy. One child per couple is proving socially unpopular throughout China. The diminishing control of the Communist Party and spreading corruption among officials is encouraging many to thwart this rule. It is not difficult to assume that once Communist military oppression is gone, the population will explode. Industrial wealth, increased life spans and improved nutrition and higher living standards will encourage the desire for more children in a land where social customs and religion are based on the large, extended family.

But even one child per couple is enough to offset economic stability and overwhelm China's environmental carrying capacity. The country has had to begin importing large portions of its food needs as farm lands become settings for rampant factory and housing development. A severe lack of water and the disappearance of organic farming methods in the onrush of commercial farming are also speeding up erosion and sterility of soils. Food production is falling steadily.

Industrialization as the solution to population control ignores the very nature of development and improved living standards, creating a two-part dilemma: It causes population growth, it does not diminish it; and both of its components, improved living standards and industrial expansion, depend on overconsumption and unlimited use and degradation of environmental resources. These conditions cannot sustain a nation's inhabitants over the long term. Even small industrial nations can be classified as overpopulated once they begin importing the bulk of their food supplies and raw materials.

Industrialization Is a Temporary Solution at Best

Often forgotten in this myth of population control through universal industrial development and better living conditions is that industrialization is, after all, only a temporary economic state which peaks and gradually diminishes, much of the decline brought about by overuse and abuse of economic advantages and the environmental resources. What must be considered is how long does an industrial state remain alive before it peaks and declines into debt, inefficiency, poor quality production and labor unrest? How long can a nation exist on a high technology base which employs less than 20 percent of its people and must compete on a world market of cutthroat competition? If the industrial cycle is growing shorter, can industrialization be seen as the answer to population control in the long term?

During a nation's industrial rise, the prosperity of all citizens has been possible in the past. Governments could safely tax both industry and workers, share the wealth of production and build a rich, highly progressive democratic society with much purchasing and investing power. At the height of industrial development, the redistribution by governments of national wealth generally leads to unsupportable costs in worker benefits, medical care, education, infra-structure and government bureaucracies. The state bureaucracies, bloated on economic prosperity, become corrupted, overtaxed and inefficient. Eventually excessive wage demands and costly conditions of production discourage entrepreneurs and deplete national capital assets. Tax bases are then eroded by fleeing investment capital. Resources are in danger of depletion and the land base is increasingly contaminated.

As overall industrial success diminishes, the affluent, expanding populations encounter an increasing decline in social programs. Quality and security are sacrificed in health care, pension plans, education, public works, transportation systems, security of person and property, law and order, all essential to prosperous, industrial democracies. Governments, having lost the large tax base of peak industrial times, begin endangering the nation by borrowing to maintain the expensive social and political infra-structures. They take great risks so as to get re-elected and to attract foreign investors and entrepreneurs. Without social benefits, a nation's economy enters a state of chaos and mass poverty as happened throughout the republics of the former USSR during the early 1990s. In the end much of the remaining industrial base is financed, owned and controlled by foreign expertise and investors whose interests are profits and cheaply produced commodities, not the welfare of the nation's people nor the preservation of the environment.

Unemployment in the developed nations has come to mean widespread emotional and physical insecurity as well as a drop in living standards. At present tens of millions of workers in Western Europe and North America have lost well-paying, full time jobs and must rely on parttime work or jobs paying minimum wage. Even these are now very scarce. The frequent downturns in Western economies is affecting a larger and larger percentage of the population. Women, both skilled and unskilled, are the first to be laid off, returning them to the previous status of struggling to afford ways to prevent pregnancies or to survive as single mothers while they sink into poverty. It is easy to understand why families are breaking apart and spousal abuse and neglect are on the rise.

Urban overcrowding and social breakdown are now symptomatic of the older, declining industrial societies. Each of the above conditions reduces living standards for a growing minority and creates "inner city" populations who are suffering from deepening poverty and all the ills and violence inherent in urban decay. As the industrial tax base shrinks and populations grow, governments fail to meet the emotional, educational and employment needs of young people, especially those whose "ghetto" existence is not conducive to turning out highly educated, technically-skilled workers.

Once again fertility rates rise among the unemployed and the poor, especially among teenagers. Young women, if they cannot get work, have been able to get government handouts to care for any number of children. Statistics in the United States for the year 1990 report that 913,000 unmarried women between 15-44 years of age gave birth, a total of 23 percent of all babies born that year. 229,000 of them were born to unwed teenagers.[9] Widespread unemployment inherent in old and declining industrial nations has become the harbinger of social decay, reducing the number of women employed, therefore, minimizing the role of industrialization in reducing populations.

Today, Western manufacturing of basic goods has all but been superseded by foreign competition. Skilled jobs in hi-tech are moving to Asia and mass production lines of basic commodities are moving to Third World countries. This has vastly reduced employment opportunities for unskilled and semi-skilled workers who still comprise a dominant sector of Western workforces. Economic pillars such as federal and state governments have been weakened by debt, and the gap between rich and poor is widening at an unprecedented speed.

North America and Britain are attempting to forestall such an economic crisis by forcing unrestricted free trade on global markets. This course tends to benefit the rich in their well established industrial nations, while impoverishing the middle classes and deepening the suffering of the poor. The poor by the very essence of their poverty and lack of skills are superfluous in the hi-tech economy of a declining industrial nation, but an increasingly expensive tax burden to the nation as a whole.

Industrialization, like any evolutionary concept of our civilizations, must be seen as a very short term solution to population control as its continuing expansion is rapidly curtailed by the overuse and abuse of its basic principles. Western dominance over industrial and agricultural technologies and production during the last two centuries, for instance, is giving way to Asian development where new ideas, advanced technologies, specialized commodities, lower prices and improved production and quality equal the West's and in many cases surpass it in sales on the international markets.

Important to the theory of industrialization and population control is that each industrialization now happens on a shrinking time scale. Japan peaked in 40 years, Taiwan and South Korea in less than 30. China became a universal challenge within ten years. Does the decline side of the cycle arrive as quickly? Global forces reveal that as one group of nations advances through the many stages of industrial development, other nations are forced into decline. At the same time, many nations attempting to industrialize and catch up with the modern world are unable to develop successfully for many social, religious and economic reasons. Many are dependent on the sale of their raw materials and natural resources which is not conducive to long term prosperity because the high rate of technological extraction and consumption reduces the resources of a landbase within decades.

Several Economic and Social Factors
Assist Industrialization As a Population Control

Admittedly, many factors of an industrial society eventually work to improve lives and reduce the birth rate. Several factors of industrialization contribute to this difference: improved nutrition, advanced medical technologies, high infant survival rates, employment benefit programs, welfare and public infrastructures among others. The overall effect is that while birth rates in the Third World expand at more than three percent a year, they have fallen in the industrial nations to just under two percent.

However, several cultural and political influences contribute more to Asian social trends than economic conditions. These nations are generally highly structured patriarchies, governed by authoritarian leadership and a military or police support system which can enforce population control as in China. Eastern religions and cultural teachings differ widely from Western traditions, the primary difference being that Asians believe what is good for the community must take priority over the needs and wishes of the individual. Therefore, religious traditions in eastern Asia sanction the welfare of the group or the community, as opposed to the rights of the individual. This tenet gives governments enough leeway to establish economic and cultural practices. Where overpopulation is threatening social stability, governments are generally free to promote contraception and access to abortion and sterilization.

While Asia slows her fertility rates by political and cultural pressures, overcrowding and industrial decay in the developed world are beginning to prove far more instrumental in slowing fertility rates then industrial expansion and technologies ever will. Russia, for example, has had a negative birth rate during the past 40 years. The hardship, the lack of food, housing shortages, the fear of persecution and the loss of individual purpose persuaded many Eastern Europeans and Russians to keep their families very small. Aided by government incentives which encouraged birth control through abortion, most families had only one child. The poverty and repression under Communist governments proved to be major restraints against the desire to have large families. Only Islamic religions in the southern republics of the USSR proved more influential over the fertility rate than did the harshness of the Communist state. Muslim populations maintained high fertility rates throughout the Communist regime and still do.

Eastern European populations are declining not because of industrialization or the employment of women, but because of the past deconsumerism policies of Communism which resulted in the decay and corruption of their industries. Widespread unemployment, mass poverty, a lack of business knowledge, environmental pollution, the loss of public infra-structure and fewer government services discouraged women from bringing children into their difficult world.

Government leverage over birth rates has generally disappeared from the former Communist countries, but the pervasive lack of employment and food, the horrors of industrial and chemical diseases and birth defects among children, the easy access to abortion and the growing chaos within these nations continue to persuade the people to limit their families to one or two children. In this case physical deprivation of mind and body caused by negative forces of industrialization are controlling fertility rates. Until Eastern Europe re-establishes its social and economic institutions, they will remain deprived of most technological advantages. Recent reports out of Eastern Europe suggest that nature's many forms of population control are in effect: famine, disease, overpopulation, corruption, violence and early death.

In actuality, industrialization in several nations is now instrumental in increasing populations as well as fertility rates. As Third World populations grow and their economic poverty deepens, they are migrating in large numbers to the industrial nations. Economic and environmental refugees are adding their numbers plus their future offspring to industrial nations. In this way industry contributes to rising birth rates; it does not decrease them, a trend which will expand many times in the 21st Century. Canada, for example, increased its population through immigrants by over 250,000 newcomers in just one year, a 1.1 percent growth from 1993 to 1994.[10] Filling up the rich nations with immigrants from poor countries may be very humanitarian, but it will have its price in the near future as the rich nations overcrowd their land bases beyond the carrying capacity.

Industrialization creates its own increase in population, Industrial nations, short on highly skilled workers in hi-tech industries, search the world for the most educated and skilled, bribing them with riches to leave their impoverished nations and immigrate to the rich. By depriving the poorer nations of their educated and skilled, the industrial nations keep the poorer nations dependent on Western expertise, handouts and food aid, while increasing their own populations. Both industrial and developing nations lose in the process, only the entrepreneur gains. But populations mount in both rich and poor countries.

Industrializing farming has also created a monster. Within all nations, developed and developing, tens of millions of people have left the land for the cities in search of jobs. In many countries highly mechanized farming techniques have made farm labor redundant while destroying the fertility of vast farm land areas. Exploding rural populations, overcrowded farm lands, a lack of jobs, slave economies and glutted markets are forcing men and women in every nation to become economic/environmental refugees, the flotsam and jetsam of the industrial age.

In Asia, migration from the farms to the urban centres may be freeing women from rural traditions of having large families needed to work the land, but it enslaves them in unwholesome manufacturing, poorly paid jobs and houses them in small, cramped city apartments or slums not conducive to child raising. The amount of physical and mental suffering associated with leaving the land and moving to the city is traumatic. Indirectly these mass migrations are contributing to a decline in birth rates as malnutrition, disease and abject poverty cause high infant mortality rates among the refugees.

Granted harsh employment conditions and overcrowding force the use of contraceptives, abortion and sterilization. But where the law does not allow their use or women cannot afford them, the death toll on mothers from illegal abortions is rising annually. Most abortions in the Third World are still forbidden by law, but women who find work cannot afford pregnancies if they hope to keep their jobs. Industrial conditions for working women in developing nations are generally very harsh. Tests for pregnancy are given frequently. The woman who fails these tests may be beaten, starved and fired. In the United States evidence emerged recently that factory managers were locking women up in a California factory to prevent pregnancies. If it is happening there, obviously it is occurring world wide. Most industries and businesses in the industrial nations as well as the Third World refuse to support expectant mothers through maternity leave or provide child care. Such conditions are inhuman solutions to population control. Their existence stands firmly against the myth that mass industrialization should be sought as the humanitarian path to population control.

In the small nuclear family of industrial societies, stress destroys family unity and the divorce rate rises. Divorce now affects 50 percent of families in Western nations. The difficulties of the single parent raising children alone are daunting. High costs of living and the scarcity of jobs for women forces most single mothers to depend on welfare. Parental neglect, physical abuse, a lack of direction and training in the home drive children and teenagers into the streets to seek identity and purpose among their peers. The results are anti-social patterns of behavior: increasing crime, violent activities, drug cultures, gang warfare and murder. Life on the streets has little value. These are dangerous precedents for civilized society and more so, as overcrowding abets violence which can become civil war.

Recent studies of family breakdown and increasing violence among working people in industrial nations suggest another evil side to industrialization. The mobility and economic self-sufficiency of parents has destroyed the role extended families play in raising the children. The bulk of children in industrial nations are now raised by one or two parents, removing them from the physical help and spiritual strength of the extended family. This, too, turns children to the streets to find direction and strength among their peers. Parents on their own generally experience excessive stress on their time and energy, decreasing their ability to nurture their children. If this industrial trend reduces fertility and obviously it does, the psychological impact is extremely unsavoury. Foremost, it is the escalating factor in the breakdown of families. Not an acceptable solution to population control!

More people now live in the industrial cities of the world than in the cities of the undeveloped nations. Technologies in urban areas provide everything one needs to live well if one has the purchasing power. Obviously family values and ties are lost when so many individuals can live without the support of the extended family. Urban life permits the young to escape family obligations and restrictions. Technological independence waives responsibility to families, leaving increasing numbers of unemployed youths to haunt city streets in search of work, unable to commit themselves to family life. Their sexual needs inflate an already unmanageable social problem of too many illegitimate children. In Africa promiscuity knows no bounds, that was until AIDs became such a scourge. Left to fend for themselves on city streets, untrained in the values of good family and communal living or sold into slavery and prostitution, the superfluous and illegitimate children of our many different societies suffer inhuman existences, none of which are likely to reduce fertility rates or produce a generation of productive, peaceful citizens.

Every industrial nation in the world is now watching as its homeless populations grow in shanty towns and on the streets. Social decay is fostering the power of gangs and warlords. Drug cartels are powerful multinational corporations, controlling governments. Corruption in business and government is the norm and violence rules on city streets. Industrial pollution is damaging the health and welfare of industrial workers and placing an horrific form of control on pregnancies as still births and physical defects proliferate. Respiratory diseases and cancers are bringing early, unnecessary death to the young. If these are the means by which industrialization controls population growth, it suffers far more from ethical immorality than the technologies of birth control, sterilization and abortion.

Recently, an alarming new dimension to human reproduction caused by industrialization has been revealed. Nearly 25 percent of men and women in industrial nations are sterile. Whether they are working or not, it is estimated that one in four women in the rich nations are unable to conceive and over 25 percent of males have less than 50 percent of normal sperm count. Sterility is a maverick social factor which may be helping to lower the birth rate, but its disturbing genesis is just coming to light. It is apparently caused by industrial pollution. The villains are the many toxic chemicals in our drinking water, in the air we breathe and in the foods we eat. They are in the plastic containers in which we cook and store our foods. The effect of chemicals common in the many manufactured items which make every day life so much easier is to mimic oestrogen and upset the natural reproductive forces in human beings.[11] Destroying human fertility and genetic health may be a dangerous consequence of the industrialization myth.

The crucial contribution industrial development can offer women is the universal power it gives them to decide how many children they will have. Knowing one has the largesse of government to turn to in times of unemployment or illness reduces the need to have large support families. But most of these are advantages few people will ever experience because the planet cannot sustain billions of people at the required level of environmental destruction needed to give the majority of people a living standard high enough to control their reproduction.

In lieu of the growing number of social and environmental problems incumbent in the industrialization solution to population control, a much wiser course would be for the rich nations to provide all women in their fertile years with birth control, basic education in nutrition and health care, access to abortion and elemental employment. Perhaps then we would stave off extinction much more efficiently than if we set our goals to industrialize the world!

Global Industrialization and Social Collapse

If the aim is to reduce global population growth, the route through industrialization is the most dangerous to take. Believed to be socially and economically progressive, industrialization is proving to be politically and internationally destabilizing and environmentally destructive.

Present day commercialism and cutthroat competition, basic causes of increasing economic inequality and ethnic hostilities, are dubious solutions to advancing worldwide cooperation aimed at achieving equitable industrial development, improved living standards for the vast majority and a reduction in fertility rates. At present economic and social forces are running against equitable trade and development among nations. The African continent is generally collapsing into mass poverty, overpopulation and political chaos. Much of Latin America is economically improving, though overpopulation and widespread poverty still offset national progress and general living standards, while the upgrading of urban infra-structures and the preservation of the environment remain low on the list of economic priorities. Moreover, the mercantilistic competition coming from newly industrialized nations in Asia is forcing the economic decline of Western industrialism. At the same time American free-wheeling market forces are proving brutal to democratic social structures of established industrial workforces world wide, including their own.

In viewing industrialization as the most widely accepted means to reduce global birth rates, several logistical questions must be broached: Can the earth supply even the basic quantity of resources needed to industrialize the Third World nations where 95 percent of the additional population will live in the next century? If industrialization is to be developed on the scale required to control Third World population growth, how much of the resulting pollution will be safely absorbed by the air, the water and the land? Do some nations, like India and China, already have too many people? Does even China's "one child per couple" rule still increase the population beyond any useful industrial impact on their growing numbers? Have industrial consumption and waste in the developed world already exceeded the carrying capacity of the earth's resources and ability to absorb industrial wastes?

In steaming ahead to industrialize all nations, we ignore the limitations of the planet's finite environment. It will not tolerate unlimited resource consumption and environmental pollution. Nor does the employment or social space exist for so many bodies. Human suffering from hunger, disease and civil war indicate there are already too many people alive to be sustained productively and peacefully.

Modern technologies make it possible to measure and compute recent world food production and estimate the amount available to any given population. Computer models of the planet's carrying capacity reveal that the addition of 90 million bodies a year is outpacing increases in food production. Somewhere in the very near future we will reach that condition described by Malthus two centuries ago when he foretold of the ability of populations to outrun food supply. Currently, over 68 nations depend on imported food commodities to feed their populations. Increasing poverty, widespread malnutrition, frequent droughts, floods and famines, the return of epidemic diseases such as malaria and tuberculosis, the debilitation of populations through polluted environments and the widening of racial and ethnic wars over land bases may already be far beyond the capacity of global industrial development to undo.

Third World populations, many of them faced with unemployment and starvation, are rapidly destroying their lands as they struggle to sustain life from one day to the next. Industrial populations continue to clearcut the shrinking forests of the earth and people and industry have damaged or used up much of the fresh water reserves. An unsolvable dilemma for humanity grows daily. The more babies born who survive infancy, the more people there are to consume the existing reserves of fresh water, forests, arable soils, fossil fuels and ecosystems. At whatever standard of existence our billions live today or tomorrow, ranging from the very rich to the starving poor, all will permanently diminish the resources of the environment and ultimately threaten human existence.

The 95 percent of the next five billion people who will be born in the Third World will be among the least able to raise healthy, intelligent, productive offspring. This means that an increasing majority of people in the world will be nonproductive. Their numbers will far outpace global industrialization. They will give birth to debilitated children who will survive to child bearing age to produce more sickly, mentally debilitated children to suffer the raft of health and social problems which accompany unemployment, overcrowding and poverty.

As global trends continue to enrich the few and impoverish the majority, the ratio of "haves" to "have-nots" will grow ever more out of balance. The needs of the poor will become so unmanageable and intense, the social stress they create will force the able, healthy people of the world to live holed up behind protective walls, manned by military guards. The paradigm is already with us in the chaos and anarchy which plague West Africa, even several American cities.

The pressures Third World overpopulation and industrial nations' place on consumption of resources pose a frightening dilemma: If the global environment is to be saved from total collapse, we must stop our agricultural and industrial expansion and actually reduce our output. Unfortunately, the consumption of resources and food supply is growing at an exponential rate; whereas, global reserves of renewable and nonrenewable resources are rapidly diminishing.

Nearly half the nations of the world are dangerously dependent on the surplus food resources of a few nations. Demand will soon exceed export supply. Predictions show that China alone will be capable of absorbing all available food supplies on the export market in the next few decades, proving that neither population nor industrial expansion is environmentally sustainable now or in the future. Food aid will become too costly for food-growing nations to provide indefinitely. The industrial nations, while presently enjoying unnecessarily high rates of production and good markets, are exhausting the fertility of their lands beyond sustainable levels of resource regeneration.

Governments, various economic and scientific experts and the general public are still driven by hope, not reality. They put their faith in technologies and those elusive "scientists" who will solve all our problems or in religious doctrine which leads us to believe we will eventually resolve all our problems with God's help. Unfortunately, those able to do the most to save us, the industrialists and politicians, are grounded in profit motives and self-fulfilment, not altruism. Furthermore, the religious forces

Bullshit I do believe if there a point to life.

which promote large families, the Catholic Church, Islam and the pro-lifers, stand firm in their refusal to reform outdated credos. Only a minimal portion of the world's billions will be willing or in a position to make the needed effort to save the planet. The greatest irony of our dilemma of survival or extinction is that those who categorize themselves as environmentalists, actively involved in saving the planet, are more often seen as the "enemies" of labour, not the "friends" of future generations.

Perhaps if we had less than half the population now in existence and could be assured of a decline in human numbers during the next 100 years, humanity could outwait the transition to higher living standards and eventually control populations and solve their survival problems through industrialization. Should we reach an average fertility rate of one percent over the next 100 years and reduce our reproductive desires, populations will still increase not only through the rising birth rate and the frequent spurts of population explosions that have followed wars and famines, but through the number of existing generations already alive which will reproduce and then survive into old age. The reality is we are facing a doubling, even a predicted tripling of human populations within the next century no matter what course we choose. Only catastrophic forces of nature such as uncontrollable epidemics or the return of an ice age have the power to ravage our numbers sufficiently to reduce them to a sustainable level that the earth's biosphere can endure.

To those who still choose to believe this planet with the right technologies can feed and house 10 to 14 billion persons, I would say they are projecting fantasies on the future which stand up there with the idealistic concept of equality, opportunity and brotherhood for all. We have learned all three of the latter are impossible by dint of the failed Communist experiment, the rising violence over social space in numerous civil wars and the many extremes of racial/ethnic cleansing now in progress.

We can glimpse the future and the folly in our actions by observing much that is happening in the many battletorn and impoverished nations today. Their suffering and disarray are the harbingers of future world struggles for land, food and water supplies as populations grow and landbases become overcrowded.

In trying to help the Third World deal with its problems, Western governments imposed impossible debt loads on them during the 1960s and 1970s. Poor nations were encouraged to borrow billions of dollars to purchase advanced technologies and hire foreign expertise with which to build vast dam and irrigation projects. The result was massive dislocation of local and indigenous peoples and impossible tax burdens. Once relatively stable, these agrarian economies became the domain of unscrupulous dictators who let foreign investors and developers take control of their economies and resources. And their populations exploded!

The realities of the future are that if nature doesn't reduce our numbers through severe climatic changes, universal starvation, thirst and epidemics, we will certainly do it for her by the misuse of our technologies and our overwhelming presence. The struggle to survive in a depleted environment will culminate in so much hatred and anger that we will unwittingly lease nuclear and biological weapons onto our neighbors, destroying us all.

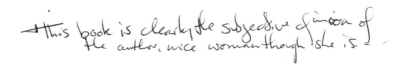

PART THREE

Dilemmas Of A Technologically-Determined Existence

Dilemmas of a Technologically-Determined Existence

The Neolithic Revolution changed life 10,000 years ago from a nomadic existence within small groups of 30 or less to communities of perhaps 50 and up into the thousands. A far more complex social and political structure gradually emerged which consisted of a centralized authority, political and religious elites, a diversified labour force, an exchange of labour for goods or coinage, a trade and commercial class and a military.

The development of such a complex social fabric of authority and labour set in place the many interdependent human activities which have grown increasingly diverse over the millennia. The distribution of responsibilities and the variety of skills required for a community to function effectively have risen out of the technological improvements in community production, distribution and consumption of goods and services. Diversity of employment and responsibility has not only facilitated societal organization and improved human living standards, but it has intensified our utilization and degradation of the natural environment.

As our dependency on technology grew, it increased our facility for turning the resources of the earth's surface into the myriad of commodities which have made our existence more viable while permitting the exponential growth of populations. Several commodities stand out as critical to daily survival. These are the basic necessities which every individual, without exception, requires for a healthy, productive life: a nutritious, adequate diet, clean fresh water for drinking, washing and growing food, sufficient fuel or energy to cook foods and heat homes and workplaces, clothes appropriate and adequate for the climate and shelter from danger and chronic suffering. Without these, life becomes a wasteful struggle to survive from day to day.

Deprivation in its many forms then destroys lives and social harmony.

Modern dependency on industrial technologies to support exploding populations began in earnest only 250 years ago. In the 18th Century technological production and trade anywhere in the world was limited to hand manufacturing and trading at local fairs. Few ventured beyond their farm villages or small urban centres, and foreign goods were extremely rare in the majority of households. Life in pre-industrial Europe showed little change from life in Roman times for the craftsmen and the farmer.[1] Since then the development of new farming technologies have increased the output of one farmer a hundred fold. "Today a grain combine harvests more than one hundred acres in a day, compared with about one acre for a man with a scythe."[2]

Living conditions prior to the Industrial Revolution were by modern standards poor at every level of society, including that of the very rich. But then it might also be said that today the rich are enjoying variety and consumption of commodities beyond all rational necessity. The developed nations with less than one-fourth of the earth's population consumes three-fourths of the planet's resources which include fresh water reserves, soils, forests, minerals, oil, gas, coal and the many life forms in the seas.

Once underway, the Agricultural Revolution, which began in the latter half of the 18th Century and expanded into the Industrial Revolution of the 19th Century, brought major agricultural changes from the use of land to the production of machine-made goods such as textiles. The distribution and sale of the growing surplus of agricultural and manufactured commodities fashioned capitalism which, in turn, fuelled the industrial expansion of the 19th and 20th Centuries.

The accumulation of food surpluses and manufactured commodities in the first half of the 19th Century in Britain initiated the need to export them and to find the capital investment to finance such large scale distribution of goods. Long term investments associated with world trade required banking and contractual systems which would guarantee the delivery of goods and the return of profits. It took only 50 years for the industrial complex in England to establish its export markets throughout its colonial empire. Europe and America followed suit in the latter half of the 19th Century.

New technologies to facilitate trade followed in rapid succession. Railroads were built, steamships designed and put into use, roads paved, telegraph lines and telephones sped up communications, planes and airports facilitated the movement of people as well as goods. Within the last 200 years these technologies have brought far more goods and services to those who could afford them than they could usefully consume.

Today we depend on technologies to enable us to live and work in every part of the world, under every climatic condition. We have spread our domination of the planet through industrial expansion, scientific intervention and highly sophisticated transportation and communication systems. The ease with which we adapt the environment to meet our needs encourages scientists and entrepreneurs to produce an expanding multitude of technologies which constantly move us further from nature's grip. Our technical ingenuity has made us incapable of leaving anything untouched on the planet. We see the environment and we judge it first and foremost in terms of human occupation, jobs, profits, medical components, usable resources, tourist attractions and reservoirs for our wastes and pollutants.

All human societies now function within the parameters of their technological competence. Political bodies legislate and police their societies with the technologies of communication and transportation. Nations ensure national integrity with arsenals of highly sophisticated weapons. Farmers depend on tools, machinery, chemicals, transportation systems and processing plants to get their crops to market. Our cities function only because of the rapid movement of goods and services which feed and protect their populations. Underground water reserves are available to farmers and homes because of massive pumping systems which have raised water from deep within the earth to make the deserts bloom. Everything in our lives is a product of technological innovation and application.

International trade, movement of capital, transfer of technologies, currency and commodity marketing, instant accessing of information, industrial development and the expansion of democracy are all made possible by the technologies of the 19th and 20th Centuries. Communication technologies have brought us the Information Age and the ability to contact any place in the world instantly through satellites. We can see into the tiniest atom and out to the furthest galaxy. Nothing in our lives except the sunshine, the rain and the air we breathe come to us where we live without technological assistance.

The more dependent the human world has become on its technologies, the more our intellectual capacity has grown to understand and use the skills of mathematics, science, economics and philosophy. The degree of complexity and sophistication of these disciplines reflect the degree of technological-determinism of any given society. Sadly a nation's technological capacity and its living standards are also reflected in the amount of environmental destruction it has done to both its own land base and to those of other nations which it exploits for resources. The greater the technological development, the more intensive and permanent is the damage our technologies do to the biosphere.

What is crucial about our modern technological determination is the recent leap forward in universal living standards and the ease with which goods and ideas are exchanged internationally. It has raised our expectations so high that we are not only unwilling to lower them but are unable to do so. Attempting to reverse the human benefits of industrial expansion creates its own extensive list of economic and social dilemmas.

Human activities over the last four decades have exposed the realities of overcrowding and overdevelopment with only 5 billion people of which less than one billion live well. Examining the impact of this inequality in the distribution of resources and wealth leads to many unsolvable problems and dilemmas: At what point must the manufacture of "useless things" stop and the consumption of resources diminish if the planet's environments are to remain habitable for our species? When does population plus technology surpass a sustainable employment capacity? If the majority of the working forces cannot be gainfully employed, can and will the "haves" carry the "have-nots"? Will the presence of so many unemployed people around the world lead to unmanageable violence and the loss of civilization as we enjoy it in the Western world? Are technologies progressively more destructive than constructive? Are we hastening environmental collapse through massive technological projects world wide? Can this planet sustain 10 to 14 billion people, or are the existing 6 billion already proving too much for the global biosphere?

To believe human growth and industrial expansion can continue without end has no historical precedence nor any scientific basis in fact. Much proof now exists that the opposite is true, indicating the folly of our ways. Under free booting capitalism, technological innovation is promoting population and industrial growth, leading to environmental collapse. For example, the introduction of the computer has multiplied the number of trees cut down to provide the mountainous quantities of paper used to spew out the data. Furthermore the computer, the new presses and the speedy delivery of newspapers, magazines and flyers has multiplied paper consumption beyond anyone's capacity to read the mounds of unwanted material that comes into Western homes.

These are the realities of our economic future which must make major political leaders as well as the public unite against industry to restrict its unlimited exploitation of the resources of our badly abused planet. Allowing corporate expansion into every corner of the earth is akin to playing Russian roulette. Each additional industrial development could be the one which initiates the final stages of environmental collapse. Moreover, to believe that our scientists and engineers can invent the "right" technologies to enable industrial development and resource consumption to expand endlessly, yet be "sustainable" is folly of the worst kind.

Looking at the earth as we exploit it mercilessly, few panoramic earthly views remain to us which do not have their horizons blurred or hidden in smog, just as there are few bodies of water that are not toxic to the life forms which inhabit them. No land masses remain which are not subject to human destruction of the natural vegetation and wildlife. From the smoke hidden vistas of all cities and countryside to the contaminated, overfished rivers, lakes and oceans to the barren, rocky hills and deserts, the entire biosphere of our planet is being polluted and devastated by human activities. What Nature created for our existence, we are relentlessly plundering by overuse and abuse.

We choose to blame recent dramatic changes in climate, vegetation and eco-systems as occurrences to be expected within nature. Granted natural forces are always at work changing climate patterns, building and eroding continents and creating new life forms while instigating their ultimate extinction. But what took nature billions of years to accomplish in creating climates and environmental conditions conducive to the evolution of life forms and the arrival of species Homo sapiens on earth has taken us less than one and a half million years to undo to the point of no return, the bulk of which has been done in the last 10,000 years and continues at an ever increasing rate. We are changing the climates of the earth so dramatically and damaging the biosphere so excessively through technological innovations and population growth that this planet is becoming inhospitable to the majority of life forms now in existence. We threaten to make it uninhabitable for ourselves within the next century.

All scientific and ecological evidence points to the 21st Century as the time in which the consequences of 5 million years of human evolution and 10,000 years of civilized progress will reach their climax. A universal crisis is fast approaching which will determine whether or not we will survive another century.

Our greatest barrier to rational solutions lies within our own minds. Because, with time, we can change and improve our political, economic and cultural institutions through leadership and revolution, the same reasoning has led us to believe we can manipulate the environment for our benefit alone through technologies. This myth ignores the fact that political, economic and cultural concepts are manifestations of the human mind, with no basis in the physical environment and tend to run in cycles; whereas, our expanding occupation and abuse of the environment are linear and ongoing.

Irrationally, with little foresight, we continue to allow our natural instinct of reproducing ourselves to the maximum to dominate our expansion while we ignore the viable limits of environmental sustainability. The rapid progress of our industrial and agricultural technologies during the last 200 years has aided and abetted maximum human reproduction rates with minimum death rates in a finite space: the planet earth. To date our technologies have supported the survival of nearly six billion people, but a growing percentage are already in difficulty as they face increasing water shortages and decreasing food supplies.

The immediate threat to our continued existence arises from a multitude of dilemmas which our technological dependency has brought to every aspect of our lives. They extend across the entire gamut of political, economic, social, cultural, psychological and physical struggles of human survival. Whichever direction we chose to go to overcome these dilemmas, the solutions are proving self-defeating, primarily because any solution is offset by our exploding numbers and our expanding industrialization.

Among the foremost dilemmas facing the human species in their struggle to survive is the dilemma of preventing our activities from destroying the biosphere as a whole. If we continue to overheat the atmosphere, deplete the tropical and temperate rain forests, increase the desertification of the remaining arable lands, expand existing industrial and agricultural production, pollute the biosphere with toxic emissions and wastes, diminish and pollute the remaining fresh water resources at the present rate of overuse and contamination and increase our populations above the carrying capacity of the planet, we will not only annihilate the bulk of living species on the planet but will endanger the whole human race in the very near future.

Humanity has been slow to face up to the truth of its destructive behaviours and attitudes towards the environment. So often it has been said that the earth and all that's on it was created for human use. A frightening philosophy. Natural law decrees that species survive in numbers sustainable within their given territories. For the human species to live within the boundaries of a given land base would require a marked reduction in populations and in present consumption rates. The pressures exerted by excessive consumption and overcrowding are reflected in the diminishing quality of life for a growing majority world wide.

Survival in the 21st Century will be much more difficult than anything humans have undergone in the past. All people, rich and poor, will experience varying degrees of food and water shortages, starvation and related diseases, global warming and harsh climatic changes, ultraviolet damage from a depleted ozone layer, destroyed eco-systems and food chains, international and racial wars over land bases and resources, and perhaps the ultimate - nuclear holocaust. As long as we remain on our present course of population expansion, universal industrialization and environmental exploitation and contamination, all of the above will contribute to the ultimate extinction of the human species.

Every human activity from the simplest things in our daily lives to the most complex of industrial and agricultural production exploits the natural world. To grow our food crops through the millennia, we have had to cut down vast forests, plough up dry grasslands or drain wetlands and open up precious wilderness to permanent erosion, desertification and lost eco-systems. Our cities may house and provide for millions of people, but every home, every job, every vehicle, every road and every building has been constructed out of nature's reserves. Billions of tons of mineral ores, oil, coal, gas, forest products and fresh water have been torn out of the earth, then remoulded and redirected to furnish our cities so that millions of people may function there.

Entire eco-systems and thousands of square miles of arable farmlands disappear annually beneath our megalopolises, the natural environment lost beneath seas of concrete and asphalt. All our technologies either extract resources from the environment, dump toxic wastes onto the land and into water sources or open the land to drought, flood or salinization. Even the simplest standards of human existence in the poorest countries deplete the soils, the forests, the wildlife and the vegetation, ultimately, changing world climates for the worse.

Survival practices over the millennia have developed strong exploitive habits in Homo sapiens. Perhaps these destructive habits also played a major role in developing our evolutionary character. It cannot be too unreasonable to believe that the struggle to survive ingrained exploitive behaviours and attitudes within our natures, just as the progression of technologies we designed enhanced the evolution of our large brain and the shape of our bodies. Unfortunately, inherent physical behaviors and mental attitudes towards the environment complicate any attempts to reach a universal consensus that might solve the dilemmas of our present existence. For instance: Could we lead satisfactory lives if we reduced our technological dependency and our standard of living in the rich nations? Can we make changes in our life styles which would put us more in balance with natural regeneration and conservation? Has our existence become totally conditional on

unceasing technological change and advancement? The economic, political, social and environmental roadblocks against humanity changing course are horrendous.

CHAPTER EIGHT

Economic Dilemmas of Employment and Industrialization

If humanity is facing so many dilemmas of existence, the reasons are surely intrinsic in our choice of survival activities. Over the millennia we have progressed through our technologies and our complicated economic systems which have risen out of human ownership and exploitation of the planet's land and resources. The production which has followed settlement and domestication of food supplies, the expanding variety of tasks and the sharing of communal workloads not only improved human standards of living but ensured our continuity and expansion in both the natural and the manmade worlds.

Basic to the wellbeing of the individual and the community has been our predilection for employment as the means for sharing both the workload and the production. Employment has become the medium of exchange in which we trade labor or the products of our labor for money, goods and services. Consequently, survival of the individual has long been dependent on his/her ability to obtain employment and fulfil the requirements of the job. A person works, is paid for the work and then uses the money to purchase food, clothing, fuels and other goods, according to one's ability to pay. The more skilful and valuable the labor, the more money received; the higher the pay, the better the individual's standard of living. A simplistic view, but the quality of one's life does depend on the opportunity to work and the value received for the products of that labor.

To date, the only organized basis of human livelihood that has functioned effectively in any society has been employment and the exchange of paid for goods and services. This system has encouraged production, efficiency, dispersal of goods and wealth and built self-responsibility. No social group nor government can function effectively without its people employed and producing goods for sale, both tolerating a degree of taxation with which to finance government administration and community infra-structures. Living standards in any country depend on the percentage of a nation's people who are at work and the quality of that employment and its accumulative purchasing power.

Advancing technologies are taking the world into a new economic age. The present highly sophisticated revolution in communications, production and distribution of goods and services already enables entrepreneurs, investors and corporations to ignore national governments along with their banking systems and their borders. Capital, technologies, expertise, labour, raw materials, patents, finished products and profits flow freely from one nation to another, largely without government interference or regulation.

As a result governments and national states as we have known them over the past two to three centuries may soon become, if not obsolete, certainly weakened institutions. The world is undergoing an economic revolution which is destabilizing all human institutions, not just governments. The impact of visual communication and the instant transfer of information are all but destroying traditional employment patterns. Electronic innovations have the power to create "jobless societies" in which machines and computers do the work of people faster and more efficiently.

A popular notion exists in Western nations that world capitalism and free trade lie just ahead. Together they will bring the consumer universal access to any commodity at the lowest possible price. However, the consequences of this freebooting capitalism is proving to be a mixed blessing. The capitalist view of global free trade ignores the interdependent duality of governments and their national economies. Free from government regulation and taxation, the global economy tears at the stability and well being of societies. World free trade is proving totally exploitive and lacking in moral commitment towards workforces or the environment. It does, however, fulfil the rich and powerful entrepreneur's dream of freedom to make money by any means.

The 20th Century has been a period of great wealth in the Western democracies, wealth which was distributed over all levels of society. If one worked hard or was willing to take an entrepreneurial risk, fortunes were made. Unions protected workers and forced capitalists to share their huge profits. Corporations saw the benefit in well-paid workers buying their own production. Western governments collected unprecedented revenues and spread them over their entire populations through public infra-structures, education, medical care, unemployment benefits and welfare. Capitalist oppression was reigned in by the power of liberal governments whose mandates came from an increasingly influential public by dint of their buying power. Both governments and businesses saw the value in helping everyone attain a higher and higher living standard through the production of more and more goods and services, which, in turn, made the workforces major consumers of industrial production.

The freebooting capitalistic structure of today's global economy, set loose by the revolution in electronic communications, has developed as a backlash to the high costs of maintaining the "socialistic" infra-structures in Western nations and the chaotic failure of Communism in Eastern Europe. Under the tyranny of Communism and the financial collapse of Eastern Europe's protected, antiquated economies, both socialistic human values and economic welfare states have fallen into disrepute. The Communist failure in Eastern Europe was so horrendous that any social program which depends on government subsidies and regulation is now suspect and vulnerable to being dismantled.

The debts and tax burdens accruing in Western nations to maintain social programs gives weight to those reactive policies which would destroy "big government" and end entitlement programs such as medi-care, welfare, unemployment insurance and universal pensions.

Aided by the technologies of modern transportation and instant electronic communication, the global economy works largely outside of national boundaries, emasculating governments and strangling their ability to promote the public good. But as several Western nations are experiencing, the cost is extreme national indebtedness, entrenched unemployment and the spectre of national bankruptcy.

Consequently, conservative, antisocial governments are gaining control in most industrial nations where their power depends on pandering to the multinational forces of the global economy. A nation's economic health is now dependent, not on the purchasing power of one's own workforces, but on its capacity and willingness to bribe multinational corporations into setting up business in one's country at great cost to the tax payers through subsidies and special tax privileges: very low corporate tax rates, excessive exemptions, few environmental restrictions, paid-for research and development and as little social responsibility to the public or to their workers as will be tolerated. Unregulated capitalistic goals seek only constantly rising profits and stock market values.

The failure of socialism in all its forms is giving way to the brutality of cutthroat capitalism. But will this alternative prove any better? The change from failed socialism to mercantilistic capitalism is motivating a universal trend towards fewer and fewer but larger corporations through mergers and "buy outs", free trade policies, "down-sized" employment roles, low minimum wage rates and fully automated production.

These conditions enable the very rich to move their wealth beyond the controls of the industrial nations and encourage them to develop the poor nations only so far as exploiting their workforces as slave labor and gaining free access to the natural resources. A loss of social compassion is now manifest in both industrial and developing nations as the gap widens between rich and poor. Human behaviour among both rich and poor grows more self-centred, more anti-social, more violently aggressive as greed and social poverty take over from 20th Century humanitarianism.

The Summit on Economic Development held in Copenhagen, March 12, 1995, demonstrated these trends very clearly. It was hoped that the major agenda of the rich nations would be to promote a free market structure based on generating economic growth in the poor nations. Few success stories have arisen to validate this policy either in the past or in the present. Chile's is perhaps one of the exceptions, but its success is purely economic, as the social and humanitarian gains are few. Most poor nations have actually been sacrificed to the dictates of IMF policies which demand large cuts in education, medical services and public infra-structure until their foreign debts are paid in full. Experience is showing that success where it occurs tends to enrich the rich and exploit the poor.

Economic components of the capitalistic global economy are interlocking to generate social problems which grow more destabilizing with each passing year. The primary negative force is the disappearance of millions of manufacturing and assembling jobs within industrial societies as machines and computers make human labor redundant. This comes at a time when tens of millions of additional jobs are needed if we are to manage the needs of another five billion people over the next 50 years.

What is needed in the long term is less automated technology and more human employment opportunities. To do so is to return to labor intensive manufacturing which is inefficient and costly and holds little appeal for the investor or the entrepreneur who has more to gain with technological efficiency. Altruism based on providing jobs for people will not be part of the capitalistic philosophy of the 21st Century.

Meanwhile, the rush to globalize industry and trade based on automation and cheap labor puts jobs and purchasing power at risk everywhere. Well-paying jobs in industry demand a workforce that is educated, healthy and not held back by grinding poverty. As wondrous and universal as the Communications' Revolution is for industrial development, it is globally disruptive of traditional employment and social patterns. Primarily, it ignores the reality that few people have the health, the intellectual capacity or the opportunity to be trained in computer sciences or biotechnologies. A survey of workers made in Canada in 1994 showed that 36 percent of all workers were functionally illiterate either because they could not read, interpret instructions nor follow directions. A lack of English language skills eliminated many from good paying jobs and added to the welfare lists. Illiteracy rates in the United States were even higher. The direct losses to industry and business ran into the billions.[3]

Even more so it is unlikely that the majority of those trained will find work in these highly technical fields. The Industrial Revolution uprooted the rural masses, but employed them in the factories. The Communications Revolution has not only uprooted them from the farms, but also from the factories, the assembly lines, and soon from all manner of services.

The present global economy is widely based on automation and the importation of cheaply produced goods and services. This trend is registering a highly detrimental effect on industrially developed nations. As the rich investor/owner in the industrial nation hides his money in offshore banks and builds his industrial plants in impoverished nations, he amasses an ever increasing share of the world's wealth and political power.

While the investor gathers in the monetary rewards, he has few scruples about letting the middle classes pay the costs of training the "hi-tech" workers vital to the functioning of the multi-national corporations. The excessive tax burden this places on the middle classes is forcing a significant drop in their living standards. They have had their purchasing power sharply reduced, all but eliminating the national wealth which normally buys the many "luxury goods" which create the bulk of an industrial nation's employment. The declining tax base also produces a sharp drop in contributions to foreign aid and development programs for Third World countries. The tax burden the "offshore" rich are forcing on the middle classes becomes counterproductive and builds an attitude of resentment towards charitable outlays.

At the same time, developing countries must accept near slave conditions for their workforces imposed on them by international banks, global corporations and their own governments. The extreme lack of purchasing power in poor nations results in low productivity, low living standards, poor health and high birth rates. Poverty deepens and the magnitude of inhuman conditions expand exponentially. Human waste and environmental damage multiply where poverty flourishes.

The deepening dilemma of the human condition and the degradation of the planet are intensified by the exploitation of industrial development and unemployment. Both deny widespread conservation of the remaining environmental resources and eco-systems. But if we stop expanding industrially and lower consumption, then unemployment skyrockets. This translates into mass migrations of economic and environmental refugees and intensifies urban overcrowding and chaos.

Nations which have damaged and contaminated their resource bases beyond regeneration are experiencing unprecedented social and medical problems. The political collapse and environmental degradation of Eastern Europe and Russia are perhaps our most conspicuous examples. Radio active farmlands surrounding Chernobyl in Ukraine, for example, cannot be used safely to grow food for thousands of years. Furthermore, the shortage of hydro power in Eastern Europe necessitates many nuclear reactors be kept running even when they stand ready to explode in a cloud of radiation as happened in Chernobyl.

As populations expand and the costs of national infra-structures grow, finding money and public approval to protect diminishing resources comes far behind the needs of industrial societies and developing nations. Cleanup costs and most recycling programs are delayed until recycled commodities prove to be better and cheaper to produce than original goods. They come into their own only when the original resources and manufactured products are no longer available or the public will not buy "environmentally unfriendly" commodities.

Scientific research has shown that only one fifth of the world's population, those who have enjoyed industrial affluence, are responsible for most of the permanent damage humans have done to the earth. One billion of us are responsible for putting six billion beyond the carrying capacity of the planet. This raises the opposing side of the dilemma: Should the Third World expand its industrial output to raise the living standards of its people to a comparable level with Western standards? If they do then the amount of production of "useless commodities" needed to reach those standards will create unmanageable pollution and consumption of resources. It also begs the question: Does the earth have the resources to provide the entire world with modern technologies and standards of industrialization?

Unemployment, Poverty and the Environment

Having to survive through the medium of gainful employment is an increasingly negative factor as human work destroys the environment. If a person is hungry and destitute, he will not give priority to saving a forest or a wetland if that destruction enables him to grow enough food, graze a few animals or illegally cut down trees to sell on the black market to survive. Extremes of human suffering do not promote moral or rational behaviours towards the environment. The hunter who kills or captures rare species for their furs or for sale as pets often cannot afford a conscience in killing the creatures as long as it is his only means of survival.

Surviving from one day to the next takes priority over conservation. Consequently, forests are disappearing on every continent and vast marginal drylands are turning into deserts where hungry families overgraze and overcrop the land, failing to protect it from sterility and erosion.

The island of Haiti at the present time exemplifies the ordeal of a nation forced to consume and contaminate its own environment because its economic base cannot sustain the population. Ruled by a tyrannical military junta and isolated by trade sanctions for three years, (1991-1994), Haitians were forced to earn money by cutting down their forests, then turning the wood into charcoal which they sold locally as fuel. Sadly, charcoal became the source of 70 percent of the nation's energy. As a result the islands forests have been reduced from 60 percent coverage in 1915 to 3 percent in 1995. Over 6 percent of the island has lost its arable soil base where nothing will grow and most of the remaining soils are so thin that plants which do grow remain very small. Forests are gone and cannot be regenerated on eroded hillsides.[4] Meanwhile, the people grow poorer with each passing year and their health diminishes through malnutrition. The population is conscious of its misuse of the forests and the land, but immediate desperation is a far more powerful motive than conservation. Saving it from itself has meant that Haiti's people are now dependent on foreign aid and the importation of its food. The island has become subject to foreign control and crippling debt.

The dilemmas of unemployment, poverty and environmental destruction we are now witnessing are occurring with less than six billion people on earth, 4 billion of which were added only in the last 50 years. Most of this latter 4 billion cannot be employed or cared for within the carrying capacity of their nations without total destruction to their land bases. But can they be sustained by the other two billion indefinitely?

A sense of self-preservation precludes a desire for helping others or for conserving the natural environment. Conservation comes into its own only when it offers employment and survival. Such is the case with several African nations where it is proving more profitable to protect the animals for tourists to see, then to kill them for their meat, hides or tusks. But conservation is expensive and employs few. It requires education, investment, strong policing and a long-term commitment. As populations grow, these conditions are not easily accommodated.

Even in the affluent nations loggers continue to fight to retain the right to log the few remaining old growth forests because there is more money and employment in the short term in cutting down the forests than in preserving them. Most people do not look beyond this month's or this year's pay cheques. Few will accept that in saving ecological systems over the long term they are ensuring their children's survival. They are even less concerned with long range weather changes which result from clearcutting. Self-preservation is a powerful, instinctual force. It exists in the "here and now" and drives our actions in self-destructive ways, despite all inherent dangers to our future survival.

With populations expanding and consumption rising, sustainable management of the environment becomes nothing more than fantasy. The environment in taking the brunt of the needs of the unemployed, gives up more of its resources than it can afford, weakening its powers of regeneration and deepening the problems of over-consumption and overcrowding.

Denied land, an education, employment skills, investment capital or self employment, the poor find poverty a powerful incentive to turn to hostile, violent behaviour. Criminality has become the alternate route to survival for growing numbers of people as drug sales, robbery, fraud, extortion, prostitution, slavery, illegal arms deals and terrorism furnish their needs and challenge their energies and ingenuity. This trend to crime, terrorism and gangsterism could lead an observer to conclude that crime, anti-social behaviour and violence are an integral part of the capitalistic, technologically-determined economy.

As technology reduces employment opportunities and purchasing power while concentrating the bulk of the world's wealth in the hands of the few, crime is proving an anti-social but effective means to redirect some part of that wealth to many more people. For example, the growing, harvesting, refining and distributing of narcotic drugs involves a large network of farmers, carriers and peddlers. A situation anathema to the concept of social order, but cutthroat capitalism and the "jobless" society are proving natural provokers of crime and terrorism. Displaced, impoverished and without hope, people have strong incentives to take what they can't buy in a world which cares nothing for their suffering.

Unable to share in the legal economic exchange of goods and services, a growing segment of self-made entrepreneurs find themselves taking a share of the global trade and commerce through theft and coercion, illegal trade in drugs and commodities. The Mafia in the United States, for instance, purchase government contracts for garbage collection in most Eastern States. These criminal organizations have few moral qualms and think nothing of dumping toxic wastes in rivers, landfills and on ocean beds. Some drug cartels are so wealthy and powerful, as in Columbia, they have indirect control of the national government. Aided by modern communication and transportation technologies, crime syndicates are able to move vast sums of illegal money and contraband with little interception and very little legal retribution. Some crime cartels are gaining financial influence over international market trends and national businesses as their wealth and power grow. The international market in weapons and drugs comprises the largest source of purchasing capital in the world. Both lead commodity sales in total world trade.

Defining Solutions to Economic Dilemmas

Finding and implementing solutions to our economic dilemmas is less and less realistic. Our need for employment is forcing us to sacrifice the natural environment for industrial expansion. This course, condoned by those powers who preach that industrialization is the best way to reduce birth rates, are powerful enough to decide humanity's future. Their greed will only increase consumption of resources and pollution of the biosphere. At the same time, in their rush to make profits, they will use automation, high technologies and "slave" labor, reducing the number of well-paying jobs to a minimum and diminishing purchasing power, basic to building markets on which to sell production.

Yet in the present race to industrialize every nation, to raise the standard of living of billions of people and to rush technological advancement which panders to human hubris, there is nothing which suggests a universal desire exists to reduce human expansion and prevent environmental collapse. Industrial growth, free trade and unlimited manufacture of commodities have become the economic policy of nearly every nation. Universal political and economic propaganda portrays a glowing future where jobs and affluence will be paramount in our technologically-determined lives. The belief persists that human destiny is to produce an unlimited variety of commodities so that the living standards of all people can be raised and in the process millions of jobs will be created.

No matter how good our technologies and their capacity to produce, future industrialization and employment opportunities will consume the earth's resources and pollute the biosphere. If we continue at the present rate of population and industrial growth, we are putting our survival at risk. Donella Meadows, author of BEYOND THE LIMITS, expressed it clearly: "In the past 40 years, 11 per cent of the Earth's cultivable soils have been eroded to uselessness. Most forests are being cut faster than they grow. In arid regions, ground water is pumped faster than it recharges. Fossil fuel burning is 60 per cent above the rate at which the atmosphere can absorb the resultant carbon dioxide ... The consequences for (societies) that know how to think only in terms of perpetual growth are...unthinkable.'⁵ And the price to be paid for unsupportable growth is human extinction, arriving within a shorter and shorter period of time.

In fact, we are facing the extreme conditions of our dilemmas as soon as the 21st Century. While our increasing numbers will be ever more dependent on technologies for survival, to date, many of those technologies have been more disruptive and destructive than useful. The Green Revolution in many Asian countries, among them India, Malaysia and the Philippines, has reduced the productivity of the soils and driven once successful farmers to the overcrowded cities. The massive dam projects in Africa and South America have displaced hundreds of thousands of people and flooded vast eco-systems. The diversion of rivers away from the Aral Sea in Russia destroyed one of the most productive inland bodies of water in the world to grow cotton on flat, desert land which was rapidly sterilized and salinated by this monoculture and irrigation.

As semi-skilled and unskilled jobs decrease, the technologies and the wealth they produce are allowing a very small, but very rich elite to control the manufacture and trade of all commodities sold both on domestic and international markets. A few hundred million middle class, highly skilled workers, small businessmen and professional groups are flourishing. Seeing this social change in many nations of the world can cloud one's thinking into believing this trend will ensure a good future for all nations, but it overlooks the reality that a few hundred million well-to-do people are a small part of 6 to 10 billion, most of which will be living in extreme poverty in the 21st Century.

Devastating for the planet, this elite, still small but growing, is chasing a constantly rising living standard which will consume as much as 500 times more resources than the poor will use. Common sense tells us the amount consumed by this elite in the present 27 industrial nations is too much for the planet to withstand. The impact of the entire 180 to 193 nations (each year there are more nations coming into being) industrializing is beyond comprehension. Furthermore, every annual addition of 90 million souls puts an untenable stress to the earth's environment. Neither short term nor long term solutions can be found because each problem and solution form an unsolvable dilemma exacerbated by our present course of rapidly changing technologies.

It is crucial that immediate universal recognition be given to the demands industrialization now and in the future will place on the remaining renewable and nonrenewable resources. Present demands are no longer commensurate with the planet's ability to support the human species. Even if "sustainable management" programs were in place on every continent in every aspect of manufacture and consumption, the exploitation of the environment and its resources would be too much. It is now only a matter of how soon the environment and resources collapse.

The economic viability of most nations is already at risk as their populations explode. The evidence can be seen in the millions of people on every continent who are without jobs and whose livelihood must come through government welfare programs or foreign aid. The only way to ensure enough employment is to allow industrialization to grow horrendously. This would mean a more rapid degradation of the planet than is already underway. The existing environment cannot withstand the degree of exploitation necessary to accommodate humanity.

To summarize the dilemma: Survival of the individual and the community depends on employment, which in turn, depends on industrial and agricultural development. The greater the productive employment of a nation's people, the higher the living standards in general. But employment and industrialization depend on the exploitation and consumption of the earth's diminishing supply of resources which our numbers are rapidly overwhelming.

CHAPTER NINE

Political Dilemmas of Technologically Determined Societies

The last hundred years have brought an abundance of technological changes to our lives, especially in the industrial world. In the process we have learned that technologically determined societies function well only when governments have access to large amounts of capital on a continuing basis to afford costly infra-structures and social programs.

No private enterprise no matter how large can afford to finance, and in most cases, subsidize the technologies of an urban society: public transport, highways, bridges, dams, sewage and water systems, airports, seaports, hydro and irrigation projects, medical facilities, military defenses and many others. Few of these necessities can be financed profitably through public "user pay" systems. Only national taxation spreads the financial burden equitably across all people within a nation, making the services affordable. Unfortunately, the government role as national provider is now under threat from many directions by the constant expansion and costs of public programs and technological innovation.

As with everything we humans design to improve our living standards, overuse and abuse eventually destroy the advantages. So it is with national technologies of scale. Their variety and quantity not only increase exponentially, their size and costs do also. Science and industry are dedicated to "bigger and better" technological infra-structures for which governments must pay.

And yet, if the tax payer cannot afford them, why do governments continue to indulge nations in so many expensive technologies and projects? Their excuse more than rational reasons: new technologies provide jobs, buy votes and encourage corporate and foreign investment[1].

However, inventing new infra-structure projects and implementing them is proving of short term value in creating jobs and buying votes. Once in place, they must then be regulated, administered, policed, maintained and rebuilt over the long term. Moreover, all must be paid for with government taxes. The numerous inherent costs also inflate annually and grow with the demands of exploding urban development. Expenditures climb as available natural resources diminish and national currencies inflate.

The costs of today's technologies of scale now reach beyond the capacity of most government coffers to meet the tax burden without nations going deeply into debt. The problem is further exacerbated by present global economic circumstances which have forced the burden of paying for them onto an ever-dwindling middle class. The real source of international wealth, increasingly inaccessible to national governments, is amassing in the hands of fewer and fewer entrepreneurs and investors who are escaping with every nation's capital into offshore banks, world currency markets and foreign investments. Untaxed, this horde of money is loaned back to our governments and industry for large interest payments.

Meanwhile, economic and social dilemmas are on the rise as modern urban societies attempt to deliver technologies of scale that not only provide jobs, goods and services, but raise living standards beyond all justification. Neither our environments nor our economies can afford the extremes of consumption and luxuries our industrial producers and traders are coercing us into buying in the name of progress and good living.

In the process, the general public has allowed governments and corporate structures to take control of our lives. We have surrendered responsibility for ourselves to the powerful and rich. We are essentially "wards of the state", controlled by the whims of the rich and powerful. The trade-off has taken away the public's right to share equitably in the nation's land, resources, wealth and production, assets we own by rights of citizenship.

The sad irony is that the majority of us can no longer survive in our technological societies without this dependency.

As national economies approach the extremes of the struggle between governments and the corporate structure to control national wealth, production and distribution, the majority among us believe that government or that amorphous "they" now "owe us a living" and what is worse, the same governments we depend on so totally are held captive to the global corporate structure which controls the world's wealth. The reality of the 1990s is that those who control the production, distribution and consumption of the world's commodities and capital have the power to determine where and how we live and work and the value of the money we earn. Recently, the term "economic totalitarianism" was coined to describe this corporate take-over of the world's economic and political systems.

Moreover, adjusting to the loss of jobs to automation in the present Information Age is economically and socially destabilizing, even more so than the Industrial Revolution of the 19th Century was to Europe and North America. At least in the Industrial Revolution millions of labor-intensive jobs were created in urban centres, benefitting the general public and producing a national affluence. In sharp contrast jobs were created by the millions in the Industrial Age; whereas, jobs are disappearing by the millions in the Information Age.

The present trend leading into the 21st Century is for industry to mechanize its output, "down-size" its work forces and go global. Computerized technologies are eliminating basic production jobs in highly industrialized countries while electronic communications are abetting the escape of the world's wealth to offshore havens. At the same time industrial corporations have farmed out manufacturing of all basic commodities to the Third World. The impact of this globalization on industrial nations has been widespread unemployment which is deepening the dependency of industrial workforces on government welfare.

The impact of this dramatic shift in production and wealth is that it hordes Western capital and savings and directs it out of the country while diminishing major tax bases. Managing and sustaining the growing number of unemployed in the industrial nations is pushing governments beyond their capacity to function as the protector of the people. Consequently, governments must reduce their financial spending by cutting back sharply on public assistance programs and curb their outlay for expensive infra-structures. The combination is ominous for the developed nations of North America and Europe.

Forced to balance their budgets, industrial nations, especially those of the West, are less and less able to maintain the affluent living standards they achieved during the last half of the 20th Century. Cracks in the democratic structures of these nations are appearing as multi-national corporations dictate world economic policies, citizens violently protest the loss of jobs, governments tax their middle classes into poverty and money for welfare, education and medical services evaporates. It is estimated that as much as 50 percent of the world's wealth is now in the hands of less than 358 billionaires.

Dynamic economic and political changes have fused to create three basic dilemmas threatening the stability of democratic industrial nations:

1) How much responsibility must national governments accept for the burgeoning load of technological and social costs involved in building, maintaining and administering a technologically-based urban society while providing for a growing, increasingly dependent public sector?

2) How does a nation finance the costs which enable it to remain economically viable and still provide the necessary social programs and public infra-structures without going into bankruptcy?

3) How can governments protect and conserve the environment and still provide jobs and resources?

Dilemma 1. **Are Today's Technological and Social Responsibilities Too Great and Too Costly for Governments?**

Every additional technological change or expansion is an added stress on government coffers. The stress results from the costs that arise in training a workforce capable of handling the rapid changes and constant innovations in technologies that are ongoing. Governments must be prepared to provide the teachers, the schools and the equipment needed to train workers in such areas as computer technology, electronic communications and bio-technologies. They are also expected to fund research of the cosmos, genetics and defense weapons. Most governments still pay the largest share of financing research and development through grants, loans, subsidies and tax breaks.

Added to these are the costs of a plethora of public services which the developed nations take for granted: piped water, sewage disposal, garbage collection, transportation systems, legislative and judicial systems, police forces, prisons, not forgetting the costs of museums, libraries, universities, schools and job creation. The list is very lengthy.

The greater part of government largesse is dispensed through social programs. For example, every citizen is in need of medical care at some time in his/her life, some much more than others. But present costs of medical services and expertise are very expensive because of the excesses of technology and facilities used by the profession. The repercussion is that a large sector of the population cannot afford to pay for its own medical care and, in the case of the United States, often fails to get medical services. The corollary of this is that if a nation is to have a healthy, productive workforce, medical care must be made available to all and financed by governments. What is of growing concern in Western nations is that as the corporate structure makes human labor redundant to machines, then the need to keep the workforce healthy also becomes a superfluous factor.

Another aspect of a healthy population is the accompanying longevity. Keeping a population healthy may add 25 to 30 years to their lives after retirement. These are non-productive years which are subsidized through pensions and increasing amounts of subsidized medical care. These two items alone comprise a staggering cost in government entitlements, running as much as 40 percent of national budgets in some countries. Canada's medical and social services, for instance, absorb over 38 percent of the annual federal budget. In 1994/95 borrowing money to meet the overrun in federal budgets added $47.8 billions in interest payments to the annual budget or 27 cents of every tax dollar went to finance a national debt which approached $600 billion by the mid 1990s.

Western industrial nations seeing their medical services costing more than the taxes they can take from their citizens, are now inundated with large influxes of refugees seeking free medicine and bringing with them a sharp increase in population numbers who expect entitlement to all the social benefits. California reported in 1995 that over a billion dollars a year in government medicare is paid out to medical facilities and doctors for the care of illegal Mexican and Latin American refugees.

Absorbing these immigrants into the education and welfare systems accrues additional expenses that are absorbed by national and state budgets. At the same time housing, job creation, urban infra-structures and social welfare programs are also overwhelmed and must be expanded to accommodate the newcomers if social peace is to be maintained.

Where universal medical programs do not exist, medical costs are inflated by corporate ownership of medical facilities and services or medical insurance programs. They do not permit affordable preventive care for a growing majority. Governments have been paying the difference, greatly deepening national debt. The U.S. government, for example, covers medical costs for an estimated 39 million people in the United States who have no health insurance because of the prohibitive monthly payments. Those who can afford a minimum amount of health insurance are generally unable to pay for specialized or chronic care. Governments have had to pick up the tab for this group. And again with constantly increasing costs in dispensing medical care, the number of people dependent on government medicare programs grows with every increase in unemployment and inflation.

The inefficiency of the insurance system and the high costs of private ownership forces the U.S. government to pay more than twice as much for medical services as any other democratic nation. Sadly, the social and economic decline of a growing sector of the nation is entrenching poor health, deepening drug addiction and criminal violence and setting the stage for the return of several deadly epidemics such as tuberculosis among the unemployed, the impoverished and the homeless.

These problems of the United States may soon be incumbent on several of the other Western governments who will have to relinquish much of their responsibility for the care of the general public if their tax bases decline much further. Governments may be unable to maintain a stable social structure in the future in nations so used to affluence, unless they resort to tyrannical rule.

Meanwhile, governments of rich nations attempt to meet their obligations to their citizens by including the protection and conservation of the environment. Billions of dollars are spent annually to clean up nuclear wastes, oil spills, toxic dumps and polluted rivers. Subsidies must be afforded for recycling used commodities and wastes as well as replanting forests and regenerating eco-systems. The ever-expanding list of obligations democratic governments find themselves financing is so huge it makes annual tax burdens capable of sucking all the investment capital and savings out of an industrial nation. Annual increases in income tax and sales taxes are impoverishing the middle classes. Business tax levies, compounded by high wages and benefits to workers continue to drive away major entrepreneurs, corporations and wealthy investors who escape with their money and manufacturing plants to offshore havens where they can evade the taxman and indulge in greater profits.

These "haven" nations - Switzerland, Leitchtenstein, Bermuda, the Cayman Islands, among many others - allow vast quantities of money to flow in and out of their banks, free from regulation and taxation. The small service fees they charge to handle the accounts and register companies have made several small nations very wealthy and politically stable. With the aid of electronic communication services, global investment capital and profits easily evade not only the tax assessor but the economic and environmental regulations of their national governments.

Consequently, with opportunities so prolific abroad to make large, untaxed profits, the rich, in their scramble to get their money and investments out of the industrial nations, are essentially refusing to share the natural wealth of their nations with their people. Most critically they have rejected the role of public benefactor. With so little tax revenue coming from the investor or the corporate structure, governments are incurring unmanageable debts, public infra-structures are falling into disrepair and much needed welfare programs are being cut back.

An additional threat underlies the investment of a nation's capital. At present, the bulk of domestically invested money in stocks and bonds is pension funds amassed over the latter half of the 20th Century by Western workforces. Should national stock markets fail or governments be unable to meet its pension obligations, the majority of disabled and elderly will be reduced to penury. The dimension of this possibility becomes a catastrophe when one realizes that the elderly will comprise one fourth of the populations in the fully industrialized nations within the next 20 years.

The Canadian federal government in 1996 in trying to eliminate deficit spending threatened to shelve several pension funds such as the Old Age Security pension and the Guaranteed Income Supplement for all middle income earners. They felt that savings plans such as the Canadian Pension Plan (CPP) and Registered Retirement Savings Plan (RRSP) should be privatized and run by the big banks so as to be more efficient. What has yet to be proven is that private corporations are more efficient, more free of corruption or more publicly inclusive than governments.

The dilemma is further exacerbated by the hording of the bulk of the world's wealth invested not in new industries and jobs but in offshore currency markets where profit is made by forcing financial ups and downs in the value of national currencies, transactions which have cost governments large sums of money in the past to protect their currencies from collapsing. An estimated $19 to $20 trillion is held in these offshore accounts, of which well over $1 trillion is traded daily on currency markets, making money the number one commodity in the world.

The growing gap being created by this trend is swelling the relentless dependency the populace of advanced industrial societies has on its governments. This inequality now threatens serious economic decline and stability both in the industrial world and the still very dependent developing nations. The trend is well entrenched for the rest of the 1990s and into the 21st Century.

Ironically, if the corporate structure is to continue to succeed in the highly competitive global markets it has created for itself, it must still demand that national governments provide the very expensive education and medical facilities necessary to educate and train healthy, hi-tech workforces for their industrial enterprises. Furthermore, the industrial base of corporate companies does not function efficiently without highly developed transportation systems, large supplies of fresh water, good sewage disposal systems, excess hydro power or electric energy, highly honest and efficient justice and policing systems, a minimum of corruption, efficient contract and banking systems, government regulatory bodies and the huge bureaucracies needed to implement, administer and maintain these systems, --all those capitalistic facilities that a true, well funded democracy can guarantee.

And yet the corporate structure rages ahead, destroying democracies, robbing nations of their resources and merging companies into ever more powerful foes of the very systems which make them viable. They forget that every excess of unbalanced abuse leads to eventual self-destruction. In destroying the labor forces, they destroy labor's purchasing power. Without this buying power, profits rapidly diminish and deflation sets in. Recession and depression can become permanent economic conditions.

Can the world as we have known it in the 20th Century survive when every civilized nation is no longer able to maintain its democratic advantages because it has no industrial advantages?

The impact of this reality is already upon us. North American roads, bridges, railways, airports and harbors are in need of extensive, costly repairs and updated technologies. Education systems are so inept and underfunded that they are unable to equip their nations' students with the knowledge and skills they need to gain employment in the rapidly changing hi-tech economies. Fewer and fewer workers, skilled or unskilled, are finding jobs in hi-tech manufacturing. With robots and computers making human labor redundant and resources and services shipped to low wage nations for manufacture, costly government education programs are increasingly superfluous. Those who actually prosper from the very progressive education programs in democratic nations form a shrinking elite group of professionals.

On the other hand, the very essence of democracy itself becomes a dilemma. As we now practice it in the West, it is an unworkable institution financially. Its very nature of equal opportunity and responsibility for all citizens presents a Catch 22 situation. While democracy nurtures technological initiative and development, it is also the most expensive form of government in use today. Supporting huge affluent bureaucracies as well as providing the public with expensive social and welfare programs, democracy places an unsustainable drain on national economies. The added costs of regulating and policing this huge network of people and services against corruption or outside takeovers require governments to build vast administrative and judicial systems and stockpile defensive weapons and provision military forces to defend it. The financial burden grows with the ever-expanding welfare state and the constant search for weapons superior to those of other nations.

Ultimately, high living standards for a growing, increasingly dependent population, combined with a comparable rise in unemployment and costly infra-structures, are too expensive for even the richest nations among us. It would appear that Western democracies are sinking deeper and deeper into debt with no way out except total disavowal of the public's needs, which negates the very concept of democracy. The decline in democratic values are hurried along by the flight of capital and the impoverishment of government social programs. With suffering from the loss of government assistance becoming universal, the public sees itself as victims of an international corporate structure which is absconding with the wealth so necessary in maintaining a successfully industrial democratic nation.

Add to this the demands of the Third World which state that the rich nations should provide the poor nations with technological advantages equal to their own and free of charge. The Third World nations see themselves as entitled to a fair share of the world's investment capital, technological expertise, jobs and consumer goods as they sacrifice their resources to the industrial world. Out of poverty and hardship, the poor nations are choosing blackmail to gain their ends. Unless they are provided with the means to industrialize and can enjoy the benefits of our modern technologies, they will do nothing to reduce their birth rates and conserve the natural environment. And yet, like those of us in the industrial nations, they realize that few of us will survive, much less prosper, if their populations and consumption are not dramatically curtailed in the immediate future.

It is very clear that the ability of governments to meet unlimited obligations with limited largesse in the 21st Century will be a major challenge for all industrial democracies. Public demands for modern infra-structures and government welfare programs will grow apace with population expansion and automation. But jobs and services will fail to keep up. Political instability will grow as social decay spreads and public demands erupt in violent protest against governments who fail to keep their democratic promises. The West is already manifesting these trends: political parties are turning to policies of neo-conservatism, economic policies favor mercantilism and cutthroat capitalism, and anti-social programs seek an end to public welfare.

Dilemma 2:   Can Governments Afford a Technologically Determined Society and Still Provide a Viable Social Climate?

The major challenge of governments in the developed nations is how to finance the myriad of technological and social obligations of the modern world. Only their accessability will slow the process of democratic decay and reduce political instability. Solutions begin with finding ways to increase revenues without destroying a nation's purchasing power or losing its entire industrial tax base. Solutions also begin with several dilemmas.

The first dilemma is how to offset the cycle of economic downturns that advanced technologies are producing in industrial nations. As more and more workers lose their well-paying jobs in production to computer technologies, they must accept low paying jobs in services. As their purchasing power declines, their inability to buy the luxury goods of an industrial society then slows the economy. This, in turn, produces fewer jobs in all areas and less government tax revenue.

Pressure on governments to prevent recession by putting borrowed money into the economy through welfare and unemployment insurance programs can only be financed through increased taxes on businesses and the employed. The cycle becomes "lean and mean". With less purchasing power, both employed and welfare groups reduce their buying of homes, cars, luxury items, entertainment, holidays and general basic living standards. The impact is then felt by manufacturers and service providers who are unable to sell their production domestically. They turn to foreign markets, export both expertise and capital, transfer technologies and lay off more domestic workers. The price of governing continues to rise beyond the capacity of the tax base to carry it. Once this cycle is in place, recession follows and unemployment rises rapidly.

Western nations now emerge from recession only when the manufactured production of growth years prior to the recession is finally in short supply. But it would seem that once those supplies are sufficient to meet demand, the national economy falls back into recession to await the slow consumption of the existing production once again. Eventually, the economy recuperates and a slow growth period returns. The high growth rate and boom times of an emerging industrial nation are no longer there.

This cycle in the old industrial nations covers a period of recession lasting two to three years, followed by two to three years of growth, followed by two to three years of recession, ending with a much deeper recession than the previous one.

During periods of restraint and recession, savings within a nation drop dramatically. Yet governments must still meet the costs of social programs, infra-structures and government bureaucracy. Few nations any longer have domestic capital reserves large enough to meet their government's borrowing needs as well as those of the private sector. To meet the difference between tax revenues and budget costs in the 1980s and 1990s, governments turned to foreign investors to buy long term bonds at high interest rates. Of course, all domestic interest rates rose too.

The problem is that any sharp rise in interest rates deters domestic entrepreneurs from borrowing capital to invest in job creation. The end result is higher unemployment, heavy fiscal debt, excessive borrowing, higher interest rates, diminishing public buying power and reduced domestic production. The array of social programs a nation enjoys becomes unmanageable and government debts threaten economic and social stability. This economic cycle is now entrenched in most developed nations.

The drive of the industrial nations in the 1990s has been to balance their budgets so as to halt government borrowing. To accomplish this social programs and infra-structures must be sharply curbed. The impact is added stress on the already troubled social and political sectors. Civil protests, increasing economic crime, homelessness, social abuse of women and children, widespread poverty, a decline in health standards and a political return to extremes of conservative values are symptomatic of nations in economic turmoil.

Conservative policies, however, are not a popular solution in nations used to full employment and the benefits of a socialistic welfare state. Neither are unemployment, increasing welfare and escalating government debts conditions liberal governments can sustain for any length of time. A strong, politically stable nation depends on a productive, quiescent electorate. Without jobs, the unemployed become hungry and restless, blaming governments for the lack of jobs and welfare. Hungry mobs can become an especially explosive force.

But the dilemma does not end there. When government coffers must sustain the welfare of a large number of unemployed, resistance spreads among the middle and upper classes who find the excessive tax burden destructive of their way of life. Overtaxed, their purchasing power rapidly diminishes and their living standards are put at risk. At the same time, the rich want their investments to return a profit, not become swallowed up by public welfare. To avoid this unwanted consumption of their capital, the rich, abetted by modern electronic communications, move their money out of the grasp of industrial governments, tucking it away in "offshore" banks where they are free to spend it or invest it as they choose. The flight of so much wealth intensifies national economic instability.

Government revenues are also at the mercy of the global economy as jobs and large pools of capital are exported to low wage areas where worker benefits are negligible and environmental laws are either unenforced or non-existent. Unemployment then contributes to "underground economies" which are presently mushrooming in industrial nations and another economic sector escapes government taxation.

The picture is clear; the reality frightening. National governments and their citizens want all the benefits of socialism and modern technologies, but neither can they nor do they want to pay for them. The rising neo-conservative parties would all but eliminate the social services and public infra-structures as they now exist. They would end the government's role as regulator and social provider while expanding those services which benefit the entrepreneur and the corporate structure. This neo-conservative leaning in the United States and Britain goes so far as to put its faith in the pretext that jobs and government taxes would increase if only governments would refrain from regulating industrial production and let the economy be governed by the free forces of the market. But global economic policies, aided by the excessive technological powers of communication and transportation to escape national controls, have created an unprecedented amassing of wealth in the hands of too few people and stripped the nations of their savings and investment capital. None of the traditional views of how to run an economy or what role governments should play seem to fit the new model.

What can be evaluated, however, is that without sufficient employment and an expanding economy, governments and industrial corporations run the risk of causing widespread social upheaval. Human nature is quick to riot if denied access to food, work, security, justice and self-esteem. Their reactions are made more powerful and effective through the use of the vast variety of lethal weapons now available and affordable to any group in the world. Terrorism, the manifestation of civil dissatisfaction and displacement, is a common weapon of 20th Century rebellion, enabling a few individuals to do great harm. Dozens of incidents and civil wars have demonstrated the frustrations which plague the impoverished, tribal nations of Africa, Asia and South America.

To prevent an irreversible economic descent, developed nations will need to be more vigilant of economic forces. With the ever-expanding number of economic and social responsibilities industrial governments must manage, several Western nations are teetering on the brink of national bankruptcy and economic decline. While the dilemma of entrenched recession constantly looms, the unprecedented accumulation of unmanageable debt grows, creating the next unsupportable dilemma. In struggling to sustain the high living standards gained since World War II, Western governments have borrowed vast sums against national savings and foreign capital.

Although many economic experts claim a nation such as Canada or the United States can easily manage a high debt ratio, the increasing drain on national wealth to pay the interest on those debts without ever paying them down puts far too much of the world's money into the hands of too few people who feel no moral obligation to help their nations. Human greed is a destructive force. It has never been known to build a sense of democratic equality among people. Its historical genesis through the inception of property ownership has produced few rich magnanimous philanthropists, whose charities generally benefit themselves.

As national debts grow in several developed nations, the fear of bankruptcy spreads. This forces other governments to bail them out. The United States, for instance, could not afford to let Canada's economy fail, no more than she could allow Mexico's economy to collapse in 1995. Canada and Mexico are America's largest trading partners. But how much can the United States afford to spend on these nations in view of its own multi-trillion dollar debt? The difficulty experienced in raising just $40 billion to save Mexico should be enough to prevent these "band-aid" solutions in the future. The costs in tax dollars and investment capital to the contributing nations are highly detrimental to the overall financial status of these nations as their own tax bases diminish for the many reasons stated above. The price is paid in lost jobs, decaying infra-structure and fewer social services.

With technologies replacing human labour and national purchasing power declining, economic solutions that might be found in a return to basic manufacturing are escaping to nations who permit slave labour to produce the bulk of the world's basic commodities and services which means that few workers are able to find jobs or build careers in developed nations. Furthermore, domestic manufacturers and distributers are down-sizing their work forces while increasing production. Where machines cannot replace the human totally, many workers are known to be doing the work of two people. The parallel decline in the tax base has forced Western governments to impose unsustainable tax burdens on their people and grab up what little domestic savings remain in the hands of their middle classes. Disappearing jobs, indebted and incompetent governments, totally dependent workforces and an increasingly enriched elite are leading the old, established industrial nations towards bankruptcy, poverty and technological backwardness.

The dilemma of the Western world and increasingly of some of Asia's Newly Emerging Industrial nations (NEIs) remains: Governments of industrial nations cannot sustain the costs of the multitude of public demands our highly technological societies require to remain progressive and stay ahead in the Communications' Revolution of the 21st Century. Forcing this dilemma, technologies of the 21st Century may prove the undoing of most industrial nations. Those on the rise will prosper, if only for a short time; those on the decline stand to become bankrupt in the immediate future. What is needed is a new economic policy designed to regain and more equitably redistribute the world's wealth which now lies in the hands of the very few. As previously stated, nearly half the world's wealth is in the hands of fewer than 400 billionaires, most of who prefer to play the stock and currency markets rather than invest in the future welfare of the earth's unmanageable populations.

Analyzing historical economic events reveals a distinct pattern of development that is repeating itself in Third World nations today. As an economy grew in the past, the bulk of the wealth fell into the hands of the most able. The majority were left in extreme poverty, providing slave labor, paid little for it and receiving no worker benefits. Death on the job from diseases related to the toxic chemicals or accidents from dangerous machines was very common. Many workers during the early years of the Industrial Revolution lived in abject poverty and received no medical care. The government members were also industrial entrepreneurs. When these inequalities became so intolerable and self-defeating in the past, they were stopped either through heavy government taxation of the rich or through revolution. However, today these are not likely solutions, primarily because modern communication technologies simply bypass government controls and escape revolutionary situations.

Governments today have little if any taxation power over their own citizens' wealth when it is held in offshore banks and currency markets. Taxation as a means of redistributing this wealth is not possible at present as few if any international laws and agreements exist which allow national governments to tax international monies. Each must devise some form of legislation that traps at least a small percentage of the wealth as it passes through their country. The second solution, revolution, is so costly to the general public, as many recent civil wars have shown, that open rebellion succeeds only in frightening and killing unwitting civilians and increasing the costs of police forces, making the general citizenry poorer while destroying the environments in which all must survive.

Dilemma 3.   **The Dilemma of Employment versus Conservation: How Do Governments Protect the Environment and Still Provide Jobs and Access to Resources?**

In the modern world a nation's political and economic stability varies according to the degree of technological expertise it has in use and the extent of its markets in goods and services. The more advanced the technological manufacturing base and the greater the output, the better the national wealth, education, living standards and trading income, all qualities of the economically sound nation as well as the politically stable. Until very recently, these were also the qualities which assured full employment.

Past national economic success required cooperation between governments and their economic sector to manage investment, industrial development, public infra-structures and trade to the benefit of all citizens, not just the few. The dualism that developed between these two sectors in democratic nations gave government the authority to regulate industrial practices, equitably distribute the wealth gained from the sale of national resources and stand guardian over the environment. Above all, it had the power to protect the workforce from unscrupulous exploitation by management.

However, this division of authority is waning as communication technologies aid the economic sector in escaping government control. As a result government is no longer an equal partner with the economic sector. Attempts to regulate big business or legislate against environmental destruction are viewed by the public as interference with much needed jobs.

In this tug-o-war between national governments and the global economy, efforts to reduce physical consumption and environmental destruction will always be offset by overpopulation. The degree to which they will be offset will expand yearly with each additional 90 million people. Over the next few decades those numbers will reach 8 billion and the majority will be seeking some form of earning power, legitimate or criminal. Their survival needs will far outweigh government attempts at conservation. What will happen is that industrial and agricultural consumption will skyrocket.

Deepening the universal problems inherent in so much industrial expansion and environmental degradation is the marketing of goods and services by international trading monopolies. To increase output and profits, global trade and multi-national corporations are forging ahead to build world wide markets in "luxury" goods throughout the Third World and the newly emerging industrial nations (NEIs). They are creating this desire through television advertisements and programs which expose the poor to riches they never knew existed. At the same time they are building their factories in these countries, using the poor as slave labor, but paying them just enough to raise their living standards just enough to give them the chance to buy a few of these desired luxuries such as a television set. Individually, these economic slaves may not buy much, but overall 5 to 8 billion people buying just one or two luxury items project a very large market for future investments.

What is not calculated into their international marketing policies is the huge consumption of diminishing resources that will follow if these newly emerging markets are supplied. Nothing will hasten environmental collapse faster. Also in seeing what luxuries they might have in their lives, those without jobs are dismantling their environments to earn the money to buy the tantalizing commodities.

In the initial stages of supplying Third World markets, these nations are open to extremes of foreign exploitation of their resources and people. The poor are used as "slave" labour and raw materials from the land are extracted and exported in return for little gain. The governments of poor nations are easily corrupted into abetting foreign developers in pillaging their lands and people. They willingly displace their farmers in exchange for foreign financed mega-projects, agri-business monoculture and as sinkholes for the contaminants of the developed world.

As overpopulated nations prepare for their industrial development and dream of affluence, experience is proving that their environments will likely move towards collapse in the process. The former USSR, Taiwan, South Korea, Japan, India, among many others contaminated their rivers and sea ports, some like China even drained several of their rivers dry. All began by dumping toxic wastes on their lands and clearcutting their forests. North America and Europe are no exceptions to these practices.

Pollution and destruction of the biosphere are already out of control in both developed and developing nations. Much of the Third World, including India and China, are in the early stages of industrialization and have yet to enforce any form of control on their toxic wastes and greenhouse gases. Their nations suffer massive escalations in urban smog caused by hundreds of city factories and the millions of new vehicles added each year to already overcrowded roads.

The idiocy of how extreme this situation can become is happening in Thailand. Industrial wealth has produced a growing middle class who can afford cars. But the country is so short of roads or space to build roads that cars are bumper to bumper on busy streets, moving at a pace slower than the passengers could travel on bicycle or foot. Yet those who can afford a car refuse to walk or cycle anymore. The car embodies the new industrial status as it displays the extent of its owner's wealth and prestige. Families are well prepared for the time they will spend on the road each day, trapped within their vehicles. They take along bedding, food, school work and entertainment to fill the hours it will take them to get to work or to school, motors running all the while.

Governments in every nation, rich and poor, remain blatantly ineffective in reducing vehicle traffic. Only when the smog is so thick it impairs vision and makes hundreds of adults and children ill are bans placed on the number of cars and trucks allowed on the road. Mexico City imposes several of these "car free" days each month, the smog is so thick. But the road ban lasts only as long as it takes for the smog to ease up. The Mexican government has yet to find a way to reduce the number of old, highly polluting automobiles, trucks and buses on Mexican roads. Greece, another country where the smog is so thick in its cities, had to outlaw cars from entering the centre of Athens at any time in the summer of 1995.

More and more people living in industrial towns and cities must cope with deteriorating health caused by their polluted environments. In fact, death, especially in industrial nations, is occurring in ever more dramatic forms of illnesses, accompanied by much pain and incapacity. The rising mortality rate among children, the elderly, the frail and the unhealthy is motivating a growing opposition to unrestricted industrial development. The rise in human suffering which directly adds to the costs of social infra-structures may be enough to force governments to face their responsibility.

And yet with the present global dash to find riches, both industry and governments remain largely unwilling to afford the inconvenience and costs of protecting the environments or allowing time for its regeneration. A forest takes over several hundred years to grow to the size which produces good wood for manufacturing. It also takes the ecology of a healthy, natural forest to guarantee the trees will not be destroyed by insects or blights. Only over long periods of protected isolation will forests grow strong enough to withstand the increasing strength of winter winds, land erosion and varied seasonal rainfalls.

As entrepreneurs and investors in the NEIs purchase resources such as trees, they escalate environmental destruction. They justify this exploitation by promoting the myth that birth rates can only be lowered if living standards are raised through full employment. Governments tend to fall in behind this reasoning as they must help to provide jobs and gain greater tax revenue. The situation is worsened by an electorate demanding jobs, expensive infra-structures and social programs. We are all to blame.

To stay in power, elected officials must first raise public funds and win elections. These conditions alone make them bend to the will of corporate power and unemployment lines, consequently environmental conservation and protection laws are always at the mercy of profit and loss. In the summer of 1995, the Canadian Environmental Protection Act was still largely in the rhetorical stage of 'good intentions'. Since its inception few toxic substances have been controlled, hazardous wastes continue to pollute the environment, toxic smogs threaten human health and the ecosystems are the victims of development and pollution.

Admitting that economic health is totally dependent on environmental health does not slow consumption of resources. Over the past few decades much has been discussed about conservation both at the domestic level and at world conferences, but very little has been accomplished.

In attempting to protect the environment for future use, politicians have learned they cannot preserve its viability and still accommodate a universally profitable and progressive human existence. Elected governments bend to the economic needs of their citizens or they are voted out of office. A devil's choice emerges: Sustain human development or protect the environment, either way humanity loses.

Governments do not enforce restrictive measures that might antagonize the economic sector. The majority of people in a nation must first be willing to accept penalties and job losses if the environment is to be protected from overdevelopment. Farmers in the United States in the mid 1990s, for instance, threatened by government moves to turn lakes and cattle ranges into protected parklands, saw the move as interference with their property rights and freedom within the constitution. Political intentions to save the eco-systems of these private lands was good. But the farmers who stood to lose the use of these lands as ranges whipped up enough political backing to get the American Congress to consider changing the National Environmental Protection Act to release their lands from the designated conservation areas.

The coercive forces at play are financially so critical to a politician's future that while the politician openly supports conservation in their speeches and promises, most of their promises have yet to be turned into action. If public opinion is against industrial development, governments will seek a compromise solution. More reluctant to anger the electorate than please the developers, they will turn an environmental area into a state park.

Again government leadership prefers to wait until the consumption of natural resources and environmental degradation are severe enough to move entire populations to support conservation laws. Having nothing to lose, governments will finally take a stand against and attempt to prevent total extinction of a resource. Generally they lose.

The fish war of 1994 and 1995 between Canada and the state of Alaska over salmon quotas exemplifies this reality. In June of 1995, Canada's Minster of Fisheries, Brian Tobin, just victorious in protecting the Atlantic turbot from being overfished by the Spaniards, wanted to save migrating salmon stocks on the Pacific Coast by enforcing strict quotas. The Governor of Alaska responded to this restriction on American fishermen by declaring open season on the salmon, assuring his fishermen they were free to catch all the migrating Canadian fish they could while the fish were passing through American waters.

In the process of establishing political power and electing for economic gain over environmental conservation, government authorities favor their corporate hierarchy and workers over resource conservation measures. No action demonstrates this more clearly than the stand the government took during the protest event in the summer of 1994 in the province of British Columbia. Over 800 men, women and children tried to prevent clearcutting of one of the few remaining valleys of old growth forest on Vancouver Island. All were found guilty of obstruction and given short term jail sentences for putting their bodies in front of trucks and machines in an effort to stop the logging.

Granted democratic governments are hamstrung by the many demands placed on them to allow development. They are also hard pressed to raise the billions of dollars in taxes needed to pay for clean up and repair costs of existing environmental contamination and destruction. Therefore, most governments, rich and poor, are delinquent in enforcing conservation and anti-pollution laws. Many can only hope industry will have enough at stake that they will need to develop their own sustainable conservation programs.

With so many differing interests involved when regulating conservation practices, most politicians prefer to obfuscate on environmental policies then to act definitively. "Fence-sitting" allows their citizens to exploit the environment and provide employment and taxes. A general lack of legislative and judicial interference against polluters and exploiters has assured governments of relative public quiescence while encouraging economic growth, political stability, social harmony, public security and human survival. The poor quality of life that can result or the permanent damage inflicted on the environment are secondary to jobs, profits and taxes.

Together government, industry and labor have turned their backs on environmentalists and made them the enemies of society. They are dismissed by loggers, fishermen, hunters, miners, developers, excavators, chemical farmers and industrial polluters as doomsayers and ecological terrorists. This defines a serious social dilemma: Do we allow unlimited consumption of the environment and its resources so that we can enjoy the advantages of immediate financial gain and universal affluence, thereby overriding the future survival of all other species and the preservation of the environment; or do we stop our exploitation of the few resources left and give the remaining natural habitat over to wilderness species. Either way species Homo sapiens has much to lose and is very unlikely to accept the idea of giving the advantage to nature.

But perhaps the diminishing state of natural resources and the environment are reaching that crucial limit of consumption when governments will stand up for nature against the human exploiter. It took the total collapse of the Atlantic cod stocks to make the Canadian government legislate an indefinite moratorium on fishing off Newfoundland. Although it meant thousands of fishermen had to accept the end of their traditional way of life, Mr. Tobin believed if he acted quickly, he could stop the same thing happening to the turbot which were being overfished by Spanish fleets bordering Newfoundland's 200 mile limit. But the battle was not his alone. It was between two governments, the Canadian and the Spanish, with the whole European Community supporting the Spaniards right to continue fishing.

As expected, the environment lost. Homo sapiens won. The United Nations insisted the Canadian government accept a compromise. The Spanish fleet was immediately allowed back to fish just beyond Newfoundland's coastal limits on the promise they will keep their catches to within a set quota. Ironically, everyone involved knew they would cheat on those quotas. They are also aware that any amount of commercial fishing will soon deplete the turbot stocks.

It is obvious that the costs in environmental destruction are outrunning the gains in industrial production. While North America's report card on pollution remains among the poorest in the developed world, participation in recycling and anti-pollution programs is on the rise. With the biosphere rapidly deteriorating, governments are less and less able to ignore the growing need to give priority to conservation.

Government Management and Exploitation of Resources

Overburdened with public expectations, governments often find themselves among the desecrators of the environment in trying to create jobs, develop natural resources and expand their national industrial bases. To do so they undertake mega-projects such as the construction of huge dams, irrigation systems, hydro electric projects and commercial agricultural programs. In many cases as with the world's largest dams, the effects have proven more permanently destructive than useful both to people and the environment.

One of the most devastating government undertakings was the diversion away from the Aral Sea to a local desert in Uzbekistan of two large rivers, the Syr Dar'ya in the north and the Amu Dar'ya in the south. The rivers were used to irrigate one of the most water-consuming crops in the world: cotton. The Aral Sea, once a beautiful body of water, filled with fish and surrounded by vegetation and inhabitants, is now all but gone. What remains is a desert of salt, strewn with derelict fishing boats. Those who remain are sick from the concentration of salt in their environment. Thousands more were forced to migrate in search of work and better health conditions.

Such experience shows that if governments themselves assume the role of entrepreneur in exploiting natural resources so as to create jobs and economic production the results often prove unparalleled disasters. Nationalized farming and industrial manufacturing in former Communist nations created vast inefficient industrial plants, large polluted land water areas, destroyed ecological systems and bankrupt national treasuries. The Arctic Ocean and adjoining lands of Northern Russia and most of Eastern Europe have been permanently poisoned by radio active wastes, industrial contaminants and toxic emissions, the result of the Russian Communist regime's habit of pouring billions of gallons of radio active and nuclear wastes into their northern rivers which run into the Arctic Ocean. Many parts of East Germany, Czechoslovakia and Poland are also contaminated wastelands where industrial toxic chemicals were disposed.

Mistakes aside, the role of governments must be to control environmental exploitation, not partake in it. They still remain the only human institution that can gather the necessary capital wealth, power and consensus to bring order out of chaos and enforce environmental restrictions. It is up to them to slow the race to destroy the earth. They must take the responsibility for curbing industrial expansion and reducing resource consumption, if not administering it. Most of all they must remain vigilant and responsible to humanity in preventing pollution and degradation of the biosphere if we are to forestall our own self-destruction.

How can this be accomplished? Efforts to balance human activities with conservation practices to date continue to be offset by the costs in lost production or of recycling as well as the heavy expenditures that must be afforded to police industry effectively. Few industries can be expected to police themselves or afford the heavy costs of most existing forms of pollution control and still be competitive. The recycling of waste products, increased use of energy, expansion of available storage, equipment, plants and transportation are all inherent costs in ending the emission of toxic wastes and boosting recycling. Most nations have found these conservation measures make industrial production non-competitive unless all nations impose the same environmental laws with similar monetary costs on their industry and agriculture.

Germany is perhaps the most advanced in regulating its industrial recycling of materials and protecting their environment. But the costs have been so prohibitive to employers, that several major manufacturers have moved their plants to developing countries to avoid the expense of recycling and environmental protection. Only in this way were they able to remain competitive in a world market flooded with goods from countries whose policies ignore pollution and environmental degradation on the argument they will stop once they are fully industrialized and can bear the costs.

In the end funding for conservation will be met by the consumers either through taxation or high retail prices. The dilemma for governments is just how much they can safely regulate and tax their people to protect the environment. Is any economic system strong enough and rich enough to withstand the loss of jobs, the price of recycling, and the reduced living standards which must accompany serious conservation programs? Will the industrial nations sacrifice their affluent life styles for the sake of the environment? And can ways be found for governments to finance and enforce a sharp reduction in birth rates in developing nations?

Larger populations will increase exploitation of every nation's environment. As human needs expand, employment will continue to take priority over environmental protection. Government cannot protect the environment and at the same time, subsidize workers and companies not to exploit it. The costs are too high.

Efforts to conserve are often frustrated by a lack of technology needed for reprocessing, purifying or recycling. Another method for saving resources is to restrict the use of raw materials and demand recycled materials be used first. Unfortunately, this approach often makes production too expensive for the producer to continue manufacturing and he will close down. Governments prefer to back away from this situation. Again, using the threat of closure to penalize the polluter as opposed to heavy fines produces the same effects. Should governments punish industry for their failure to follow environmental codes or use recycled materials, they may be penalizing themselves. Official interference through closure of plants raises unemployment and welfare costs and loses tax revenues.

Refusing multi-national corporations unlimited exploitation of rivers, land and resources brings a backlash so expensive and economically retributive that governments acquiesce to corporate demands. Corporate industries, now global and easily moved from country to country, threaten to close their plants or stop resource extraction and sue for multi-million dollar compensation payments. This form of blackmail quickly forces governments to give priority to their demands. Multi-national forest companies in British Columbia, for example, continue destructive clear-cutting on a large scale while governments pass laws against such actions just to placate the public. Whether they are enforced is questionable. B.C. government leaders found themselves trying to convince a watching world that they had stopped the practice of clearcutting. When British Columbia was dubbed "Brazil of the North", the government attempted to offset this view by turning a few virgin, old-growth valleys into parklands, promising to save at least ten percent of the province from logging. But clearcutting still stops only when a valuable forest is gone and what remains is of little or no economic value.

A more nationally defined problem also influences how and where environmental protection programs are imposed. Getting elected to government office depends on the largesse of the same corporate structures which are among the worst polluters. Staying in office means keeping promises to those who finance the politicians' elections and to those who elect them. Consequently, protecting the environment sits low on the list of most politicians' priorities. Governments cannot promise their people jobs while at the same time passing environmental laws which prohibit the use of a nation's resources to provide those jobs.

Governments may give the appearance of restricting exploitation and environmental degradation by passing legislation against offenders, but most infractions of these laws are ignored or the laws themselves are rescinded when a different government comes into power. The Republican Party in the United States in 1995, promised to amend, if not do away with, the Endangered Species Act because it hinders resource extraction and human occupation of the preserved habitat of protected species such as the forests of Washington and Oregon.

Many governments are increasingly helpless to prevent pollution or destruction of their environments. In Third World and in developing nations such as Mexico, even direct effects of pollution have not stopped the poor from working and living in contaminated environments where their drinking water runs thick with chemicals and human excrement. The Maquiladoras of the U.S. Mexican border is rampant with intolerable contamination, yet thousands of people live in these conditions because they are assured of more income (as little as it is) than they have ever had before if they work in the plants of multi-national corporations owned and managed by the First World entrepreneurs.

If Governments could Really Protect the Environment

If governments were free to impose conservation bans wherever needed and were capable of managing the earth's natural assets as well as its human populations, they would have to have unlimited rights to restrict human activities. In fact, they would need enough power to undo much of our economic development and reverse the direction of our technological dependency. Most of the commodities which so enhance our lives but damage the environment would have to be sacrificed or their use sharply curtailed.

Conservation would have to include a total ban on logging old-growth rain forests, a reduction of commercial farming and its use of fertilizers, pesticides and herbicides, a sharply reduced consumption of fresh water reserves, a stop to ocean fishing, the closure of industries which produce toxic emissions and wastes which cannot be reabsorbed into the environment naturally and almost a virtual end to burning fossil fuels.[2] People would have to be prevented from migrating both within nations= and to other lands where their presence would escalate environmental damage. Governments would of necessity have to prevent the growth of mega-cities which are gobbling up scarce farmland. More important, governments would need the power to curtail our use of vehicles by banning fossil fuels or any other form of energy which produces ozone and greenhouse gases.

All peoples would have to offer their governments unlimited rights to restrict human activities. In fact, they would have to cede to governments enough power to undo much of our technological advancement and reverse the direction of our technological dependency. All the luxuries of high living standards would need to be sacrificed: paper, cars, sea foods, many varieties and excesses of foods, machines burning fossil fuels, increasing consumption of resources, the manufacture of plastics and refining of oil.

To impose these restrictions would require totally repressive, omnipotent regimes. They could not allow one person to break the rules, or all will fall apart. It would mean a complete reversal of human activities and habits: the subjugation of the human spirit and its creative abilities. It would be Orwell's "1984" many times over. Bluntly, there is no way in which we can prevent self-destruction because we cannot sufficiently change the human character to accept the repression that would be involved in preventing us from exploiting and destroying the remaining viability of the earth's environment.

This expresses the enormity of our basic dilemma of survival: employment or conservation? Protecting the environment reduces industrial consumption of natural resources and pollution of the environment, but eliminates jobs and reduces living standards. National governments would be impoverished. A decline in production and consumption would produce a growing underclass of unemployed poor who would be reduced to robbing the environment just to survive.

The dilemma is that governments must sustain their economies by allowing the natural environment to be exploited, permitting an expanding economic climate in which large workforces are employed. Consequently, few governments will force their industries to reduce their environmentally destructive practices. They recognize the prohibitive costs in lost production, unemployment, lost trade, diminished purchasing power and forfeited government revenues if their restrictions or penalties force a company out of business or to take its employment to another country where taxes and environmental laws are not intrusive. Most countries welcome the employment opportunities and accept the pollution. In this way governments are forced to put jobs and industry before the environment.

But could our exploitation ever be less harmful and more efficient of human labour?. Recent attempts by governments and industry to regain its credibility in environmental protection have been directed towards "sustainable management" programs. Small, localized attempts have been made here and there to work with the environment instead of against it. The old industrial nations of North America and Europe have passed many good laws to restrain development in fragile areas and wildlife habitat. Clean-up programs have restored some rivers and lands to their natural state. Science research has been financed to discover ways to dispose of toxic wastes and pollutants and protective measures have been taken to reduce greenhouse gases and CFCs. Unfortunately, population growth, demand for more resources, industrial expansion and the new chemicals added annually offset the gains, especially in the newly developing nations and the Third World.

To be truly cost effective, conservation of resources must be profitable. It is not. Rather, it is an excessive cost added to production. Management and shareholders view conservation as an expense that cannot be afforded in a world where markets are glutted with commodities and only the cheapest of the best quality can compete, a situation that has arisen in the last few decades and shows no chance of lessening well into the next century.

Few sustainable management programs have been successful in the past or over the long term whether from a lack of scientific research, expertise, technologies, money or inefficiency. More often they are costly failures, which makes the public sceptical of government's role in environmental management. Government participation is seen by the capitalistic sector as an unwanted interference in the natural flow of market forces. Some nations such as the United States and Great Britain, prefer that market forces determine economic policy rather than governments regulating and restricting industrial growth. Other countries like Japan have shown that governments working in partnership with industry can be far more expansive and successful economically and environmentally.

As pressures mount against conservation programs and the global internet of electronic communication weakens governments, budgets for environmental studies and conservation are constantly shrinking. Environmental departments are classified as a government handout which can be reduced or eliminated in times of recession or high debt. Trained and experienced staffs of knowledgable inspectors are dismissed and environmental subsidies to industries discontinued.

Attempting to save the planet through a moderate course of solutions still depends on a universal willingness of governments and their people to impose restrictions on themselves which will decrease, if not bring an end to the most destructive activities which threaten the planet. At the top of the list of priorities must be the reduction of greenhouse gases and the protection of the ozone layer. Equally important is an enforced rationing of fresh water, trees and fish as well as a sharp decline in the use of toxic chemicals. We survived in the past without the plethora of chemicals we have today; we could certainly live without most of them in the future.

Unfortunately, the necessary list of "do's and don'ts" in the name of conservation is all inclusive of our technological existence. For governments to stop development and consumption of resources would be to retract the thousands of years of mechanical progress which we have enjoyed. To give them such power would be to sanction repression beyond all human sufferance.

The reality is that governments are more and more emasculated by their inability to control global economic trends or to regulate environmental exploitation. Their weakness will continue to emerge as they fail to ensure social stability and natural resources disappear. The rich will grow richer and good jobs and living standards for the majority will no longer be possible.

CHAPTER TEN

Social Dilemmas
Of Our Overcrowded Planet

Only half a century ago, most of the world's two billion people coped on their own in small family units, centred around small villages. Eighty percent lived on farms which provided them food and animal protein. Without doubt some existed at a subsistence level. But most Third World people lived, gave birth, raised their children and died on a small plot of ground, their success determined by varying degrees of soil fertility and organic farming practices. Some moved their families and animals with the seasonal changes and the return of fresh vegetation. They were largely independent of modern technologies, using their hands, farm animals and a few simple tools to grow or craft their basic needs of shelter, clothing and simple cultivation. Some fell victim to unscrupulous landlords, but the majority were responsible for their own existence. Life was generally difficult and short. Their consumption of resources and use of soils was far less threatening to the entire planet and its people than they are today.

Self-sufficiency is rare anymore. "Going it alone" in this overcrowded world is left to the social recluse who chooses to escape the trappings of civilization. For the majority, it is impossible to live without manufactured goods and processed foods. Even in some of the most isolated areas, the local people can be seen wearing machine-made clothes and live in houses built with processed materials. In times of famine, food is brought to them in ships, trucks and planes.

Less than one percent of the world's people are still able to exist in the self-sufficient hunter-gatherer state, living off the bounties of the forest and the seas. But as their reserves of edible plants and animals disappear from overuse or climate changes and their tribal territories are invaded by civilization, even this small vestige of humanity must turn to modern technologies to survive. For example, the once totally self-sufficient North American eskimo now lives in wooden houses, heated with oil burning stoves, wears imported parkas made with synthetic materials and eats food caught with guns and nets, imported from urban centres.

Humanity is now totally dependent on its technologies to provide employment and enable the universal exchange of goods and services. It is not only an economic but a social dependency that only thoroughly competent governments can manage. Very little remains that the individual can furnish for himself. Without modern technologies of communication, transportation and public infra-structure, urban living would not be viable. This is already self-evident in the slums of most cities in South American, Africa, Asia, even North America where extremes of poverty and disease are the norm. Hundreds of millions of people exist there without public utilities, jobs and health care. Life is generally non-productive, subsistent and chaotic. Few are able to fulfil their human promise. As world populations double from the estimated 5 billion in the 1990s to 10 to 14 billion in the 21st Century, human numbers will continue to create vast ghettos harboring a plethora of unmanageable social conditions.

The failure to provide technical infra-structures in decaying inner cities exacerbates unemployment, poverty, diseases and violent crime. Without efficient technologies to overcome these problems through employment and a more equitable distribution of goods and services, nations risk popular unrest. Young men, forced to wander the streets in search of work and self-esteem, gravitate towards gangs which have become a constant threat to the functioning of every urban society, rich and poor. This is a dangerous trend, one that can only increase as 60 percent of the world's people will soon be children under 16 years of age. Able to view the luxuries of the industrial world on television, even the poorest and most primitive are experiencing extreme dissatisfaction with their own poor lives. They see that the many luxury goods available in the global economy can be attained if only one has the money. This encourages them to acquire such goods through any means, including violent criminal activities and the sale of drugs, both of which are on the rise.

Humanity's dependence on technologies for survival is now so total that when they fail us, nations fall into social chaos and political disintegration. Tribal/ethnic wars soon follow. In their extremes, the lack of technologies and widespread unemployment initiates terrorism, guerrilla uprisings, political coups, assassinations, bombings and the loss of human rights. Life reverts to rule by the gun.

When workforces have no jobs and existence has no purpose, they have little to lose. Human life comes to have little value. Violent death is then an everyday occurrence, carrying little fear or trepidation. Armed death squads, whether they are gangs, "mafia" styled organizations, warlords or the military of dictatorships, become the arbiters of law and order, ensuring the spoils of power go to those who are the strongest and best armed. Under these conditions, trade and commerce are quick to decline. Workplaces, homes, schools, transportation and communication systems are bombed out of resentment derived from a common sense of futility. The anger is directed at governments through social infra-structures which, when destroyed, capture worldwide attention and reparations may be forthcoming. However, many nations at this point sink into anarchy and non-productivity; poverty, fear and violence take over.

Events in Somalia, Africa, in 1992, exposed the many social horrors which befall any nation that loses its technological base and falls into the hands of warlords and rebel gangs whether through chaos or in this case, tribal wars for national control. Out of a Somalian population of 4.5 million, 1.5 million starved, over 150,000 died. The largest toll took the lives of children under 5 years of age. In the capital city of Mogadishu, an average of 1500 persons died daily, many sprawled on the streets, in alleys, dead or dying from hunger, infection or bullet wounds. Hundreds also died daily in the villages and outlying areas. [1]

In the cities of Somalia, people lacked water to drink because the water pipes under all the roads had been torn up and traded for food. No electricity and no phones remained. Their cables had been cut and sold for their copper content. Garbage, the carcases of dead camels and donkeys, smouldering and rotting, blocked the streets. Fires raged from explosions and looters. There was no government, no police force, only roaming gangs with guns, indiscriminantly killing while stealing and black-marketing any food aid supplies which reached the hungry people. No life was safe, including those of foreigners who, under United Nations' protection, tried to distribute food and medical aid to the starving.[2] Drought, warfare, and a destroyed technological, political and social infra-structure produced a dying nation, where the gun ruled and life for the millions hung by a slender thread of foreign aid which generally failed to arrive in time. Civil war and famine had forced the destruction of all manmade technologies of survival, leaving an entire nation vulnerable. Add mass migrations of starving refugees and epidemic diseases and the metaphorical image of the Four Horses of the Apocalypse is complete: War, Famine, Pestilence and Death.

Only the foreign aid distributed by non-governmental organizations (NGO's) and the food and medicines brought by the United Nations to alleviate the hunger and disease caused by crop failures and war saved the people, if not the nation, from total social catastrophe. The UN's attempt to keep the peace among the tribes proved disastrous, forcing the nation to accept foreign military rule which was incapable of restoring civilian authority. The situation remained calm only as long as UN peace keepers were present. But once they withdrew their forces in the spring of 1995, anarchy and brutality returned as warlords resumed their struggle for power. Feeding the people had failed to solve the problems of tyranny, lawlessness and tribal wars, in this case, as in many others, a war which pitted child soldiers against child soldiers.

In present times, a flourishing society is one whose majority of citizens has living standards commensurate with its degree of industrial/technological innovations. These assure food production, employment and purchasing power while raising the living standards of the majority to a viable level. Without constantly improving its methods of production and its living standards, a society tends to become authoritarian and as a whole degenerates. Rising birth rates then become catalysts for violent, destructive behaviours, and life becomes unbearable, especially for women and children.

The complexity of our industrial social structures are now such that unless governments and their economies afford public assistance for the unemployed and the unemployable, nations risk civil protest and destructive violence. Education, medical care, law enforcement, national security, an employed workforce and a government bureaucracy are the price of stability and improved living standards. Without these the social fabric decays. Violent protest becomes widespread, riots erupt, cities are burned and civil wars soon follow. Justice is lost, and criminality, depravity and brutality rise.

A profound dilemma. We can no longer survive without our technologies, yet those same technologies which make our lives fruitful are threatening our very existence as they destroy the environment and permit the survival of nearly an additional billion people in each decade.

Price of Our Dependency on Technologies

The modern industrial world requires an unprecedented amount of resources to maintain the growing populations and produces an unmanageable quantity of pollution and environmental degradation. It is commonly recognized that earthly resources are finite and will never ensure 6 to 10 billion people a productive life. This reality is already with us as hundreds of millions of lives are moving towards a severe state of poverty. Increasing unemployment, housing shortages, a loss of privacy, a growing underclass of poor, failing infra-structures, food and water shortages, unmanageable wastes and a polluted biosphere are already reducing the survival rate of both the productive and the dispossessed. The point of sustainability was passed in mid-20th Century when population numbers began to exceed two billion and technology gave us the power to consume and destroy the total environment.

Increased technological consumption and production now make every nation dependent on every other nation. Each becomes enslaved to the output of the other. Self-sufficiency of landbases no longer exists. For example, all industrial nations depend on imported oil. Japan and the United States could not function as super powers without the billions of barrels of oil and gas they import. Between 65 and 70 countries rely on imported food or food aid to compensate for what they cannot grow themselves. The largest nations, India and China, whose populations and industrialization are expanding rapidly, are no longer self-sufficient in food supplies to provide the people with living standards equal to the purchasing power they have gained through industrialization. With only 250 million of her 1.2 billion people able to afford a better living standard, China is now importing 30 to 40 percent of its food needs, an amount which grows annually with increased industrialization.

This huge new market for large quantities and varieties of foods is putting an added stress on diminishing world supplies of food grains and a corresponding strain on the natural environment. The scramble for food production is reflected in the overcutting of tropical and temperate rainforests in search of farm land to grow crops. Supplying the new Asian markets has produced a corresponding rise in the use of chemicals and fertilizers in the Third World. Critical wetlands are being drained and fragile, marginal lands which should never be touched are being opened up to intensive technological farming. The greatest impact increased crop production is having is the speed with which it is using up underground reserves of fresh water and sterilizing the arable soils.

Just how much overcrowding of a land base can humans tolerate and still remain relatively acquiescent. Where cultures and traditions have promoted large families and ingrained the rights of the community above those of the individual, overpopulated lands have experienced relatively stable societies, but there is a limit. The Communist regime in China, for example, imposes the occupation of single dwelling houses by several families. One room is allotted to each set of parents and their children. The kitchen and the bathroom facilities are shared by all families in the house. This extreme sharing of living space, even in China with its legacy of closely knit, extended families, led to family squabbles over diminishing privacy. Harmony was maintained only through fear of being reported to the local authorities which could mean public humiliation, severe forms of interrogation, indoctrination and brain washing sessions, beatings or years in prison, among many other forms of punishment.

The same forces of overcrowding, a lack of materials, money and a shortage of houses became severe in Eastern Europe during the final stages of the communist regime and its collapse. Many families had no choice but to share one house, cut off from each other by blankets for walls. The strain proved socially debilitating and often explosive. Only the greater fear of being reported and persecuted by the police kept these overcrowded people from attempting to displace those with whom they were forced to share.

In the West, on the other hand, where religions and cultures promote individual rights above those of the community, living without private social space is neither conducive to social harmony nor to individual happiness, especially where populations are of so many mixed cultures. Nerves are frayed and ethnic hatreds are quickly aroused when people are crowded into tenement buildings or even city blocks. The overcrowding of different races in the inner cities of New York and Los Angeles reflect the self-imposed segregation which takes place among races as each ethnic group isolates itself within their chosen city blocks. These blocks are then considered gang "turfs", controlled by youths of the particular ethnic group living in that city block. For example, the Koreans of Los Angeles do not occupy apartments or homes in the same blocks as African Americans. They may buy goods in each other's shops or work together, but they avoid living side by side.

Rapid decline is symptomatic of the quality of life the vast majority of people living today must endure. A parallel rise in social unrest and violent behaviour is occurring, generating from poverty, overcrowding and deprivation. As millions of people are forced to migrate to the cities in search of jobs and housing, the infra-structures of schools, hospitals, public transportation, water, sewage, electricity, roads, railways, bridges, airports and seaports can neither be built fast enough nor afforded by the state to handle the influx of millions of immigrants.

Few cities today in both developed and developing nations have sufficient land or resources to sustain a stable, industrial society. The symptoms of overcrowding can be seen in any large urban area, intensifying the level of social stress: highway gridlock, inner city decay, economic decline, "drug economies", malnutrition, the return of fatal epidemic diseases, low self-esteem, lawlessness, ethnic violence.

Many overcrowded nations have seen their economies destroyed in ethnic/tribal struggles to gain control over scarce resources of water, food, forests and arable lands. Much of Africa has had large areas of the continent engulfed in civil wars lasting decades. Growing populations and constant desertification are reducing employment opportunities and destroying resources of food and water at a much faster rate than they can be replaced. The Middle East is a powder keg which could explode at any time as nations vie for the water of the Nile, the Euphrates, the Tigris and the Jordan to meet the needs of the millions of farmers who cling to the river banks and the millions of city dwellers whose supplies of drinking water depend on the diminishing flow of fresh water in these rivers. Over the last 20 years Arab states on the Persian Gulf have tripled the amount of underground water they pump to the surface, causing water tables to fall and the water to become brackish. At the same time, dozens of desalination plants are adding to the salinity of the gulf waters, threatening fish and coral, while proliferating algae which consume the oxygen in the water, killing off all other life forms.[3]

Continuing to rely on industrial expansion and downplaying the environmental consequences is making human survival totally dependent on industrial and agricultural output no matter what the cost in human health and environmental degradation. The prognosis is we will go out of existence in an irrational, violent manner because of our destructive survival techniques.

Obviously, we are digging our species deeper and deeper into an unsolvable dilemma. Industrial and agricultural consumption of water is crucial to the everyday production of human needs demanding its output be increased daily. Food supplies must run apace with population growth. Unwisely, we have placed our faith in scientists to bring us new hybrids and genetically engineered crops which will multiply food output and tolerate drought, pests, salty soils and rising temperatures. At the same time technological production must be expanded so that more and more people can be employed and their consumption of goods and services expanded to ensure economic growth.

Historically, human survival has depended on the earth's capacity to provide unlimited reserves of water, soils, trees and fuels. The rate at which humanity now consumes these natural elements will multiply several times in the 21st Century, presenting problems which are paramount to our future existence. Three economic realities have taken shape which must begin to prevail worldwide: Improvements to technologies must be geared to producing only goods basic to human survival, not luxury spending, and must be done more efficiently with a heavy emphasis on recycling and environmental conservation. Second, new technologies aimed at manufacturing luxury goods must be seen as superfluous to our existence, serving only to flatter our intellectual egos and assuage our greed. Third, most research and development of technological innovations will be confined to undoing the massive damage our hubris has already committed against the planet and discovering ways for us all to live more simply.

However, several socio/economic problems are inherent in any of these solutions. All three of them entail a dramatic drop in commodity production and resource consumption, causing an equally devastating rise in unemployment. The dilemma would then deepen as unemployment spreads. Housing shortages would increase, the underclass of poor and homeless would expand, social space would decrease and a universal decline in the quality of infra-structures would permit the accumulation of human wastes and urban pollution to grow both physically and financially unmanageable.

The point of equilibrium between environmental carrying capacity and human consumption of resources was passed at mid-20th Century when population numbers began to exceed two billion and technologies were able to produce more commodities and services than existing purchasing power could absorb. During the last half of the 20th Century, military weapons and manufacturing technologies, capable of destroying the total environment, were invented and widely distributed.

In the future, human demands for goods and services will be so massive they will overwhelm the earth's ability to sustain even present rates of industrial and agricultural expansion. The stress on farmlands has already reduced the annual increase in production. Even the most advanced technologies cannot force much more out of the soil, nor prevent the yearly escalation in desertification. As more nations become industrialized, the stress on the planet will make societies, even civilizations, topple. The extent of unemployment, declining purchasing power, overpopulation, political and economic instability, economic migrations, civil wars and environmental collapse will bring universal anarchy and civil chaos to the majority of nations.

Technology and overcrowding have already done excessive damage to the earth in just the last forty years. Much of the physical environment of both rural and urban areas is now unfit for human habitation. Former Communist countries are quagmires of toxic pollutants. Industrial nations continue to degrade their farmlands and pollute their rivers, lakes and ocean shores. The loss of farm lands and soils to erosion and overcropping destroys an area equal to that of Ireland annually. Underground water supplies are dwindling rapidly and many are contaminated. Air is polluted with toxic emissions from factories and cars, and drought and flooding constantly threaten many nations with economic and social financial ruin.

Communication and transportation technologies have gone far beyond meeting our basic needs. They now have the power to undermine our social and cultural fabrics. For example, the international computer network (Internet) puts the greatest weapon of human control in the hands of the fanatics, the xenophobic and the criminal without any universal means at present to police them. Pornography, race hatred, monetary and literary theft, all run the full gamut on the electronic internet systems, unabated by censorship or judicial punishment. The possibilities of this technology puts it among the most disruptive, most corruptive technological innovations known to humanity. It has the power to reach hundreds of millions of people with millions of bits of information both good and bad. No other form of communication has ever had this capacity nor been able to flaunt civilized authority so freely.

Humanity is now caught up in a dire predicament. All nations in the 21st Century, dependent on a technological/industrial existence, must either choose to enjoy an affluent life style at the cost of a destroyed, nonviable environment and an early demise of the human species; OR all peoples will have to endure a large degree of deprivation and a sharp rise in the annual death rate. Obviously neither choice is morally preferable nor economically feasible.

Our exploding populations may soon make it impossible for any nation's citizens to live in relative affluence and safety as it becomes increasingly difficult to prevent the poor from seeking redress for their unemployment and poverty. The end of human tolerance for excessively rich elites may be approaching as communication and weapons' technologies put enough power into the hands of small guerrilla bands to defeat national armies. Living with double the present population in the next century in even more crowded and deteriorating environmental conditions will not bring about rational solutions. Rather it will embroil us all in struggles for social space, food and water supplies. Racial and ethnic groups will kill each other in a scramble to control landbases. Several nations will pose a nuclear threat as they build nuclear arsenals either to invade other nations or to protect themselves against encroachment. The present state of chaos and social collapse of West African countries as described by Robert D. Kaplan in the magazine article, "The Coming Anarchy" may be a preview of our universal future.[4]

Even the poorest among us with enough courage and daring can assemble highly destructive weapons to mount civil wars capable of destroying a nation's entire economic structure within days and replace political authority with warlords. Inequality, injustice and inhumanity now lead to technological wars which destroy the land, human institutions, civilization's heritage and civilian populations. Civil violence and terrorism in war torn countries such as the former Yugoslavia are leaving a disgraceful legacy of destroyed structures which eventually necessitate huge quantities of resources to replace them. The lesson of Easter Island tells us that the price in environmental destruction is not sustainable.

Migrations: No Place To Go Anymore

The most visible indications that our world is already overcrowded and unmanageable is the unprecedented migrations of tens of millions of refugees at the present time. Such desperation has many origins: resource depletion, lack of land, water shortages, crop failures, pollution, eco-extinction, overpopulation, ethnic violence, civil wars. Motivated by these conditions, millions, in escaping the horrors of oppression, privation and hunger and aided by the technologies of mass transportation and communication, have uprooted their families to go in search of personal security and a better life.

By 1992 over 100 million people around the world were attempting to migrate to new homelands or to regain previously lost lands. The list of causes for so many refugees must begin with laying blame on the international money community which was experiencing a world glut of oil money in the 1970s and decided to finance the Third World through industrialization. The money managers worked on the belief that no nation could go bankrupt; therefore, it was safe to loan even the poorest nation huge cash sums at high interest rates. By the 1980s financing these debts was so destructive of Third World economies that the only way to repay them was to accept excessive construction of dams, mines and roads, and unlimited resource extraction and monoculture farming of vast areas of peasant farm lands. Millions of peasant farmers were displaced and robbed of their livelihoods. The majority still live as refugees in search of jobs and land.

The human flood of refugees expanded in the late 1980s and early 1990s when the Communist states of Eastern Europe collapsed, freeing millions of impoverished economic refugees. At the same time, hundreds of thousands of political refugees from the impoverished, repressive Third World nations invaded Europe and America. By 1995 UN estimates put the total number of world refugees at 125 million.

For several decades legitimate governments have competed with crime syndicates and black marketeers for the world wide trade in weapons and drugs, aiding in uprooting whole civilian populations through tribal wars. Racial genocide re-emerged in full force, causing millions to flee their homelands. Many more became the dispossessed of overcrowded land bases, oppressive governments, drought, abject poverty and chronic starvation. A good percentage fell victim to food aid programs as their survival grew to depend entirely on handouts.

Internal migrations of refugees are also adding tens of millions to the numbers seeking a place to live and work. The armies of unemployed, dislocated, insane, sick and addicted homeless grow annually within both the industrialized nations and the Third World. City streets have become home to millions, many of them children, who must beg, panhandle, prostitute themselves and sell illegal goods and drugs to eat. They suffer all forms of physical and psychological deprivation.

In the 1970s and 1980s, before the problem of refugees became massive and beyond solving, such suffering did not go unnoticed by the Western nations of Europe and North America. Governments who attempted to "lock them out" risked defeat at the polls. Public guilt in the "have" nations, which were enjoying the highest standards of living and industrial production in history, was building a vocal majority which believed they owed the refugees of the world a better chance at survival. Such moral obligation was borne out of the horrors of World War II and enshrined in the Constitution of the United Nations stating that asylum was the right of the persecuted and dispossessed.

Western governments continued to abide by this policy until the 1990s. As the world's population exploded from two billion to 6 billion in just 50 years under the pressures of crowding and oppressive governments throughout the Third World, the bulk of the refugees and illegal immigrants entered Western Europe and North America, where, initially, they were welcomed and made citizens.

The United Nations' Population Fund estimated that some 15 million people entered Europe from 1980 to 1992 and continued to run at one to two million a year.[5] By 1993 Europe was flooded with immigrants and refugees from North Africa, Yugoslavia, East Germany, Turkey, the former Communist countries of Eastern Europe and Russia, as well as thousands of refugees from Asia who had entered Europe through the Eastern countries. The United States in the same period had absorbed over 7.3 million legal immigrants and an estimated 10 million illegal aliens from Central and South America and Asia. Cross border migrations throughout Africa, Central and South America were in the tens of millions.

While people fled North to avoid persecution and hunger, large movements of migrant and contract workers flowed into the oil producing states of the Middle East and the newly industrialized nations of Asia.[6] Of notable importance in these migrations is that among the millions of homeless refugees, statistics in 1993 estimated 75 percent were women, and most of the remaining 25 percent were children.[7]

By the 1990s processing and settling large numbers of refugees was at the root of several dilemmas for the host nations. Their constant influx was jeopardizing social stability. Thirteen European countries plus Canada, Australia, and the United States had to process and financially assist over 900,000 asylum seekers in 1992 alone. Only one third were truly in danger of their lives in their own countries.

Germany, for example, was flooded with 400,000 refugees who had to be kept on assistance for as long as it took to screen them which was generally two to three years. What resulted in this "holding" policy was a backlog of migrants who put their names forward for asylum in several countries, thus enabling them to move from one nation to another until they found a country that would accept them. In this "delaying" process they were living at the expense of one Western nation after another.

Their assimilation into their new homelands was further hindered by their lack of familiarity with the cultures they encountered. Unable to adapt quickly to the laws, languages, environmental practices and social mores of their new homes, they continued, sometimes for years, accepting public money to assist them in training, finding jobs and housing them. The costs of "holding" them still constitutes an enormous drain on national budgets, not withstanding the pressures and costs of public protests and violent destruction that has ensued where local movements against their presence has caused the deaths of many refugees as well as landed immigrants. Violent bombings of immigrant homes in Germany in the early 1990's and the riots in Los Angeles in 1992 were only two among many incidents of public violence against the newcomer that has devastated urban areas of housing and sources of employment.

The moral, humanistic intention behind the postwar "open door" policy which allowed any and every needy refugee to find asylum in the Western nations was a very humane, altruistic approach in assuaging world suffering. But it has proven to be a solution with many repercussions among the host nations. It took less than twenty years before the flood of refugees and illegal aliens became unmanageable. Europe and North America, struggling in the 1990s to emerge from the deepest recession since World War II, experienced a vast increase in unemployed, homeless people. Public opinion turned against refugees as anger and violent protests erupted in the media and on the streets. The sheer volume and diversity of ethnic backgrounds of these migrants was causing an unwanted impact on already shrinking employment opportunities, housing, resources and public funding, while disrupting local cultures and traditional values, all culminating in a renewal of racial animosities and public resentment against the "outsiders".

To prevent widespread public protests and violence against asylum seekers, deportation is now the legal practice in Western nations. Ships and planes of illegal aliens trying to enter European and North American countries are stopped, impounded or sent away, returning the refugees to their homelands. In the summer of 1993, several shiploads of Chinese refugees attempted to land illegally in the United States and were forced to dock in Mexico, take on fresh water and supplies, then return to China with their human cargo.

Where the opening of a nation's borders to refugees was once felt to be a moral right and obligation, many nations have had to pass laws preventing the uncontrollable flood of unscreened immigrants from landing, destroying their documents and claiming refugee status. Article XVI of the German Constitution was removed ending the provision which allowed all refugees to claim asylum in Germany as a compensation for Germany's activities during World War II. France has declared a "zero immigration" goal and eliminated a two hundred year old rule allowing that anyone born in France is automatically a French citizen. Britain will now accept only immigrants with special, desirable skills or immediate family members and Austria has made asylum next to impossible to claim. The United States at time of writing was in the process of returning illegals to their native lands and organizing legislation against the right of any refugee to tear up his/her documents so as to gain sanctuary while the case is processed through the courts.

However, "closed borders" have not stemmed the flow of refugees. Many still enter illegally and remain hidden in the underground economies. The Southern United States is populated with Mexicans and Hispanics who have crossed the Mexican/US border in search of work or have been smuggled in by labour contractors or criminal organizations.

Estimates made in a Geneva study in 1994 revealed smugglers in "human cargoes" around the world are profiting by as much as $9.6 billion a year, twice the income of the Colombia drug cartels. Of the "125 million migrants throughout the world... as many as 15 million of them were transported to their present countries by professional smugglers."[8] Traffickers moved over 4 million migrants from poor to rich countries in just the first four months of 1996. Entire family fortunes are turned over to the smugglers without a guarantee the migrant(s) will arrive safely and find asylum in a new country.

As technologies of communication and transportation become more sophisticated, people are smuggled from one country to another over circuitous routes. Travel by car, small boat or plane, or even by train, offers relatively easy conditions to evade customs. Consequently, catching smuggled refugees is proving increasingly difficult and costly. With the help of fake passports and documents, the "illegals" are quickly hidden within the social enclaves of their own ethnic people. They either remain hidden permanently, finding jobs in the underground economy, living off the charity of their own race, some through extortion or theft, or they go through the legal system to get immigrant status. Others stay only as long as it takes them to move on to another country of preferable choice. A few arrive to carry out terrorist missions as in the bombing of the World Trade Centre in New York or to exchange drugs for money.

Of great concern to political and judicial authorities is the movement into Western nations of illegal immigrants by unscrupulous traffickers who make them pay extortion rates for their transport. If they cannot pay, they are forced to work as indentured "slaves" to ethnic criminal gangs or prostitution rings.

As the powers and criminal activities of these gangs spread nationwide, the large numbers of indentured refugees are proving dangerous to every nation that must deal with them. Their criminal activities are undermining national law and order as well as public safety. The Chinese and Vietnamese gangs in Vancouver and New York, for instance, have become so powerful and wealthy within the Asian communities that attempting to seek out and punish their members for crimes according to Western judicial law is proving fruitless. Gang members hide behind laws which protect their human rights and within ethnic communities who are terrified by the ease with which gang members can get away with torturing and killing informers. Police forces in North America are almost impotent in finding ways to deter the insidious social power of these new "mafias".

Although refugees with forged documents cannot enjoy the many rights and privileges of citizens, life in the underground in a "rich" industrial nation is often better for the majority than the life they have escaped in their homelands. As it is seldom possible to trace the backgrounds of people from poor nations because their governments keep few records and it is even more difficult to gain information from hostile regimes, many refugees receive permission to stay and are eventually swept up in amnesty programs which accept them as landed immigrants.

While 125 million refugees are presently unsettled around the world, in another 30 years, with 10 billion inhabitants trying to cope on diminishing landbases, this number may surpass a billion. Anarchy of the worst kind can only evolve. Eventually the mounting xenophobia of those occupying habitable land areas will choose to kill newcomers. When there is not enough physical space to secure the survival of one's own social gene pool, just as all creatures in nature do, humans will fight the intruder to the death for the possession of "territory".

Ethnic cleansing is not a new phenomenon in the 20th Century. History is riddled with genocide. But the extent of the practice today in so many countries certainly is. Pol Pot of Cambodia had his army put two million Cambodians to death in 1975-1979 on ethnic grounds. Perhaps we are seeing the re-emergence of our most primitive natural instincts. When the physical survival of a social group is threatened by loss of food supply or domination and overcrowding by another social group, the instinctive response is to bring a violent death to the intruder or conquer other lands through warfare and ethnic cleansing.

During the rise of civilizations, humanity generally overcame the limits of nature by growing food crops and redirecting natural aggression into productive work. But if our social space which offers security to ourselves, our families and our ethnicity is threatened by the intrusion of too many outsiders, our instinctive territorial aggression resurfaces. There are few examples anywhere in the world where all races and ethnic groups are living happily together, especially where land bases are overcrowded and one ethnic group has superiority over another. The bulk of this xenophobic anger is now falling largely on those unfortunate refugees who cross our path in their search for freedom from hunger, torture, death and war. They have no immediate preference of destination; they are just escaping to find better conditions in which to survive. Slow to recognize this unfortunate truth, we confound the problem even more by refusing to admit that the return of racism and xenophobia is the result of shrinking social space, overpopulation and excessive consumption of diminishing resources.

With increasing numbers of persecuted ethnic groups forced to escape the threat of "ethnic cleansing", their plight has been difficult for the West to ignore. Western humanitarianism still moves us to protect those facing civil wars fought for the purpose of "ethnic cleansing": Kurds in Iraq, Muslims in Bosnia, Mayans in Guatemala. Their numbers now swamp immigration offices as bureaucracies fail to cope with the backlog of asylum seekers. As "holding" periods grow longer, more and more unscreened immigrants disappear into Western societies. Will the rich nations be able to stop the flow of hungry refugees?

Using the Roman Empire as a paradigm of possible future events, the most obvious parallel is that of the inability of the Romans to hold back the "barbarians". Roman society by the 5th Century had grown moribund. Government changed property law to give inheritance rights to the government over family rights. This plus the excessive drain of taxes robbed the rich of their wealth and destroyed both their desire to invest in trade and commerce or have children. Roman civilization began to collapse. The barbarians who had been welcomed initially for their labor and military manpower were beginning to outnumber the Romans. As the Romans declined in number and in health, the barbarians moved into the periphery of society, waiting to overrun the remnants of Roman Civilization, which they did in 476 A.D.

Many similarities exist between a declining Western civilization and the final century of the Roman Empire. Just as the Romans declined in numbers and military supremacy throughout the Mediterranean, so has the white race and its dominance over Western Civilization. Paralleling the massive movements of the barbarians into the lands of the Roman Empire and Rome itself in search of a better life, the refugees of the modern world are entering the West in growing numbers. Rome fell under its excessive weight of national debts, tax burdens, declining production and trade, a shortage of resources (especially forests), failing military strength and a corrupt, inept governing elite who cared only for their own self-indulgence. The similarities today in the Western nations are frighteningly obvious. The West is in danger of disappearing beneath the "barbarian" onslaughts of refugees from Asia, Africa and Latin America whose numbers in Western countries will outnumber the white races within the next 20 years. It is estimated that by 2010, the non-white races of North America will comprise more than 50 to 60 percent of the population.

The worldwide population explosion which continues to reduce the living space of both the individual and the social group and reduce the chances of survival of the bulk of humanity is not a phenomenon that can be solved simply by growing more food. What is of key importance in assuring a liveable future is preventing an identity crises based on the right to belong to a landbase which permits the individual to seek employment, build a sense of self-worth and contribute to the community in which he resides. These have become rare circumstances for large groups of itinerant refugees. The loss of an identity related to a land base tears at every person who must suffer oppression at the hands of an ethnic majority, flee from destroyed environments or escape death from the weapons of war.

Technologies of agriculture, transportation, resource exploitation, manufactured commodities and life saving medical treatments have given the bulk of humanity the power to reproduce themselves to an non-viable state. Living for most is becoming a state of sufferance, neither productive nor natural. Vast numbers of unemployed young and old endure a sense of low self-esteem and having little purpose in their lives. Seeking some reprieve, they turn to the many available forms of transportation which moves them to new locations, new countries.

Unfortunately, their migrations in the 20th Century are threatening the social stability of the entire world and place an excessive strain on the rich nations which have become their prime destination. In the near future they will overcrowd all landbases
and, in turn, weaken the nations they flood by overwhelming the viability of their new homelands. Coping with their numbers is already sapping the wealth of the rich nations and dissipating the energies of invention, initiative and cultural progress.

Through much of history migrations were instrumental in building societies, adding new blood, spreading new ideas and introducing new commodities. The space and the opportunities were there. Today they are not. Modern migrations, especially of those who are illegal immigrants, bring unmanageable problems of overcrowding, mixing of hostile cultures, promoting religious and racial xenophobia and accumulating unaffordable national costs to process, assist and assimilate unwanted numbers of people.

Most nations are already occupied beyond their sustainable carrying capacity. The overwhelming presence of migrating economic and environmental refugees in the future can only be instrumental in lowering living standards in all nations and causing a ruinous decline in production and infra-structures.

Refugees now exist on every continent. They are the dispossessed beings of environmental collapse, poverty, and civil war. Their numbers represent most nations: Vietnam, China, Ethiopia, Iraq, Mozambique, Somalia, the former USSR, Cambodia, the oppressed and persecuted of Central and South America, the economic refugees of Mexico, Eastern Europe, Africa and Asia, the displaced ethnic and religious sects of Yugoslavia and the Middle East, the victims of flooding and cyclones in Bangladesh, the homeless of earthquakes and civil war in Armenia, the chemically poisoned of Bhopol, the radiation victims of Chernobyl and the millions of people, freed and impoverished by the collapse of the Communist world.

One of the many stories depicting the desperation of these refugees were the ongoing attempts in the 1970s and 1980s of thousands of Vietnamese to escape poverty and political oppression in search of finding new homes in the rich nations of the world. Most attempted their escape under life threatening circumstances in boats that were not seaworthy over seas that were ruled by pirates. On arrival at destinations such as Hong Kong, those who survived drowning, hunger, thirst and pirate boardings, were immediately imprisoned in overcrowded, violent refugee camps from which few were to escape to new homelands. Most have since been returned to Vietnam. They had failed to penetrate the societies where they believed they would have a better chance at life. A token-few were accepted by the United States and Europe, but even these societies are no longer able to absorb, employ, house or offer welfare to millions of destitute, unskilled and unhealthy refugees. It might be said, "The world is full. Sorry, no more room at the Inn."

Throughout our historical past, faced with a depleted environment, people simply moved on to neighbouring lands or sent out vanguards of colonists to explore and settle virgin territories from which they returned with food supplies and other products to the "homeland". Both the old and the new centres of civilization were able to prosper once again. But today and in the future, this choice is gone. Virgin lands and unexploited resources of forests, soils and ecological systems are negligible prospects; almost all have come under human "management". Few wilderness areas are left untouched by humans, of which most are not conducive to human habitation or use.

Millions of people continue to be forced from their territorial lands by drought, floods and wars. Millions more continue to join the 125 million refugees that now wander the earth. Civil wars plague the peoples of the Third World and of the former Eastern European Communist states, --Afghanistan, Yugoslavia, South Africa, Somalia, Mozambique, Sri Lanka, and Haiti,-- to name only a few. Yearly, large numbers of refugees and civilians die in ethnic wars from malnutrition, disease, wounds, starvation and hopelessness. Hunger persists in India, Bangladesh, the Philippines, Malaysia, Africa, Brazil, Mexico, Latin America and even the United States where large urban areas of extreme poverty exist, often referred to as Third World nations within a nation.

Mass migrations of refugees and international aid programs have had far reaching effects on the economies and social structures of nearly every nation. These alone cannot solve the problems of several billion people whose existence and needs depend on a rapidly deteriorating environment, which, in turn, cannot be saved because of the stress the human population places on it. Dilemmas of existence are multiplied by the ignorance and general apathy of the majority who are absorbed in their own stressful struggle to survive. People generally follow the habit ingrained over the millennia of migrating in search of solutions rather than staying and working them out at home. Unfortunately, solutions are expensive, limited in success and thwarted by aggressive, corrupt leadership and exploding populations.

A photograph in several magazines and newspapers in August of 1991,[9] showed thousands of young men attempting to flee the poverty and harsh existence of life in Albania by trying to enter Italy illegally. It was a startling, if not frightening, look into the future. A freighter, every inch of its decks crammed with refugees who had left their country with nothing but the clothes they wore, approached a pier that was equally crammed with thousands of refugees. Below them dozens of men swam towards the pier in desperation to reach the Italian shore. I was reminded of pictures I had seen of lemmings rushing headlong to their deaths in their desperate search for food and living space. All sense of human worth, individuality and dignity were lost in that photograph. I felt as though I were looking into the future when every inch of living space will be occupied by human bodies, forming a solid, undulating mass poised as if on a precipice, ready to be dropped into the ocean's depths, some already thrown into the sea, suggesting there was no other direction for them to go except to their deaths.

Some would argue that the Third World still holds much untouched land and many unused resources; that these nations must be opened up to migrant peoples to develop agriculture and industrialization. They must be allowed to improve their living standards, because only if they can overcome unemployment will they decrease their populations. Where such attempts have been made in the Third World to introduce technologies and industrial projects, open up vast forest areas to farming and give access to untapped resources, populations have generally exploded, the lands degraded and the eco-systems left permanently damaged (Amazon Basin, Sahel, Northern India) Those who believe that higher living standards can be "imposed" on Third World nations fail to recognize the influence environmental limitations and indigenous life styles have on many Third World peoples. In vast continental areas of the Southern Hemisphere, modern technologies and industrialization have eliminated the wise use of the land which primitive methods had successfully evolved, while interfering with tribal methods of population control.

What this trend means is that even well-organized, industrial nations among the developed countries are reaching a point of being overpopulated. Western nations are discovering they cannot sustain large numbers of refugee immigrants at a healthy, productive standard, free from the welfare rolls. Their infra-structures, job markets and welfare systems cannot assimilate the hundreds of thousands of immigrants and refugees fast enough to cope with their needs.

Forced into hiding to endure an existence in large enclaves of poor, malnourished, uneducated, non-working people, they unwittingly repeat many of the social practices of their native lands such as having large, unsupportable families that contribute to the problems of overcrowded cities, further environmental destruction and pollution, and add to the social decay and growing violence of the Western cities. For example, since the collapse of the Communist bloc in Eastern Europe, the Gypsies of Rumania have moved en mass into Germany where their life styles of begging, stealing and adhering to clannish behaviours are at odds with German social behaviours. Germans saw their "open door" policy to refugees as the cause of growing social unrest and violent protests among the working people who demand the "doors" be closed. Weeks of bombings, beatings and angry protests often shattered the safety and peace of Germany, as right wing protestors took violent actions against non-German immigrants and refugees in the early 1990s.

The cost of absorbing refugees is becoming a crushing financial burden on the Western nations whose national debts are exacerbated by the influx of hundreds of thousands of immigrants and refugees, the bulk of whom must be kept on welfare. The Western nations are plagued with thousands of illegal refugees, living in hiding on the outskirts of society and reducing the standard of living of the cities that must accommodate them in overcrowded housing, medical plans, schools, poverty conditions and in illegal, low paying jobs. Their increasing presence is also reducing the general sense of security of most democratic nations. The race riots of the 90's in Germany, England, France and the United States were manifestations of this growing xenophobia.

Return of More Virulent Epidemics

While technology has aided and abetted our overcrowding of this planet, it has also structured environmental conditions favourable to the return of more virulent epidemics and bacterial infections as well as setting free a variety of lethal viruses. Although these "predators" of our bodies may be invisible to the eye, they are powerful and implacable enemies which have the potential to kill billions of people in the next 50 years if remedies are not found. Vaccines for most viruses remain elusive to scientists and most infectious bacteria have developed immunity to antibiotics.

Attempts to control and eradicate strains of bacterial infections through pesticides, medications and antibiotics has worked for a short period of time, but failed to eradicate the diseases. Instead the bacteria have built an immunity to the drugs and returned more deadly than ever. Malaria is an example. The parasite which spreads it has developed immunity to DDT and quinine medicines. The human dilemma is that before chemical technologies were used to control malarial infections, many died of the disease, but many more survived because they had developed a natural immunity to the disease. The new bacteria, now immune to chemical cures as well as human anti-bodies, are much stronger and capable of producing much higher death rates than in the past.

Various deadly infectious diseases, --tuberculosis, cholera, hepatitis, streptococcus pneumoniae, bacterial meningitis, gonorrhoea,-- have all produced more lethal mutations that are proving resistant to known antibiotics.

Cholera, an historical pandemic, thrives on the lack of employment, housing, medicines and nutrition among those who must live in slums. It strikes where the simplest practices of washing food and hands with clean water and soap cannot be followed. It thrives in the polluted waters the poor and homeless drink. It has been found in the fish caught in polluted waters, running with sewage and human excrement. It grows in the food sold by the street vendors who stand all day in the hot sun. Only those who have access to water purification systems and proper sewage disposal can protect themselves against it.

South American countries, whose populations are growing faster than their economies and environments can assimilate them, have been battling a cholera epidemic that began in January of 1991. It originated in Peru where over 300,000 cases were reported by February of 1992 and more than 2000 deaths. At the same time the epidemic spread to other nations, among them Brazil whose over-crowded cities of vulnerable poor could not prevent its spread.[10] Over 3000 deaths were reported throughout South America from the disease. Cholera now turns up frequently throughout Latin America and has even reached as far north as the barios of New Mexico.

While bacterial infections are the pandemics of overcrowding, poverty, migration, ignorance, drugs, prostitution and slum conditions, most highly lethal viruses have remained undisturbed until recent human occupation and technologies upset wilderness eco-systems and set the viruses free. Humans, having developed little if any immunity to these unknown viruses over the millennia, are proving a very successful medium for their spread. The most lethal viruses are emerging in Africa and South America where deforestation, heavy use of agricultural pesticides, climatic changes and human settlement are occurring at an unprecedented rate. Some viruses are even activated by the increase in ultraviolet light.[11] Among the most deadliest are the philoviruses which include AIDS and Ebola which recently emerged from degraded tropical forests in East Africa. "In a sense the Earth is mounting an immune response against the human species"[12]

"Viruses are little more than bundles of genes of DNA or RNA, the molecules that carry the blueprints for all life." They are not "composed of cells...(only) floating bits of material which move into body cells where they manufacture themselves."[13] Although viruses cannot reproduce without a "host", they make new viruses by "commandeering the reproductive machinery of cells they invade". They gain entry by "precisely fitting their molecules on their surfaces to those on the membranes of targeted cells."[14] Viruses once inside a cell begin to replicate themselves and bloat the cell which eventually erupts, releasing the virus to attack other cells. If the immune system fails to recognize the virus in time to fight it, it spreads rapidly and the host becomes sick.

Viruses spread through the transfer of blood, urine, even through the air in several cases. By slightly altering their shape, they can fool our defense cells and any vaccines used to prevent their spread. Some of the deadly varieties such as Lassa fever kill their victims swiftly. Their "entanglement with host cells makes viruses very hard to kill without murdering the host as well."[15] Furthermore, vaccines, if they exist, are able to control only one form of the virus. This explains why each of the annual flus which spread around the world must have its own vaccine.

Demonstrating the impact that technological invasion of natural habitat can have on isolated environments is the bout with the philovirus, Ebola, in Zaire in 1995. Transmitted through the air in coughs or sneezes, it is spread by any form of contact with an infected human being. Hospitalization of the very ill can prove fatal as many Africans have found. The plague was contained in the past by removing the infected from the technological world of the hospital and returning them to the isolation of their homes to wait out the course of the disease. Primitive practices necessitated that the bodies of those who died were burned along with all their household belongings. Those who emerged alive and well from quarantine had their lives, but all their property was burned. In this way the disease was contained in the past.

The source of the Ebola disease has not yet been isolated, but the epidemics seemed to originate with the monkeys of Zaire whose numbers are rapidly diminishing because of the ferocity of the disease. Transporting monkeys from Zaire for laboratory use to the United States in 1989 could have caused a world outbreak capable of threatening all of mankind. The American experience was contained only by the vigilance of one scientist working on a group of infected monkeys.[16]

Diseases are nature's way of restoring ecological balance when a prolific species gets out of control. For example, viruses decimated the millions of rabbits and mice which exploded in their numbers upon importation to Australia, a continent where food was plentiful and they had no natural predators. Similar threats are now facing humanity with newly emerging viruses - AIDS, Hepatitis B, the annual flu forms, Ebola, Lassa Fever, and several viruses produced in the faeces of rodents. Each has the capacity to decimate populations on overcrowded land bases. Dr. Joshua Lederberg, a winner of the Nobel Prize, has warned us,"

We live in evolutionary competition with microbes. There is no guarantee that we will be the survivors."[17]

No less threatening are the many diseases and infections caused by industrial and agricultural poisoning. Working and living near industrial plants, drinking water from polluted rivers and lakes, breathing in toxic smogs and eating poisoned foods are proving as deadly as any virus. Pesticides and plastics are now suspect as major causes of reducing human intelligence and aiding the emergence of violent behaviors. Chemicals such as dioxins, PCBs and pesticides, already in the environment, are showing up as contributors to brain disorders, seizures, learning problems and brain tumors. These chemicals interfere with thyroid hormones which are critical in brain development. Changes in the human brain forebodes dangerous changes in human society itself.

Cancers, the loss of immunity to respiratory and organ diseases, underdeveloped lungs in children, infertility in men as sperm counts drop, general malaise, radiation poisoning, anaemia, asthma and toxic syndromes are taking more and more lives, especially in poor areas where the populations must live near their industrial jobs. Genetic inheritance is now in the balance as our industrial chemicals change or destroy the DNA of our genes.

Anarchy, Civil Wars and Environments

Economic deprivation, generally accompanied by political repression and social chaos, is symptomatic of degraded landscapes, weak economies, endemic poverty and environmental refugees. Under these circumstances any size of human numbers is overpopulated. This can be seen in the tribal/ethnic wars around the world being fought to establish claim to the habitable lands and resources both within national boundaries and in neighbouring countries.

The more difficult survival becomes, the more fierce are the tribal wars. They spread their terror and suffering as they spill over borders. The war in Rwanda in 1994 exemplified the problem. Hundreds of thousands of tribal refugees flowed over the borders into Zaire and Burundi. Enroute, tens of thousands were slaughtered or died from cholera and other diseases. In civil wars, hostilities and hatreds between tribes intensify. Having to share the same land base in peace, they do not let go of their hatreds, building xenophobic fears which remain for years. As former nations break down into warring tribal enclaves, implementing a safe, peaceful resettlement of refugees or re-establishing a workable government is proving difficult and costly for the United Nations.

With populations exploding and poverty and social inequality spreading, civil wars and ethnic cleansing have become the chosen course to gain tribal power in many poor or ethnically divided countries. The United Nations' failure to stop so many of these wars and impose a political peace has raised universal scepticism that leading military powers cannot contain civil wars. The list of failures is growing: Russia's failure in Afghanistan, more than four years needed to bring peace to Yugoslavia, UN incompetence in preventing the death of millions from starvation and ethnic cleansing in Africa and the refusal of the United States to go to the aid of the Timorese who were invaded and decimated by the Indonesian armies. In the latter case, the U.S. preferred to honor its economic agreements with Indonesia rather than prevent the mass killing of over 100,000 Timorese, wiping out more than a third of their entire population.

Unable to bring an end to wars as envisaged by the United Nations' charter, the latest policy is to let tribes fight among themselves until they run out of soldiers or weapons, which ever comes first. When the flow of modern weapons and technologies cannot reach the fighting partners, wars generally come to an end. However, this solution is now hindered by the technological capacity of black marketeers and criminal organizations to move weapons and supplies around the world undetected in exchange for drugs and drug money.

In response, international financial and military support for civil wars is dwindling. Future civil wars are unlikely to receive little more than food aid distributed by non-governmental organizations, and little of that, if the carriers of food supplies continue to be killed by those they are trying to help. In 1995 UN troops in Yugoslavia began losing so many of their trucks, weapons and soldiers to Serb guerilla attacks that they themselves became embroiled in defensive actions.

But what is the price of non-interference? Ethnic/tribal wars are pulling many nations into their web of anarchy. Modern wars destroy social and political structures which opens the way to gangsterism and rule by warlords who thrive on crime and the sale of arms. This is not a situation the international community can ignore. Excessively powerful explosive, chemical, biological and nuclear weaponry are falling into the hands of the warlords, creating a universal dilemma of unimaginable proportions. Should they choose to use them to blackmail the rich nations into meeting their demands, the way to the future is dangerous and strewn with political chaos and lawlessness that threatens all of humanity.

As governments and nations fail to meet the threats of our highly technological future, repression, economic chaos and rapid social decline will quickly follow. In periods of economic decay and social anarchy, the dilemma between employment and environmental conservation is highly exacerbated. More critically any solutions aimed at reducing the pressures between human existence and the declining carrying capacity of the earth are delayed or unlikely to be enforced.

The course and ferocity of wars has always been determined by the destructive powers of the technologies employed. At the same time large numbers of lives are lost in battle, most human structures of civilization are destroyed. Whole cities are bombed into rubble as happened in Chechnya and Yugoslavia. It has torn apart most countries in Africa. Nearly a hundred civil conflicts are in progress around the world at this time of writing of which 30 have been major wars. Tens of thousands are killed annually in violent power struggles.

Social disorder has become the bane of national governments and a drain on United Nations' finances. The UN budget for peace keeping rose from $300 million in 1988 to $3.6 billion in 1993. Arms comprise the largest trade in any commodities in the entire world. At least the natural environment and the human environments would stand a better chance of remaining in tact if modern weapons of destruction were withheld. But the power to stop the illegal trade in arms is as illusive as trying to stop the drug trade. Too much money flows through too many hands when arming soldiers and civilians for civil wars. Human greed tends to win every time.

One has to wonder about the state of mind of those living under civil war conditions and daily violence. The stress and trauma experienced by soldiers in wartime and recorded for the public after the many wars of the 20th Century suggests they are undergoing madness, uncontrollable fears, nightmares and psychological dementia. If this is true, in what state must all the orphaned children of civil and racial wars in Africa be? What of the impact on the millions who live through wars and guerilla attacks in Asia, Africa, and South America ? What is the state of sanity in children forced to take up arms at the age of ten, or of those children who have had to stand by and watch their parents hacked to pieces in Rwanda? What trauma pursues those who are sold into slave labour and prostitution? The world is becoming rampant with madness and fear, with diseases caused from overcrowding and psychological stress.

Hundreds of millions have and will undergo the horrors of ethnic cleansing and racial wars over the next century. Will our bestial aggression resurface and our civilized veneer disappear entirely? Will we, in our horrendous numbers and with our xenophobic mentality, return to basic violent aggression against all outsiders?

Preserving or regenerating the physical environment of many of the embattled nations will require billions of dollars so that humans can return to work the land once again. In many cases the damage has become permanent and beyond human ability to regenerate it. Added to the costs of rehabilitating the land is the rebuilding of industries and re-establishing employment for millions of unskilled, poverty stricken people who must live on these lands. The costs are so prohibitive in consumption of materials and resources that the amount of technology and money needed to clean up the accompanying pollution is unlikely to be available for many years to come.

PART FOUR

Increasing Consumption Is Threatening Environmental Collapse And Extinction Of Species

Increasing Consumption
Is Threatening Environmental Collapse
And Extinction of Species

When humans first settled the land to grow their own food crops and domesticate animals, they did so because the natural food resources of the hunter-gatherer were fast disappearing, the result of overhunting, the end of the Ice Age, the spread of deserts and the growth of human populations. Today we are running a parallel course of declining food production, disappearing ecological species, extremes of climate and exploding populations. Just as the early hunters with their improved weapons killed off the wild herds of Europe and Asia, the fishermen of the 20th Century have all but destroyed the ocean fisheries with their purse seines, drag nets, sonar tracking devices and large factory ships.

Domesticating crops and animals saved the Neolithic farmer, but what will save those living in the 21st Century? Human settlement over the millennia has consumed nature's gifts at spiralling rates. Overpopulation, industrialization, resource extraction and human consumption are destroying those very features of the planet which made continued survival possible for the hunter-gatherer and the first farmers of ancient times.

The human species evolved under relatively consistent environmental conditions much as they are today. Once we radically alter these elements, survival may be impossible. Just one example is global warming. It is believed that if the average global temperatures rise as little as 3 degrees Celsius, weather conditions will change sufficiently to threaten food and water production. Some scientists estimate that a 3 degree rise in temperature would reduce most of the presently farmed marginal lands to deserts. It would be sufficient to melt the ice caps enough to raise the oceans as much as three meters, inundating all low level coastal regions where over a third of the earth's populations now live and from which they would have to be evacuated and relocated. A three degree rise would produce rainfall at the wrong time of the growing seasons and a temperature increase would intensify wind storms, drought, cloud-cover and flooding. Higher temperatures now felt in the subtropics will be experienced well into present temperate zones.

As we alter the planet's biosphere, all the interdependent parts of the environment, --climates, vegetation, life forms and soils,-- will either change their present functions dramatically or stop working as a habitable eco-system. In the event of either occurrence, present environmental conditions will change radically enough to threaten the existence of present life forms, including Homo sapiens.

The environment will collapse in that it will no longer provide for human physical needs: moderate temperatures, seasonal rainfall, sufficient days of sunshine at the most beneficial time of the growing seasons, moderate weather patterns and limited flooding and windstorms, adequate growing seasons for local crops, arable productive lands, sufficient ground and surface supplies of fresh water, edible food crops in adequate quantities, a balanced system of oxygen and greenhouse gases and a healthy eco-system of millions of plant and life forms.

There are those who choose to believe severe climate changes will not occur, except by natural forces beyond our control. They continue to conclude that human impact on the entire biosphere can only be minimal; that humanity's food and water needs can be met by genetic engineering and massive desalinization of sea water. These are the same people who would have us believe we will always be able to increase production of goods to correspond with population numbers. They loudly declare: Didn't the Agricultural Revolution of the 18th Century prove we could support millions more on this planet? Yet over 15 millions die annually from famine, over one billion people are chronically hungry world wide, and at least another two billion suffer the many ramifications of varying degrees of malnutrition. What will these statistics look like in 40 or 50 years when populations have doubled and the environment is correspondingly diminished?

Each collapsing environmental area places a limitation on human survival. Dehumanizing conditions become visible.

Desertification, erosion of farmlands, deforested hills and valleys, water shortages, all mean little or no human carrying capacity. When populations of any size overcrowd such areas, they come to depend on foreign aid to sustain them or they are forced to migrate. Those who stay behind may starve or become embroiled in tribal wars over the few remaining resources.

Our future is filled with the probabilities of several dilemmas: If we stop industrial and agricultural expansion to conserve the remaining environment for future use, then we must limit our present day employment opportunities, reduce our standard of living and force billions to live in even greater poverty than they do now, all of which would lead to a more violent, unstable world than it already is. But if we do not stop our present industrial and agricultural expansion, we hasten our extinction as we will soon be living on a planet whose deteriorating climates and disappearing eco-systems begin to kill, not nurture us.

CHAPTER ELEVEN

The Evolution and Extinction of Species

To believe we can exist totally outside nature and actually control eco-systems to suit human needs alone is foolhardy in the extreme. We may have learned to help nature increase our food production and extend our lives, but we must never make the mistake of believing we can take control of the natural processes governing life and death, nor that we can exist in a world devoid of other species. We are, however, proving we can destroy them enmass. Therefore, it is wishful thinking to believe we can forge a distant future for unlimited human populations surviving on genetically engineered foods, managed forests, protected endangered species, farmed fish stocks and artificially produced fresh water.

We can consume and destroy the bounties of nature, but we cannot create them. Once they become extinct, they are lost to us. Genetic engineering may be able to transfer genes and produce species more adapted to slight changes in the environment, such as drought or salinity, but the basic species from which the hybrid is derived is a product of natural evolution.

The insurmountable factor against human management of species is that natural evolution is very slow and random in its production of species. Furthermore, their successful survival is tied to environmental conditions to which they have adapted over thousands of years, if not millions. Just how crucial a factor environmental adaptation is has come to the fore in recent years as the ozone thins and excessive amounts of ultra violet B rays reach the earth, threatening all forms of flora and fauna. A few species may be able to mutate and actually flourish on ultra violet rays, but the proportion of these species is infinitesimal compared with the number which will perish.

Science has shown that if any species survives a markedly changed environment, it will have reproduced itself in a mutated form capable of digesting mutated "food" species. This disposes of the possibility that humanity could engineer foods which would allow Homo sapiens to survive on this planet if the majority of presently available plant and life forms which we can metabolize should die out. Several question arise: Can the human species adapt, evolve or mutate successfully to eat and metabolize the newly mutated animal and vegetation species while physically withstanding the radically changed environmental conditions? If we could, would the time left to us be too short for our mutations to adapt before the earth is no longer habitable for our species as we now exist? What would be the parameters and chances of Homo sapiens evolving as an "adapted" species?

Recent discoveries in British Columbia, Canada, have found that 250 million years ago most life on earth vanished abruptly, probably caused by a colliding asteroid. But "geological evidence suggests it took 50,000 to 100,000 years for the planet's biological productivity level to recover to pre-catastrophe levels".[1] It is this excessively long period of recuperation that humanity should be calculating into its cavalier devastation of the natural environment and our false convictions that nature can be repaired easily if only we put the money and technologies into the task. We have neither the time nor the means left to us to trust to such solutions. But we have the technological power and human numbers to cause a "mass extinction".

Evolution and adaptation of species are a mix of several forces: mutation, gene flow, natural selection and genetic drift.[2] In order to become established as a species, a mutation must come into existence in an environment that encourages its survival and supports its reproduction at a controlled rate which allows for the development of a genetic tradition.[3] Natural selection then adapts the new species to its environment as it takes the mutation from the chemical level to the biological level of adaptation.[4] It is at this point the mutation must develop into a strong, reproductive species of which the newly evolved group must then have time to develop a gene pool which produces superior members, adapted to the conditions of the environment and able to cope with the forces of survival. The success of a mutant species depends on whether or not it can parent the next generation as many things produce barriers to that success. Evolution has produced millions and millions of species, few of which exist today as a result of mutant failures or of the inability to adapt to the environment which it has entered. Once established, a gene pool composes an ecological unit that occupies a definite area to which the members are tolerant and all make the same demands on the environment. The numbers within such groups vary from a few members to millions, occupying small areas to hundreds of square miles.[5]

As a gene pool becomes firmly established within a given territory, its continued development and population expansion depends on its access to consistent, sustainable, uncontaminated supplies of food and fresh water. The regeneration of an ever present food supply, in turn, depends on a limited, sustainable population of species members. If either gets out of control, that is, if food supply is diminished or lost, or the competition for it is too great, then the species usually dies out.[6]

Homo sapiens evolved through this evolutionary process as did all other species. The arrival of Australopithecus, the first of the hominids which evolved into "Homo sapiens", was that of a new species suited to a given set of climatic conditions in that they were endowed with adaptive abilities that were mainly mutational.[7] Human survival was guaranteed by the competitive physical advantages which included the ability to walk upright on two feet, freeing the hands for other uses, and a large brain which continued to increase several sizes through a number of mutational changes over more than 5 million years.

The intelligence our ancestors were given was an "adaptively valuable trait...undoubtedly favoured by natural selection,"[8] which provided the evolutionary forces that made "Homo erectus" the ancestor of Homo sapiens, considerably more intelligent than our first ancestor, Australopithecus. In turn, Homo sapiens was much more advanced than Homo erectus. The advantages of increased brain size and intellectual capacity were so great that the emergence of Homo erectus led to the extinction of Australopithecus, just as the arrival of Homo sapiens led to the disappearance of Homo erectus, but in a much shorter time frame.[9] Our physical attributes and evolving intelligence established our hominid ancestors as a dominant predator species, ensuring their survival and their place at the top of the animal chain.

The important point to be made here is that Homo sapiens as a mutational species fulfilled all the criteria of a successful adaptation. But under impending climatic and ecological changes in the future, could we do it again in the short time we may have left to us? It is well documented that mutational adaptations do not occur overnight. In fact, it took Homo sapiens nearly five million years to evolve, adapt to our present physical form and the environment, then reach the degree of civilization and technological sophistication humankind has achieved since the Neolithic Agricultural Revolution. Furthermore, if the failure rate of mutations which survive runs into the millions, the odds are very large against the emergence of another human mutation similar to ourselves that would be able to adapt to the dramatic changes in climate and vegetation our present activities are forcing on the environment. As Hoimar and Ditfurth point out "...drastic changes will not accelerate genetic adaptation any faster.[10]

Closely related to the survival of a species is its reproductive propensity. Biologists tell us that all species reproduce their numbers to a maximum, wherein loss of breeding territory, starvation, predation or disease will then reduce their populations and their reproductive capabilities to a viable number that can survive within territorial carrying capacity. When food is overly abundant, species multiply; when food is scarce, their numbers are decimated, sometimes to the point of extinction.

Homo sapiens, although capable of improving the environmental conditions which sustain life, are ultimately prone to the same natural dictates as all other creatures. Increases in food supply and general health of the populace have been responsible for marked increases in human birth rates at various times in human history just as famines and epidemics have decimated large populations. As previously mentioned, women during the time of the hunter-gatherers generally had one child every four years; the early farmers increased this to one every two years and the women of the Industrial Revolution averaged a pregnancy annually. In the past, infant mortality rates were exceptionally high by comparison with modern survival rates. This meant reproduction rates and population increases remained relatively low in proportion to the number of conceptions. With modern technologies of food production and distribution as well as medical care, natural attrition rates have been widely decreased allowing survival rates to exceed death rates by a much greater margin than at any other time in history.

Humanity like any other species must compete for food supply. The smaller, weaker, slower creatures always lose out to the stronger, more dominant species in a competition for food. The same struggle faces large numbers of people who must survive on smaller and smaller farms or low yields of poor quality crops as they crowd increasingly degraded farm lands, while much of the remaining rich arable land is owned by the few or disappearing beneath urban development. This inequity of land and food distribution annually adds more nations to the list of those who have come to depend on imported food supplies. All species must cope with the critical limits of their immediate environment; for humans it is the diminishing carrying capacity of the planet.

With all other species, conservation, not extinction of prey species is innate. Survival of one species depends on a healthy reproduction of new generations of prey. All animals and birds are programmed to leave enough prey to regenerate future food supplies. Without this instinctual control on their appetites, they would have eaten themselves into extinction long ago. A clear warning to fishermen and loggers who refuse to practice what the simplest creature in nature does unwittingly.

Unfortunately, humanity seems to have lost its sense of species' preservation when we changed from being creatures of nature to a species of self-determination. The more civilized we become, the less motivation we have to preserve other species, especially if they are of any commercial value or occupy space we want for ourselves. Our rationale is that we can always replace one disappearing food source with another. Our hubris leads us to believe those species we do not eat are unnecessary to our well being and can be sacrificed. Such attitudes have left us with little sense of conservation or regeneration of eco-systems. Their destruction is merely an inconvenience to us.

In nature most extinctions tend to be die-offs of single species from everyday causes in localized circumstances: a failure to adapt to environmental changes in climate or vegetation, a loss of digestible foods, a die-off of prey, competition for available food supply, loss of habitat, excessive predation or virulent disease. Many millions of species have emerged and then disappeared from a variety of these causes.

Prolonged changes in annual temperatures and weather patterns are sufficient to eliminate existing vegetation and life forms. Constant cold temperatures will retard growth just as desert conditions will cause most plants to die off, eliminating the bulk if not all of the indigenous life forms that depend on the vegetation either directly or indirectly.

Obviously then, the greatest threat to humans, who are, after all, an animal species subject to natural laws, will be the dramatic changes in climate and vegetation resulting from our expanding interference with the natural workings of the planet's biosphere. Marked climatic and vegetation changes will mean widespread losses of digestible foods. In the very near future we may have reached that stage in our occupation of this planet that we cannot grow food crops which our digestive systems can assimilate.

Our rapid degradation of the biosphere through pollution and desertification has accelerated the number of species' extinctions in the last 100 years on a scale that equals past extinctions over thousands, even millions of years. Today one species is lost every 25 minutes compared with one species lost every 2000 years in the past. A mass extinction similar to those of distant geological times may already be in progress.

Continued evolutionary existence for the human species demands that we learn to live in harmony with nature. Unfortunately, from the nomadic hunter-gatherer's relentless destruction of grazing herds to the recent genetic engineering of food plants, species Homo sapiens has been so all-consuming, so oriented to exploitation of environmental resources that any harmony with nature has been increasingly lost over the millennia since the last Ice Age and magnified a thousand fold with each century. Our extinction as a species now rests on the speed at which we bring about environmental collapse.

CHAPTER TWELVE

Climate Changes and Their Impact on Environmental Carrying Capacity

Scientists of the 20th Century recognize that nature is a complex ecological system which is self-regulating and very interdependent, a system presently endangered by human activities and technologies threatening the natural balance and functions of the many components which produce global weather and climate patterns.

In 1979 James Lovelock, a British scientist, theorized that climates, vegetation and all life forms are vital players in a "complex entity involving the earth's biosphere, atmosphere, oceans and soils."[1] According to his hypothesis, it is "life itself," that "has evolved the capability to regulate the exchange of heat between Earth's surface and outer space," creating and maintaining the optimal conditions which sustain living organisms on our planet.

Climate is the first major component of this self-regulating system. It determines the existence and distribution of all vegetation and life forms over the face of the earth. Climatic weather patterns bring the seasonal rains, warm temperatures, sunshine and growing periods required by vegetation to germinate, develop and mature. All life forms on land, from the smallest microbe to the largest animal, directly or indirectly depend on vegetation for their food and oxygen supplies, on rainfall for their moisture and fresh water, and on sunshine for their well being. Destroy the bulk of the earth's vegetation through deforestation, desertification, excessive ultra violet-B rays and induced extremes of cold and warm temperatures, then climates become lethal to human existence.

This complex system which Lovelock named Gaia began to establish itself on earth over three and one-half billion years ago. Meteors in great numbers bombarded the planet during the earth's early formation period. The high temperatures which resulted turned the rocks into boiling magma, releasing the water vapour stored within them. As the moisture escaped, it rose to form a thick blanket of clouds, eventually cooling the earth's surface by blocking out the sun. When the cooling was sufficient, the moisture fell as rain, filling the oceans. The beginnings of the hydrological cycle were in place and conditions set for the first forms of life to emerge.

The atmosphere at the time life began contained an estimated 2000 times more carbon dioxide than it does today. Lovelock believes that carbon dioxide formed a thick blanket over the planet that "let light through but retained the shorter-waved, less energetic heat radiation."[2] This phenomenon kept the earth's surface heated to an average year-round temperature of 23 degrees Celsius (75 degrees F) which with the massive presence of carbon dioxide helped bring about the advent of microscopic blue-green algae in the oceans. These earliest forms of life originated the process of photosynthesis to manufacture their food. In the process they gave off oxygen which over millions of years enabled other life forms to evolve.

As life expanded under these temperate conditions, the carbon dioxide in the atmosphere was reduced to less than 1 percent of the atmospheric composition (78% nitrogen, 21% oxygen and 1% carbon dioxide, gases and vapours) mainly through absorption by the oceans. Billions of microscopic organisms and new forms of marine life used it to manufacture their skeletons and shells. As they died off, their skeletons were stored in vast mountains of limestone in coastal waters whose weight, in past eons may have been a major force in the upheaval and movement of continental plates.[3]

The process of absorption of the carbon dioxide by the ocean is now under threat as increases in ultraviolet-B rays reach the earth through the thinning ozone layer. Tiny marine organisms called phytoplankton absorb more carbon dioxide than all vegetation on land, collecting as much as 100 billion tons of carbon dioxide annually. Spread out over the surface of the oceans, phytoplankton are particularly vulnerable to lethal UV-B rays, now reaching earth in greater quantities, destroying the microbes and their power to absorb carbon dioxide.[4]

Not only was the blanket of carbon dioxide reduced by "dumping" it in the oceans, but vegetation, appearing on land, was breaking the chemical bonds of carbon dioxide and water with the aid of the sun through photosynthesis, then storing the carbon in plants and freeing up oxygen and water vapour. Water vapour which transpires through leaves during photosynthesis is a major source of moisture in the hydrological cycle which brings us our weather and provides vital rainfall.[5]

Free oxygen, a by product of photosynthesis, made possible the appearance of living organisms. Life forms use oxygen to metabolize the plant carbohydrates they eat to produce the energy which sustains life. Two by products, carbon dioxide and water are given off during metabolism. In this process hydrogen is stabilized in water molecules, helping to prevent it from burning up or disappearing into space, a very necessary chemical reaction which keeps the planet from becoming arid.[6]

At the same time that these self-reproducing microscopic life forms began to emerge, a parallel species of micro-organisms developed whose task was to decompose accumulating dead vegetation. But they had a second purpose as important as the first. Had it not been for these micro-organisms producing methane and carbon dioxide, both "greenhouse" gases, during decomposition, the complete absorption of carbon dioxide from the atmosphere by photosynthesis might have occurred.[7]

From the beginning a fragile but relatively stable interdependence of climate, vegetation and life forms was established. Temperatures and weather patterns directly influenced and regulated vegetation, vegetation controlled global warming and cooling, and life forms depended for survival on climate and vegetation. The atmospheric temperatures, controlled by the amount of greenhouse gases in the atmosphere, have since stayed within a range that promotes optimal growth in plant and life forms which, in turn, control the production and absorption of greenhouse gases. At the same time enough excess oxygen is produced in this symbiotic process to maintain a 21 percent share of the atmosphere, the precise amount needed to sustain life fully and safely. It also ensures the continuation of the oxidation and reduction processes which keep the planet clean and productive, while preventing everything combustible from bursting into flames.

Consequently, this interdependent system has many crucial operations which must function with consistency. The cycle begins with the production and control of the quantity of greenhouse gases in the atmosphere which determine the temperature ranges on the earth's surface. When the proportion of carbon dioxide increases, the greenhouse effect increases, raising the earth's temperatures because more of the sun's heat is held within the atmosphere, unable to escape back into space through the thicker blanket of carbon dioxide.

As the atmospheric temperatures rise beneath this blanket, the warmer air evaporates larger quantities of moisture from the oceans and forests which then rise into the atmosphere where they are cooled by lower temperatures at higher altitudes. Here the moisture forms clouds. The amount of cloud cover over the planet is then increased world wide, reducing the amount of sun which reaches the earth's surface, lowering the temperatures over the lands and oceans. This prevents the atmosphere from becoming too hot and destroying the earth's vegetation.

The combination of cooler temperatures, increased rainfall and carbon dioxide available at the earth's surface then brings an increase in vegetation to the land as well as cooler temperatures to the oceans' surfaces. Together the oceans and vegetation absorb the excess carbon dioxide until the atmospheric blanket of carbon dioxide is reduced and the global temperatures cool down. The cooler the oceans the more carbon dioxide they can absorb. Warmer ocean surfaces give off vast quantities of carbon dioxide which adds to the accumulation of this gas in the upper atmosphere.

As the amount of vegetation grows with greater moisture and cooler temperatures, the methane and carbon dioxide escaping from their decaying matter are released into the atmosphere, once again building up the content of greenhouse gases. As the greenhouse effect increases, global warming conditions result which produce drier, hotter weather patterns in the tropics and cooler, gradually wetter conditions in northern and polar regions.

More importantly as recent studies have shown, the warmer the atmosphere, the warmer the ocean currents become. These currents are revealing themselves as the main generators of world wide weather patterns. El Nino and its extremes of weather patterns are the manifestation of this effect.

A natural phenomenon may also have as much influence on climate change as manmade causes. Long periods of warming and cooling of climates are intensified or weakened according to the changing location of the earth's orbit about the sun. The orbit expands away from the sun and then contracts towards it over a period of 100,000 years. While the earth's orbit moves away from the sun, the planet undergoes a gradual cooling period that eventually becomes cold enough to bring about continental glaciation in the Northern Hemisphere. Ice ages over the past 3 million years are estimated to have lasted on average 80,000 to 90,000 years. Glaciers covered North America, Europe and Asia while causing dry savanna conditions in the sub-tropical zones that changed tropical forests into grasslands, even deserts.

As the earth's orbit contracted towards the sun, the last Ice Age began to disappear over 19,000 years ago. Since then, the last 10,000 years have proven to be the most habitable time on earth for all life forms and vegetation. As continental glaciers melted, human expansion and development in the Northern Hemisphere correlated with the effects of interglacial warming. Obviously the fact that we are reaching the end of this warm period and could be returning to glacial conditions is of great concern. Scientists are hard pressed to determine how much our own contributions to global warming will forestall or escalate this climate change.

Whatever the forces of climate change, natural or manmade, it is generally agreed that industrial and vehicle production of green house gases, aerosol particulates and acidic compounds are interfering with the physical and chemical balances within the biosphere of "evolutionary process." Lovelock sees "the evolution of the species of living organisms so closely coupled with the evolution of their physical and chemical environment that together they constitute a single and indivisible evolutionary process."[8] Should the self-regulated system of gases in the atmosphere be radically changed, then climate, vegetation and life forms will undergo forces of extinction and evolutionary change.

Climates and Population Growth

The self-constructed biosphere of the planet is crucial to human occupation of the land masses. Population growth, cultures and industrialization show a direct correlation to climatic conditions.

The bulk of the developed nations lie mainly within the temperate zones of the Northern Hemisphere where climates are cool to cold in winter and the annual summer growing season is relatively short. The greater distance of the land in the Northern Hemisphere from the sun's direct rays, the greater the seasonal temperature ranges. The harshness of winter and the cold of spring and autumn rains demands sophisticated technologies to provide the people with well heated, insulated homes, reserves of food and appropriate clothing to maintain good health. Northern inhabitants are not only forced to maintain extensive building accommodations for living and working, they must also have sufficient transportation and energy resources to move them about. Temperate climates are also very physically and mentally stimulating so that northern people are generally energetic, active and innovative. They are able to work harder for longer periods of each day than people in tropical zones.

People living in hot, tropical lands have their physical energy debilitated by high temperatures and moisture laden air or desert dry air. Life tends to be lived at a slower pace, one day at a time. The peasant farmer in the tropics is forced to rest or remain indoors during much of the day so as to avoid the hot sun. On the other hand, little preparation for the future is necessary where food can be grown the year round. Consequently, throughout much of Africa, Asia and Latin America, families can exist on small plots of land, grow what food they need to live almost on a daily basis, and sell the surplus in exchange for those things they cannot make or produce themselves.

Until the late 20th Century, existence in most tropical lands remained relatively primitive. Life flowed with minimal changes of temperature from dry to wet seasons. Herders simply moved their animals and families in harmony with the seasonal rains and vegetative growth, keeping only as many animals as they required for their family's sustenance.

Hot, moist climates permit housing to be simple and keep clothing and use of fuels at a minimum. Amazon regions of South America, Africa and Asia have allowed for relatively primitive living conditions for large numbers, offering ready access to forests for fuel and rivers for fresh water, as well as fruits, birds and wild animals. If the people husband their local resources carefully and live in balance with nature, they can live simply but relatively harmoniously within their environments. In relatively few jungle areas, stone age hunter-gatherers can still live off the natural environment, employing the simplest of technologies. Their future, however, is endangered by encroaching civilization.

In recent decades primitive populations have lost much of their natural habitat which supplied them with fruits, nuts, roots, game, birds, fish and edible vegetation. Deforestation, peasant farmers and cattle ranchers have clearcut much of the forests and burned off the natural vegetation. Eco-systems are disappearing. Those, living as hunter-gatherers within nature and dependent on eco-systems, fall easy prey to land hungry marauders with guns and chain saws.

Over 80 percent of the world's population lives in Third World nations located in the Southern Hemisphere where tropical and subtropical climates predominate. At present their human populations are rising at an average of one billion every ten years, an annual fertility rate of 2 percent. 1990 United Nations' estimates stated that 3.9 billion people now live in these nations and will increase their numbers to 4.9 billion by the year 2000. By 2030, this annual growth rate will bring Third World populations up to 8 billion.[9]

Where modern technologies have moved in, the simple, "environmentally friendly" natural farming techniques of primitive life has disappeared. Their lands are now the victims of deforestation, massive agricultural and irrigation projects, agricultural chemicals, exploitation of mineral resources and fossil fuels, desertification, destruction of natural grasslands and overuse and pollution of water supplies. Once in place unsustainable environmental practices and extremes of poverty levels are proving intransigent.

Another aspect of land destruction comes with mining and oil drilling. The horrors of life among the Brazilian gold miners who dig mountains of earth with little more than their bare hands will not stop until the exploding peasant population can be employed elsewhere. Meanwhile the miners are tearing down whole mountains in the Amazon basin and poisoning the river systems as well as the local populations with the mercury they use to extract the gold from the ore.

Destructive climatic changes always follow the arrival of technological commerce as forests disappear to the axe and the plough. Where deforestation and land erosion have scarred the land, seasonal rainfall is less reliable. Drought is common and water stored by the roots of the trees is lost in runoff. Extremes of droughts and flooding occur regularly and crop failures are common. Until the 1980s, Zimbabwe, for instance, always grew enough food to feed its people with sufficient left over to export. Now drought is both frequent and widespread, bringing famine to many Zimbabweans.[10] The life giving monsoons of Asia, once so welcome, are now more devastating than useful, flooding fields, destroying crops and washing away millions of tons of topsoil each year.

Sources of Weather Phenomena

Increasing evidence exists to prove that human survival depends on climate, vegetation and ecological systems remaining as stable and unchanged as possible. The increasing severity of weather patterns on every continent in recent years has caused massive waste through the loss of crops, homes, property and wildlife to drought, fire, wind and flood.

Hydrological Cycle: Tracing the human influence in these recent extremes in weather phenomena begins with realizing that all major weather patterns originate with the hydrological cycle over the band of forests at the equator, 15 degrees North and 15 degrees South. The cycle begins where the direct rays of the sun create high temperatures at the earth's surface, evaporating millions of tons of water from the oceans and the tropical rainforests. The hot, moist air rises and expands high into the atmosphere where it cools, condensing the water vapour into heavy clouds and falling daily as tropical rain storms. The moisture is held in the soil by the vast stretches of forests and vegetation, then absorbed by the trees and plants.

The moisture in the ground dissolves the nutrients in the soil which are taken up by the roots of the plants and trees, pulled up through their stems to the leaves where it is used during photosynthesis and then returned to the atmosphere through the leaves. As water vapour, the moisture then rises into the atmosphere until it is cooled in cloud formations, and once again returned to the earth as rain to repeat the process. This hydrological cycle works with the winds of the planet to produce the seasonal rainfall and weather patterns of the continents, vital to annual vegetation growth.

Ocean Currents: Not all the moisture evaporated in the equatorial areas is returned to earth at the equator, however. As the hot air rises, it flows outward in convection currents which form the prevailing winds and ocean currents of the planet. These winds drive the clouds and spread the moisture to all areas of the globe, evaporating more moisture from the oceans and vegetation of the lands as they pass. With the aid of oceans, land masses and mountains in their path, these prevailing winds and ocean currents produce the many variations in climate and seasonal weather patterns of the planet which determine the location of all life forms and vegetation on both land and in the oceans.

Next are the global forces of winds, temperatures and atmospheric moisture which are closely related to the movement of ocean currents. These are massive internal waves in constant motion, moving both upwards from the ocean floor and outwards along the surface and down again as they cool. The Gulf Stream, for instance, might be compared with a warm river crossing the Atlantic. As it flows northeast across the Atlantic, its warm surface temperatures keep Britain and Western Europe from suffering frigid winters in continental areas which should by their location be cold, polar lands. Global warming now threatens to turn these temperate effects of world ocean currents into destructive weather patterns explaining why recent summer and winter weather conditions world wide have grown more severe with each passing season.

El Nino: El Nino, an ocean current now infamous for bringing extremes of weather to the Pacific nations, is the result of repeating patterns of internal waves in the oceans. As warm water rises to the surface near Indonesia, a large warm pool of water forms, reducing the atmospheric pressure in its path and creating more westerly winds. The ocean current begins to spread along the equator towards South America where it brings heavy rains to Ecuador, Peru, Argentina and parts of Brazil.[11] But when the El Nino effect is particularly severe, the westerly direction of its winds move it north along the coast of North America. It is powerful enough to alter the jet stream and "disturb half the globe's climate, altering rainfall and temperature patterns over South America, North America and parts of Africa and Asia."[12]

El Nino brings increases in temperatures and moisture which may result in torrential rains and high winds. In 1992 it caused tornadoes and winds in Texas up to 100 kilometres per hour. Heavy down pours accompanied the winds, flooding large areas and damaging crops. At the same time it brought drought to Australia and parts of Africa.[13]

Many natural disasters followed in El Nino's path as it moved eastward in 1981-83 and 1991-94. As much as a 75 percent drop in monthly rainfall on the Pacific islands of Fiji occurred. New Zealand in 1995 experienced unseasonably cold weather, even freezing temperatures, caused by cold fronts from Antarctica. Australia suffered droughts and the worst bush fires and fire storms in its history in 1982 and 1994. Deserts in Peru and Chile have been flooded. Pacific storms continue to bring frequent floods to California with longer periods of increasing drought.

The severity and impact of this phenomenon grows as the pool of warm water increases almost yearly in temperature, size and duration. Should the effect continue to worsen, either through global warming or through the beginnings of a new Ice Age, world agricultural production will be disrupted. Freezes, high temperatures, droughts, floods, wind storms, all reduce crop output and force changes in the types of crops that can be grown. Fisheries are lost as marine life migrates with the warm water or escapes it as Peruvian fishermen learned when the rich anchovy schools disappeared from their coastal waters in 1982-83. El Nino's impact on local fisheries was felt on the Pacific coast of Canada in the 1990s as large schools of mackerel migrated with the warm waters and ate large quantities of salmon fry returning to the ocean from spawning grounds on British Columbian rivers.

Hotter growing seasons which accompany El Nino cause drought conditions which reduce seasonal rainfall, lower rivers and lakes and reduce crops in one location. At the same time heavy cloud formations develop in another part of the globe bringing more frequent, excessive rainfall and flooding during growing seasons. The unparalleled flooding of the Mississippi River Basin in July and August of 1993 kept temperatures unseasonably cool and heavy cloud formations were a constant presence throughout the summer. Australia during the summer of January, 1994, experienced its worst drought and fire season ever.

El Nino and its varied effects on world weather conditions may be receiving a lot of help from human activities. Scientific studies are beginning to show a correlation may exist between the increasing "greenhouse effect" caused by the burning of fossil fuels and the cooling over large industrial stretches in the Northern Hemisphere caused by excessive amounts of aerosol particulates of sulphur dioxide, the source of acid rain. Sulphuric acid and ammonium sulphate form as droplets in the clouds, reflecting sunshine back into space and increasing the moisture content of the clouds. The clouds tend to remain heavier and more reflective of sunshine than normal cloud cover, cooling the land beneath.[14]

While summers have been extremely dry in some areas and very wet in others, the winters of 1990 to 1996 in the Northern

Hemisphere were colder then previous years with increasing ice formation on lakes and rivers. 1992 and 1993 remained cold enough to prevent spring from arriving in the Western Arctic. Areas surrounding Hudson's Bay and on Baffin Island remained covered in snow in June, making it impossible for the tens of thousands of migrating geese and swans to nest there in the summer months. They were forced to return south without having raised a generation of offspring. Temperatures in these Arctic lands in June were on average 3 degrees Celsius lower than normal.[15]

A third natural force determining climatic changes is the seasonal expanding and shrinking of green vegetation in the temperate zones. When the Northern Hemisphere enters the summer months, the abundance of leaves on trees and vegetation then plays a major role in the amount of oxygen, carbon dioxide and water vapour in the atmosphere. Through the hydrological cycle, wide continental bands of deciduous trees and shrubs in the spring and summer months provide much of the seasonal rain vital to the growth of crops. As the vegetation increases, it absorbs vast quantities of carbon dioxide from the warming oceans and the air and releases large amounts of oxygen into the atmosphere during the warm seasons when most species are reproducing themselves and are the most active. In cutting down the vast forests of the Northern Hemisphere, we have endangered both this vital source of oxygen and the hydrological cycles. To date, humanity has destroyed two-thirds of the planet's forests which is rapidly deteriorating the delicate balance between climate, vegetation and life forms which took billions of years to perfect.

Under "normal" atmospheric conditions when water evaporates from the oceans and is given off by vegetation and other chemical processes, the amount of moisture the air can hold is determined by the degree of warmth in the air above them. By adding industrial gases to the atmosphere through burning fossil fuels, emitting chlorofluorocarbons (CFCs) and increasing the production of methane gases in the upper atmosphere, the heat of the sun's rays cannot escape into space. In burning fossil fuels alone, each car on the road, averaging one and a half to two tons in weight, emits three and a half times its own weight in carbon dioxide. An estimated 50 to 60 billion tons of carbon dioxide (and rising as 10 million more cars come onto the roads of the world each year) were produced by vehicles and other burning processes when a record 6.1 billion tons of fossil fuels were burned in 1995. This amount of carbon dioxide added to the atmosphere annually is accepted as sufficient to trigger weather phenomena destructive of the natural environment and human life and property. The heated atmosphere, able to hold increasingly larger quantities of moisture, moves it into the wind systems of the earth.

Internationally, a consensus to reduce carbon dioxide emissions receives no more than a promise to discuss the matter again in a few years as demonstrated at the Berlin Conference held in April, 1995. Every possible means to finagle extra quotas for toxic emissions in the developed nations or to allow poor nations any amount of pollution until they are industrialized make a mockery of international co-operation to be environmentally responsible.

Scientists now know that higher temperatures and greater evaporation produce extremes of weather. The warmer the air in one area of the globe, the greater the speed of air flow from high to low pressure areas, creating much stronger winds and accompanying storms that tear up trees and powerful enough to flood the land. The temperature differential, growing between equatorial areas and the poles as temperatures increase at the equator, could become instrumental in producing rapid cooling in the polar regions, initiating colder winter conditions and eventually a build up of ice and glaciation, not forgetting the planet is reaching the end of its 10,000 year interglacial period. The cool, rainy summer of 1993 throughout middle North America and the coldest winter temperatures on record in January of 1994 across the entire Eastern half of North America suggest such a trend may already be happening.

This cooling trend in the northern hemisphere causes global temperatures in equatorial regions to rise and produce even more moisture to be transported toward the poles by the prevailing winds and ocean currents. As the moisture laden air cools and moves poleward, it condenses into heavier and heavier cloud formations which prevent the sun getting through to the earth for longer and more frequent durations, cooling the land as they pass overhead and falling as snow in polar regions. This cooling, reduced only in the years El Nino moves into the Northern Hemisphere, may soon be sufficient to prevent the summer melting of the accompanying heavier snowfalls.

The phenomenon has an added twist. Scientists, Gifford Miller, a geologist from the University of Colorado, studying glacial deposits in the Arctic, and Anne de Vernal, a micropalaeontologist at the University of Quebec researching fossils of microscopic animals from the ocean floor, correlated their finds to report that the last Ice Age was preceded by a period of global warming.[16] Put this newly acquired knowledge together with scientific studies of glaciation and they suggest the return of an Ice Age. Reports during the 1980s of glacial melting in high mountain areas and at the poles showed an increase in the rate of annual melting. Warmer than ordinary temperatures, some as high as 40 degrees Celsius, were reported in Arctic lands during several summers in the 1980s. The land actually heated up enough to melt some surface permafrost. The warm, black land areas were able to absorb enough heat from the sun to melt some glacial deposits. Perhaps weather phenomena during the 1980s signalled a similar intervening period of global warming is in progress: exceptionally warm summers, but colder winters.

Adding to the impact of this phenomenon are the extremes in winter weather patterns. For example, in January of 1996, freak warm temperatures in the middle of winter rose high enough to hatch the tadpoles all along the coast of Cape Breton, Nova Scotia. Soon after the temperatures dropped again below freezing, killing them all. Scientists fear the area's entire frog population may have been frozen to death by this extreme in local weather conditions.

Although the average world temperature as a whole has not increased more than 1/2 degree Celsius over the last 100 years, increases in particular geographic areas have experienced as much as an 8 to 10 degrees rise or fall in annual averages. This may be because global warming is making itself felt primarily at night. Temperature records kept at 1,000 weather stations since 1950 showed an average daytime rise of only 0.3 degrees F., but a 1.5 degree rise in nighttime lows. The increase in cloud cover resulting from air pollution and high levels of smog over urban areas may be responsible for the small change in daytime temperatures.[17] Air pollution increases cloud cover which reflects more sun back into space during the daytime while preventing the warmth of the land accumulated during the day from escaping into space at night.

In tropical and temperate zones, warmer temperatures are increasing evaporation and cloud cover, producing heavier rainfall which erodes away greater amounts of topsoil each year and drowns lands which cannot absorb or channel enough of the run off to prevent flooding. Catastrophic floods in Asia, Europe and North America are becoming annual climatic events. At the same time, higher temperatures are expanding the spread and frequency of droughts on several continents. Large central areas of Africa have suffered extended periods of drought. Lake Chad, once a large inland body of water, is rapidly disappearing as drought reduces its boundaries and depth each year. In 1984 its area was only one tenth of what it was in 1973. As the Sahara moves south, Lake Chad will disappear entirely. Timbuktu, once a thriving inland river port in Africa, is now an almost deserted village amid the sand dunes. All of these conditions are reducing world food supplies and degrading the quality of human existence.

The facts of climatic change are confusing, however. We do not know if the planet is headed into a period of global warming and all the weather changes that implies, or whether it is entering another 90,000 years of glaciation? Volcanic eruptions send massive quantities of dust and greenhouse gases into the atmosphere which interfere with the global weather patterns by adding more cloud formation and more seasonal cooling. The explosion of Mount Pinatubo in the Philippines in 1991 caused a sulphurous haze which reduced the sunlight reaching the earth, slightly lowering the upward trend of temperatures in 1992 and 1993. In 1994 the seasonal temperatures were once again on the rise.[18] As yet we cannot be certain that our contribution to the greenhouse effect will delay another Ice Age.

There is little we humans can do to stop the return of an Ice Age. But this does not mean we can continue to pollute the atmosphere and destroy the biological components of the evolutionary process as we are doing. However, if we are answerable for global warming, the ozone depletion and the destruction of the natural balance among climate, vegetation and life forms which makes our existence possible, then we are responsible for the present threat to our future survival.

Scientists continue to map very definitive changes in the atmospheric composition. These include a decrease in ozone, an increase in carbon dioxide, a large volume of CFCs, methane, nitrous oxide, and several other greenhouse gases in the upper atmosphere. Methane in recent studies, for instance, appeared in record quantities in the atmosphere, originating in the stomachs of the hundreds of millions of ruminant animals we raise around the world for food. With development has come more buying power and a demand for animal protein. As a result, cattle and pig farming are thriving and will expand as long as there are enough grains to feed them. In the near future this major source of methane production will be vastly increased as improved standards of living in the Third World encourage widespread animal domestication. The huge amounts of methane produced by termites and microbes as they digest our escalating quantities of composting crop residue must also be calculated into the accumulation of this greenhouse gas. Presently enough greenhouse gases - carbon dioxide, methane, nitrous oxide and chlorine - have accumulated in the upper atmosphere to raise the average world temperature 4 to 8 degrees Celsius within the next 50 years -- or to bring on another ice age.

Impact on Humans of Changing Weather Patterns

Which ever climatic change comes about in the near or distant future, whether it is a return to continental glaciation or to extremes of warmth accompanied by hotter, drier climates, the planet is at present experiencing "unnatural" climate phenomena and cataclysmic weather events which do not bode well for humanity in either the present or the future. Prevalent droughts where once seasonal rains could be relied on, widespread

flooding, cooler, rainy summers, colder winters and remaining El
Nino effects are changing weather patterns to the detriment of
human occupation and food production on every continent.

Weather patterns began showing a marked change for the
worse during the 1970s. Temperature extremes in the Northern
Hemisphere in 1972 increased the extent of snowfall by an
"enormous one-and-a half million square miles over the previous
year. It was estimated that only seven such winters consecutively
could establish an ice cover, not yet in depth but the equivalent in
area of the last ice age."[19] We have seen violent wind storms blow
over thousands of trees, floods ruin millions of acres of crops,
hurricanes destroy billions of dollars worth of property and
thousands drowned or killed by raging rivers, hurricanes,
mudslides and tornadoes. The coldest winter temperatures up to
1977 struck the Eastern United States in that year, bringing the
first ever recorded snow fall to Miami. Granted our overcrowding
of vulnerable areas such as river plains and mountain valleys
contributed to the number of casualties, yet the frequency and
ferocity of recent storms surpassed any previous records.

Spring frosts on the Atlantic and Southern coasts of North
America destroyed vast areas of fruit trees and vegetable crops
while drought, summer freezes and autumn flooding killed
millions of livestock throughout the world. Snow fell on Florida
in 1970, and for the first time in history, it also fell on the Sahara
Desert.

The decade of the 1980s produced seven of the worst years for
temperature extremes on record world wide. It began with El
Nino which swung north along the Pacific coast, intensifying
weather patterns and producing higher than normal ocean
temperatures. The warmer ocean waters killed plankton, which
are at the bottom of the food chain so that millions of sea
creatures starved to death. 1984 was warmer than 1983, 1985 was
warmer than 1984 and so on up through the decade. Drought in
the early 1980s destroyed vast acreages of grain and corn crops
in North America. Record high temperatures of 85 degrees F.
occurred in early March in North Eastern United States and
Canada, followed by devastating tornadoes, some in areas which
had never before experienced them, just as record high summer

temperatures in the Arctic caused rapid glacial melt and increased warming of the land, melting the permafrost to deep levels.

Hurricanes in the Caribbean uprooted millions of citrus fruit trees while summer frosts destroyed millions of trees in Texas and Florida in 1989. Europe experienced as many as three violent destructive storms and floods in less than one month in 1990 and extensive flooding again in the winter of 1992. Bangladesh is now inundated annually with flood waters that pour off the barren mountain slopes of Nepal during the monsoons. Summer drought in Britain emptied the southern rivers in 1992, then flooded the same areas in 1993. Hurricanes battered the United States, Mexico and the Caribbean in 1992. Eastern North America passed without a summer in 1993 as the Mississippi and Missouri Rivers over flowed their banks and consumed the river basin and surrounding farmlands during July and August. At the same time the Southern United States sweltered under its worst drought in a century.

The summer of 1994 brought heat waves to Northern Europe with temperatures reaching 36 degrees Celsius. These "high temperatures hatched insects and algae that used up the oxygen, littering beaches with suffocated fish."[20] Excessive heat and dryness caused the largest forest fires on record in B.C., Washington and Oregon. Japan sweltered under a heat wave which parched large areas of the country, resulting in water rationing and the death of over 110,000 chickens from heat prostration. Air pollution in large cities throughout Europe experienced deadly smog conditions.[21] At the same time a three year drought, the worst in memory, continued to plague Eastern Australia, caused by the waning influences of El Nino.[22] Each year brings more devastating weather as the winter of 1996 proved with some of the lowest temperatures on record in Canada and Europe.

These are no longer weather occurrences to be viewed as rare anomalies. Erratic, disastrous rainfalls and excessive temperatures are more common with each passing year, bringing flooding, drought, heat waves, frosts and wind storms to every continent. During recent years in North America, thousands of homes and businesses have been lost or heavily damaged, food crops wiped out, thousands of domestic animals drowned, property in the billions destroyed or ruined and tens of thousands of people left homeless and unemployed for the duration of the floods. Should such weather conditions recur on a regular basis, it will make river and coastal plains too expensive for farming and too dangerous for living. In poor nations, drought and flood have already increased the number of starving and homeless in Africa and Asia.

On the other hand, the return of weather conditions severe enough to initiate an Ice Age will be too onerous for societies in the Northern Hemisphere to withstand. Just how severe such climatic changes will be on large population centres can be studied through the experience of those living in the Eastern United States during the winters of 1976-77 and January-February of 1994. Both periods brought record cold temperatures. In 1994, temperatures between minus 19 and minus 25 degrees F and heavy snows over 44 days in many large urban areas resulted in a near shut down of entire cities. Buffalo had 80 inches of snow, 14 inches above normal, and Boston had 61 inches, 35 inches above normal.[23]

A shortage of energy fuels was the worst problem because deliveries of fuel could not be made. The heavy drain of electric power night and day proved unmanageable. Lacking sufficient power supplies, businesses had to shut down, a number of people froze to death, and nearly all suffered from cold in their homes. Food shortages ensued as transportation systems and roads closed down or were difficult to maintain. The economy stalled as businesses closed for weeks and people could neither get to work, nor earn money or shop. The old and sick were generally unable to reach hospitals. Cold temperatures, electricity blackouts, thirty foot snow drifts and almost daily snowstorms closed roads and trapped people in their homes. Winds so strong made getting outside nearly impossible. Over half a million workers were laid off because of fuel shortages and millions were in jeopardy of freezing and going hungry. Existence was reduced to waiting out the cold and trying to stay alive for however long it lasted.[24]

Should such winters occur frequently, then these living conditions would become an annual event. Only Arctic vegetation can grow under extended winter conditions. Food crops which now occupy the vast prairies of North America and Europe will fail as the snow line moves further and further south. This could happen within our own lifetimes. The impact on human societies would be horrendous. Large concentrations of people would be forced to move south into subtropical lands which are already overpopulated. The degree of overcrowding that would occur would lead to racial/ethnic battles over control of land bases, food supplies and resources. Perhaps the only geographical advantage to an ice age would be the amount of land that would rise out of the oceans as the glaciers held back the rain as ice, and sea levels fell exposing large areas of shoreline.

In view of the few real changes the world's societies have made to reduce their destruction of the environment over the past 30 to 40 years and the exponential growth of populations, it is doubtful humanity will be prepared to manage its survival rationally and efficiently under ice age conditions. Those Homo sapiens who survived the last Ice Age did so because there were so few of them and most were scattered in warmer lands. Today's exploding populations only magnify the problems future generations will have to face on this overcrowded planet whether it be under glacial conditions or global warming.

Tens of millions of people suffer today from disruptive and unseasonable weather patterns. The United States has undergone much hurricane, flood and fire damage in the past ten years. Fire storms of 1992 destroyed over 1000 homes in Oakland, California and an equal number in and around Los Angeles in October of 1993. Repairing the damage and caring for the victims has become a financial burden beyond the carrying capacity of insurance companies and their insured. Coping with the cost of replacing the billions of dollars in property losses has even the American government unable to provide all the money they promised to reimburse the thousands of victims. Loss of jobs, reduced retailing and destroyed industrial plants add to the uncertainty and misery of those dislocated by the many natural catastrophes.

For those forced to live on lands which have lost their former balance of climate, vegetation and life forms, human existence grows more difficult. Excessive drought and flooding bring with them dislocation of populations, huge property loss, unemployment, poverty, starvation, disease and epidemics. Bangladesh, built largely on the flood plains of several large rivers, undergoes yearly flooding which brings widespread hunger, disease, abject poverty, even death to many of its overcrowded citizens as they cling to the shifting and eroding soils of the river plains.

The number of deaths caused by weather extremes both to humans and wildlife rises on every continent. While flooding takes its share of human victims, the decimation of wildlife is unparalleled as fires and floods have damaged vast areas of pristine wilderness. Drought now dominates summer climates in both hemispheres which multiplies the size and number of forest fires. Fire storms in Australia in January of 1994 destroyed 90 percent of the 37,500 acres of the Royal National Park near Sydney. "Out of tens of thousands of animals that had lived in the park, only five (were) found alive."[25] Those which survived by escaping the fire were then eaten by predators or forced to compete for remaining wilderness space and food supplies. In all, the fires burned over 1.2 million acres of mostly bushland, killing the majority of wildlife. Given five to ten years the various species can regenerate their numbers, but the fires in Australia are recurring on a more frequent basis than five to ten years. Australians are wondering if the wildlife can survive constant devastation.

Increasing seasonal temperatures, heavier cloud cover and hurricanes are diminishing wilderness habitat. The nesting grounds and food supplies of whole species of wild life and birds are disappearing as grasslands, wetlands and forests are destroyed by drought, fire and flooding.

Lands once nurtured and protected by the eco-systems of the planet are turning into unproductive, uninhabitable wastelands where poisonous weeds replace edible vegetation. Drought and overgrazing of mountain meadow lands in B.C. in recent years brought an infestation of uncontrollable knapweed which continues to push out and replace the grasses and natural flora of the range lands. Knapweed is poisonous to grazing animals and does not attract valuable insects. Its presence is a plague that has come as the climate grows drier and hotter.

If humanity has any choice left to prevent further degeneration of both local and global climates, then we must act immediately to reduce our impact on the temperate, rain abundant climates on every continent or accept that we are sacrificing them for dry deserts, high winds and extremes of temperature. The choice we make will depend on how we manage regional industrial development, urban expansion and toxic pollution.

Effects of Human Activities on Climate

Wherever people have settled, they have destroyed most of the immediate vegetation and life forms whose loss then radically alters climatic conditions. Total removal of vegetation and extensive erosion of land creates desert conditions, reduces local rainfall, changes wind patterns and often increases temperatures. Industrial and agricultural development may affect local weather patterns that may not be of global consequence, nonetheless, they can have disastrous results.

Greenhouse Effect: The burning of billions of tons of stored carbon in fossil fuels and forests not only returns the ancient reserves of carbon dioxide to the atmosphere, increasing the greenhouse effect, but it pollutes the air we breathe with toxic smog and acid rains which kill vegetation, life forms and human beings if the chemicals are concentrated enough. Many urban areas, especially those in Eastern Europe, and the newly industrializing nations of China and India are presently sinkholes of toxic smog. The premature death of thousands of people in these cities is directly related to tiny particulates in the smog which lodge in the lungs, and in extreme cases cause death. It is estimated over 64,000 people in the United States die each year from these particulates and the respiratory diseases they cause. People at greatest risk are children, especially those with asthma and the elderly who have lived most of their lives in industrial areas.

Acid Rain: Other poisonous emissions - sulphur dioxide, and nitrous oxide - combine with the moisture in the air to produce acid rains of sulphuric acid and nitric acid. As they filter through the soils, they upset the Ph balance, hindering the ability of the trees to absorb nutrients from the ground. Acid rain is acknowledged to be the major cause of forests dying across the Northern Hemisphere. As it falls to earth, it collects in lakes where the acidity destroys plant life and starves the small creatures of the food chains. The larger fish soon die out from a lack of food. Gradually any life that survives starvation, dies off from a lack of oxygen in the water. Massive algae blooms which thrive on acidic waters absorb the oxygen in the water and smother the plant and animal life. Many northern Canadian lakes which may look beautiful in their crystal clear state are dead lakes. They are clear only because they are empty of life. Acid rain travels on the prevailing winds which means even the remotest landscapes are affected. Once a pristine wilderness, the Arctic is now yellow with the acidic smogs spewed out into the atmosphere from the refineries and industrial plants of Europe and Asia as they float on the prevailing winds over the Arctic poles.

Ozone Depletion: While human activities are increasing the greenhouse effect and causing acid rain through toxic emissions, another group of emitted gases are destroying the upper layer of atmosphere which protects our health and that of all growing things: the ozone layer. This layer prevents the deadly ultra-violet B rays of the sun from reaching the earth where they can kill nearly all ecological species.

Emissions of CFCs, gases used in refrigeration, air conditioners, industrial solvents and cleaning compounds, seep into the air and rise to the top of the atmosphere. The sun splits the CFCs and sets free chlorine molecules which combine with the oxygen of the ozone, forming chlorine monoxide. Two chlorine monoxide then combine to produce chlorine and oxygen, destroying the ozone molecule of three oxygen atoms. In this way, one chlorine monoxide molecule can chew up 100,000 ozone molecules.

Ultra-violet B rays originally formed the ozone molecules in which three atoms of oxygen combined to form one molecule of ozone. The historical extent of this process eventually produced enough ozone to build an atmospheric barrier to the harmful

Ultra-violet B rays, preventing the harmful rays from reaching the earth's surface. The rays, however, are not powerful enough to offset the ability of the chlorine atoms in the CFCs from breaking up the ozone molecules. Ultra-violet B is then free to pass through the atmosphere to the earth's surface.

During the winter months, when the air is very cold, large clouds of crystals form. CLO (chlorine monoxide) molecules stick to these ice crystals. In the spring when the crystals melt, the CLO molecules are released, setting free large amounts of chlorine monoxide which continues to tear apart the ozone molecules.

Scientific studies mapping changes in the ozone layer show it is diminishing and actually disappearing over the poles and adjacent land masses during the spring and summer months in each hemisphere. Measurements of ozone taken by the space shuttle, Discovery, in 1992, reported a 10 to 20 percent loss over the United States and much of Europe. Estimates of ozone depletion over Canada during the winter of 1993 indicated a loss as high as 30 percent in some areas.

In March of 1996, temperatures in the Arctic fell as low as minus 100 degrees Fahrenheit causing large clouds of ice crystals to form. The crystals prevented the CFCs and other chemicals which deplete the ozone from sinking back to earth. The result was a loss of 20 to 30 percent of the ozone over Greenland and the Russian Arctic and as much as 40 percent over parts of Britain, before weather changes blew the ozone depleted air over the Canadian Arctic.

Permanent holes in the ozone layer are now appearing over the Arctic, much of Canada, Europe and Australia. In 1994 tests of the ozone content registered an expanding hole above Antarctica. Most recent discoveries have found the ozone is now thinning over equatorial lands.

Should ultra-violet B rays reach earth in vast quantities, particularly during the growing season, they would eventually damage or kill most life forms, especially the smallest creatures and plant life at the bottom of the food chains, both on land and in the oceans. Ultra-violet B rays prevent the growth of many forms of vegetation by interfering with photosynthesis. They are already damaging the oceans' ability to support the phytoplankton which absorb billions of tons of carbon dioxide annually and are the mainstay at the bottom of the food chain in the oceans.[26]

While ultra-violet B rays burn the skin of living species, growing numbers of humans in recent years, unprotected from the sun's ultraviolet rays especially during hot summer months, are suffering immune deficiencies, skin cancers, eye cataracts and blindness.

The same physical symptoms have been found in rabbits, sheep and salmon in Australia, New Zealand and South America where the ozone loss over Antarctica is most severe. Blindness is common among the Australian kangaroos which makes them vulnerable to extinction. Ultra-violet B rays are now being blamed for the disappearance of frog populations world wide.

The loss of the ozone layer is our most immediate threat to survival. As the ozone is depleted, the ultra-violet B rays reaching the earth's surface will weaken the human immune system. Reacting with DNA, they produce foreign cells which attack the body, leaving it open to all infectious diseases. As a result, certain diseases and allergic reactions are already on the increase. Furthermore, the devastation those rays can do to life forms at the bottom of the food chains threaten humanity with starvation should they begin killing off microbes and bacteria, as well as small plants and animal species.

Urban Development: New weather phenomena are developing that are credited to high concentrations of human populations and extensive urban development. One is the effect of reflected sunlight from tens of thousands of buildings, concrete roads and sidewalks which heats up the atmosphere above and around them. The air above our large urban centres is generally several degrees warmer than that of the adjacent countryside, building an artificial differential in air pressure which increases wind strength and velocity between city lows and country highs. The result is more violent wind storms than would be normal, with the capacity to do much damage to both the city and the bordering countryside.

The second weather change is the result of massive manmade changes in natural landscapes. In February of 1995, Western

Europe, under circumstances similar to those experienced throughout the Mississippi River basin in 1993, weathered the flood of the century as the Rhine and the Moselle Rivers overflowed into villages, cities and onto farm lands. The rivers have been artificially straightened and confined within cement channels to improve the passage of barge traffic. These massive constructions changed the riverbeds and flood plains so much, the land cannot absorb the unusually heavy winter rains nor disperse the sediment the river would normally deposit on the river plains.[27] Instead, the high water levels are forced to overflow the river banks and flood onto surrounding lands.

Humankind has done more damage to the atmosphere and the surface of the earth in the last 50 years than in the previous 5 million. It is a key argument in proving that we have rashly taken charge of our own evolution and extinction. The changes we are causing to the earth's climates have the power to threaten us with mass starvation and water shortages on every continent within a few decades. Long periods of drought and extensive flooding have destroyed the crops of many nations both in the past and in very recent years, leaving millions to die of starvation. As extreme as recent weather aberrations have been, governments, corporate leadership and sycophant scientists and economists still maintain they must have more proof that these are climatic changes caused by human activities and not just isolated occurrences of natural phenomena caused by sun spots or the earth's distance from the sun.

In 1995, the scientific community publicly announced its consensus that the self-regulating system of greenhouse gases in the atmosphere is being unduly influenced by the emission of billions of tons of carbon dioxide, methane and nitrous oxide produced by human activities. Universal agreement is slowly admitting to the role humans are playing in raising seasonal temperatures through the emission of greenhouse gases. Less and less credence is given to those who try to refute the scientific data in order to promote industrial development and ignore the consequences. Finally, when catastrophe strikes, the media no longer shies away from defining the human role in having destroyed the natural processes of Gaia.

Throughout human evolution climate and local weather patterns have controlled our survival. Overuse and abuse of environments and their eco-systems brought climatic changes which threatened isolated civilizations and now threaten the entire planet. Unless we reduce, if not cease, those industrial and agricultural activities which permanently damage the natural balance of the biosphere, we stand to increase the anomalies in weather conditions which erode soils, kill food crops, destroy property and wipe out eco-systems.

CHAPTER THIRTEEN

Destruction of Land, Soils and Forests

In November of 1994 torrential rains in Alessandria, Northern Italy, caused heavy flooding in which 60 people died and over 7000 lost their homes in landslides. The major cause: soil erosion on hillsides where the trees had been cleared to make way for farming, housing and tourism.[1]

People have been abusing and destroying the land and its indigenous vegetation through deforestation and progressive cultivation technologies since the first Homo sapiens emerged as efficient hunter-gatherers capable of setting fires to flush out animals or cutting the trees for wood and living space. However, the impact of the hunter-gatherers on the earth was minimal compared with that of our settled forbearers or present day agribusinesses. "The seeds for today's ruthless exploitation of the natural world were undoubtedly present at the beginning of the Neolithic Revolution some 12,000 years ago, when mankind first embarked on permanent agriculture and created large, fortress-like settlements to keep out nomadic invaders."[2]

The effects of 10,000 to 12,000 years of human settlement characterize the Middle East and the Mediterranean basin. The Nile River plain, the Tigris-Euphrates Fertile Crescent and the Indus River system of Northern India and Pakistan are today deserts, still much the same as the ancients left them.

As ancient civilizations expanded and moved out around the entire basin of the Mediterranean, the forests disappeared. With the rise of the Roman Empire, land was given away to colonists for the price of clearing the forests. Consequently, vast numbers of trees were cut down to be replaced with crops. Roman villages, cities. ships and aqueducts were built with timber. Over 200 million trees were cut down in Spain alone to make charcoal used in the manufacture of Roman swords and other metal objects. The ancients gave little, if any, thought to conserving the forests, the wildlife or the soils. To them nature was a storehouse of natural resources to be plundered as they chose.[3]

The collapse of the Roman Empire was hastened by the collapse of the natural environment. Deprived of forest cover, the climates of the Mediterranean changed. The loss of trees sharply reduced local hydrological cycles reducing seasonal rainfall and preventing the natural absorption of moisture into the lands where it is was previously held by the forests. The seasonal rains failed and the soils grew infertile. Grazing animals, particularly goats, tore up the vegetation cover and compacted the soil with their hard hoofs, leaving nothing to hold the water or soil in place. Water poured down hillsides, taking the soil with it to the seas. Abuse of the forests, farm lands and seaports left the Romans without timber for their ships or charcoal to make weapons. Militarily and economically weakened, Rome was vulnerable to encroaching barbarian invaders.

Exhausted from deforestation, overgrazing and erosion, North Africa and most of the Mediterranean lands became deserts, bearing witness to thousands of years of exploitation and vanished civilizations. The decreased carrying capacity of the Mediterranean lands was instrumental in moving the centres of civilization north into Europe and Russia. As Western civilization emerged throughout Europe, the same mistakes as the Romans made were repeated as Europeans abused their forests and lands.

Destruction of the Mediterranean environment did not end with the Romans. As late as the 17th Century, several islands were still covered with trees. Today they stand as barren monoliths to human exploitation over the last 400 years. Only a few pockets of the original forests still remain on the European and Asian continents. Most existing stands of trees were put there by human hands to meet human specifications, not nature's. With the loss of the post-glacial forests throughout the European continent, a great variety of species have disappeared or became extinct.

Viewed from a satellite today, these landscapes show up on the screen as arid, uninhabitable lands. Exposed rocks, dotted with sparse clumps of grass, empty of life except for a few hardy goats, dominate the landscape of Turkey, Greece, Lebanon, Israel, Southern Italy, Spain, North Africa and most of the Nile valley. The lands lie stripped and bare, at the mercy of sun, wind and rain, unable to recuperate. Only fragments of temples and buildings of ancient civilizations and outposts mark the places where lush forests, farmlands and towns once flourished. The wide bands of fertile plain along the Nile which nurtured ancient Egyptian civilizations no longer exist. What remains are narrow patches of farmland fed by the myriad of dams and irrigation canals which consume the Nile river.

Degradation of Mediterranean lands continues even today. Fertilizers, herbicides and pesticides poison the soils and the rivers of the Mediterranean while goats graze on remaining pockets of vegetation. In Spain the goats have learned to climb trees to eat the leaves, destroying even the few hardy varieties of scrub trees which cling to the land, despite the ravages of drought and wind.[4] Desert conditions, largely caused by human occupation, prevail over large land areas of Southern Europe and North Africa.

Where climatic changes and desertification have not yet destroyed the natural environment of all six continents, clouds of toxic fumes, spilled oil, toxic chemicals, fertilizers, herbicides, pesticides, manures, toxic run-off from industry and landfills are completing the destruction as they descend on the land from refineries, factories, vehicles, power plants, farms, contaminated rivers and burning forests.

Soil Erosion and Desertification

It took close to 10,000 years to destroy the Mediterranean and North African lands, but it took less than 500 years to spread this destructive process worldwide. As the food growing capacity of much of Europe and the Mediterranean Basin decreased, Europe became unable to sustain its expanding populations. Explorers were sent out in the 16th and 17th Centuries to find new lands suitable for occupation to absorb the excess populations and find new supplies of resources. Their invading armies ransacked the Americas, Africa and Asia.

With colonization and the introduction of fenced farm lands, the process of intensive farming over less than 500 years has led to depleted soils, thinning vegetation and forests, erosion and desertification. Satellite views of North and South America reveal a profile of clearcut forests, burning vegetation, overgrazed grasslands and vast land areas which have been irrigated, have a high salinity content and are eroded. The satellite photographs and computer models define large areas of disappearing farm lands in need of serious conservation programs. "In the last 50 years, the Earth has lost 11 percent of its vegetated land to human-induced soil degradation, an area about the size of China and India combined. Most of the lost soil is irretrievable".[5]

From ancient times to the present, human beings have looked to the horizons and believed the earth's lands and resources to be infinite. However, this is no longer true. Civilizations now span the globe and occupy nearly every acre of arable or marginal land that exists. What remains lies beneath the few forests still standing or in marginal drylands or wetlands, all under seige by developers.

In the last 30 years attempts have been made to increase the agricultural output of land beyond its seasonal cycles of growth and regeneration through irrigation, hybrid crops, the excessive use of fertilizers and now genetically engineered foods. This has led to several major agricultural failures and the rapid soil degradation on most continents. The Sahel of central Africa, the grasslands of Australia, and the farmlands of Asia, forced to use technologies of the "Green Revolution", have become the victims of the heavy hand of human exploitation.

Dry lands, whose sole source of water supply is through irrigation, fall victim to water logging and/or salinization. Flat lands which do not drain become waterlogged and sour. Constantly irrigated dry lands bring vast quantities of salts up to the surface which collect as a white crust, poisonous to vegetation. Anyone who fertilizes their house plants and discovers a white crust on the surface of the soil has seen this salting effect. It is a condition that can only be cured by pumping huge quantities of water over the heavily salted and chemically degraded lands to dissolve them, and then only if there is an abundance of fresh water which once contaminated with the dissolved salts can be forced to drain away from the area. Large tracts of formerly arable land in the Imperial Valley of California have had to be abandoned because of the salt buildup.

Irrigating large areas of dry lands for intensive farming also entails prohibitive construction costs. It is seldom attempted unless government subsidies are available to build the irrigation systems and farmers are given large shares of available water reserves. Few farmers can afford the costs on their own. Much the same can be said for organic farming. It demands nearly a third of the crop vegetation be returned to the soil, a loss in revenue the farmer must be able to sustain. Not too many farmers are so productive and financially secure that they can withstand this decrease in output. Organic farming also tends to be more labour intensive, especially in agrarian nations. Once common throughout the Third World, organic farming enabled the growth of a greater variety in crops and animals which cannot survive where heavy use of chemicals and mechanized farm machinery are popular.

Deforestation has also played a major role in turning fertile lands into deserts by changing global and local weather patterns. Without trees rainfall is inhibited and increased temperatures occur in areas that never before experienced prolonged heat waves and droughts. Hotter, drier growing conditions are more widespread and common than at any time before this century. High summer temperatures reduce crop output, and drought conditions eventually destroy natural vegetation until it disappears. Increasing drought also eliminates forest watersheds needed to hold large reserves of fresh water in the soil and disperse it slowly over the year.

This capacity of ours to impose climatic changes which destroy the fertility of the earth's major farm lands will soon equal our power to destroy the same lands through erosion, chemical technologies and the practice of monoculture. The degree of abuse humanity imposes on arable soils is leaving the farm lands of the world in danger of failing us in the very near future.

There are approximately 37 billion acres of land on this planet; only one-fifth of them have been classified as arable and able to provide good sustainable growing conditions. The rest are either marginal farmlands, pasture, desert or rock, a total of about 16 to 18 billion acres. Only 3 to 3.6 billion acres will grow crops and 6 billion are suitable for pasture. But these lands are disappearing at a dangerous rate. Annually, some 77 billion tons of topsoil are being lost to erosion, pollution, salinization and desertification. On average 6 to 10 million hectares of new desert are formed by mismanagement and erosion each year. The existence of arable lands is further endangered by an annual loss of 11 million hectares of tropical forests and 31 million hectares of temperate forests, damaged by acid rain, pest incursions and deforestation. The total permanent loss each year of farm land averages over 10,000 square miles.[6]

Worked out mathematically, all things being as they are, this annual loss of farmland leaves only 250 years before we will have destroyed all the arable lands on the planet. To date Central America has destroyed 24 percent of its fertile lands, Europe 17 percent, Africa 14 percent, Asia 12 percent and North America over 4.5 percent.[7]

Admittedly these statistics do not account for the numerous variables, such as the rise in conservation and organic farming practices which are catching on. However, there is no indication that these efforts will not remain minimal and be offset by the demands of a population that will exceed 10 billion by 2050. Nor does this estimation of time include the impact of the "greenhouse effect", ozone depletion, acid rain, contamination of soils, water pollution, loss of eco-systems, warmer and colder seasonal temperatures, longer periods of drought, increased flooding and windstorms, rising sea levels and the many other variable changes of climate, vegetation, soil and ecology we are causing, putting our farmlands and capacity to grow food at great risk.

The most productive farm lands which remain anywhere in the world lie in North America. But just as in Sub-Saharan Africa and South and Central America, ill-conceived farming methods and technologies continue in use, induced by the profit motive and a persistent belief in the human right to despoil the land. Intensive use of farming technologies, employing large machinery and heavy doses of chemicals have ruined over 120 million acres by erosion and salinization in the United States. Although new tilling methods have saved one billion tons of topsoil from disappearing annually since 1980, two billion a year are still being lost. This has cut the annual loss by only one-third. Over 60 percent of all U.S. croplands need conservation treatment to protect the soils from exhaustion and erosion.[8]

In Canada the loss of arable soils through destructive policies also adds to the world wide degradation of croplands. First, only 11 percent of Canadian territory is suitable for farming of which less than one-half of one percent is classified as excellent growing land. These high quality farmlands exist almost exclusively in valleys and river areas where populations have settled and built their cities, creating a strong conflict of interests between urban and farm use. Urban development is proving an uncompromising adversary. For example, the Niagara Peninsula in Southern Ontario has some of the finest land and climatic conditions for mixed farming and fruit growing, but it is disappearing beneath urban construction, housing and roads. An original 23 million acres of rich farm land in Ontario is now down to less than 14 million acres and disappearing to development.[9]

Across Canada approximately 165 million acres are still farmed. During the 1980s and early 1990s this number dropped yearly. Mechanized farming, increasing costs, subsidized competition of other grain growing nations, frequent seasonal extremes of drought, rain or hail and increasing carrying costs and debts drove many Canadian farmers into bankruptcy and off the land. More so, the high costs of financing production fostered the use of poor farming practices.

Unable to meet their annual expenditures, many Canadian farmers ignored such things as rotating crops to keep the soils fertile. Instead they grew crops which were in demand and paid well, among them rape seed which rapidly depletes the nutrients in the soil. Neither could farmers afford to let the land lie fallow for a year or grow a high nutrient crop of little return. This practise exhausted the soils and degraded the organic content. Many farmers escaped bankruptcy by selling their farms to developers or to profit-oriented farmers.

In 1995 poor growing weather produced fewer crops. At the same time increasing world demand reduced existing inventories. By 1996 wholesale grain prices had doubled, stimulating the opening up of an additional 4.5 million acres to wheat across Canada, raising the total in wheat production to 32.6 million acres. The Canadian farmer had a reprieve, but the costs of refurbishing and protecting their lands from future overcropping may prove as harmful as low demand and bankruptcy.

Protecting the land takes sacrifice and much hard work, with a minimum of technologies of heavy machinery, herbicides, pesticides and fertilizers along with the return of a third of the harvested vegetation as compost. This takes time, labour and a willingness to sacrifice profit to farm the land organically. Adding to the farmer's problems is the victimization of the Canadian farmer by government and multinational grain handlers. As an Alberta farmer told me, "Farming is the only business where the costs of production are at retail prices and the return on the grain is at wholesale prices."

The second or third generation farmer who cares for his land is an anachronism. The futility of working so hard, only to fall further into debt each year, forces him to give up the land to those "farmers" who are motivated only by quick, short term profits and "mine" the land with heavy machinery and chemicals. The land is soon degraded, its fertility gone, crops diminished, erosion set in and tons of topsoil blown away on the winds. The true caretakers of the soil are dispersing and the farmland is under threat of the natural forces of destruction, --weeds, drought, flooding, erosion and wind. An estimated 10 tons per acre are lost on many North American farms annually.

Cattle ranchers are the major cause of desertification of the pasture lands. They overgraze the drylands or areas of poor soil around the globe. Large herds of cattle and sheep compact the soil and chew the vegetation to the roots. The soil then loses its friability and turns to dust. Its capacity to grow grass is reduced and the soil is swept up by the winds.

Often the cattle rancher damages the grasslands further by refusing to curb the size of his herds. The amount of feed needed to meet the demands of the domestic animals of the world now surpasses sustainable yields of grasslands. In southern Africa, for example, the number of cattle exceed the carrying capacity of the savannas by 50 to 100 percent. When drought occurs, millions of cattle die. Drought and land shortages have driven farmers into marginal lands which erode rapidly, create their own drought conditions, become infertile in a few years and end in permanent deserts. Savannas are becoming endangered marginal lands where human populations are presently generating deserts in 22 countries in Africa alone.

Widespread destruction of arable lands presents a dismal future for food production and human use. Obviously, arable land will be in ever decreasing supply in our lifetimes, causing incremental drops in annual world food production. Thousands of acres of farmland throughout Canada and the United States are now covered with houses, roads, railway beds, cement, dam reservoirs, industrial sites and sprawling urban development. These are lands that may never be re-utilized for growing crops as they are lands occupied by people and their activities, people whose numbers are growing and forcing construction further and further onto farmlands, reminiscent of Malthus's observation of rural England in danger of disappearing beneath urban development during the 18th Century. We have come to see land only in dollar terms, believing idle land must be developed for human use, not left wild or for environmental protection and conservation. Arable land is environmentally costly to farm and it is economically costly to leave idle.

Effects of Climatic Changes on Soils and Crop Production

Good farm lands are not only diminishing with human exploitation, but with increasingly hostile climatic changes. Much of North Africa, once a major granary of the Roman Empire, is today a hostile, infertile desert that is increasing its size by 40,000 acres a year as the continent's climates grow more arid.[10] Droughts lasting several years plague Africa from the Mediterranean to the Cape of Good Hope.

Some prognosticators believe diminishing crop production in present agricultural zones will be offset by the effects of "greenhouse" warming. Warmer year round temperatures should bring northern lands, now unusable because of cold summers or very short growing seasons, into temperature ranges and longer growing seasons sufficient for producing food crops. But most northern areas that have arable soils are under cultivation now, albeit for short growing periods and for very limited varieties of crops. A few small pockets of alluvial soil in scattered areas can be found near small settlements, but most northern lands beyond the areas that are now farmed are primarily rock outcroppings, left barren by the last ice age, dotted with lakes and covered in muskeg which will grow very little. Even the best climatic conditions will not grow food on barren rock. Believing that existing farm lands in North America and Russia could become areas of mixed farming, able to produce crops the year round as global temperatures rise ignores the fact that world climates and wind patterns would have to change drastically to produce sufficient seasonal rainfall to turn the prairies into gardens of plenty.

Accordingly, the possibility of increasing northern crop production if world temperatures rise is only surmised at and remains at the whim of the vagaries of time and natural phenomena. If, on the other hand, global warming should trigger an ice age through vastly increased cloud cover, already existing crop production will be widely reduced as cold and glacial ice return to present grain growing areas in the Northern Hemisphere. On the other hand, the Southern Hemisphere may become dryer and its growing lands become deserts as so many are in Africa and Australia.

Forests Under Stress

Stress on both old-growth and regenerating forests has been intensified in recent years by the high levels of industrial development and fossil fuel emissions of sulphur dioxide which have combined with water vapor in the air to form weak solutions of sulphuric acid. This "acid rain" leaches into the soils and interferes with tree growth. Most varieties of trees and vegetation are unable to take up nutrients from overly acidic soils and process them. The effects show up in both the original and planted forests in Europe and Russia where vast areas of trees are dying from pollutants and heavily acidic soils.

The beautiful European Alps of skiing fame epitomize the impact overcrowding and chemical abuse of forests can have on an entire nation as well as its neighbours. The inhabitants of the Alps have dammed their rivers, replaced their forests with roads and ski runs and filled their valleys with resorts. This is particularly true of Switzerland where over 100 million visitors arrive throughout the year to enjoy the beauty and the recreation offered by the mountains.

Traffic passing through the country pollutes the air with fossil fuel emissions, the effect of which is seen in millions of dying trees. Wild animals and birds that once favoured the Swiss mountain slopes have largely disappeared and rare alpine plant species, though protected by law against picking or cultivation, are under attack. Mountain slopes, once held in place by thick forests, have become destabilized by roads and diverted watercourses. Floods and heavy snowpacks threaten the villages and resorts with frequent mud slides and snow avalanches. Rock and cement walls must be constantly built and replaced along railway lines and roads to prevent these slides.

This loss of slope stability has a most vital long term impact. Without the slow melting of mountain snows and ice packs, there is less and less water to feed the major rivers of Europe, the Rhine, the Rhone and the Po which supply the drinking water of hundreds of millions of people, irrigate the farms of Western Europe and keep the rivers navigable for the thousands of tons of shipping that supply the heartland of Europe. Frequent low water levels along the major river routes have slowed river traffic and reduced carrying capacity, particularly during the busiest summer months when tourism is at its height.[11]

Trying to protect the environment from the erosion and instability caused by clearing and farming forest lands has led nations to encourage large plantings of trees. However, producing viable forests and eco-systems is still beyond human knowhow. To date, manufactured eco-systems, based largely on mono-cultures in preparation for future logging, continue to produce an inferior quality of forests. Planted forests lack variety, ecological diversity and biological resistance to diseases. They tend to suffer a general decline in the health of their trees and a dying-off among most varieties within 150 years of being planted. The wood products are generally inferior to those of old growth forests which have withstood the ravages of varied weather conditions and natural diseases for hundreds of years.

As human populations grow on every continent, their struggle to live must of necessity increase the stress on forest lands and arable soils. The danger to lives are an added element. The following news story in April of 1996 clearly demonstrates the contest between nature and humans:[12]

"At least 70 Bolivians were missing after a landslide in a La Paz suburb unleashed tons of dirt and rocks on a dozen homes. Officials had planted trees in the area during recent years to prevent such a disaster, but authorities say that peasants had cut them down to use as firewood."

The jungles of South America are also disappearing beneath the chain saw to grow coca for cocaine, to raise cattle for the North American markets and to provide meagre, very short term sustenance for land-poor peasants, struggling to grow enough food to stay alive.

The worst possible methods of land clearing are used. In the Amazon River Basin in South America, trees are clear cut, then the vegetation and stumps are burned. Few farmers can afford the machinery to dislodge and remove stumps and debris, so they burn them. In the process the nutrients in the soil are destroyed and most of the life forms which make the nutrients accessible to the plants are killed by the heat. The trees which were the sole source of nutrients for all jungle vegetation have been destroyed, leaving the soil open to erosion and poor crop production. The soil, so low in nutrients, will produce only two or three years of poor crops, then the peasant with his very primitive methods of farming must move on to clear and burn another patch of forest. Thousands of square miles of exhausted soils and vanished eco-systems have followed in their wake.

The process is duplicated by those farmers who produce cocaine for the large drug cartels. Vast areas of the Amazon forest have been cut down and burned to plant the coca shrubs. No organic material is returned to compost and refurbish the soil as the plants are stripped four times a year and no leaves are left to fall to the earth. As a result the soil is rapidly exhausted so that chemical fertilizers must be added in larger and larger amounts, killing off all life forms in the soil, rapidly making it sterile. Coca production drops and the farmer moves on to destroy more acreage.

Over 10 percent of Peru's rainforest has been lost to coca farming. Furthermore, the land is now toxic from the chemicals and acids used to process the cocaine. Police often add to the destruction of the soils in that, rather than transport the confiscated cocoa leaves long miles over difficult terrain to dispose of them, they burn the stores of leaves and coca plants where they find them growing, leaving the residue chemicals to contaminate the farmland and pollute the air. The coca growers' contest with police and with nature expands as poverty deepens among the people. They cannot afford any drop in their coca production or the lost employment involved as coca farming pays 18 times what any other crop does.

Thousands of farmers and logging companies both in the rain forests of the tropics and in the temperate forests of the Northern hemisphere are guilty of similar destructive deforestation practices. Both groups clearcut their forests to provide timber, fuel, jobs, cash and land as did their forefathers. Their actions are seldom regulated or curtailed by local governments who may benefit directly through taxes or have few enforcement powers to stop them. Millions of people living in urban poverty in the Third World are migrating to forest wilderness areas where they believe they can clear the land to grow enough food to feed their families, garner sufficient wood to meet their fuel needs and illegally sell the timber of the trees they fell. In the process they are laying waste forests and exposing the land to erosion.

By 1980 over 1.2 billion people in the Third World were meeting their firewood needs by cutting down trees faster than nature could replace them. With their forests disappearing, women and children must walk long distances daily to collect wood for cooking their food. The long treks, carrying heavy loads on their heads, burns up energy needed for other tasks of daily living or the earning of money. The effect is increased poverty and malnutrition with an ever growing delay in conservation and reforestation.

In India, for example, if local people are to practice "sustainable forest management" so as to ensure future wood supplies, they must restrict their annual wood use to less than 40 million tons. But their actual requirements are 135 million tons. The deficiency of more than 95 million tons must then be made up by burning cow dung and crop residues. But both of these are critical sources of compost if the overworked soils are to remain sufficiently fertile to grow nutritious foods. Consequently, the forests are the first to be sacrificed.

In areas of high seasonal rainfall, deforestation for whatever reasons poses a threat to human habitation and health. Heavy run off from deforested mountain slopes floods valleys and river plains, endangering the lives and property of tens of millions of people around the world annually. The seasonal monsoon rains which pour off the denuded slopes of Nepal and overflow the banks of the large rivers of Bangladesh take thousands of lives annually and leave the populace short of living space, housing and food. The destruction of the natural environment has made many nations like Bangladesh more and more dependent on other nations to provide their basic survival supplies of food.

Our Destructive Stewardship of the Land

Environmental degradation is obviously not restricted to the 20th Century. Destructive practices have been carried on over the millennia. Many of them might be assessed as a "necessary evil" of human development and survival. To state it even more honestly, environmental exploitation and degradation have been inherent in our evolution and now in our extinction. What is recent is the magnitude of the damage our exploding populations and technologies have inflicted on the land and its environments during the past 100 years and the rising speed at which it continues.

Human populations have always settled in concentrated numbers where the best soils and water resources are located. During their occupancy, humans have reduced fertile lands into varying degrees of deserts. This pattern of human settlement and expansion over the earth has shown up in ever-widening circles of land degradation, beginning with the earliest centres of civilization in the eastern Mediterranean and Persia and reaching onto every continent today. Our latest photographic technologies in space clearly show a correspondence exists between the destructive use of the land by ancient civilizations and the degradation of millions of square miles each year through desertification and urban development today.

The desertification process is synonymous with deforestation, overgrazing, chemical sterilization and urban sprawl. Creeping deserts now threaten every continent. Preventing this extensive annual degradation of the land and its soils may now be impossible to stop. Growing populations will exploit their environments as long as those environments can grow food.

Our earliest settled ancestors struggled with a "cruel" nature which often seemed more of an enemy than a source of sustenance and survival. As primitive peoples they tried to live in harmony with nature, afraid to anger the powers of natural forces, practising primitive methods of hunting, herding and simple agriculture. With time and the development of civilization, the demands of their expanding populations abused the land to the point the inhabitants could not overcome the damage they had done to the soil, the forests and the water supplies. Most were forced to move on to "greener pastures", or as in so many cases in ancient times, their civilizations disappeared and their people died or were scattered.

The modern scientific idea of escape from collapsed environments is either to find another planet or build artificial environments here on earth and isolate ourselves from the natural flow of life within nature which sustained us in the past. In assuming human mastery over the earth and its natural powers of life and growth, we have put our faith in science and technology to carry on with the stewardship of nature which we usurped. What we must stop to consider is that we may have exceeded our reach and created a world of steel and concrete which has become our "prison" rather than our "home".

More importantly, we are failing to recognize that nature can no longer tolerate this massive attack on her forests and lands. There simply is not any land left that we can "mine" safely without doing harm to some other part of the earth's eco-systems. Nor is there land that can withstand years of "sustainable development" as we chose to practice it. If human populations continue to take more from the earth than they put back or conserve, we will turn the remaining habitable lands of the earth into deserts in less than a hundred years.

Ironically, our devastating impact on the earth was recognized by an individual as long ago as 2000 years. Isaiah is quoted in the Bible as having told his people "Woe unto them that join house to house, that lay field to field, till there be no place, that they may be placed alone in the midst of the earth!"

CHAPTER FOURTEEN

Overuse and Abuse of the Earth's Fresh Water Reserves

When the Egyptians settled their ancient cities along the Nile valley, fewer than 7 million people occupied the fertile plain. Today, those numbers will approach 70 millions in the next decade. With overdevelopment and unrestrained use of the land, both the fertile plain and the Nile River are shrinking rapidly. At the source of the Nile are Sudan and Ethiopia who share control of 80 percent of the water that reaches Egypt. The Sudan agreed to give Egypt two-thirds of the annual flow, but both the Sudan and Ethiopia are in need of more water themselves. Egypt finds itself at the whim of these nations. As the amount of water in the Nile shrinks annually, the shortage has come to mean life or death for the millions hugging its banks.

The above scenario repeats itself on every continent, some situations much more desperate than others. With the constant parade of innovative technologies to capture water and distribute it thousands of miles away, 20th Century technologies continue to intensify the struggle for diminishing reserves of fresh water. The contest for supplies threatens most large populations.

While human contamination of fresh water reserves and growing overuse and abuse of supplies were instrumental in the disappearance of ancient civilizations, the shortage of fresh water in the immediate future is becoming the most internationally destabilizing social force on the planet. The growing shortage of fresh water on every continent threatens civil and international wars in many overcrowded lands.

Water shortages already play a major role in climatic changes, causing widespread drought and desertification. Dwindling underground reserves, diverted rivers, irrigation projects and dried up lakes are major catalysts in environmental collapse and economic chaos. The repercussions may prove so intractable that they will paralyse most chances of universal cooperation in seeking ways to facilitate equitable sharing of remaining reserves.

Meanwhile modern technologies give us the power to collect, store and transport billions of gallons of water from one place to another, while draining, depleting and contaminating the sources of origin. Few nations today have water reserves that are not in scarce supply or over allocated for human use. Even more catastrophic is the amount of contamination existing reserves must endure from human waste, deforestation and toxic pollutants.

We have learned to grow vast quantities of food year after year and distribute it anywhere on earth to hungry populations. But we continue to ignore that the regeneration of fresh water supplies cannot keep up with our overuse and abuse of it.

Distribution of Fresh Water over the Globe

To live all species must have access to fresh water daily; however, nature makes fresh water available in very few ways and in limited quantities. Seventy percent of the planet is covered with water, but 97 percent of it is salt water, leaving only three percent as fresh water, two percent of which is locked up in ice caps and glaciers. Of the remaining one percent, 15 to 20 percent of the volume is in Canada and another 20 percent is in Lake Baikal in Siberia. Both of these water reserves are located in isolated, sparsely populated areas. This leaves little more than one-half of one percent of fresh surface water available to the rest of the continental areas and the bulk of the population.

Supplementing this scarce resource are the estimated 10 million billion cubic metres of underground water stored in aquifers and wells, an amount equal to one hundred times the water held in the world's lakes and rivers at a given time.[1] Fortunately, for many countries, underground water reserves are more equitably distributed around the globe and often more pure than surface water. Modern technologies have enabled us to pump billions of gallons of this fossil water to the surface for use.

The location of fresh water supplies has influenced human settlement and population expansion since prehistoric times. Nomadic hunter-gatherers set up camp next to fresh water. As more and more of our ancestors were forced to take up farming to survive, archaeological excavations reveal they established their farms and villages on the banks of rivers and lakes where, as time passed, they learned to build small dams to redirect water onto their fields. The earliest "empires" such as those of Sumer and Babylon on the Fertile Crescent of the Tigris-Euphrates River system and Ancient Egypt grew up near large river systems with adjacent arable lands.

Early methods of irrigation ensured a supply of fresh water for drinking, agriculture and general purposes which eventually led to more sophisticated technologies for collecting, storing and transporting water, especially where settlements were heavily populated or facing encroaching deserts. Later civilizations built reservoirs and aqueducts to store and carry water to expanding urban centres as well as to the fields.

The more adept a civilization was at providing its people with adequate fresh water, the more advanced, productive and stable their societies tended to be. The Romans built large aqueducts to transport millions of gallons of fresh water over many miles to where it was needed, enhancing agriculture while enabling their cities to sustain relatively large numbers of people. At its peak Imperial Rome is estimated to have had a million residents, among whom the rich elite had water piped directly into their homes.[2] Advanced sanitary practices of bathing regularly as well as a varied diet added to the energy and stamina of the Roman people. The distribution of fresh water and the disposal of sewage through piped systems as well as technologies to drain lakes, swamps and wetlands facilitated successful urban existence for large cities like Rome.[3]

Many of the engineering feats of Roman times were lost in the chaos of the Dark Ages. The knowledge of advanced technologies of water disbursement returned slowly over the centuries in Europe. Real advances in storing, distributing and using water and then the introduction of hydro power came with the Agricultural and Industrial Revolutions in the 19th Century. The harnessing of water to produce electric power and the use of it in the textile industries were instrumental in accelerating the invention and use of machines to manufacture a myriad of commodities. Electric power inspired the 20th Century mania for erecting large dams and reservoirs.

As commercial agriculture and manufacturing gain headway, human dependency on technologies, enabling the storage and dispersal of large reserves of fresh water, grows constantly. At present two-thirds of the fresh water consumed world wide irrigates farmlands, one half of which is used in Asia whose share alone will rise to two-thirds of the total yearly water consumption by the year 2000.[4] Clean fresh water is fast becoming as valuable a resource as oil and will soon cost as much to obtain. Many already drink bottled water which is an expensive commodity.

Populations Overwhelming Fresh Water Reserves

Fresh water resources are finite although generally classified as "renewable". They must be divided up and meted out for city use, irrigation and industries. Small populations place much less stress on water reserves than large concentrations of people and industries, permitting a natural, sustainable rate of replacement.

However, exploding populations on every continent have meant smaller and smaller shares of available water supplies per person. World demand for fresh water is already outstripping population growth. Annual consumption tripled between 1950 and 1990, while population doubled. Experts estimate that 2,744 litres for every person per day is needed to meet the present demands of agriculture, industry and populations. This is a rise of 800 cubic metres a year per person over the past 40 years. Total annual world consumption now stands at 4,340 cubic kilometres and continues to increase at a rate three times that of population growth.[5]

While overall consumption has risen, the actual amount used per person has dropped by a third since 1970, the result of increasing populations, especially in "water-scarce" countries.[6]

At the present time, over 26 nations can be categorized as "water-scarce" in that they have yearly supplies of 1,000-2,000 metres per capita which in drought periods often shrinks to less than 1,000 metres per capita.[7] The majority of these nations are in Africa and the Middle East, among them the heavily populated countries of South Africa, Kenya, Somalia, Sudan, Egypt, Israel, Jordan, Lebanon and Iraq.

The most stressful situations are occurring in nations such as Iraq, Syria, Lebanon and Egypt where water allocations must be raised to meet the needs of an added population rise of 3 to 4 percent annually. Egypt, for example, must have water for an added two million people each year. In these nations river flow is sharply reduced by the number of dams along their courses and the amount allocated to irrigation. The registered annual drop in their water tables reflects the growing loss in underground reserves as well.

These and many other "water-scarce" nations are experiencing a deterioration in the quality of their water as it registers a sharp rise in salt content. This salt reduces annual output and lowers the farmer's living standards. Increasing numbers of farmers, impoverished by poor crop production, have left the land in search of work. The decline in crop production must be covered by national spending of foreign credits and borrowing from other nations to purchase food imports. This cycle of water scarcity and deepening poverty gradually worsens in that "scarce-water" nations, in using up their foreign credits on food, have little or no money left to purchase technologies with which they could recycle, desalinate and purify their contaminated reserves of used water.

Growing populations are a major contributing factor in the diminishing capacity of nations to protect and conserve their fresh water resources. Overcrowding the land must be accommodated by deforestation, irrigation projects, dams, river diversions, erosion and drought, most of which have turned large land areas in Africa, the Middle East, North America and Asia into deserts. As populations grow, large settlements are built on drylands and deserts to which water must be either pumped from aquifers or transported long distances. Arizona, California, Israel, the Sahel in Africa have deserts where life is sustained by pumping billions of gallons of water to the earth's surface from aquifers.

Wetlands are nature's prime means of cleaning contaminants from river water before it reaches the oceans. Yet thousands of hectares of wetlands have been drained to make way for housing and farming; thousands more are threatened. Extremes of environmental changes such as destroyed wetlands ravage the natural eco-systems and interfere with the natural forces of weather and water runoff which replenish surface and underground resources. As the forests have disappeared, the hydrological cycles have failed. This has reduced the amount of surface water which seeps into wells and underground reserves or is retained by the residual soils.

Of even greater humanitarian concern are the increasing periods of drought which plague most of the continents. Water shortages in central and Eastern Africa have caused horrendous suffering and brought death to millions of displaced environmental refugees who have no food source other than foreign aid during extensive periods of drought. The resulting chaos, economic breakdown and tribal warfare in many African nations are intensified by starvation and wandering refugees from drought. Australia, the U.S., various areas of Asia and South America are also prone to extremes of weather which bring crop-killing droughts. Overdevelopment and settlement of the land on every continent has increased the frequency and length of droughts, conditions which worsen catastrophically whenever El Nino disrupts the earth's weather systems.

As populations reach 6 billion in 1997, total world consumption of fresh water is predicted to increase by 25 percent and continue to rise on an annual basis into the 21st Century along with populations.[8] Commercial agriculture, urban development, industrialization and higher living standards will come to the developing nations through the activities of the global economy in the next few decades. Obviously, the demand for water will escalate even more rapidly than at present. Meeting the demand may soon prove impossible.

A parallel rise in world poverty exists where diminishing water capacity and pollution are critical. Scarcity of clean water usually causes a drop in productivity, a rise in unemployment and a general decline in the health of populations. Forced to use less water than they need for a healthy existence, they must endure poor sanitation, filthy living conditions, malnutrition, reduced mental capacity and a rise in infections and endemic diseases. At present over 1.3 billion people, 30 percent of the world's population, use contaminated water to drink, wash their clothes and irrigate their crops. The annual rise in epidemic diseases such as typhus and cholera is a constant threat where water is scarce or contaminated and where sewage and garbage disposal are generally inadequate or non-existent.

A comparison of life expectancy and infant mortality rates with access to safe water and sanitation in Africa, Central and South America and Asia shows that the infant mortality rate and a short life span coincide with unsafe water and poor sanitation conditions. For instance, in African nations where less than 40 percent of the population has access to clean water and safe sanitation, the average life span is 40 years and the infant mortality rate is 140 out of every 1000 births. This is the case in Guinea-Bissau where only 23.3 percent of the people have access to clean water. In Sierra Leone the life expectancy is 42 years and the infant death rate is 122 in a 1000. The improvement is because 38.5 percent have access to clean water. In Mauritius, on the other hand, 98.8 percent have access to clean water and 97.6 percent to safe sanitation. This is reflected in the average life span which is 62 years and the infant death rate which is as low as 20 out of every 1000 births.[9]

Water shortages are also a prevalent cause of the declining health of domestic crops and animals. Contaminated water, if they do not kill the vegetation, will pass on the poisons to all local life forms through the food chain. Domestic animals, having no other choice but to drink polluted water and eat contaminated vegetation, are then infected with diseases and toxic chemicals which may destroy their immune systems and reproductive abilities. The toxins in their meat and milk is also passed on to humans.

Trying to reverse these effects requires large investments in purifying or recycling plants. In poor nations people themselves are the major cause of contamination in their water resources.

Without sewage systems, human fecal wastes, even bodies, are deposited or dumped directly into rivers and streams for disposal.

As populations rise to 10 billion over the next 50 years, 95 percent of them in the Third World, the majority of people will consume contaminated water and the health problems entailed will multiply manyfold.

Consequences of Abusing Fresh Water Reserves

Universal dependency on fresh water is obviously immense. Although the largest share of fresh water is allotted to farming and irrigation, all human activities depend on water either directly or indirectly. Large quantities of it are particularly crucial to economic development and the high living standards which come with industrialization. Through modern technologies distribution of fresh water to urban and farm areas from distant rivers and lakes has facilitated urban development on an unprecedented scale. Pumping technologies have also made it possible to drill deep into the earth and bring up vast reserves of fresh water from aquifers where surface reservoirs are scarce. Today more than half of the United States is supplied with drinking water from underground sources in urban areas and 96 percent in rural areas.[10]

Our dependency on fresh water is now total for daily existence. Without it modern societies come to a standstill and essentially disappear. Hydro-electric power, for example, is indispensable in the operation of hundreds of technologies from running the machines of industry and commodity processing, to heating and lighting our homes, streets and workplaces, to providing the social and public services of hospitals, transportation systems and the bright lights of entertainment. Unfortunately, few nations today have sufficient hydro capacity to meet all these demands. Many produce power through burning coal or using nuclear power, both dangerous to the environment.

Industries are large, dependent users of fresh water for cooling, cleaning, diluting and flushing, especially in the major industries of paper manufacturing, chemical production, petroleum refining and metal processing. An average 36 billion gallons of water are used daily by industry in the U.S.

In recent years a few industrial nations have managed a marked reduction in their industrial consumption of fresh water by developing new technologies that improved efficiency in recycling used and contaminated water.[11] Among these nations are the 25 fully industrialized members of the Organization for Economic Cooperation and Development (OECD). Together their populations total approximately 610 million people, one-tenth of the world's 6 billion. As OECD nations presently manufacture and consume the bulk of the world's industrial output, their use of water reserves is far greater per capita than the rest of the world. The minimal amount of water conservation and recycling they do puts into perspective the impact coming as the Third world catches up industrially. At present 15 Newly Emerging Industrials (NEIs) in Asia and South America are undergoing rapid industrial development. In these nations live the largest concentrations of populations in the world, those of China and India where water scarcity is looming as the most threatening problem of their industrialization.

A brief look at China's situation illustrates the array of problems associated with diminishing water resources. In China, empty rivers are common. For example, the Heaven River dried up over 20 years ago and its canals no longer bring water to Beijing.[12] Overused wells are drying up in Northern China. Over 82 million people in rural areas find it difficult to get water. Industrial pollution and agricultural chemicals are contaminating more and more of their rivers and wells so that the quality of existing supplies is rapidly dropping. Over 300 cities throughout the nation are short of water, 100 of them very short.[13]

The industrial development of China, the wealth it is generating and the ensuing rise in living standards for a growing sector of the population, magnify the problem of future world water shortages. Concern is spreading that their water supplies and crop production will not keep up with either population growth or industrial development. Farmers and workers in rural areas who have already overwhelmed the carrying capacity of their farm lands and water supplies are migrating in the tens of millions to the urban areas in search of work. Over nine million men left the farm for the city in 1995 alone. China today has over

280 million non-farmers out of a population of 1.2 billion. Although her newly found industrial wealth means she can afford to import food, it does not bode well for that future that at present she must import as much as one-third of the nation's food needs to support her 1.2 billion people. This new dependency is establishing a dangerous precedent in a world where food and water supplies are rapidly declining.

The water problems of China are exacerbated by the local destruction over the centuries of eco-systems. This has reduced the hydrological cycles and caused dangerous climatic changes, such as the 10 to 20 percent drop in annual rainfall in Northern China in recent years.[14] Thousands of square miles in Eastern China, where the bulk of the people live, are devoid of trees, let alone forests. Paul Therroux in writing of his travels through China points out that trees are not grown because they make shade which reduces crop growth.[15] Unfortunately, this full exposure to the sun dries the land and prevents the natural retention of water which trees would offer. This interferes with natural evaporation which is almost negligible, producing little rainfall in the bulk of growing areas and a heavy dependency on aquifers.

Only 40 years ago there were 5200 large dams in the world, eight of which were in China. Today, over 36,000 dams restrict the rivers of the world, half of them in China. Yet this has not alleviated either China's water shortages nor fulfilled its power needs, especially now that industrialization is spreading so rapidly. The need for hydro power to replace power from burning coal is leading the nation towards precarious decisions about its environment.

The highest hydro-electric dam in the world is to be built at the Three Gorges on the Yangtze River, which environmentalists say will create a reservoir that will inundate 26,000 hectares of farmland and force over a million people to relocate. The hazards associated with this, the highest dam in the world, cannot be measured. The river at present receives millions of kilograms of waste from steel mills and cement, chemical and fertilizer plants which would "instead of discharging into the East China Sea, pour into the reservoir, creating a cesspool stretching 580 kilometres behind the dam. Water used for farming, drinking and bathing could become deadly."[16] The weight of the water stored behind that dam could also trigger huge earthquakes. A weakened structure would give way and a massive deluge of water sweep down the canyon, drowning thousands of people and flooding miles of rice fields.

Problems are universally inherent in hydro-electric projects. Initially they flood vast treed valleys, destroy eco-systems, cover hundreds of miles of arable farm land and displace hundreds to millions of people. They require vast quantities of water be stored by holding back normal seasonal flow which stops the natural flooding of river plains and prevents the replacement of worn out soils with new silt and nutrients. While dams in the past have ended much of the disaster associated with regular flooding of the Yangtze River in China for those living along its banks, it has also reduced the fertility of the soil and the amount of crop production.

Continued damming of river water also decreases the supply of fresh water available to people along the river banks. The Nile river, for instance, is heavily controlled by a series of dams. The irrigation systems supplied by these dams increase the areas on which crops can be grown, but the soil suffers from the lack of annual renewals of sediment. Crops require larger and larger doses of chemical fertilizers. Fish, once prolific in the river and at the river mouth, have all but disappeared as the natural ecology of the river and its valleys have changed with the reduced flow of water and the fish killed off by toxic waste. Also local diseases, parasites and malaria have increased because of low river flow. Drinking water taken from the Nile is highly toxic, carrying several bacterial forms which debilitate human health.

Perhaps the most distressing aspect of dams is that most of them last less than 100 years before silt and river debris pile up behind the walls, stemming the flow of water through the turbines and making them inoperable. The costs of building a dam plus the damage done to the environment and the displacement of people for such short periods of use is finally deterring many nations from building large scale dams and dissuading the World Bank from making huge loans to Third World countries to build them.

While advanced technologies of water collection and distribution are crucial in attaining high living standards, they encourage the misuse of supply. Overcrowding and overuse of the land follows where water and power are easily available. Problems are increased as mismanagement and the careless waste of fresh water is common. Distribution generally falls under political control, giving those who are strong party supporters or members of the elite priority of supply. Subsidized farmers in California, for instance, tend to grow inappropriate crops such as rice and cotton on drylands or use their allocated share inefficiently and profligately just to ensure their future quotas will remain high. The lack of expensive, efficient technologies which permit "underground" watering keeps farmers wasting large amounts of water through evaporation, especially where they depend on irrigation in hot, dry lands.

Several large nations, some with relatively good water supplies in rivers and lakes, have water shortages because their surface supplies fail to meet the demands of expanding agriculture and urbanization. They now depend more on underground reserves from aquifers and wells than on surface reservoirs. China and the United States are the largest crop growing countries in the world, but they are also among the most heavily populated. This makes them intensive users of all surface and underground water reserves. In the United States 65 percent of the nation's irrigation water is drawn from continental aquifers.[17]

Surface wells or deep wells can be drilled thousands of feet into the earth, tapping aquifers whose water, known as fossil water, has been collecting over tens of thousands of years. In our extravagant use of it, we tend to forget this water is a non-renewable resource. It is generally very pure and excellent for irrigation. India pumps over 150 billion cubic meters of water a year from her aquifers. The same excessive drain is put on the large aquifers underlying the Midwestern United States where billions of gallons are pumped to the surface yearly from the Ogallala aquifer. The replacement rate from seasonal rain input in minuscule.

Most nations dependent on deep aquifers have little or no replacement water to rebuild their underground reserves and using them at present consumption rates will soon drain them "dry". Saudi Arabia depends on her fossil reserves to provide 75 percent of the nation's water needs. Using this water the country works to remain self-sufficient in wheat production, growing enough extra grain through irrigation to place them among the world's top exporters of wheat. At the present rate of use, the Saudi Arabia's aquifer will be drained within 50 years.[18]

As populations grow and overflow existing land bases, fragile drylands and wetlands are opened up to agriculture and industrial development. Billions of gallons of water are then transported into dry areas where a disproportion of people take up farming and industry in artificially enhanced environments. The demands place an unsustainable stress on the environment both where the water originates and where it is consumed. Industries then follow. With the aid of modern technologies, they develop local water supplies or import them to the extent they require to meet their needs. In so doing, they become the main contributor to the overuse and contamination of local surface and underground water reserves.

Agriculture also expands as water supplies are increased until all aspects of environmental deterioration set in: the loss of arable soils, deforestation, and pollution of water and land, all the result of over-farming, overgrazing and abuse of chemical technologies. Eventually local reserves of water fail to maintain the expected living standards and high intensity crop production. Newer, more destructive technologies are then introduced to capture and transport water from distant sources, initiating projects to harness or divert rivers in neighbouring countries. Long distance storage and transfer of water supplies increase the damage to eco-systems and wilderness through the intrusion of construction of dams, canals and pipelines.

The megalopolis of Los Angeles in Southern California depends on billions of gallons of water reaching it through hundreds of miles of pipelines and canals which bring fresh water from the many rivers and lakes of California. Nearly 85 percent is directed to agriculture. The importation has permitted the growth of especially heavy consumers. Rice, for instance, a grain that must be grown in several inches of water, is raised on a large scale in flooded fields of California's deserts. Another extreme example is tomatoes which require over 8 gallons of water for each tomato. And then there is milk. The production of one gallon of milk directly or indirectly uses over 4 gallons of water. Obviously the California farmers' demands on water supplies are now so great that visionaries have designed elaborate plans to divert rivers, dam mountain valleys and extend pipe lines from the Canadian Rockies to California to provide as much water as is needed to assure such crops will continue to be grown.

On every continent, existing fresh water supplies are now overtaxed wherever populations are the most dense. In continental dry areas existing surface and underground reserves are fully allocated for vast urban areas, irrigation systems, hydro-electric power, industrial needs, disposal of wastes, recreational activities and the maintenance of ecological systems and indigenous species. The problem is exacerbated by the many rivers and lakes which are not usable because they are contaminated by human waste and toxic pollutants or have dried up with overuse and drought. The universal demand on existing supplies is so heavy that many nations are at risk of depleting their available supplies within the next few decades, a predicament which will reduce industrial growth and increase poverty at a time when employment and production are seen as the major solutions to population control and world stability.

Drying trends on all continents have been a natural phenomenon since ancient times. The 20th Century has been one of the longest periods of temperate climatic conditions in civilized history, but it is changing now for the worse. Deserts are expanding and forests are shrinking. The result is a greater frequency of droughts and flash flooding. Africa is particularly prone to long, extensive droughts. Existing lakes and rivers across the continent are drying up permanently and imported technologies are enabling populations to overpump their wells. Water reserves are threatened as continental underground sources shrink and existing resources are damaged through contamination.

Both greed and need promote over exploitation of fresh water resources. Most experience with human nature and survival indicate we are more strongly motivated towards destruction than to "sustainable management" no matter how difficult our daily existence threatens to become. Such attitudes are reflected in the personal observations of Cheri Thiessen while in Zimbabwe in 1992.[19] She wrote of Lake Kyle, once a large, beautiful lake that supported a wide variety of wildlife, birds and fish, but today is nearly dry. It has been shrinking for years as the water is drained to irrigate the local sugar cane fields. "The pathetic pond (which remains) is still the only supplier of water to millions of local people" yet in the lodge where Ms. Thiessen stayed, cars were washed daily, toilets ran constantly, taps dripped 24 hours a day and huge bathtubs (75 litres to fill) were used in every guest room. "We cannot look at the lake without wincing" she writes. "Its wasting death, devoid of birds, lacking the splash of fish, the grunts of hippos, is too painful to bear. The water coming from taps of (the) lodge is the colour of blood." She listened sadly as the locals shrugged off her concerned inquiries as to what they will do when the Lake is totally dry in the near future. No one she met had given any thought to the future.

How soon we will begin to respect the efficient and equitable use of remaining reserves is of growing universal concern as shortages and problems mount. Where water shortages are severe, people cannot grow their own food, raise livestock, fish, replant forests, conserve eco-systems or develop industries to supply growing populations and raise their living standards. Fresh water shortages force people to use less water than they need for daily care and good health. It reduces food production, increases unemployment and multiplies the number living in wretched poverty.

Tapping the earth's remaining reserves of fresh water to meet future needs has several drawbacks. The largest reserves are in glaciers and wilderness rivers. Both remain inaccessible and too high in economic, social, political and environmental costs to be fully developed. But the time is coming when even these will be exploited, no matter the cost. Water shortages will be so severe that desperate measures will have to be taken.

Meanwhile, efforts to conserve or recycle fresh water remain in their infancy worldwide. In developing nations where economies are still reliant the exploitive policies of multi-nationals development grows where environmental regulations are not enforced and conservation of resources have no priority. The consensus among developers is that a nation must industrialize first and worry about cleaning up the mistakes after it is accomplished. Environmental protection is to be effected only after development is successful and a nation's people are rich enough to afford the luxury of conservation and recycling.[20]

Tensions Over Shared Rivers and Aquifers

Expansive agriculture, industrialization and rapid urbanization throughout the 20th Century now threaten existing surface and underground fresh water reserves on every continent. Competition for river water grows annually between Canada and the United States as they plan and negotiate deals over hydro power, dam reserves, fresh bottled water and redirecting river systems. Mexico and the United States compete for water allocations of the Colorado River which ends up a mere trickle by the time it reaches the Gulf of Mexico, changing the ecology and salinity of the ocean where it enters. The Danube and the Rhine, each shared by many European nations as their major water source, are over allocated, polluted by industries, contaminated by the thousands of boats and barges which plough their waters and are the purveyors of urban sewage. Exploding populations in Africa, India, the Middle East and China compete for shrinking reserves of river water. The Nile, the Tigrus-Euphrates and the Jordan Rivers must meet the needs of annual population growth averaging 3 to 4 percent. Scarcity and pollution are raising tempers around the world.

In subtropical drylands high birth rates demand large water supplies for both home use and farming. As populations rise upstream on a river system, they divert more and more water for themselves, leaving less and less for those downstream. As more land is brought under cultivation and industrialization develops upstream, more water must be harnessed for hydro power, irrigation and urban use. The amount of water which gets through to those downstream decreases in proportion, threatening their supplies of water for drinking, irrigation and industries.

The Tigris-Euphrates river systems in the Middle East support large, rapidly growing populations in Turkey, Iraq, Iran and Syria. Turkey, located at the head of these rivers, has built some of the largest dams in the world. Just filling the Ataturk dam, one of 21 dams, was estimated to take five years of closure periods of flow from 1990 to 1995. Turkey has chosen to store large quantities of the annual flow of the Euphrates River to irrigate thousands of acres of drylands in Southeast Turkey and to provide the nation with huge reserves of hydro power.

This excessive share of the river water comes at the expense of the downriver nations, Iraq and Syria. Decreased river flow reduces both the quantity and quality of crops as it increases water salinity and concentrates pesticides and fertilizers which drain off the farm land. When hydro power downstream drops on these large river systems, all general use of water is disrupted. Living standards decline and huge debts are accrued to cover the costs of imported food supplies. Severe water shortages bring famine.[21] Where the problem is severe enough, the tendency is for the hungry people to migrate into neighbouring countries in search of food and water or take what they need by force, creating political instability and leading to war.

The economic and social costs accumulated because of water shortages in Syria and Iraq are escalating historical and ethnic tensions. Syria, for instance, had to import food to compensate for lost crops during the periods Turkey closed off the river. Further, to meet future food needs as its population grows from 13 million to 22 million over the next 20 years, Syria plans to irrigate 100,000 acres of new land which will require 15 million cubic meters of water. As Syria rapidly depletes its aquifer, the demand this will place on the Euphrates is way out of proportion to the amount of water that will be available to the nation. Tensions between Turkey and Syria over control of water supplies could eventually lead to a war of desperation.[22]

Historically, shortages of water supplies in the Middle East and African countries come with a parallel decline in climatic conditions, deepening drought cycles and increasing the inefficient use of existing water supplies.[23] Spreading desertification, caused by longer, more frequent periods of drought, threaten irrigation of croplands; just as the allocation of river and lake water down to the last drop reduces adjacent forests, marsh lands and local eco-systems. Adding to the problems of climate change and surface water shortages is the use of alternate underground water reserves or diverted river systems which encourage a tendency to overcrop and overgraze the land, speeding up the desertification process and deepening drought conditions. This is particularly true of the Sahel in Africa, where the aquifers are being drained to raise food and animals on lands which have been turned into deserts by human abuse. The civil wars which plague Africa are exacerbated by the shortage of water and crops as large numbers of environmental refugees move across tribal borders in search of food and water.

The tension over water supplies has become endemic in large areas of the African continent. Water shortages, reaching crisis levels in the Nile Basin, one of the world's poorest and most populated regions, threaten an existing population of 240 million which will double to nearly 500 million in the next 40 years. Should more dams be built to catch and store water on the upper Nile to meet the needs of drought ridden Sudan, they would increase the present threat of disappearing water supplies to millions of Egyptian farmers downriver who already take too much water from the river for their crops. The amount of water now reaching the millions of city dwellers in such urban centres as Cairo is much reduced and highly polluted.

Supplies from the smallest river basin, the Jordan, supplying Israel, Jordan and Syria, has already led to bloodshed. Allocating its supply constantly threatens peace in the West Bank and in Gaza.[24] Israel has two main sources of fresh water, the Jordan and the aquifer which underlies the West Bank. The Jordan River is little more than a trickle and the aquifer which underlies Israel, Jordan, Lebanon is diminishing rather quickly as its used up for irrigation. In 1967, Israel decreed that water is a strategic resource under military control. Since then, the Israelis have enjoyed the bulk of water available to the area while curtailing Palestinian use. "The 100,000-odd Israelis who have settled in the West Bank now use almost as much water as the million Palestinians living there."[25]

As Arabs and Israelis draw off more water in the Gaza strip than nature can replace, the water table has dropped many meters, allowing seawater to seep in, turning the water brackish. Settling the strife between these nations is complicated by water allocations. Both nations have burgeoning populations living on a desert, attempting to feed themselves on lands whose climates gobble up water through evaporation and fail to replace it with sufficient rainfall.

With water an increasingly scarce but vital commodity in so many nations, and populations exploding so that every acre of land is needed to grow food for them, fresh water is becoming the most valuable resource. Nations forced to share disappearing water reserves equitably are vulnerable to the demands of their own greed, development ambitions, lack of population controls and climatic changes. Human nature seldom admits to its own failings or errors in judgment during the course of making those errors. As a result, solutions and rights of possession are more readily sought through warfare then through equanimity. Wars arise out of the ego of the racial gene pool and the inherent belief in the rights of the property owner.

Technological Pollution of Fresh Water Resources

Every human activity employing progressive technologies to remake the landscape affects the earth's water supplies. For instance, cut down forests to provide timber or clear farm land and the watersheds are destroyed, reducing the amount of water held in reserve on the land. Reduce this holding capacity and rain pours off the barren slopes, filling water reservoirs and rivers with silt and debris. As the run-off water rushes across farmlands, it carries with it arable soils, plugs up rivers, lakes and coastal areas with precious topsoil, destroys marine and fish life, pollutes lakes and coastal areas, floods urban settlements and farmlands, ruins crops and drowns livestock and people. Water, once held back by forests is being lost to the oceans from every continent. A case in point is Bangladesh , a vast heavily populated river plain which is annually inundated by monsoon floods that roar down from the deforested Himalayan Mountains, wash away crops, topsoil, homes, animals and people. Life there is a constant struggle to survive starvation, disease, poisonous snakes and polluted water.

Continental water resources in our rivers, lakes, ponds and underground are poisoned by run-off from farm lands carrying pesticides, herbicides, fertilizers, fungicides and vast amounts of manure, all waste products of agricultural technologies. Carried away in run-off, heavy concentrations of chemicals flow down rivers into lakes and oceans where they contribute to massive blooms of algae which smother other life forms. Food chains which provide nutriment for larger species of marine life may die beneath the algae from a lack of oxygen, starvation and/or the ingestion of toxic chemicals. Summertime in the Mediterranean has brought vast billowing masses of green algae to the beaches of the Adriatic and the bays of Italy, turning coastal areas into polluted wastelands.

Billions of tons of toxic wastes and sewage have been disposed of in local rivers, lakes and coastal waters in the industrial nations. Annually the North Sea and the Mediterranean receive hundreds of tonnes of chemicals from industrial plants. The North Sea and Atlantic coastal waters are constantly under stress from billions of gallons of untreated sewage and liquid sludge. Britain alone averages 5 million tons of sewage to be disposed of every day. Added to this output of toxic wastes are the thousands of tons of solid industrial and incinerated pollutants, as well as radio active materials which are dumped from ships at sea. The Arctic Ocean bordering Russia has been contaminated irremediably from years of dumping nuclear and radio-active wastes and storing contaminated nuclear ships and submarines in coastal waters. Dumping continues and ocean currents carry the radioactive ocean water to all parts of the world.

Few nations can still boast of being able to supply their people with clean, uncontaminated supplies of drinking water. Heavy metals, toxic chemicals, human sewage, pesticides, herbicides, oil products, all exist in unsafe quantities in the water resources of rural and urban areas. The industrial nations are particularly troubled with contaminants as pollution of water resources is endemic with manufacturing and processing. Clean drinking water is not only rare in major industrial areas of North America, Europe and Asia but water pure enough to meet the requirements of factories and industries is often unattainable.

Industries, manufacturing and processing plants, paint factories, coal burning and nuclear power plants, chemical and oil refineries, old and new mines, ore dumps, plastic and glass industries, pulp and paper producers, all require vast quantities of clean, fresh water in their production, manufacturing and clean-up. Millions of gallons of water are then drained off, mixed with industrial by-products and wastes of toxic and radio active materials, heavy metals, chlorine compounds, cleaning fluids, dioxins, PCBs, DDT and many others. Removed and diluted in fresh water, they are poured into local waterways from which many nation's draw their drinking water. Each year in the U.S. alone over 5 trillion gallons of industrial waste are dumped into US coastal waters[26]

Added to the chemical pollutants in continental water resources are the millions and millions of tons of unprocessed human sewage and household products, -cleaning fluids, medications, garden pesticides, paints and paint thinners,- which are dumped down the drain into the sewers, leaching into fresh water reserves. In some areas sewage is dumped unprocessed into rivers and oceans by governments who cannot afford to build sewage treatment plants or believe oceans are much more efficient processors of human and chemical wastes than are sewage plants. There may be some truth in this. Efforts to purify effluent before it is dumped into waterways produces a sludge that is more highly concentrated and toxic then the original sewage. Disposing of it is usually done by pouring it back on the land as fertilizer or into landfills from where it eventually works its way into surface and underground water systems.

A lack of space on land to dump garbage and toxic waste leads to dumping them in the oceans, a dangerous practice which is causing frequent "die-offs" as well as abnormalities and sterility in marine life. In 1987 over 700 dolphins suffering from large, active lesions, came ashore to die along the New Jersey and Virginia coasts. At the same time unprecedented amounts of garbage washed ashore. Over one thousand of the poisoned dolphins also died at sea. Examinations of their carcasses showed a wide variety of bacteria in their bodies, the result of suppressed immune systems. The die-off continued, reaching as far south as Florida, finally ending in March of 1988. They had been killed by a nerve poison which accumulates in fish which eat red tides, but there were no red tides in the area, only large amounts of PBCs and toxic chemicals such as chlorinated hydro-carbons which had been dumped into coastal waters.[27]

Ocean waters are polluted by an average of 3.2 million tons of oil yearly which is either dumped or accidentally spilled into them, deliberately pumped from bilges or flushed off land by rain into rivers and underground reservoirs. Vast quantities of oil, lighter than water, spread out in a thin layer over the water, poisoning the plankton and small creatures which live near the surface. Oil from tanker spills or pumped bilges take an enormous toll of animal and bird life. Unable to clean the oil from their coats or feathers, they die of exposure and oil poisoning.

Despite advanced purification systems in industrial nations, heavy metals and other pollutants remain in the water and are ingested by all who drink supplies taken from lakes and rivers shared with industries. The poisons are also transmitted to humans and animals through crops raised on irrigation water polluted with industrial wastes.

International laws were passed against dumping garbage at sea. Still, ships and garbage disposal companies continue to risk fines and public censor as they surreptitiously dump their contaminants in the ocean. The problem is generally a very limited choice of where to dump, as few landfills are equipped or willing to accept toxic wastes. Incinerator plants are rare because of construction/management expenses and toxic emissions. Finding places to dump toxic wastes or set up incinerators on land must also include overcoming the power of NIMBY protests (Not in my back yard).

Consequently, industries are forced to find illegal methods of dumping their toxic wastes. One dangerous solution had truckers from the United States moving toxic wastes across the Canadian border in fuel trucks and dumping the contents legally in landfills until Canadians realized what the contents contained. Only then was the practice stopped. The problems of disposing technological wastes is so huge that illegal trade-offs, long distance transport and deep sea dumping occur on every continent. And the problems continue to expand as population and industries grow.

In industrial nations toxic wastes are piling up in holding tanks, in ponds, in landfills and in metal containers. Large quantities are still dumped daily into rivers, lakes and oceans. Studies of disposed toxic wastes reveal that over two million kilograms of chemicals were dumped each year into the Great Lakes by Canadian and American industries throughout the 1980s and an estimated 100 contaminants are poured into the North Sea from industries and manufacturing plants in several countries along the Rhine and the Elbe Rivers annually.

Reduced use of toxic chemicals, recycling and high fines for polluting are on the increase in the Great Lake area, but most industries continue to dump their wastes on a daily quota system which manufacturing companies would have us believe is at levels the Lakes can safely absorb. What is coming to light is that the water may be less polluted, but the accumulation of material and chemicals on the lake and river beds is extremely concentrated and continues to affect all life forms in the lakes and rivers and pollute drinking water.[28]

The excessive polluting of rivers and coastal waters is inhibiting fish reproduction and adding to world food shortages. The stress of toxic pollutants affects the smallest life forms in the oceans, the plankton at the bottom of the food chain which indirectly feed the very fish humans catch to eat. These basic creatures also ingest toxic waste, chemicals and oil. Many die as a result. Those eaten pass on their toxicity to larger fish, and larger fish concentrate the poisons in their bodies which are then passed on to larger fish which eat them and, in turn, concentrate the toxins. Contaminated marine life at the top of the chain often ends up in the nets of fishermen and is sold as food. The concentration of toxins in fish is proving harmful to human health in areas where fish is a mainstay in the diet. The native Americans living on islands in the Great Lakes depend largely on the fish they catch for their protein. The fish are disappearing, but those caught and eaten are destroying the health of the natives who eat them.

Consumption of contaminated fish is now taking many human casualties. A high rate of birth defects, cancers, liver failures, miscarriages and still births are common among people who eat a lot of fish taken from polluted rivers and lakes. One public school along the Mississippi River has over forty children with birth defects where catching and eating river fish is prevalent. Congress ruled as early as 1977 that the river was to be cleaned up by 1985, but it has not been done yet because the law is not enforced and the costs and restrictions too inhibiting to trade and commerce.

Dangerous to all species, the burden of absorbing so many toxic wastes continues to be borne by water bodies, most of them very limited continental reserves of fresh water such as the Great Lakes. As industry is unlikely to reduce production and endure the loss of jobs necessary to reduce their output of toxic wastes, contamination of water resources is bound to increase world wide. Nations such as Canada and the United States can afford to recycle and purify their water supplies, but the costs and the lack of technology in developing nations along with the resistance of big business are unlikely to permit this to happen for some time yet. Even though we have become very aware of the damage our activities are doing to the environment, jobs and profits still override conservation programs. The players in the global economy prefer to ignore the environment and are powerful enough to avoid government regulations or taxes.

Too much public resentment over waste disposal has induced many manufacturers to move their plants to Third World nations where governments accept pollution as a necessary part of industrial development. In this way recycling and reprocessing of chemicals can be avoided and the costs of production can remain very low. This allows the elite of most developing nations to have higher living standards for themselves while ignoring the dangers to the health of their people and their environments. Even more dangerous for the planet is that poverty and the need for foreign credits entices most Third World nations to accept toxic wastes for dumping or storage in exchange for cash payments or foreign credits.

Excessive pollution of water systems tends to accompany industrial development. Taipei, capital of Taiwan, one of the richest industrial nations, had rivers flowing through the city which were open sewers, clogged with garbage, toxic chemicals and human excrement during its first industrial years. The tens of thousands of Taiwanese living and travelling along these waterways suffered from diseases, infections and poor health, all related to the pollution. However, their economy, now well developed and enriched, is attempting to reduce most of this pollution. But the damage to rivers and oceans has been done and the amount of toxic waste is huge and costly to dispose of on a very small island. Where does it all go? What can they do with it?

Fresh water reserves are affected everywhere by air borne contaminants which fall as acid rain into lakes and rivers, causing excessive algae growth which smothers all other life forms. Many North America lakes, once active with life and normal conditions of vegetation and life form decay, now lie "dead". Nothing lives in them and nothing decays. There is no oxygen supply left in the water for the normal functioning of food chains. The necessary micro-organisms have been killed off by the highly acidic water. Only the skeletons of dead trees occupy many of these lakes, preserved in a sense by the lack of life that would normally break them down into soil. Thousands of these "dead" lakes dot northeastern Canada and the United States where millions of tons of sulphur dioxide and nitrous oxide have poured into the atmosphere from industry and coal burning plants to combine with the hydrogen in water vapour to form mild solutions of nitric and sulphuric acid which return to earth as rain and by natural gravity.

Where efforts have been made to reduce toxic waste, recycle the chemicals and purify the water used both in industry and in households, some rivers have recovered. The Great Lakes are cleaner, if not yet "alive" with life. Yet the loss of species, the immensity of the damage already done to fresh water reserves and the continuing expansion of polluting industry, especially in newly industrializing nations may remain beyond any powers of regeneration of world water resources far into the next century.

The amount of industrial and nuclear pollution that exists in the former Communist states of Eastern Europe and Russia alone goes far beyond the technological and financial capacities of those nations to clean up their many polluted domestic water resources. Major rivers, ponds, lakes and coastal waters are sinkholes of toxic wastes, chemicals and sewage. It has been said by citizens interviewed in these countries that many of their lakes and ponds are so contaminated that they use them to get rid of unwanted dogs and cats. The toxic water kills them instantly and dissolves their fur and bones.

Another negative side to anti-polluting and clean-up campaigns exists other than preventing straight forward dumping of wastes into rivers. These are the frequent accidental spills that can undo all the previous clean up attempts. During the hot summer months of 1988, the Thames River in England, considered a cleaned up river and model of regeneration, had to have oxygen pumped into it to keep the fish alive. When the river goes "dead" the fish die and have to be restocked. Frequent accidental spills of toxic materials in the river have set back several attempts to maintain its health. A spill of "20 tonnes of aluminum sulphate were accidentally dumped into the wrong tank at an unstaffed treatment works in Cornwall...(Such) water pollution incidents average more than 21,000 a year in England and Wales."[29]

Impact of Water-Borne Pollution on Human Health

Humanity is paying a heavy price for so much carnage as people suffer and die from water pollution world wide. Contaminated drinking water is a major cause of heart defects, blood disorders, limb anomalies, cancers, spina bifida, genetic disorders and overt symptoms such as skin rashes, sore eyes and throats. Increased mortality rates among infants and children, thyroid malfunctions, headaches, anaemia, allergies, lung and respiratory illnesses, lead poisoning, chemical and pesticide poisoning, blindness, muscle failure and a rise in cases of cholera and malaria. Unprecedented forms of death stalk many of us for just living near industrial centres.

Yet industrial expansion and economic growth remain priority factors. Protecting and conserving clean water reserves must bow to profit and jobs, creating one of the basic threats to human survival as soon as the 21st Century. Pollutants will be created as long as industry and agriculture exist. These wastes must be disposed of somehow and somewhere which generally means into the environment either through liquid runoff or as gaseous emissions. Not all can be recycled, neutralized or encapsulated; nor will industry afford the costs of disposal as long as free markets and cutthroat competition are the global rule.

Unfortunately, the human body can neither safely absorb nor slough off the quantities of toxins which have accumulated in much of the world's drinking supplies. What is most horrifying is that we have water supplied directly into our homes under the auspices of municipal and national governments, those whom we are supposed to trust to protect our lives. Obviously, these authorities cannot always do the job safely. Although bacteria can be filtered out or destroyed through chlorination, most toxic by products from industrial manufacturing remain in suspension in the water or collect on the river, lake or ocean beds. Consequently, many river systems and lakes are contaminated beyond being safe for drinking or preparing foods.

Most people living in highly industrialized river areas must now depend on imported bottled water for drinking. But not everyone bothers to buy it and many cannot afford it. These people drink tap water from municipal supplies or from their own wells. The combined effect of drinking contaminated water and breathing polluted air is producing a growing list of incurable cancers of the lungs, the stomach, the pancreas, bladder, thyroid, oesophagus, intestine, liver and the skin.[30]

The millions of residents living along the Mississippi River system depend on the river and its tributaries to provide water. But "millions of pounds of toxic chemicals go directly into the river each year. Millions of pounds of toxic debris have been buried, dumped in landfills, stored in surface ponds or injected through underground metal pipes deep into the earth".[31] The Mississippi is contaminated by the pesticides, herbicides, fertilizers, oil, sewage, chemical and toxic wastes of over 600 companies along its banks. Hundreds of land sites along the river are used to hold and absorb sludge or toxic landfills. 16,000 tons of pesticides from just one outlet is dumped into the river annually, and the city of St. Louis has the worst record of any city along the river in that it pours millions of tons of polluted effluent into the river on a daily basis. Chemical industries and oil refineries pour PCBs, heavy metals, oil, vinyl chlorides and benzene into the river system, chemicals responsible for cancer in nearly every body organ. The stretch between Baton Rouge and New Orleans in Louisiana, polluted by over 100 chemical companies and refineries, " is better known as Cancer Alley, with the highest concentration of manufacturers, users, disposers of toxic chemicals in the United States."[32]

Buying bottled water as a precaution has turned into a nightmare in many cities where some bottling companies take their water directly from local water sources and claim it is pure. Some bottled brands have been found to have greater amounts of contaminants than municipal water supplies. Regulating and guaranteeing the safety of the water used by billions of people both in cities and in rural areas has become an administrative nightmare.

The seriousness of the Mississippi example is that similar situations exist throughout the industrial world. Multiply this situation several times in the United States and Canada alone. Every industrial nation which produces plastics, uses oil or refines it, manufactures chemicals, uses chemicals in its industrial processes or pours chemicals on its farm lands is contaminating its lands, air, rivers, lakes and oceans to rid themselves of industrial wastes. Europe has all but destroyed the Rhine and the Danube; every nation in Eastern Europe including the former states of Russia have contaminated rivers, lakes and oceans. The planet is already very sick from previous industrial pollution. The expansion of industrialization into the Third World, where four times the population live, can only poison us all as they begin to enjoy a technical but more deadly existence.

At present 60 percent of the world's people presently live in poverty in the Third World, necessitating very primitive methods of water storage and collection, often contaminated by unsafe waste disposal and few efforts at sanitation. Although they still have more reserves of clean water than the industrial nations, the developing nations do not have the fresh water reserves where they are needed and cannot afford to build the canals and pipelines to transport it, store it or deliver it to homes.

Remembering that problems of supply, purification, storage and transportation of fresh water exist for rich as well poor nations, humanity is already deep into a major crisis facing future consumption. At what point does our immunity and genetic composition break down under the wide range of ingested filth, human effluent, toxic chemicals, radio activity and heavy metals absorbed by human society through the water we drink? Are there universal trends of chromosome damage which are bringing chronically ill or malformed babies into the world in rising numbers?

Are the poisons of industrial and agricultural development producing a plethora of biological horrors? Ten years after the explosion of the nuclear reactor at Chernobyl in the Ukraine, not only are the children suffering multiple defects and diseases related to radiation poisoning, but scientists have discovered children born eight years after the explosion to parents exposed to the radiation have twice the number of mutated genes than other children. The significance of this discovery is that genetic alterations caused by radiation are passed on to the next generation and can become a permanent part of the human make up. The genetic possibilities could be horrific.[33]

Radiation releases, oil and chemical spills and toxic waste dumping, both accidental and intentional, occur daily in every part of the world. We just don't hear about them unless they cause large fish or bird kills or cause the deaths of dozens of people as did the explosion in Bhopal,India, in 1984, when over two thousand people were killed by the escaping gases and over 6000 died of related causes over the following years.

How long before these poisons destroy the genetic strength of our species and the human race is unable to reproduce itself? The evidence is already with us as sterility becomes common, children are born without proper genitalia and males ingest chemicals which cause their reproductive organs to behave like female organs in the older industrial nations of Europe and America.[34]

Conservation and Sustainable Management of Fresh Water

Conservation and sustainable management of water resources, both fresh and salt, is now critical to human survival. But overpopulation, overuse of supplies and widespread pollution are preventing the reduction of water use as our consumption and contamination grows much faster than fresh water can be produced in nature.

The most obvious solution is population control and reduced industrial and urban development, especially in marginal areas. Populations must not be allowed to grow on drylands and deserts. This includes the American West and Midwest states such as California, Arizona and Nevada, the African drylands from the Sudan the Sahel, the Nile to South Africa, all the Middle East countries from Egypt to Turkey and the vast marginal dry areas of India, China and Australia.

The irony in this restriction is that these are the present areas of greatest population growth and should be the least. Between the easy movement of goods and technologies and the innovations which permit the transferral of billions of gallons of fresh water over long distances and the ability to raise equally large quantities from underground reserves, these dry areas have become the only available living space on which the burgeoning populations can live and grow crops.

But does this trend to desert irrigation cause greater harm in that such innovations have a very short future and allows vast populations to build up in areas of rapidly diminishing water resources? Drought and deserts are expanding outward along every desert border which will mean a continuing reduction in surface water and a heavier demand on underground fossil reserves.

Imminent collapse of these drylands lies in providing large populations with an abundance of food and water supplies for a short time. In nature, abundance brings on species' explosions, only to kill them off in times of scarcity.

As long as fresh water can be procured either on deserts or in megalopolises, migrations into urban and dryland areas will continue. But if sustainable management programs are to work, governments will have to be empowered to restrict human movement and reduce water usage with an eye to future supplies. This will entail using water far more efficiently worldwide as spreading deserts and drought reduce hydrological cycles and diminish seasonal rainfall, extending the severity and length of droughts.

Conservation and sustainable management of any resources comes at a very high price few nations can afford. In most cases it entails a marked drop in crop production and expensive methods of purifying and recycling used and contaminated water. Above all else, water conservation requires a drop in population numbers which not only use up resources, but contaminate both surface and ground water with toxic run offs, oil spills and human and industrial sewage. As there is no where else for these contaminants to go, they will always end up in the water supplies.

CHAPTER FIFTEEN

Population Outrunning Food Supply

In 1798, Thomas Malthus, an English political economist published his "Essay on the Principle of Population" in which he theorized that humanity was doomed never to be able to grow enough food to keep up with its own birth rate; that is, human populations increase geometrically, whereas, the food supply can only be increased by adding new sources of production. To Malthus it was obvious that to keep up with food supply required increased farmlands, and England was a small, finite land base.

He came to his conclusions as he observed that England's population was rising steeply and overflowing the cities, spilling out onto the farmlands, threatening to gobble up arable lands and, thereby, reduce crop production at a rate that would leave much of the expanding population without available food supplies. "How (can) a nation survive if it demands more food on the one hand and (destroys) its farmlands on the other?"[1]

However, when Malthus submitted his theory for public scrutiny, the Agricultural and Industrial Revolutions were just beginning in England. He could not foresee or else chose not to include in his theory that The Enclosure Acts and the many improved agricultural technologies of the 18th Century had already ensured an annual increase in food production. Neither did he have the accumulated statistics, visual experience and foresight to predict future trends which our modern computers can correlate for us. However, if he had the opportunity to analyze the planet from space as we now have, he would have decided he was fully justified in his forecast. World wide today people are outrunning food production.

United Nations' assessments in 1994 showed that a billion people are malnourished or bordering on starvation.[2] Over 15 million die annually from famine and at least another two billion suffer various ramifications of diets short in nutrition and a necessary variety of foods. Population growth is outpacing the food production of world fisheries, rangelands and croplands. World commercial catches are dropping as fish stocks are diminishing. Tuna, cod, salmon and several lesser species have all but disappeared from the oceans. World grain stocks continue to decline as water shortages spread, farmlands are lost to misuse and drought hinders plant growth. Vast areas of farmland are degraded annually through erosion, salinization and agricultural chemicals. Rangelands are believed to have reached their maximum carrying capacity and with overgrazing, will decline in animal production until cattle will have to be grain fed.

But feeding grain to cattle may soon have to end. The world grain production in 1995 was the lowest since 1988 and grain reserves left world inventories at enough to last only 48 days. Pressure will soon fall on using all grain output to feed people, not animals. This reflects a dire reality. With the loss of our major sources of protein, --fish and cattle,-- the problems of feeding the world will increase with every additional billion people.[3]

Diminishing food supplies reduce the quality of life for burgeoning populations. The World Bank claims "about one billion people are ill or disabled because they didn't eat enough of three vital nutrients...Vitamin A, iodine and iron which causes blindness, goitre, anaemia, retardation and death." Furthermore, "at least twice that many are at risk."[4] Poor diets and low living standards result in poor health, a marked drop in intellectual capacity, loss of concentration and impaired working capacity. The reproductive quality in the offspring of the malnourished is also diminished. Malnutrition, disease and the general filth which the hungry poor must endure take a heavy toll on their chances of gaining opportunities to improve their living standards.

Only 30 years ago these conditions did not ravage the multitude of nations to the extent they do today. National populations were fewer and their use of the land more natural and "environmentally friendly". Living was not such a fierce life and death struggle for the majority because there was only a third as many of us.

A United Nations' report released on July 13, 1993, stated that the world may not be able to feed itself as early as the 21st Century. Lester Brown of the Worldwatch Institute in Washington, D.C., estimates that "by 2030 India will need to import over 44 million tons of grain each year to feed its 1.5 billion people ... and China will need to purchase 200 million tons of grain abroad for its 1.6 billion people - as much as is now exported by all the world's countries."[5]

The UN study faults poor farming practices for 28 percent of the soil depletion, 34 percent from overgrazing and 29 percent from overlogging. Europe with almost one-fifth of the world's total of degraded soils has the added factors of contamination, toxic pollution and acid rain contributing to the ongoing decline in agricultural output.[6]

In our zeal to commercialize farming on a very large scale, we are doing more to inhibit growing conditions than to protect them. Dams, irrigation projects, heavy farm machinery, hybridized seeds, fertilizers, pesticides and herbicides, all have increased food production in the short term, but the degree of water and soil depletion caused by these agricultural technologies over the long term is now turning success into disaster. Growing conditions are less and less reliable as experienced in the summer of 1993 which brought catastrophic floods, droughts and hurricanes throughout much of the world, a traumatic year following more than a decade of deteriorating weather patterns world wide.

Causes for Declining Food Production

To date the world's food supply has kept pace and a little ahead of the needs of growing populations. Those millions who die annually and sporadically from hunger die when local crops fail because of drought and floods, or because food aid has either not been distributed to them in time or civil wars have prevented its immediate delivery.

However, United Nations' estimates state that 1984 was the last year in which world crop production actually rose above the previous year's output. The increase in production from 1950 to 1984 averaged 30 million tons per year. From 1984 to 1992, the annual increase had dropped to 12 million tons per year and has continued to drop each year thereafter.[7] In 1995 the total annual grain harvests produced 1.7 billion tons. Brown estimates the annual increase can raise this total output to no more than 2 billion tons, an additional amount that can feed only another 2.5 billion people living at the present U.S. level of consumption, or as many as another 5 billion living at India's subsistence level of consumption per capita. With the world population approaching 10 billion people in the next 50 years, the distribution of grains will be very unequal, leaving a much larger percentage of the world's people living well below the subsistence line and facing starvation.[8]

Although food production has not increased in overall annual output since 1984, grain sales have suffered universally from an overabundance of annual output, an actual glut in proportion to the number of people with sufficient purchasing power to buy them. However, as world populations double over the next 40 years and arable lands deteriorate, the number of those who must depend on handouts will far exceed the number with sufficient buying power.

Another factor has entered the distribution of existing food supplies in recent years: the ability of workforces with rising incomes in newly developing industrial nations to buy more and varied types of foods. China and India, with the largest populations in the world, could offset any attempts at equalizing or even improving present distribution of food. Wealth is enabling them to demand a greater share of the world's annual output, a share that can only increase in the next few decades. Lester Brown believes that "China could well end up competing directly with U.S. consumers for U.S. grain. This could drive up prices of cereal foods and meat and dairy products from grain fed animals in American supermarkets."[9]

The same trend can be seen as production of other foods than grains drops. Disappearing fish stocks of salmon, cod, tuna and halibut are raising the price of fish well beyond the purchasing power of more and more people, forewarning of the detrimental effects larger populations will have on existing food supplies. Even the rich stand to face a future of poorer quality diets as variety in available foods disappears. Intense competition for basic food supplies will turn into economic and political battles. Some may develop into global wars in the coming struggle among nations to survive.

Aside from present inequalities of distribution, projecting 40 years into the future, it is obvious that exponentially expanding populations and rapidly industrializing nations will soon outrun the world's food production. Populations are increasing nearly 20 percent a decade, 10 to 12 percent faster than food production, remembering that food production is declining in its annual rate of increase.

Calculating crop output not only against population growth but also against annual soil loss, salinization, desertification and destructive farming methods would suggest that 100 percent increase in population by 2030 will result in twice as many people having to survive on less food than is now produced annually. For a while it may be possible to feed the additional 4 billion or more added mouths in the 21st Century, but for how long and at what cost to the environment? Human consumption is already outrunning world production of the more nutritious foods such as fish. Future food shortages will take a heavy toll on the health and intelligence of the majority as can been seen already in both the industrial and Third World wherever hunger and malnutrition are rampant.

1. Arable Lands Disappearing: Arable lands are shrinking as our needs expand. Poor farming methods, overgrazing and deforestation practices are causing topsoil to disappear at an average of 77 billion tons per year. A three year United Nations' study given out in 1992 estimated that " an area the size of China and India had suffered 'moderate to extreme degradation' in the past 45 years" of which a "sizable portion is irrecoverable, if not biologically dead".[10] By 1992, as much as seventeen percent of the world's arable lands were categorized as degraded. The continuing loss given in the most recent UN estimate is put at over 7 million hectares per year. This means a parallel reduction, not an increase, in the output of agricultural products worldwide.[11]

Some 250 scientists working through the International Soil Reference and Information Centre located in the Netherlands also reported that humans have destroyed the productivity of land areas equal to the area of Western Europe through deforestation and overgrazing. At the present rate of loss in Africa, for example, most African nations will soon be unable to sustain themselves. Latin America and Asia are facing the same inevitable shortages.[12] Another 900 million hectares are in need of serious regeneration.

Year round irrigation and crop production in semi-tropical and dryland areas is overusing millions of hectares of arable land which is turning them into deserts, salt flats and waterlogged fields. Crop production suffers everywhere farm land is absorbed by expanding cities, housing developments, road construction, dams and diverted rivers. Millions more hectares will be unable to grow crops because of increased drought conditions and human consumption of existing water reserves. Ground water capacity is dropping at a rate three times faster than nature can replace it.

Several recent climatic factors are having a marked influence on annual crop outputs. The expanding holes in the ozone layer and the accumulation of acid rain and toxic emissions are blamed for the loss of about 5 percent of world crop capability, a rate that increases annually as the ozone holes grow. Increasing changes in climates or adverse conditions of the biosphere are also reducing crop production. El Nino, for example, brings more frequent and excessive drought, flooding, unseasonal freezes and hurricanes when it returns north, all factors which lower food production.

Where weather extremes are severe enough, famine often follows. Many African states, especially those in the northeast section of the continent, have a climate pattern of two or three good crop years, followed by one or two drought years with no crops of any value. In the last decade, these drought years have increased in occurrence and length. In 1992 and 1994 nearly all of the African countries south of the equator experienced unprecedented drought conditions that scientists attributed to El Nino.

   2. *Poor Farming Practices:* An estimated 550 million hectares of land are losing their topsoil to the degrading practices of poor farming. China alone lost 35 million hectares of farmland

between 1957 and 1990, an "area equal to all the cropland in France, Germany, Denmark and the Netherlands combined."[13]

Overcropping, overgrazing, artificial fertilizers, herbicides and pesticides are exhausting arable soils, reducing crop output and contaminating fresh water reserves needed to grow food crops. Heavy use of pesticides and herbicides kills the beneficial life forms in the soil and destroys the balance of natural processes which keep soil friable and capable of releasing the nutrients vital to growing plants. At present there are no international policies or standards in place to reverse these destructive practices. Most governments remain powerless to control the distribution of chemicals by the large multinational chemical companies. Many governments actually support the use of chemicals in that they willing take part in the Green Revolution and its use of agricultural technologies. This program is widely promoted by chemical companies who, while selling their fertilizers and pesticides to the farmer, promise him vastly increased crop production through their use.

Sadly, using chemicals increases production, but only in the very short term. Crops quickly come to need more and more chemical aids, increasing the amount of fertilizers applied annually and the strength of pesticides used. In the process, the nutrients, the life forms and the friability of the soil are lost within four to five years of constant chemical applications and the pests have grown immune to the poisons, while the beneficial life forms have been killed off.

On the other hand, organic farming, the wiser, safer choice, is generally not the most favoured because it can be expensive. Organic farming means less crop output as it requires that nearly a third of the plant matter grown be returned to the soil as compost to remain fertile. It also requires fallow periods to let the soil rest and rebuild itself. Large scale commercial farming, short term investors and indebted farmers are seldom willing to sacrifice immediate maximum production in exchange for preserving the soil over the long term. Profit generally supersedes conservation in both rich and poor nations, until the land will no longer grow crops.

The use of chemical preservatives, growth hormones, food additives, irradiation and genetically engineered foods will grow apace with our need to increase food production to meet population growth. As food shortages grow and soils lose their fertility, both farmers and distributers will be forced to use a variety of artificial technologies and chemical preservatives in growing and handling food crops to prevent food spoilage and extend shelf life. The impact of so many chemicals on the human body will be secondary to need and profit, but they are undoubtedly a universal and ongoing debilitating factor in human health.

The effects of additives and preservatives are already producing reactions in the human body which interfere with natural functions. Chemicals such as PCBs are showing up in humans, especially in mothers' milk. Allergic reactions to food additives, preservatives and coloring used in food processing are weakening human immune systems and multiplying allergic reactions. Some people have no tolerance to any chemicals as the result of an overexposure to some particular chemical that damaged their immune systems. The result can be incapacitating, even life threatening. Children, encouraged by the television media and bright paper packaging to eat "junk" foods preserved in sugar, salt and a variety of chemicals are suffering symptoms of malnutrition in nations with the highest living standards. The impact on mind and body is often adverse, affecting both children and adults who absorb large quantities of modern chemicals.

Many of the poor farming methods listed above, plus overcropping and erosion, are now universal as populations explode and food production declines. But some dangerous practices of farming are peculiar to the Third World. Where wood or other fuels are in short supply, vegetation and animal manures are burned in their place. This practice is dangerous in that both these items are vital as composts for the fertility of the soil. In many cases such as India, they are the only available sources of organic matter that can be used to refurbish tired soils and produce nutritious crops. As a result, malnutrition increases as crop quality deteriorates.

Farmers who once farmed organically did so because they had no other choice. Now those same farmers find themselves in competition with technological farming and monocultures. Many subsistent farmers have been pushed off the land by the large commercial growers or by urban development. All this is very reminiscent of Malthus' prediction.

The human suffering which follows dislocation from rural farms quickly leads to abuse of the natural vegetation. In an area of South Africa, for instance, the inhabitants of a group of small coastal villages, removed from access to the land, learned to live by fishing. They took only what they needed from the sea. Today commercial fishing fleets have depleted those fish stocks, leaving the native fishers without a livelihood and scavenging the land for food and fuel just to survive. Worse yet, the few remaining forests of Natal where these people live are losing rare flora and fauna to this human invasion. Forty percent of Natal's forests have already been lost.[14]

Traditional agricultural methods which cater to preserving the soil and farming in accord with the seasons endows the farmer with a deep respect for nature and its eco-systems. The failure of the Green Revolution and the increased poverty among farmers that has followed the aggressive technological innovation of commercial farming is encouraging many farmers to return to traditional organic farming. In small ways and in small areas scattered around the globe, farmers are once again nurturing their soil.

Unfortunately, with many impoverished and overpopulated nations unable to meet domestic food needs, poor farming practices continue to spread, driven by hunger and the consumption of all environmental assets. Deprivation will not endure conservation. Consequently, there is a deepening dependency on food aid and the beginning of mass migrations of millions of people in search of new lands.

Solutions to Food Shortages Are Few

Few options remain for increasing food production. The major solution has been to open up drylands or cut down forests to plant crops. But even this avenue is closing as drylands and forests are finite and displaying some rather frightening consequences as a result of human intrusion. Very soon after the lands are cleared, the depletion of fresh water reserves, rapid erosion of soils, long term drought and permanent desertification follow.

Scientific studies now underway are attempting to improve farm technologies and develop food hybrids which will allow grains and vegetables to be grown in extremes of climate such as desert conditions or on lands that have little fertility. Recent developments in genetic engineering of DNA molecules produced some forms of plants resistant to disease and drought, among them tomatoes. New, more productive strains of rice and corn are in the testing stage. Genetically engineered plants that can thrive in salty soils or grow in freezing temperatures are being studied. Several new successfully engineered plant forms have yet to be grown on a commercial scale.

Genetic engineering for invitro-production in greenhouses is another means of acquiring more growing space, but the costs of materials and energy are enormous, and the production so far falls very short of the quantities needed to feed billions of people in the future.

It may also be that we have learned to squeeze as much production out of an acre of land as can be grown on a continuing basis. Food production may always be limited by the quantity of plant growth that can succeed on a given acreage. No matter how good our biological technologies become "Crop plants can be congregated only so much and no more. They must be spread over the ground in a diffuse geometry so that they can capture enough sunlight and carbon dioxide to make a crop. Plants do not lend themselves to mass production techniques..."[15]

Third World Food Production

In many Third World nations food production falls far below the demand of the present populations. The effect is malnourishment and malnutrition with all its incumbent diseases and health problems. In India, for example, millions are forced to endure disease and hunger in crowded city slums on a daily basis. Food crops in Indian villages are endangered by the increasing severity of seasonal droughts and floods. Similar conditions are rife throughout Latin America, Africa and Asia where overcrowding, overgrazing and overfarming impose a subsistence level of existence on several billion people.

In rural areas of poor and underdeveloped countries, the production of food poses many problems related to poverty. Seed is too costly; fertilizers and pesticides put the farmer in debt. If he must purchase chemical fertilizers and pesticides, the poor farmer is faced with a future of unmanageable debt, degraded land and declining crop output. Often his life is cut short from breathing or absorbing the poisonous chemicals through the skin when he spreads them by hand or uses sprays and cannot afford protective clothing and breathing apparatus. Where clean water is in short supply, the farmer must use polluted water which, in turn, contaminates the soil and the food he grows. This is particularly dangerous to those who must work in polluted rice paddies for they have the added factor of diseases which flourish in contaminated water.

Where traditional organic methods of composting and fertilizing the soils are practised, the health of the people and the soil remain relatively stable. However, wherever technologies of the Green Revolution and the pressures of overpopulation have upset the balance, the results have proven disastrous. In some countries the peasant farmers, attempting to return to organic farming, do so while risking the wrath of their national governments.

Corrupt, faced with huge national debts or incapable of meeting the food needs of their overpopulated nations, a number of Third World governments have allowed the destruction of indigenous peasant farming. They have forced the small farmer off the land and sold it to huge international corporations in exchange for debt, foreign currencies, technologies and expertise. Huge agri-business companies now own vast areas of arable lands which once supported millions of peasant farmers in the Third World. These corporation farmers grow single crops which they sell almost exclusively in the First World. The major side effect of this takeover of peasant farms is the forced migration of millions of farmers and their families to urban areas in search of work and housing. In most cases, there are none. The other effect is the rapid degradation of the arable soils through monoculture and heavy use of chemicals.

One outstanding case of a government selling out its people in exchange for the arrival of the agri-business occurred in the Philippines. In the 1980s President Marcos and his henchmen, under the auspices of the National Development Company, literally stole millions of acres of growing lands from the country's peasants. The sole proprietorship of the land was then given to transnational corporations such as the British company, Guthrie, to grow palm trees and harvest the nuts for the manufacture of palm oil which was shipped to the markets of North America and Europe.

Intimidated, and in many cases, physically forced to give up their land, the peasants were robbed of their only form of livelihood. A very small number of the displaced farmers were able to get work as day labourers for the company, and they were paid so little in wages, they could barely survive. The companies only aim was to sell their production as competitively as possible in the rich nations and receive a large return of profits for the management and stockholders of Guthrie.

Those who could not get jobs with Guthrie migrated to the urban areas where unemployment, a lack of housing, malnutrition and disease meant a life of despair in shanty towns. As living conditions deteriorated for so many Filipinos, guerrilla bands and communities organized themselves into groups powerful enough to bring about the downfall and expulsion of the Marcos' regime.

In abdicating his responsibility to the entire nation and being totally self-serving, Marcos had robbed the people of their traditional livelihood, forcing them to the end of their tolerance. He had failed to meet his responsibilities as a leader. Eventually they rebelled, no longer able to acquiesce to his political corruption and economic crimes which were deepening their poverty and suffering.

Unfortunately, the new regime under Mrs. Aquino could do little to change the distribution of the farm land or alleviate the problems of the displaced farmer. Most of the land was now held by foreign agri-businesses or by a small elite of wealthy landowners of which Mrs. Aquino was one. Naturally her popularity waned rapidly. She was left with no legal means to take the land away from the large land holders and redistribute it among the peasants. Furthermore, the nation's foreign debt was so huge that she could not buy back or expel the foreign agri-businesses. Her remaining term in office was plagued with constant coup d'etats by underground organizations which continued to seek redress for the wrongs of Marcos' regime. Her good intentions went the way of so many in a world where economic power and ownership generally come before the needs of the people.

The story of the Philippines has repeated itself in varying degrees throughout Latin America, Asia and Africa. And yet the destruction of indigenous farming so that international corporations can profit from commercial crops for export at the cost of millions of lives cannot be condoned by the civilian population. When governments abdicate their responsibilities and the public passes the point of tolerable sufferance, peace and stability are soon lost and chaos and civil war ensue. The Philippines produced guerilla bands tired of suffering the loss of their farmlands, homes and dignity just as each Latin American nation has had its rebel bands seeking justice for the peasant cause over the past three decades.

With the end of the Cold War with the Soviet Union, the United States can no longer openly arm Third World dictatorships to destroy their peasant revolutionaries on the excuse these guerillas are Communist cells. In addition, military dictatorships of the Third World, once backed by the United States, are having to relinquish their power through democratic elections. The general public of Latin American states are increasingly able to speak out against the power and corruption of their elite. In time, democracy may prevail, but the solutions to overpopulation, diminishing food supplies and destroyed lands will continue to have their real roadblocks in mass poverty, hunger, degraded lands and exhausted resources. This takes some of the blame off elite power groups. They can no longer be held totally responsible for the poverty and suffering of their people. Population growth and degraded environments are more to blame and are generally conditions far beyond any government's control.

Inequities of Food Distribution

Every nation today, developed and developing, has its growing class of poor, ranging from the millions of farmers displaced by commercial agriculture, hydro-electric projects, drought and spreading desertification through to those victims of environmental collapse in overpopulated rural and urban areas. Obviously, as populations have expanded, humanity has come to depend on technologies destructive of the environment to provide food and employment. At the same time a cycle of interwoven social forces have emerged: poverty, unemployment and lost purchasing power, all of which directly increase population growth, rather than reduce it. Human existence now depends on creating jobs that use technologies which deplete the total environment and its resources. The effect has been to reduce billions of people into poorer and poorer living conditions for which a growing number must spend all their energy seeking a minimal daily food supply.

A shortage of purchasing power now exists among three quarters of the earth's population which denies them adequate nutrition and enough calories to work efficiently. Of the entire global population, the majority live at or below a subsistence level. Brazil in the 1990s, for example, has a population of 144 million, of which 20 million have no access to clean water, 60 million have no regular garbage collection and 75 million live without proper sewage and garbage disposal.[16] Conditions of widespread poverty, inadequate diet, complicated by contaminated drinking water, unsanitary environmental conditions and ignorant, unsafe medical practices have led to endemic diseases and virile plagues whose pandemic effects are rising, not only in Brazil but throughout Latin America.

Providing sufficient food and purchasing power for exploding populations will continue to be extremely difficult in the many poor countries where 95 percent of the world's people will live in the 21st Century. Here the majority not only lack employment skills, but their nations are very lacking in employment opportunities. Conditions are worsened by the shortage of national capital, industrial technologies and marketing expertise. Having too small a tax base, these nations can neither educate their people nor provide them sufficient health care which would allow the majority to overcome their poverty, low living standards and lack of education.

United Nations' estimates in 1993 stated that 40 percent or 2.2 billion people around the world are malnourished or facing starvation and all its ramifications. In Central America alone 75 percent of the children are underfed. Hunger on this scale produces malnutrition, disease and depressed intelligence. United Nations' reports have estimated approximately 15 million children a year die from malnutrition world wide, some 40,000 a day, comprising well over one-half of the annual general death total of 25 million from starvation.

Obviously, these annual death statistics will rise sharply over the next forty years as Third World populations double and children comprise more than 60 percent of the earth's populations. Rough estimates place 36 to 64 countries in danger of experiencing widespread food shortages by the year 2000, a number that will continue to rise throughout the 21st Century. At present nearly one billion people must attempt to survive without any purchasing power, government support or food aid. Without money to buy food, they ravage an already degraded natural environment in search of anything that will sustain them. Scavenging through urban garbage dumps of the Third World nations now occupies millions of hungry poor. Without security of food supply, most die young. They are the victims of overpopulation, neglect, landlessness, unemployment and incapacitating poor health.

Exploding populations on every continent may soon make it impossible for any nation's people to live in relative affluence as it becomes increasingly difficult to provide food and jobs for the bulk of their people. Among those who must endure abject poverty and chronic hunger, there is an approaching end to their tolerance for excessively rich elites who seem to respect no limits in their capacity to consume. Civil wars are already closely related to food and fresh water shortages.

Famines caused by drought and civil wars in Africa regularly drive whole tribes on treks to find food and water supplies. Their movements make them targets for roving guerilla bands who intercept food convoys for their own use; or government troops harass and kill the refugees for moving into the territory of another tribe. The horrors of this reality have dominated the 1980s and 1990s as clan wars in Ethiopia, Sudan, Somalia, Rwanda, Mozambique among many others, have terrorized most African nations as various tribes wage civil wars for political control. The power over distribution of food supplies in most African nations secures control over territories and their people. Whole tribes have been subjugated, some even wiped out by starvation imposed on them by rival tribes. By controlling food supplies ethnic cleansing of one tribe by another is possible. Consequently, tribal wars will escalate throughout the 21st Century as the endemic problems of hunger, drought, violence, tribalism and political chaos are inflamed by the scarcity of arable lands and the increase in population.

Equalizing Food Distribution

At present more nations are importing food supplies to feed their people than nations exporting food, both rich and poor. In 1990, 68 countries imported more food to feed their people than they grew. By the year 2000 the majority of them will be permanently dependent on imported food, some will be welfare nations vulnerable to their reliance on food aid. The populations of food importing countries now total more than one billion and will reach two billion within 30 years if their populations grow according to estimates. Population rates have already surpassed increase rates in food production and the demand for imported food will soon far exceed what is available for export. This growing imbalance has many serious ramifications.

National debts rise in nations which must import the bulk of their food supplies to meet the demands of their growing populations. Foreign credits are then spent on food, rather than on technologies and industrialization, rapidly depleting these credits, but people must be fed. Import trade deficits soon become financially unmanageable. National debt then forces increased productivity. This translates into excessive consumption and exportation of raw resources and manufactured goods. Domestically, fewer citizens own their own land, and the arrival of foreign owners who turn to monoculture deplete the soils and consider only the profits to be made.

Indebted nations soon lose their viability as well as their political stability. Economic and social inequality and dependency which leave people hungry generates civil violence.

On the other hand, some nations such as Japan, Hong Kong, Taiwan and Singapore have industrial bases rich enough to afford the costs of importing the bulk of their foods and raw resources. But at the same time they have built a dependency on foreign trade which brings environmental destruction to those nations they exploit for their food crops and raw materials. This is sadly reflected in the clear cutting of tropical forests, the spread of agri-businesses throughout the Third World and the overfishing of the world's oceans.

With food production on the decline, the concept of so many nations totally dependent on other nations to meet their food needs is ominous. As populations grow faster than food supply, present rates of output will be threatened by an increasing number of crop failures caused by changing seasonal weather patterns, global warming, extremes of El Nino, chronic drought and regular flooding on an expanding world scale.

Ownership of the natural resources of soil, water and food production remain most inequitable. This unfair distribution stands as a major threat to world peace. With 65 to 70 nations already totally dependent on food imports and the majority of countries in the Middle East and North Africa running out of fresh water reserves, these nations alone form a formidable bloc of large populations whose terrorists and nuclear arsenals are strong enough to threaten the safety of the entire world. The desperation of their survival may lead them to enforce demands on the "have" nations for a greater share of the world's resources. As their struggle to survive grows more desperate, nuclear blackmail will become a popular means to get what they want. It is hard to put aside the enormity of exploding populations on already overwhelmed land bases. The struggle to survive, when desperate enough, nullifies all civilized behaviours.

Food Aid

Food and water shortages in Africa during the last half of the 20th Century forced millions of starving people to go in search of help. The media's coverage of so much suffering shocked the world and initiated international food aid programs intended to bring aid to the needy in times of disaster. The co-ordination and distribution of food aid, survival supplies, money donations and military weapons became a permanent phenomenon of 20th Century philanthropy. Food Aid organizations now bring help to millions of people everywhere when they are uprooted by crop failures, catastrophic weather conditions, earthquakes, temporary food shortages, droughts, floods and civil wars.

Thanks to the technologies of transportation and cold storage, millions of tons of food and other basic needs can be moved relatively quickly anywhere in the world. This sharing of food has made survival possible for increasing numbers who without it would have died of starvation and related diseases. Aid is also intended to develop and establish modern industry and agriculture in the poorer nations through large loans and transferred technology.

Unfortunately for all, food aid has been one of many inappropriate and mishandled international activities which once in place, expanded and enriched its bureaucracy. Most of the money supplied by national governments to the large loan and aid organizations such as the United Nations, World Vision, The World Bank and the International Monetary Fund (IMF) has been absorbed in the administration of these organizations and by their agency staffs, making them among the most highly paid bureaucracies in the world. Past experience has shown that little "aid" money actually reaches people in distress.

Incompetence, arrogance, unpreparedness dog these large distributors of aid. Little thought is given to the needs of the uprooted or the victims of starvation. The real interest lies in the financial benefits that can be gained by the companies supplying the food aid as it allows them to use the donations as tax write-offs or as a means to dispose of unsold or unwanted production. More often than not, the food or other survival goods arrive as much as a year to two years after the disaster has occurred; in many cases the wrong forms of aid have been sent or the food is contaminated. In reality, aid to the disaster victims seldom arrives in time, is generally inappropriate for the needs of the victims and is often too poor in quality or insufficient in quantity to help the majority in need.[17]

Furthermore, corruption runs rampant in the aid business. The distribution of seventy percent of food aid sent to a nation in distress is left to the discretion of the governments receiving the aid to distribute it among their people as they choose, a practice that prevents much of it from ever reaching famine victims. Instead of giving it to the starving, government officials sell it to the middle classes, to their own employees and to their soldiers and police. The money is then pocketed by corrupt officials who are often no more than warlords and their terrorist gangs.

In recent years aid givers have become victims themselves to civil wars, kidnapping and murder when they appear to take sides in civil conflicts. Many have been taken hostage by guerrilla leaders to serve as bargaining chips in achieving rebel demands.

Unfortunately, food aid, while vital immediately in times of disaster, has proven more detrimental in the long run. It tends to complicate normal economic patterns rather than ease them. Studies in the 1990s have shown that international food aid in Africa often produced worse problems than the droughts that caused the famines. As aid tends to be delivered long after it is needed, the food is dispensed almost entirely in the urban areas where it is easier to distribute because of the concentrated numbers of people. It is even easier to dispose of the food supplies in seaport cities where it arrives then to bother transporting it into the countryside. Here aid supplies are sold cheaply on the black market, competing with the sale of domestically grown crops from outlying farms whose farmers must transport their crops over nonexistent roads to reach the urban markets.

Impoverished nations also find it easier to accept aid than to subsidize their domestic farmers. The farmers, in turn, discouraged by the lack of rural markets and the very low prices they receive for their crops, must compete with cheap food aid in the cities. Already living on the edge of bankruptcy in normal times, they cannot afford to hold back their crops until the aid supplies of food have been sold off and market prices improve. Defeated by so many setbacks, the farmers choose not to risk planting another crop.

In this way food aid replaces local farm production, and farmland is left to the destructive forces of erosion and weeds. In the process nations with frequent drought and flooding problems have become "addicted" to their annual "food fix" from Europe and North America.

The problem for the subsistence farmer is magnified by his need to produce at least enough food to feed his family. He is convinced he must have large families to work his fields. African populations experiencing these circumstances have exploded. The farmlands are overcropped, the ground water reserves overused and drought grows more widespread with each passing year. If the population of farm families had remained small and had they worked with the seasons instead of cultivating the land all year round and irrigating with water brought up from wells with modern technologies, perhaps the need for continuous food aid would not have arisen.

Watching people die of starvation from the point of view of the technological world is highly disturbing, and so philanthropy remains commendable. However, sadly for humanitarian intentions, the efforts of the rich nations to help the suffering in poor nations may well be among the major causes of environmental collapse.

Rather than develop small enterprises and give aid to farmers, the development loans during the 1960s, 1970s and 1980s generally went towards building large projects such as dams, roads, mines and irrigation projects, all of which devastated the environment, uprooted millions of people and generally proved fruitless in their attempts to develop viable industries in many Third World nations. Instead, the effect of so much government aid was to put unmanageable debts onto poor nations who could not repay them, while their leaders lined their pockets and hid the wealth in offshore banks.

Undoubtedly, famine may be offset by food aid at the time of crisis, but it must remain only a stopgap. On a continuing basis, it has not only destroyed local farm economies, it has encouraged high birth rates. Aid has proven more detrimental to most receiving nations than useful, increasing poverty, not lessening it. In Ethiopia in 1990 the local farmers were bankrupted when they tried to compete with food aid after the drought eased up and crops could once again be grown. Aid in most forms tends to institutionalize poverty which decreases self-sufficiency and purchasing power while building total dependence of the poor nations on the rich.

Massive humanitarian outpourings of food aid have not only proven detrimental to those people who receive it, it has become an economic drain on the donor nations. In recent years the continuing dependency and the inability of nations receiving aid to improve their economic and political viability has created a resentment among rich nations as investments have turned into "give away" programs. Too many exploding populations, too much corruption and too many destructive tribal wars have discouraged humanitarian aid. The term "compassion fatigue" describes the vastly reduced generosity of the rich when natural disasters strike the poor. A growing apathy in the industrial nations is fostering isolationist policies as their citizens come to think of unnecessary terror, cruelty and costly destruction imposed by one tribe on another as in Africa or Yugoslavia as waste and wantonness they will not finance. What is even more resented is that the poor nations expect the rich nations to pick up the costs of rebuilding after their catastrophic civil wars.

And yet a humanitarian and moral conscience motivates much of the Western world to seek ways to redistribute the universally produced supplies of food more equitably. At present we can grow enough food on the planet to contend with infrequent horrendous events of starvation as we have witnessed in the last few decades of the 20th Century. But that ability is waning. The large, food growing nations are faced with declining climatic patterns, frequent losses of commercial crops to weather extremes and diminishing arable lands to erosion and urban development. The requirements of the needy of the world are already so huge that meeting them on an equitable basis surpasses all the largesse the rich nations are willing to offer for fear they, too, fall into poverty and self-destruction.

CHAPTER SIXTEEN

Exploitation and Destruction of Ecological Systems

The laws of evolution and extinction of species do not exempt Homo sapiens. We are as vulnerable as any other species to the forces of nature no matter how we strive to prove otherwise. Although we have developed technologies to augment natural food supplies and designed weapons to curtail the threat of nature's predators, we have yet to overcome the basic conditions of territorial carrying capacity which ultimately limits the production of food and resources of fresh water on any given land base. As yet we have not developed technologies capable of regulating the earth's interdependent forces of climate, vegetation and life forms to the exclusion of sustaining our voluminous consumption of environmental resources.

Nor have we subjugated the individual's need for social space which is generating a swell of human aggressive behaviours in every society as the struggle for sustenance within "tribal" territories inflames civil violence universally with each annual addition of 90 million souls. As with all species, life and death still determine our length of stay. But increasingly, we are reducing the length of that stay by destroying the natural eco-reservoir of life on this planet.

To evaluate our continuing chances of survival is to assess our place and role within the highly interdependent eco-systems. It begins with an honest acknowledgement that our over zealous drive for human self-fulfilment is causing the rapid extinction of species world wide, along with climatic changes for which our industrial/agricultural technologies are increasingly responsible.

In past geological times eco-systems flourished and continuously maintained and improved the quality and variety of species.[1] The number of new species added to the earth always outnumbered those lost through attrition and extinction. In each case, the surviving species had adapted over thousands of years to the climatic conditions and natural carrying capacity of the land and ocean areas they inhabited.

Numbers and variety of species evolve within interdependent systems built on food chains, ranging from the smallest microbes to the largest mammals. On land, for instance, the number of herbivores a territory can carry is determined by the amount of digestible vegetative foods available to sustain them. The number of herbivores which form the food source for carnivores, in turn, determine the variety and number of carnivores which an area can support. To maintain a liveable balance among species, their individual populations are ultimately limited by territorial carrying capacity.

Populations increase only when a species' territory is enlarged or extra food supply is introduced into the system. An increase in food supply will result in a larger number of offspring born and a high survival rate. A decline in food supply and increased predation will cause a sharp decline in births and a rise in deaths among a starving population, even extinction.

The historical extinction most related to human occupation and technologies was the disappearance of the herds of large grazing animals throughout Europe and North Africa as the ice receded between 10,000 to 20,000 years ago. A direct correlation exists between the disappearance of these herds and the improving hunting practices, especially the weapons, of increasing numbers of hunter-gatherers.

Consequently, the gradual extinction of grazing animals through "overkill" resulted in widespread hunger among the hunter-gatherers. Farming the land and domesticating smaller food animals replaced the lost herds of large grazing animals. Although the human species learned to domesticate their own food animals and increase their numbers phenomenally, at the same time, they continued to destroyed other species at an irresponsible rate. Technological self-determination has allowed humanity increased carrying capacity of food supply as well as greater use of natural resources. Unfortunately, our advancement has always been at the expense of other species. Historical archaeological digs continue to turn up the bones of large numbers and variety of animals which were killed with human weapons or displaced by human occupancy throughout the Mediterranean basin and North Africa.

With every passing century, the rate of extinction of species has risen. Farming the land meant clearing it of much of its natural vegetation and life forms. The remaining small, scattered populations of birds, animals and fish on the planet are indicative of our increasing total occupation and exploitation of the planet.

In the 20th Century approximately 1.4 million species have been recognized and catalogued. Estimates of the total number in existence ranges from 5 to 80 million. Human interference with the natural processes is causing the disappearance of over 20,000 species a year.[2] "Today species vanish not over millennia but over hours. Based on current rates of habitat destruction, scientists estimate, conservatively that from one to three species are lost each hour,"[3] making a possible total of 26,000 species lost per year. "Some biologists have hazarded a guess that perhaps one-quarter of the species are at serious risk of extinction over the next twenty to thirty years.[4] We behave like demons and have become the scourge of the earth.

Agricultural and industrial abuse through chemicals, toxic emissions, oil spills, irrigation, acid rain, global warming and ozone depletion has damaged or is in the process of ruining the entire planet's supplies of soils, fresh water, oceans, forests, mineral resources and vegetation. Every type of species' habitat has been contaminated or degraded: ponds, rivers, lakes, wetlands, coastal waters, forests, grasslands and polar ice caps.

The contaminants we are adding to the natural environment through pesticides, toxic wastes and industrial chemicals cannot be degraded or broken down by the organisms which absorb or ingest them. All species evolved to use the materials of the environment to build their own bodies, but none are equipped to use the artificial chemicals we are adding to the earth. Once organisms absorb them, the chemicals remain in their bodies, accumulating and contaminating whole food chains. The result is cancers, deformities, a failure to reproduce and an inability to survive.

Recent scientific studies suggest that plastics may be responsible for a hormonal change in both animals and humans. The effects show up as an interference with the fetus that results in decreased IQ's and aggressive behaviors in later years. As species die off from the devastation of their bodies, their food chains and their wilderness habitat, their loss is setting off dangerous changes in climate and vegetation patterns which make this planet habitable. We are fast approaching a time when life on earth will be determined by an overabundance of a few commercial species in an increasingly sterile, polluted biosphere.

Preventing the collapse of the eco-systems is obviously vital to our future existence, but can we reverse our role in species' extinction? We may be hindered by elements within our own evolutionary makeup. In the struggle to survive over millions of years, our weak, physically defenceless hominid ancestors were instilled with a "killer instinct", an inventive brain and a dextrous body structure. Unable to sustain their expanding populations, these ancestors gave up their dependency on carrion and small animals and invented ways to catch and kill large, dangerous game animals. In so doing, they began the evolutionary process towards destructive dominance over most life forms.

Unfortunately, the ingrained memory of that well-armed, aggressive hunter still exists within us. It comes forth in the desire to shoot "big game", kill wild animals and birds and overfish the seas. It is there in our arrogant dismissal of the rights of other species to share this planet, especially if their deaths serve human needs. To date, few people express a desire to stop the pain or death sentence we impose on other species as we forcefully commandeer their habitat, poison them with toxic chemicals, hunt them down for captivity, fence them within small compounds, force feed them, ply them with antibiotics and hormones and kill them for their meat, hides and organs. As long as other species advance our survival, we continue to ignore their role in the ecological balance of the total environment.

The following story was extracted from a daily newspaper article dated June 30, 1990. It reflects the attitude of human authorities and the willingness of governments to support endless cruelty and decimation of animals to benefit human demands:

Capetown: South African animal lovers rallied...to block a Taiwanese businessman's plan to turn 25,000 seal pups into dog food for export to the United States and Europe. Capetown biologist, Philip Stewart, said the seals to be killed will also include adult males, whose dried genitalia will be processed as an aphrodisiac used in Asia. A businessman (H. Hsu) has paid the government the equivalent of 10 cents for each seal ... the seal pups will be clubbed and have their throats slit on a beach in the northern Cape Diamond zone, where the public is banned.

The Taiwanese Embassy economics advisor, C.H. Fang, said...that opposition to the killing is stupid. Referring to a telephone call from a woman who opposed the plan, he said, "I think she is just a stupid woman. I think she is just too fat and she has nothing better to do. She should protest against the countries that kill people ... and not against countries that kill seals ... People should worry about people, not animals."[5]

While the article shocks anyone sensitive to nature, the last sentence sums up the irrational arrogance and expediency with which so many still view other species. The major evolutionary difference between Homo sapiens and all other species is that humans continue to kill other species for the wrong reasons. Our cavalier attitudes towards and treatment of other life forms are anathema to the natural ecology, yet we wantonly slaughter millions of birds, sea mammals, fish and other marine creatures in the process of netting commercial fish or entertaining our hunters. Asian markets scour the earth for any remaining wild animals from which they can extract their organs and genitalia for medicines and aphrodisiacs. Poachers search out wild animals which can be eaten or sold for their hides or exotic value. The elephants and rhinos of Africa, the tigers of Asia, the seals of North America and the rare and beautiful birds of tropical jungles are in constant danger of hunters who see them only as a source of income to be exploited to extinction. It is estimated that over "12 million exotic wild animals a year are illegally trapped in Brazil's Amazon rain forest and sold .... Of those captured, only 10 per cent make it to the black market and stores alive, where they are sold."[6]

In their evolution species have not been programmed to wipe out others. When it happens, it is because an exotic species has been introduced into an area where it can eliminate any competition for local food supplies and it has no predator enemies or natural controls on its reproduction. Only Homo sapiens engages in the supreme brutality of murdering members of its own species and attacks its fellows with the deliberate intention of destroying them. Most species have "weapon" features to kill prey or fight off their enemies, but they do not use them for indiscriminate mass murder as humans do for profit or power. Unlike humans, other species cannot afford the energy nor the dangers inherent in frequent physical battle. Injuries weaken and destroy their capability to reproduce and find food. When a predator attacks and kills prey, this is not aggression as in combat, it is killing for food or in defense of territory, the loss of which could mean certain death to its entire social group. Even then most species avoid combat to the death over territorial rights.

"Evolution of all species except man has come about as a clear cut strategy of avoiding conflict."[7] With this inherent "killer instinct" towards our own species, it is obvious we will never fully respect the rights of other species to occupy space on this planet which we want for ourselves. Nor will we permit them to survive if their removal facilitates our existence.

Killing Species for Employment and Enjoyment

Technological advances in food production should have brought an end to humans killing wild life both on land and in the oceans. We can grow crops and domesticate poultry and animals to provide as much food as we need to maintain a nutritious diet. Yet we continue to slaughter wild species to extinction so that we can sate our desire for an infinite variety of foods, be employed through killing them, be entertained by their antics and their captivity and indulge our bodies and vanity with the luxury of furs and "natural medicines".

Instead of ending our dependency on other species, we have usurped the powers of extinction over them. Our primary method of endangering species has been our technological ability to eradicate their food sources and destroy the food chains of the land and oceans. Even worse, those we fail to kill directly, we destroy indirectly with chemicals, pollution and confiscation of their natural habitats.

Through thousands of years human societies have been programmed to believe that exploitation of the environment is critical to our own survival, a socio/economic value which reinforces the conviction that it is our right to view the environment and its eco-systems as a storehouse of resources assembled entirely for human use. This self-centred attitude towards our own survival has instilled in us a total bias for economic prosperity at any cost to the environment. Farming, logging, fishing, mining or urban development take precedence over ecological systems.

In the past, whenever the immediate environment collapsed under human occupation, former civilizations broke up and the people either died out or moved on to consume the eco-systems of another land base. It is only now that we are beginning to realize the true impact this perpetual habit is having on the planet. There is no virgin habitat left which is suitable in its natural state for our purposes unless it is radically changed by deforestation, draining, irrigating or cementing over.

A political and economic vision which would reverse ecological annihilation exists in the minds of visionaries and eco-planners; but they are generally curtailed by powerful forces of industrial exploitation, agricultural and urban development or economic dilemmas thwarting wholesale conservation. Government authorities are often uneducated in the biological and ecological aspects of the environments they permit to be exploited in the name of jobs and profit, or they are hamstrung by the financial power of corporate interests which thrive on ecological resources. Preventing environmental degradation of forests, toxic runoff or overfishing has always been secondary to economic pursuit.

Short term development, investments and tax revenues rather than conservation for future generations motivate political and corporate decisions. The powers of multinational corporations who own the millions of hectares of temperate rain forests in Western Canada and the American Pacific Northwest have generally won out against environmental concerns. Only in very recent years have governments, faced with public anger over clear cutting old growth forests, passed and enforced minimum conservation laws. Each patch of old forest that remains standing has been hard fought for by environmentalists.

Some public protests have been loud enough to overcome the development plans of powerful economic forces. Such a case was that of Alcan, the aluminum smelting company who, in need of more local hydro power, sought government permission to build another dam on the Netchatko River in Northern Canada. To do so would have all but eliminated the river's water supplies to local citizens and threatened one of the most prolific salmon spawning areas on the Pacific Coast, all in the aid of increasing aluminum output. It is not an even trade-off for the environment or the local people. Pressures, however, were great enough to put the project on hold until a thorough environmental study could be done.

Reason tells us we should not exploit species to extinction for economic profit. Unfortunately, the need to secure and indulge our own survival outweighs our concern for the needs of all other life forms. Intelligence has produced a deadly combination in us of overpopulation and technological-determination which permits us to carry on the extravagant exploitation and destruction of so many other species.

One of the most appalling examples of ecological destruction for profit in North America is that of the Florida Everglades. State and federal governments financed the artificial channelling the river through wetlands, draining an area that once teemed with the greatest variety of life on the continent. Heavily fertilized farmlands and urban development now occupy miles of drained swamp lands and most of the river water is consumed in irrigation. Contained within cement walls, the river no longer spreads out over the vast river plains, but flows through impermeable canals directly into the sea. A very small portion of the delta and its everglades remains in its natural state within a national park. It can hardly be considered as protected wetlands as millions of tourists go there each year to stare at the wild life and trod the many manmade pathways. The continuing destruction of the Everglades and its waters is especially unforgivable in a nation which boasts the greatest accumulation of ecological knowledge and habitat protection in the world.

Fresh water which once fed natural sanctuaries is now laden with fertilizers and pesticides. Water from the river and the delta poison the coastal waters and foster massive algae blooms which cause large fish kills. The shame is that those who continue to cater to human needs and pleasure in destroying the Florida Everglades know the damage they are doing. Yet in the name of development, farming and sugar production for profit the process of eco-destruction expands. Despite public disapproval, it is unlikely that development will be halted or the artificial drainage systems of the river plains removed. Eventually the entire environment on land and water will be so polluted or dried up that it will no longer be habitable even for humans. The loss of the Everglades demonstrates how rare, fragile environments have become the hapless victims of river diversion technologies.

The Tug-o-war between Environmentalists and Job Seekers

The battle to save the earth's eco-systems wages on between those who would keep all the remaining forests, wilderness and marine life from human exploitation and those who see trees, fresh water, animals and fish as cash crops to be harvested for human consumption and jobs. The environmentalists argue that the loss of even one rare species is indicative of the permanent loss of a wilderness habitat and all its other species within that eco-system.

Choosing in favour of wild life and the forests does not make sense to the economic mind. The idea persists that human needs have priority; the loss of other species is not worth the price of thousands of jobs or the loss of cash resources to be extracted from the wilderness or the billions to be made from fishing out the seas, or so the argument goes.

The number of species being driven into extinction by the belief that preservation of a few rare species cannot be allowed to take precedence over human employment and development is indicative of human self-interest. Even government agents whose task it is to protect the environment argue that there is little sense denying thousands of loggers, miners, oil drillers and fishermen jobs just to protect the habitat of one or two rare species like the spotted owl or the red-spotted squirrel, both endangered species in the United States. The idea of protecting one species has created an angry battle between loggers and environmentalists in the Northwest forests of Washington and Oregon. Environmentalists see the role of the spotted owl as an indicator of the loss of the entire old-growth eco-system in which it lives, and the loggers see the owl as a "ridiculous" roadblock to logging, jobs and healthy human communities.

The mistake lies in the Endangered Species Act itself. It is seen as an absurd law which gives priority to one small creature over the needs of thousands of workers and their families.

Ironically, the only way to date that the U.S. government could find to protect a entire endangered eco-system was to protect a single species within that system.

While a single species' protection act has gained some credibility, as in the case of saving the remaining old growth stands of Northwest forests, it remains close to impossible to convince the job hunter that the loss of one species represents the loss of thousands of other species in the interdependent ecological balance of the wilderness and oceans.

Scientists, late in the game perhaps, are "beginning to question why there is so much bio-diversity and how it is generated and lost. They are also asking whether bio-diversity has a role in the functioning of ecosystems."[8] Some duplication in ecological roles occurs in that several species eat the same things and occupy the same territories, but their contributions to the eco-systems may differ. As yet we do not know which ones we can safely do without.

What is so frightening in this contest between the human species and the natural eco-systems is that we have already destroyed over two-thirds of the planet's wilderness and brought about the extinction of tens of thousands of species before we have taken the time to evaluate their impact on our own existence.

How much of the deterioration of the planet's eco-systems is due to human interference and exploitation and how much is nature's own process of decline and decay is not known. But without a doubt, our clearcutting and burning of old growth forests, for example, can only increase the rate of ecological decline and ultimate loss. The burning of 200 million trees in Spain by the ancient Romans to make charcoal nearly 2000 years ago and the barren desert lands they left behind should be evidence enough to make us rethink the prudence of providing thousands of jobs cutting down the few remaining forests.

At present cutting rates, the forests of the world are endangered by increased logging, diseases, pests and changing climates. Infestations of insects and diseases which old growth forests previously withstood are gaining in strength as the genetic immunity of forest eco-systems is lost because of human interference and the introduction of exotic species. Dutch Elm disease, spruce bud worm, gypsy moths, borers and many more are destroying vast stands of trees. Forests planted with human hands are proving even more vulnerable to diseases, pests and fungi. Managed forests also lack resistance to high winds and fires, giving them short life spans so that they cannot replicate their eco-systems as do natural forests. Above all, bio-diversity is lost through clearcutting and monoculture.

In our haste to cut old growth forests, we are destroying the ecological interchange which exists between vegetation and life forms and depleting the genetic strength of entire eco-systems. In the process climatic changes have occurred which killed trees the world over. Human interference through trying to prevent the natural cycles of forest fires and regrowth has resulted in severely hot burns when they occur. The damage to plant and life forms has been devastating. Common sense should tell us it is time to stop cutting the forests and find other ways to produce building materials and paper products. We must end the massive role wood plays in our lives before forests disappear and we are struggling to exist on a barren planet.

As populations grow and wilderness disappears, the percentage of lost species threatens to increase so rapidly that many of us may see the collapse of the global ecology within our lifetimes. If the estimated loss of 20 percent of life forms over the next decade holds true, at this rate all major life forms will be gone within the next 50 years. Can any species including humans survive with such a dearth of plant and life forms in the interdependent eco-systems?

Two disturbing arguments are used by environmentalists to coerce the public into agreeing to protect endangered species. One argument is that we have yet to discover whether or not the millions of unknown species could be exploited to benefit human life as food sources, medications or chemical products. The second is to save the species by promoting eco-tourism so that millions of people will see the wild species and be co-opted into protecting them from human development. Both arguments only sustain the belief that all species exist for human benefit. Both concepts are highly destructive of eco-systems.

Encouraging their exploitation for human use tends to provide an excuse to consume species which may cure human illnesses. The recent discovery that the bark of the Yew tree can be used to make the chemical "taxol" which cures breast cancer has sent the opportunist out to the forests to ravage the forests of their yew trees. It is doubtful they will leave enough of these trees standing to ensure their continued existence, especially since the financial return is so high and the demand for "taxol" so great. That all other species are an essential part of the entire global eco-system, making life possible for humanity is not even a consideration when human needs are seen as of primary concern.

Such arrogance! We have set ourselves up as gods on earth. What punishments we are accumulating for our future existence. Environmental degradation is now so severe that nature is beginning to rebel and will soon have all the necessary "weapons" with which to defeat us in our battle to survive. What species we do not destroy, nature will through extremes of drought and flood.

Destruction of Ocean Eco-Systems

Much has been recorded and written on the destruction and disarray of eco-systems throughout the world. It is happening everywhere to every species. The story of our oceans and their dying eco-systems is a sufficiently shocking illustration.

Technology has played a villain's role in overfishing the oceans and polluting their waters. Millions of birds, dolphins, whales, turtles, porpoises as well as every variety of marine life in the oceans and on the ocean floor are being caught up in the "invisible" drift nets where they die of suffocation. Millions more are poisoned by the toxic wastes of industry, agriculture and urban life pumped into the oceans in the billions of gallons. Many more die from starvation as ocean food chains vanish through overfishing, warming ocean currents or ultra-violet B rays.

Commercial stocks have all but disappeared along the coasts of the industrial nations of North America and Europe, and now throughout Asia. "One-fourth of all assessed fish stocks have been overexploited; another 44 percent are fully-to-heavily exploited, according to the United Nations Food and Agriculture Organization (FAO). Fisheries everywhere are in crisis."[9] Over 200 million jobs are at stake.[10] Fish harvests which rose annually throughout the 20th Century have declined sharply since 1990.

And yet world fishing fleets continue to expand and larger, more efficient fishing boats appear on the oceans each year. Fishing technologies employing purse seines, drift nets and large sea going fishing boats, equipped with sonar and refrigeration and accompanied by "factory" ships with full scale processing plants, have been instrumental in devastating fish stocks throughout the world. Government quotas remain far too high, encouraging too many fishermen to invest huge sums of money in fishing boats. A total of $54 billion in annual subsidies is paid out to fishermen who catch $70 billions worth of fish. Such a policy at present is still profitable enough to prevent a massive drop in the number of fishermen and boost conservation programs.[11]

In Canada, the federal government aggravates the situation even further by paying out unemployment insurance to fishermen during their off seasons. Captains of large fish boats who have earned over $100,000 in two to three months of fishing, still line up for nine months of unemployment benefits along with their deck-hands who have incomes as high as $40,000.[12] This handout of free money encourages the number of fishermen to remain large and seek ways to stay in the system, despite the fact that their overfishing is rapidly depleting the stocks and governments must eventually call a moratorium on fishing. Caught in this trap, neither fishermen nor governments are backing conservation measures. The problem is exacerbated as the large, highly equipped vessels of the rich nations face increasing competition from the developing nations whose share of the annual take is now surpassing 60 percent.[13]

Unenforced regulations and quotas, inappropriate and incompetent government policies, "fish wars" over disappearing stocks, improved detection equipment and more efficient methods of catching and storing fish are practices that "mine" the seas. World commercial stocks are so depleted that fishermen everywhere are returning to port with smaller and smaller catches each year. In 1950, some 21 million tons of fish were taken from the oceans for commercial use. In 1987, 85 million tonnes were taken commercially, a fourfold increase and 24 million tonnes by subsistence fishermen,[14] a total of 110 million tonnes of fish in one year. However, in 1992 only 90.9 million tons were caught, down nearly 7 percent from the peak in 1989. By 1995 the numbers had declined so dramatically that fisheries were closing down for a lack of fish.

As fish stocks decline, tempers rise. The number of international incidents are growing. Increasingly, the lack of international laws or the imposition of them induces fishermen to ravage the stocks of open seas and coastal waters while fishing nations with the largest fleets support their refusal to follow conservation quotas. In 1994 "Russian patrol boats fired on three Japanese fish boats near the Kurile Islands... Spanish fishermen fired on French trawlers in the Bay of Biscay, wounding one Frenchman ...", and armed Canadian coastguards "seized two American fishing boats in International waters for illegal scallop fishing."[15] As populations grow, so do the number of fishermen. However, over 20 million small scale fishermen are on the brink of going out of business.[16]

New methods of dragging nets to "scrape" the bottom of the oceans and capture all types of marine life are hauling in fish that were once considered unworthy of eating.[17] This process has endangered many more marine creatures as such methods of fishing go on not only in coastal areas but in mid-ocean. Marc Beaucheasne aboard the Rainbow Warrior in 1991 described the fishing tactics of driftnetters in the Pacific. "Over 1200 driftnetters... lay out their nets around 4 each afternoon and pull them in around midnight every day of the year. They set out a total of about 25,000 nautical miles of nets".[18] They have become exceptionally efficient in their netting and even rough seas do not stop them from their fishing.

Ruthless mining of the oceans' marine life can only deplete all species and capture few of the desired squid and tuna. The same process of decimation is practised by the shrimp fishermen off the southern coast of the United states where turtle populations have all but disappeared from these waters as they are caught in shrimp nets. The turtles drown along with many other sea creatures caught in the nets. Attempts to design nets which allow turtles to escape may be too late in coming. The turtles are now an endangered species with little chance of regenerating sufficient numbers. Most of those remaining will still fall victim to the nets.

The decline in fish stocks has been catastrophic for shore birds and all other life forms which depend on fish for their food supply. The entire North and South American Atlantic shoreline, once home to massive flocks of migrating and nesting birds, now sustains a fraction of the life it once did. The abundant schools of small food fish on which both the birds and the cod fed are gone. Also the thousands of birds and fish that once lived along the coastal shores of every continent are in steep decline or have disappeared where once they flourished in the millions.

Coastal sea life is also at risk, destroyed by sewage, soil erosion and coastal construction. Oil from motorboats, ships and oil rigs, seepage from city drains, run off from industries, development of coastal resorts, all are rapidly eliminating sea life along the shores or poisoning them with chemicals that are capable of changing species' genetic structure. All varieties of fish, shellfish, molluscs, turtles, sea worms and seabirds are dwindling; many have become extinct. Hundreds of miles of coral reefs in tropical waters have been killed by divers and swimmers whose hands and feet touch the coral. The reefs are also dying around the world from the warming ocean currents which cause the coral to expel the algae on which it depends for food, oxygen and protection from sunlight.[19] As the coral dies, its marine life dies. The massive numbers of dying reefs around the world form a major eco-system succumbing to human activities and climate change.

Garbage, especially plastic wastes have polluted the oceans and the beaches. It is estimated that "each boater creates 700 grams of plastic garbage per day, merchant vessels dump at least 450,000 plastic containers per day and the world's commercial fishing fleets discard more than 30 million kilograms of packaging and 100,000 tonnes of plastic fishing gear every year, all into the oceans."[20] Plastic containers, bags, bottles, pop rings, littering the surface of the oceans, trap the sea life which eventually kills them or chokes them to death if they cannot get free. Much of this junk is swallowed by mammals and birds.

Estimates put the number of ships dumping garbage overboard daily at more than half a million. Many pump their bilges to rid them of oil, water and sewage, despite international laws prohibiting this practice. The millions of tons of garbage dumped at sea floats to shore and collects on the beaches where it endangers shoreline birds and other creatures. Some of the most beautiful beaches around the world, from every country in the Mediterranean to the Australian coastline to North America to Asia are littered with refuse which pollutes the beaches and makes them unsafe for all ocean and coast life forms as well as humans.

"On average, one bulk ore/oil tanker sinks every month". These ships, registered in Panama, Liberia or the Bahamas, travel the oceans with multinational crews who are untrained in seamanship, low paid, cannot understand the language of their officers and are often held in bondage aboard ship. Everything is done to keep operation and maintenance costs at the barest minimum. Through these foreign registries owners can avoid taxes and maintenance regulations imposed by national governments who are trying to protect the ocean from the disasters that follow the sinking of these ships.

Lost drift nets continue to "fish" on the oceans, catching millions of birds and other sea creatures which become tangled in the nets. Added to the dangers of floating debris are the millions of gallons of sewage and pollutants dumped along coastal shores by industry and sewage plants, debilitating all sea life with toxic chemicals, cancers, deformities and a loss of reproductive capacity.

Inland waters such as the Black Sea could be dead in a decade as it becomes a "landlocked... dump and sewer."[21] Human, agricultural and industrial effluent, the product of 162 million people in eleven countries, pour into the Black Sea in the rivers that drain much of Eastern Europe. They carry tons of heavy metals, pesticides, fertilizers, manure, hydrocarbons, sewage and toxic industrial waste.

Loss of Bio-diversity

All known species are believed to be interconnected and interdependent in nature. Insects pollinate flowers and provide food for birds and other small creatures. A variety of herbivores eat a variety of plants. Birds cull the harmful insects which threaten the health of the trees, and all spread seeds about the earthen floor. Trees are essential to the hydrological cycles of climate and provide homes, protection and food for birds and animals. Predators control populations of small rodents. Every plant, insect, bird and mammal appears to have a defined role in maintaining a relative balance between climates, vegetation and life forms.

Destroy too many species and the eco-system collapses. Clearcut a forest, burn the vegetation and leave the land open to the elements, and the soil will be washed away, the climates changed and the species gone. Deserts do not support life; ergo few humans will survive the desert landbases we are creating for ourselves worldwide.

Many of our technological manipulations of the natural world have heightened rather than lessened the destruction of eco-systems. For instance, pesticides and herbicides quickly decimate the beneficial birds, insects and microbes on which healthy crops depend. On the other hand, most weeds and insect pests have mutated and reappeared with immunity to the chemical poisons. While boring and chewing insects flourish and grow stronger, many of the birds and helpful insects become extinct.

As larger applications of pesticides must accompany each planting, the increased use of toxins to kill pests and weeds contaminates the soil and kills the microscopic life forms necessary for the plants to grow and the soil is left sterile. Soils, then leached by irrigation and rain water, release these chemical poisons into ground water, which eventually flow into ponds, rivers and lakes, continuing the killing of birds, fish and so many other plant and animal species which depend on the water for their survival.

Chemically caused problems are symptomatic of the "Green Revolution" in Third World countries where growing food still entails their use. In Indonesian villages, for example, the government coerced peasant farmers into growing chemically produced commercial crops which could be sold on foreign markets. To win over the peasants, the government offered them free seeds, fertilizers, herbicides and pesticides. Soon after applying the chemical sprays and fertilizers, the peasants watched as both the wild birds which lived in and around their fields and the fish which swam in the irrigation ditches died off. Both had been major sources of protein in their diets.[22]

Having little knowledge of the danger to their health, many of the farmers had applied the chemicals without protective clothing or masks. The program rapidly sterilized their soils, degraded their health and impoverished their diets. Realizing their predicament, many farmers planted vegetables and fruits in areas hidden from the road where government inspectors could not see them. By defying government laws and employing ancient forms of organic farming, they regained the health of at least some of the people and some of the land.

However, this has not stopped the use of poisonous chemicals either by peasant farmers or the large commercial monoculture growers. The "Green Revolution" continues to wipe out hundreds of native species in many lands and poison humans as they use greater and greater quantities of fertilizers, herbicides and pesticides to keep the land free of invasive weeds and pests. The result is smaller and smaller crop output.[23]

Human interference with natural diversity has produced an unsolvable dilemma for future eco-systems and arable soils around the world. Millions of species are still unknown to scientists, most of them are microbes. As chemicals and technologies are used to control known pests, they destroy and sterilize the entire ecological foundations for all species which are essential to the creation of arable soils, to keeping water clean and to ensuring temperate climates. At some point in the near future, we could unwittingly destroy the entire fabric of the natural web of species with our toxic chemicals.

Technological developments which provide only for human needs have already caused the extinction of thousands of species. But even more devastating to eco-systems is the unmanageable explosion of exotic species humans have set free, some of which are capable of destroying so many other species. A wide variety of noxious and invasive weeds, diseases, philoviruses, bacteria and destructive pests humans are spreading world wide as we move so freely about the planet, carrying them with us.

Conservationists who believe in future "sustainable management" propose that humanity can "manage" these invasive species through regular culling, poisoning or spraying, and thereby, decimating their numbers to an "environmentally safe" level. As damaging as chemicals are, they would have us believe, we cannot wait for nature's powers alone to control harmful species lest they destroy human food supplies first.

This policy, if implemented universally, has a very dangerous side. It categorizes species as renewable resources and puts their right to exist in the hands of human "resource managers". But will such experts ever be capable of maintaining a balance among natural species, especially if much of that balance is not understood or it is sacrificed for domesticated crops and animals?

The problem has surfaced dramatically in recent attempts to preserve the elephant herds in Africa. The international market for ivory during the 1970s and 1980s led to the near extinction of the herds. International restrictions were ultimately placed on the sale of ivory in an effort to save the elephant. The colonial powers chose to protect the animals in parks, thus stopping the natives from hunting them or preventing the elephants from destroying native property. These actions complicated the situation for those farmers and tribesmen who culled the herds to protect both the land and the elephants.

The changes had removed the balancing forces between elephants and native hunters which had existed for thousands of years. The elephants multiplied beyond the carrying capacity of the land and at time of writing have become a threat to the habitat of all local species. To eat, they pull up trees and feed off the leaves, fruit and seed pods. In large herds they can destroy whole forests, damaging their rangelands and its eco-systems for many years. During drought periods or in times of diminished environments, whole herds may perish. Others will migrate onto cultivated lands or into human settlements, destroying gardens and homes, trampling people. Culling the herds has again come to be seen as a necessity.

But the dilemma is worsened by human need and greed. Finding a means to cull and conserve the herds while protecting the land from their ravages has put the elephants' survival entirely at human discretion. The near extinction of the elephants (and the rhinos) during the 1980s was prevented only by an international cry for banning the sale of ivory and the killing of elephants. But once again, with the herds overpopulating their territories, should the ban on ivory sales be lifted, or will poachers once again threaten the animals with extinction?

The present world shortage of ivory due to the ban has raised its value and brought many unscrupulous poachers and traders into the black market, selling both elephant and rhino tusks. Natives who once lightly culled the herds because the task was so dangerous with the poor weapons they had to bring down such a beast, can so easily kill them today with rifles and then transport the ivory in trucks.

To the African tribesman the elephants are no more than renewable resources. "They cannot afford to set aside land and grazing for a beautiful but useless animal to live on. If the wild game is to survive in Africa, it has to pay for its supper."[24]

Poverty, ignorance, greed, hunger, drought, collapsing environments are motive enough for native tribesmen to defy national laws, kill the elephants and sell the ivory illegally. Few can afford the Western luxury of viewing the elephants from the point of view of a tourist. The money they represent for the poacher will never secure a safe future for the animals as hunting and searching technologies improve and populations grow more desperate for jobs and income.

Diminishing Habitat

The future of most wild animals in every nation is now at the mercy of human hubris. Wilderness habitat and its carrying capacity are rapidly shrinking. Habitat is also suffering under increasingly severe conditions of drought and flooding. At the same time, human dependence on rangelands grows as demand for food increases. We are ever more reluctant to share pastures and farmland with wild species. Overgrazing and over farming destroy millions of acres of vegetation and arable soils yearly, spreading deserts on every continent.

As croplands and pastures disappear, many believe competition with wild species for remaining lands must be won for human needs. The hungry, desperate peasant of Brazil or Malaysia cannot understand the need to preserve the rainforest and its species when one's family is starving from a lack of work and food. "Survival of the fittest" and strongest starts to take precedence.

Overpopulation among predatory species caused by human interference in the natural balance ranges from the locust and rabbit plagues of Australia to the seals and wolves of North America. As they reproduce in large numbers, their presence means heavy losses of crops, grasses, fish stocks, domestic animals and wild species. An integral part of the human dilemma in this imbalance exists between the protectionists who would save all life forms and let natural forces do the culling, and the hunter, farmer or government conservationist who prefer culling herds, using pesticides and providing employment, while saving the bulk of the environment for domestic animals and human occupation. Morally and environmentally, we are struggling with the dilemma as to who is right?

Either way the eco-systems are failing. Humans are overusing the productive lands, turning them into deserts. Wildlife is collapsing as their environments shrink and they cannot sustain healthy populations. Infrequent population explosions of a species always ends in widespread environmental damage and eventually, the collapse of the species, taking with them many other life forms which depend on the same food supplies. Hungry and weakened, the involved chain of life falls victim to disease, human poisons and predators. Extinction follows for thousands of different life forms.

Culling wild herds, poisoning birds and the beneficial insects while giving priority to sheep, cattle, goats and crops is destroying the earth's bio-diversity. Attempts to eradicate germs, parasites and viruses, lethal to humans have only increased the power of these microbes to bring death to humans. Mutational strains resistant to pesticides, medications and antibiotics have evolved. Malaria, once sharply controlled with DDT in the environment and through quinine derivatives in the human, is again on the rise. The parasite and mosquito which spread the disease developed immunity to DDT products. Now the new strains of malaria which have emerged from the human war on their carriers are far more deadly than any previous varieties and are totally resistant to any known drugs at the present time.

During the period when DDT was in wide use, it poisoned many other species and reduced their reproductive capacity to the danger level. Birds were unable to make eggshells strong enough to protect the growing embryo. Species, unable to raise young, were dying out. The American bald eagle was among those species facing extinction from DDT.

Impact of Wilderness Parks and Reserves

Attempts to conserve declining species and preserve bio-diversity are underway. But conserving fish stocks, endangered wildlife and wilderness habitat will continue to be offset by the enormous demand placed on all wilderness areas to provide jobs or to entertain the burgeoning ranks of tourists.

Wilderness areas designated as "protected" constantly fall victim to tourism and home builders, seeking to build a home away from the stress of urban life. We are escaping our overcrowded cities only to find overcrowded parklands and disappearing wilderness.

The decline of eco-systems in North American parklands is a barometer of the pressures large, affluent populations place on preserved habitats. Tourists, campers, hikers and developers in wilderness areas cut large swaths of forest to build roads to transport huge numbers of people. Public facilities are erected in parks to house visitors and absorb their wastes. Pollution and vehicle noise damage eco-systems.

Wilderness habitats, especially those designated as parks, must endure the damage of millions of human feet as they tramp down the vegetation and frighten off what little wild life may still be alive in the area. Human presence sharply curtails wildlife reproduction and survival. Attempts to "manage" the parklands so as to protect the majority of species, birds and animals which live there is proving only relatively successful. A few species, able to live and reproduce under human auspices, such as elk, deer, buffalo and raccoons are thriving, but most birds and small creatures are disappearing.

Few birds or animals can live and reproduce where a forest is surrounded by buildings, roads, campsites, hotels and municipal developments. There are few areas left in North America that can be honestly considered as true wilderness habitats. Human curiosity and the desire to get back to nature are abetted by an array of destructive technologies which allows us to invade every inch of this planet. Even the inhospitable Antarctic is plagued by the invasive, destructive power of our inexorable presence of human species and their pollution.

Introduction of Exotic Species

Over the millennia human occupation of the planet's natural habitats has meant the extinction of thousands of wild plants and life forms. Hunters have decimated numerous species of birds and animals with the constantly improved accuracy and deadliness of their weapons and hunting skills. Spy glasses, radar, sonar, all-terrain vehicles, large fishing boats, huge mechanically controlled purse seines, all have added unprecedented advantage to the hunter in his search for prey. Farmers and developers have lain bare the forests and lands where most plant and life forms have evolved. Species have failed to compete with goats, sheep and cattle or to survive on deforested lands. With human help, food crops and invasive exotic species have overwhelmed indigenous vegetation.

Habitat falls daily to the clearcutting of forests, the cultivation of grasslands, diversion of rivers, the draining of wetlands and the development of urban areas on the best farm lands. Nature cannot compete with these mechanical forces; consequently, species and wilderness habitat are disappearing rapidly.

While our intrusion into wild areas has destroyed many species, it has facilitated the migration of exotic species from one geographical area to another, even from one continent to another. Wherever humans settled or encroached on once pristine islands or continents, they brought with them domestic animals: pigs, dogs, cats and rabbits, as well as wild life forms, mice, rats, insects and exotic plants. Most of these species, alien to their new environments, have thrived at the expense of indigenous species which could not compete in the struggle for food or for territory in which to raise and feed their young. Where many indigenous species disappeared to the exotic invaders, uncontrolled populations of these invading species now dominate the landscape and continue to destroy local vegetation, food chains and wild life.

The recent accidental arrival of the zebra mussel into the Canadian Great Lakes on the hull of a Russian ship highlights the devastating impact such exotic life forms can have on an entire eco-system. The zebra mussel established itself rapidly. In doing so it siphoned off most of the plankton in several of the Great Lakes, killing off the natural food chains and starving the fish stocks, turning the water crystal clear. Having no natural enemies, the mussels reproduced to the optimum. They spread out thickly over the shallow spawning grounds, preventing those fish which did survive starvation from laying their eggs. Colonizing in huge numbers, the mussels soon became an invasive pest for humans as they clogged intake pipes, cutting off municipal water supplies and endangering power plants which depend on large quantities of water for cooling.

Crystal clear lakes may be beautiful to the eye, but such clarity means the waters are devoid of nutrients and life. In the process of overwhelming the indigenous eco-system, the mussels have destroyed not only all other species, but they themselves now face starvation and mass die-offs. A rather profound lesson for humanity in this phenomenon of overcrowding a land base by one all consuming species.[25]

Many exotic species have been introduced accidentally, but many more have been imported purposefully, only to get rapidly and inexorably out of hand. The kudzu vine from Asia was introduced into the Southern United States to control erosion in the 1930s. It has since taken over vast areas and destroyed the natural vegetation. Cheatgrass is an invasive plant that dominates tens of millions of acres of grasslands. Hoary cress eats 2000 acres a day of the Western plains and Loosestrife threatens most North American wetlands, ditches and marshes where wildlife still flourishes. Bindweed, knapweed and thistle from Europe, water hyacinth from South America, broom from Scotland, a wide assortment of exotics from Hawaii, all are displacing native species, "some forcing out entire complexes of native species and simplifying plant communities to the point of impoverishment."[26]

The brief but catastrophic history of European settlement of Australia is perhaps the most dramatic and visible example of the damage humans have done to an entire continental environment by introducing exotic species into an indigenous population where the exotic has no enemies and the conditions are suitable to their expansion.

Australia is a continent of many climates, ranging from areas of dense rainforests to hot, empty deserts to temperate plains and coastal areas. Isolated from the rest of the planet's land masses, Australia has species found no where else on earth. With the arrival of Europeans, the rapid extinction of many of these species followed as settlers killed them for their furs and feathers or ploughed them under. Having no concept of the size of the continent, the new inhabitants saw the land as limitless and gave no thought to conservation or the fragility of the eco-systems.

At the time of discovery, only one-tenth of the continent was covered with forests. Today less than one-half of those forests are left. Five million acres of rain forest remain, less than one quarter of the original. Rare and valuable species of trees continue to be cut down at devastating rates. Of most concern, rain forests are proving to be a non-renewable, non-manageable resource.

The plains and marginal dry lands have been largely ruined by the hard hoofs of 135 million grazing sheep. As they destroy the fragile vegetation, the soil turns to sand and dust. Recovery is slowed by increasing drought conditions, resulting from global warming and El Nino. Kangaroos of many varieties, once prolific on these plains, now compete with the cattle and sheep for grass. While a kangaroo's feet are soft and do not damage the fragile soil, their numbers have multiplied wherever cattle and sheep have eaten down the tall grasses, exposing an abundance of short grasses on which the kangaroos feed. Consequently, together the domestic and wild animals overgraze the plains, leaving them open to the effects of drought, wind and erosion.

To gain a grazing advantage for domestic animals, farmers have the legal right to cull three million kangaroos a year. But human investment and profit raises the illegal slaughter of kangaroos to include many more. Over 17 species of small kangaroo have disappeared since the English arrived and 28 more are on the endangered list as they lose in the competition for food.

The Murray River in Eastern Australia was dammed to prevent flooding of its river plains, dooming the vegetation and animals which depended on it. This also dammed large areas which were then flooded the year round. Overflow problems were solved by installing irrigation systems which opened very dry flatlands to farming. The urban poor were encouraged to move into the area after the two world wars of the 20th Century. Both their lack of farming skills and the salinization which always results when flat, dry lands are irrigated turned their farms into a salty desert which could not be flushed out.

Drought, erosion, salinization, mice plagues and locusts then destroyed wheat crops. The mouse introduced by Europeans had no enemies, but an abundance of food. Their numbers exploded into the millions. Locust plagues grew so large that at times they could destroy 500 miles of crops in one night. Poisons and sprays had to be used to control these plagues, introducing dangerous toxins into the soil.

Many other exotic pests and plants were introduced, some to enhance human existence such as rabbits and foxes for hunting, and pigs, goats, donkeys and cats for domestic use. Both the rabbits and foxes, once in the wild, quickly got out of control with nothing to stop their reproduction. The rabbits ate up the vegetation and destroyed the food resources for many small animals, several of which became extinct. Eventually a virus spread among the rabbits and nearly wiped them out. But those rabbits which survived the virus now have immunity to it and their numbers will get out of control once again.

The foxes killed off many wild birds and small mammals, the feral goats and pigs destroyed the fragile vegetation and soils, and the donkeys, set free, multiplied and took over Western Australian grasslands. Domestic cats escaped into the wild and like the foxes, killed off millions of birds and mammals. Hundreds of wild species disappeared entirely under the pressure of so many exotic species. Attempts to control large populations of domestic animals which had gone wild have gradually reduced their impact on the land, but so much of the damage already done was permanent, especially to the natural vegetation, that many wild species have become extinct.

Implementing solutions has also had serious repercussions on the native species. For instance, in the 1930s a fence 1400 kilometres in length was erected in an effort to prevent the rabbits from destroying pastures and crops. They managed to get around the fence and economic ruin followed. But the fence remains to this day. In August of 1994, extreme drought conditions in Western Australia drove tens of thousands of emus in search of food and water. In their migrations they smashed up against the fence, killing hordes of them.[27]

Australia today suffers from widespread drought. Soils, turned to sand and driven by the wind, often envelope the cities in clouds of dust. The trees and the vegetation which once held the soil have been killed off, erosion is extreme and continuing drought has driven many farmers from the land. Over stocking, deforestation, exotic species, drought, erosion have ruined the grasslands. And yet some farmers continue to overstock and overgraze the land. Cycles of drought bring starvation and thirst to large numbers of domestic and feral animals each year, mainly because they are unable to survive on the sparse vegetation and drink at dried up water holes.

Those who have settled Australia all but destroyed the fragile eco-systems of the continent. They bulldozed the plains, overgrazed the grasslands, poisoned the rivers with mine runoff, flooded river plains and turned them into deserts of salt. They hunted birds and animals to extinction, introduced exotic species which rapidly got out of control, killed off hundreds of indigenous creatures and turned the soil into dust and sand. Modern attempts to rectify their mistakes have eased the catastrophic occupation, but the changes are coming too late for the majority of unique and rare species which no longer exist.

Hybrids and Genetic Engineering

World wide the last two centuries of technological farming replaced natural food crops and vegetation with laboratory hybrids. Bred to meet specific climatic conditions and produce abundantly, these plants do not have the immunity to diseases or the hardiness of wild varieties which have survived for hundreds of thousands of years. Improving or producing new hybrids is done by crossing wild or traditional varieties. However, heavy use of arable lands for food crops over the centuries has destroyed the habitat of thousands of wild varieties of edible and medicinal plants which once flourished in open fields, ditches and forests.

Destroying wild varieties and replacing them with laboratory hybrids may endanger future food supplies should the hybrids be destroyed by pests and climatic changes. Wild potatoes, once abundant in many varieties in the Andes of South America, are becoming extinct as governments, taking part in the Green Revolution, tend to subsidize commercial varieties because they produce more abundantly. Destruction of habitat and replacement of traditional varieties with hybrids is reducing the remaining genetic varieties of potatoes to only two or three kinds. If these become extinct, the future of the commercial potato is in jeopardy. Genetically engineered crops being designed will undoubtedly replace natural vegetation just as the hybrids have done. What we cannot foresee is whether or not they will live and reproduce themselves, build an immunity to withstand other extremes of climate and survive diseases for which they have not been programmed. Perhaps they will become exotic species with the power to destroy many existing beneficial plants and insects. Will they be able to withstand new evolving varieties of pests and diseases?

In ridding the land of its traditional vegetation and destroying the bulk of naturally evolved species, what will we use in the future should our genetic experiments fail? And can we be certain that our chemical pesticides, fertilizers and herbicides will not produce pests and microbes immune and even more lethal to the newly engineered plants? Will our chemicals create mutations capable of destroying known food crops? Can we afford to destroy the myriad of microbes and bacteria which keep the earth clean and the soil productive?

Unfortunately, little care is given to the preservation of indigenous plant and life forms for future use should they be needed to reintroduce traditional food crops. A few world gene banks are attempting to save as many seeds of the traditional varieties as they can obtain. But the distribution to farmers of the seeds in gene banks is often at the mercy of unstable governments or political conflicts which may prevent a poor nation gaining access to the very seeds they provided the gene banks. In many Third World countries the farmers who try to save their own seeds, must hide them from governments who are caught up in the rules of the Green Revolution and its dependency on commercial farming technologies.

Detrimental to both commercial and traditional varieties, the use of fertilizers, pesticides and herbicides not only sterilizes the soils but destroys the immunity of both the planted crops and the wild varieties, exacerbating the loss of all forms of food plants.

Hubris and Species' Extinction

Human survival like that of any species has had its share of cruelty and suffering and is neither easy nor certain. But Homo sapiens survived with the unprecedented advantages of intelligence and technology. We have to ask ourselves whether our excessive predatory tendencies have been programmed into the human character over thousands of years of civilization, or are they the instinctive manifestations of the innate "killer ape" within us? What motivates our continuing desire to hunt and kill other species to extinction when our food needs can still be met by our farmers? Why do we refuse to acknowledge that the damage our domination of wild species threatens our own existence? Despite all warnings why do we continue our relentless consumption and destruction of species and natural habitat? Have we been programmed by nature or by our escape from the natural world into the civilized world to be the "master species" of extinction?

Obviously, both our natural instincts and our technologically determined existence have programmed us for destroying species.

The more advanced our technologies have become, the more we are separated from our natural roots. The more distant human society gets from its natural dependency, the greater the scope of the destruction it imposes on nature. The more intelligent and scientifically innovative our survival techniques, the more removed we are from acknowledging nature and its role in our existence. Bound up within the concrete walls of our cities, mechanically supplied with our everyday needs, we experience little remorse for our eradication of the natural world when human expectations are to be met. Most North American children when asked where the meat and vegetables they eat come from will answer from the supermarket. Can these be the future stewards of eco-systems they do not even know exist?

Our predatory nature has yet to be controlled even legally as most nations still license their hunters and fishermen. Few punish offenders or have the resources to enforce laws against overfishing and hunting in the wild. Although a growing number of people call themselves "caring environmentalists" in their fight to save endangered species, the number who believe that human needs come first still remain proportionately larger and will grow in number and need as world populations rise towards 10 billions.

There is no more formidable example of our self-destructive bent, nor of the role technology is playing in that self-destruction than our attitudes towards and exploitation of the natural world and other species. The ease with which humans kill other species and our extreme disregard for other life forms characterizes our hubris and prescribes our nemesis: the massive amount of suffering and death we inflict on all other life forms is reducing our viability and hastening our own demise.

It has only occurred to us as a collective whole in the last thirty years that we are endangering ourselves by destroying other life systems. Yet our choice remains: we will meet human needs first. Jobs for loggers and lumber for homes have priority over old growth forests; fishermen continue to drag the ocean bottom until all edible marine life disappears and the blame can be passed on to some higher authority. And tigers and bears will soon be a memory as superstition and hubris grinds their bones and organs to increase human sexual potency in a world already suffering from the products of too much sexual activity.

To value and preserve remaining wild species now demands a universal effort and a morality which recognizes the sanctity of all life forms. However, social conscience and social mores towards eco-systems will differ from nation to nation. The degree to which a nation destroys its ecological systems is defined by its social, religious and medical traditions, its employment patterns and its geography. The extent to which they destroy the viability of the environment will vary with their dependency on eco-systems to sustain growing populations.

Primitive people whose sole means of survival is hunting and fishing are likely to be more conservative in their consumption and destruction of eco-systems. On the other hand, people who depend on the crops they grow do not hesitate to consume the forests and the wildlife if it advances their capacity to farm. Consummate poverty and ignorance of ecological systems also ensures the extinction of marketable species.

The reality is we seem unable to produce a universal standard of morality among peoples towards other species. First, we remain the cruellest, most invasive predators on earth. This insensitivity to other species cannot be more flagrant than that shown by poachers who hunt and kill thousands of North American bears and Indian tigers just for their organs or their bones to be shipped to China or Taiwan, processed as aphrodisiacs and medications, then sold to people who still put their faith in old medical traditions. The fact that a chemical analysis of these animal parts could be easily done to show they have little effect as aphrodisiacs, or that more ecologically sensitive medications can be produced synthetically has little if any power to change the faith the Chinese have in traditional folklore.

Even stringent preservation laws, international sanctions and heavy penalties do not prevent the Chinese around the world from taking part in this illicit trade in animal parts. Viet Nam and Cambodia are a case in point. Trade in tiger bones have reduced the tigers to a very endangered species. Yet universal moral codes, validated by internationally enforced laws, are proving ineffective in changing these ingrained traditional practices. Unfortunately, billions of dollars can be earned yearly through the sale of wild species on the black market. Consequently, wealth earned in the trade of exotic animals or their parts far outweighs any sense of morality towards conservation of species. The illegal trade in species is surpassed only by the illicit trade in drugs.[28]

A deep sense of awe and concern for the natural world exists among few members of any social group, and even fewer social groups exist who are strongly drawn to the natural world. An inherent sense of superiority and predation overshadows our empathy for other species. The occupation of Tibet by China in this century is one of the most outstanding examples of this conflict in our social makeup. Tibet was once a wonderland of many species, comparable with the African plains. The Tibetans deified nature, protecting their habitat and wild species. That is, until the Chinese invaded in 1953 and killed off thousands of unique and rare animals for target practice or for meat, cut down the ancient forests and shipped millions of logs back to China, and then destroyed the wilderness pastures with large herds of yaks. That former wonderland of many rare species is today a desert of barren mountain slopes and an impoverished people.

The unique Tibetan religion which taught that all life forms are sacred and to be protected could not withstand the powerful Chinese invasion force whose cultural values taught that all life forms are created for human consumption. Unfortunately, the majority of people in most nations continue to view wild life as inferior to human life, put there to be killed and eaten or driven from lands we want for our own use.

Killing out of season or killing rare species, as well as the capturing and transferring of rare species for sale to private individuals or to zoos is commonplace. But it is surely demonstrative of our hubris and thoughtless pursuit of other species to their extinction.

The thoughtless agony we impose on other life forms extends to killing for fun or because they are easy targets as witnessed in Northern Canada where Eskimos kill the wild geese and swans during their summer nesting season on Arctic lands because their are so many of the birds.

Such callousness might be forgiven if the Eskimos shot only the number of birds they require to feed themselves, but to shoot them for target practice is hubris of the worst kind. Their actions are reminiscent of Coleridge's Ancient Mariner who shot the albatross. His senseless killing of the bird which "protected" the ship brought about the horrifying death of his shipmates and the agony of his own eternal punishment, forcing him to roam a hostile world, warning of the dangers in destroying nature. The lesson is still applicable to those who kill wild creatures for enjoyment or spite, for they may enjoy killing other species, but they unwittingly threaten human survival.

Sadly, little international will or authority exists among nations to prevent their citizens from destroying eco-systems and the wilderness they inhabit. Evolutionary and historical precedence has ingrained the ideas in our social psyche that humankind has the right to hunt, fish or clear land, no matter the costs to other species, an attitude which remains paramount over any desires to conserve other species.

To offset the foolhardiness of this behaviour, we try to convince ourselves that we can continue over-exploiting the eco-systems of the earth if we practice "sustainable development" and "resource management". In other words, the environment is to be thought of as one huge manmade and managed garden of resources being prepared for our picking. The record to date of such grandiose undertakings has been catastrophic. Most agricultural mega-projects and "Green Revolutions", wherever they have been implemented, have damaged both the land and the eco-systems as the story of Australia illustrates.

This totally cavalier mentality towards the natural environment is finally lessening as we attempt in small scattered conservation programs to live with nature rather than without it. Sadly, too many of these projects are coming too late. So much of the continental lands and eco-systems have been permanently destroyed. But can we save what remains of the earth's eco-systems? There is little being done to curb our industrial expansion, our invasion of wilderness habitat, our tourism or our poisoning of the biosphere.

Desperate for foreign currency, developing economies which depend on selling their natural resources automatically legalize their environmental exploitation as a moral right. Highly industrialized, heavily populated nations continue to sacrifice both their environments and eco-systems to advance employment, profit and living standards. Finally, the more heavily populated a nation, rich or poor, the more destructive it is of its lands, forests, water reserves, wilderness habitat and species.

Western European nations and North America have become equal destroyers of their eco-systems and marine life with those of Japan, Taiwan and South Korea. More importantly, these industrial nations are now destroying eco-systems of all developing nations with their excessive demands for exotic species and forest products.

How unfortunate that we did not develop a universal conscience and a history of environmental conservation to go along with human intelligence which might have protected other species from our predatory ways. Choosing to favour wild life and old growth forests does not make sense to many, especially those whose livelihood depends on exploiting it. Can a spotted owl be worth saving eleven million acres of prime timber for and in the process forfeit 28,000 logging jobs over the next ten years in the western states of Washington, Oregon and Northern California? Can saving the rare red-spotted squirrel from extinction have a greater priority than being able to place a telescope in their territory which will increase our knowledge of the universe? Are we to forego such knowledge for a squirrel whose territory is one of the few remaining places on the North American continent which are not smogbound with industrial emissions? What value can there be in protecting the few rare species which no one ever sees? The list of contestable trade-offs is long and growing as environmentalists and industry clash over the use of the remaining pockets of untouched wilderness.

Environmentalists, hoping to convince the general public that the loss of one endangered species is indicative of the permanent loss of an entire eco-system, face an inexorable reality of human need and greed, human realities which will continue to outweigh even the direst predictions of scientists who have learned that without the balanced contribution of a wide assortment of species, ecological systems collapse. Dr. Rick Page, a scientist with the B.C. provincial forest service described the end result of a shrinking ecological system: "The more simple the ecological system becomes through extinction, the more open to disaster it is."[29]

CHAPTER SEVENTEEN

Sustainable Management of Resources

The survival technologies we are presently using cannot continue for long before the environment collapses and all our future efforts to exist will be useless. The present order of human activities which puts human needs before the environment simply is not working. Serious attempts to reduce our expansion and give priority to preserving the remaining environment worldwide have yet to be made. What the Easter Islanders did to their island, we are now doing to the whole planet. It is of momentous concern that we identify where we are on a parallel scale of decline with that of the Easter Islanders so as to gain some real insight into just how close we are to complete collapse. In this way we may chose to change course immediately and forestall our extinction.

Essentially, in weighing conservation of the environment against human consumption, we should begin a universal program of sustainable management with a return to growing all our foods organically. But as a third of an organically grown crop must be reinvested as compost, organic farming fails as a solution because it reduces output sharply, increasing food shortages. Neither could such natural methods cope with the worldwide climate changes, ultra-violet B damage, sterile soils, water shortages, extremes of temperature, drought, pest destruction, excessive use of fertilizers and environmental pollution that our technologies are causing.

In giving priority to growing food in any sustainable management program, the most popular choice has been to put our energies towards developing genetically engineered foods. Crops which can tolerate drought, salty topsoils and waterlogged fields are already in the advanced research stages. New corn varieties, for instance, are able to grow under drought conditions which would formerly kill the corn seedlings. They are also pest resistant. Recent cross pollinating techniques have made it possible to "increase yields by 40 percent in often difficult Third World growing conditions. If widely planted, the new corns could feed 50 million people more per year than current varieties".[1] It would prove a valuable staple in the dry regions of China and Africa. 50 million? That is only one half the number of people added to the planet in just one year.

But again growing genetically engineered food crops has its negative side. Poor nations with many peasant farmers cannot afford either the genetically altered seed, the fertilizers or the sterility of their lands that follows. Also, as with the Green Revolution, this revolution in highly altered vegetation forms is dependent on expensive chemical fertilizers which sterilize the soil. How long can the environment withstand the impact of more chemicals before the crops fail?

Environmental problems will dictate that human survival in the 21st Century will depend on a near elimination of chemical technologies to grow food and the return to more benign natural farming methods which will not contaminate the air, soil and water, but replace the nutrients and hold the water in the soil.

Next, sustainable management programs should require an end to commercial monoculture and agri-businesses. Wide scale farming by machine, as efficient as it has been in increasing crop production over the short term, needs to give way to labour intensive farming. The shift away from mechanized farming would allow for the return to the soil of the hundreds of millions of displaced peasant farmers round the world. Old traditional methods of growing a wide variety of foods and rotating crops would then be re-instated. But the problems will not end here as the demand for food grows with population. Even the most primitive farming methods soon deplete the soil if the agricultural output is intensive and the land not given time to regenerate or be supplied with sufficient organic materials. Nor will crops grow without sufficient amounts of clean, fresh water. If history is any measure of what destruction humans can do to the land, use of even the simplest of tools has brought an end to many civilizations.

Farming marginal and dry lands should be curbed, not expanded as part of a sustainable management program. Only then can surface and underground water reserves be conserved and desertification slowed.

Augmenting food production by increasing animal protein is on the rise, but under a sustainable management program for the world it should not be tolerated. As industrialization improves living standards in developing countries, the demand for cattle and pigs rises. In China meat consumption from 1991 to 1994 increased 10 percent annually.[2] Industrialized Asia will use more meat and fish as their incomes grow with a rise in living standards. More meat in a population's diet means more cows and pigs eating corn crops which could feed people. It also entails producing billions of tons of methane gas and manure, -an unmanageable greenhouse gas and a major water contaminant.

Food shortages are not yet a universal problem, although over 1.2 billion people live on the verge of starvation, primarily because they do not have land on which to grow their own crops and animals; nor do they have the purchasing power to buy food. As populations burgeon and world food shortages increase, demand for food will raise prices and leave more and more people without access to food commodities.

The same problems of managing food scarcities arising out of overused technologies and excessive demand are applicable to the world's diminishing fish stocks. A global moratorium on ocean fishing is critical, but nations, unless they are willing to enter into armed confrontation with poachers, are presently helpless to stop the ships of other nations from depleting their offshore fisheries. In March of 1995 The Canadian government sent coast guard patrols into the Atlantic to prevent Spanish vessels from overfishing turbot on the tail and the nose of the Newfoundland continental shelf. European objections to this interference with its fishermen in waters beyond the 200 mile limit led to a Spanish naval vessel rushing to confront Canadian patrol boats and protect its fishing fleet from being seized. The European Union threatened to retaliate by freezing trade agreements with Canada. The Canadian stand was a moral one aimed at protecting the stocks from extinction, while the Europeans argued their rights to unlimited quotas beyond the 200 mile line. Conservation or consumption? Survival or extinction?

Sustainable management of marine life would require a morality at sea which has yet to exist among fishermen or their governments. Most governments fail to enforce total, long term bans on either their own fishermen or on foreign nations until the fish stocks have disappeared. Few governments have openly sent patrol vessels aimed at capturing or sinking poachers. Everyone involved in the fishing or processing of fish attempts to avoid responsibility and place blame on governments, saying it is they who must impose fishing bans and patrol the oceans. Little can be said for voluntary restraint among fishermen!

The general consensus is that if all fishermen do not stop fishing at the same time, why should any given individual fisherman stop voluntarily, unless his government is willing to compensate him for his boats, equipment and unemployment. Such are the weaknesses and complexities governments face in defending the environment when jobs and profits are at stake, clearly delineating the major roadblocks to sustainable management of fisheries.

Consequently world marine food resources are close to depletion. Many stocks are already commercially extinct. Realistically, fish stocks are not resources which can be sustainably managed, nor are they capable of keeping up with the demand. It is now a matter of survival for millions of fishermen. Exploding human populations will fish the seas to extinction no matter how many international agreements are signed to conserve the fish stocks. Fish wars are with us now, so is hunger.

Also at the top of the sustainable management list is the quest to manage the forests. Administering nature's resources by first destroying them and then believing they can be replaced and regenerated through human design is folly of the worst kind. Forests take hundreds of years to produce the natural diversity that grows timber useful for other than junk lumber and pulp. Monoculture forests in Europe planted over 150 years ago have produced a weak, porous product of inferior quality. Second growth forests are generally much inferior to old growth forests for logging, which explains why logging companies always go after old growth forests. The crucial factor in sustaining commercially consumed natural resources is that manmade forests and wild fish stocks take time to regenerate into useful products. Many of them never do and become extinct.

But loggers want employment now so they can feed their families and pay their living expenses. Few willingly relinquish their right to harvest the environmental resources. They argue vehemently against quotas, bans and protectionist policies. If governments interfere in favor of the resources in both developed and Third World countries, these workers will log illegally.

Food chains and ecological systems will survive only if left in tact. Thinking we can use up the natural species and then replace them successfully with tree farms, fish farms, zoos and seed banks is a dangerous form of hubris. Our interference with species is most dramatically seen in the introduction of exotic species into areas where they have no enemies in the misguided illusion these species can be utilized for human benefit. Generally they have contributed to the destruction of entire eco-systems.

It is foolhardy to believe the human species can "manage nature" en toto, primarily because nothing in past social and cultural behaviours suggest we have ever lived peacefully in a collapsing environment. Historical precedence shows that dying civilizations turned to war as a last resort to survive in overcrowded, non-viable environments. In fact, if we depend on sustainable management programs to extricate us from the dilemmas of our survival, we may hasten our decline in that such faith in science builds overconfidence in our ability to master the earth for our own use. Any conservation programs will have to include draconian reductions in most of our economic activities as well as in the living standards of the affluent nations, if they are to be truly effective.

Attempts to sustain future populations, let alone improve their living standards, will demand great efficiency and protection of fresh water reserves. This means preventing all forms of contamination of rivers, lakes, oceans and underground reserves and imposing heavy penalties on polluters. The flagrant use of water from aquifers at three times its replacement rate must stop, along with bringing an end to growing crops on deserts, especially rice and cotton crops which are heavy water users. Crops which are superfluous to human need should not be grown. We must stop the growing of corn or sugar plants for the production of gasohol or for the production of pet foods. Both crops rapidly deplete the soil and occupy precious food growing lands imminently critical to human survival.

World wide river diversions, dams, reservoirs and vast irrigation projects must cease. The ecological damage as well the displacement of people throughout the 20th Century to accommodate these modern technologies has resulted in vast areas of devastation and millions of displaced people. Farm lands should be cropped in accordance with seasonal rains and drylands left alone. Above all, cities must not be allowed to develop on deserts where water is scarce and must be pumped up from deep within the earth or transported thousands of miles. These steps would ease the pressure human needs place on water reserves that are now channelled to desert farmers and urban areas at great expense to the rest of the environment.

Urban growth, engineered rivers and canals, deforested lands, farming methods which prevent absorption of runoff, vast road systems and massive concrete structures are all technological aids for human occupation but each seriously reduces the ability of the land to absorb rain and store it. They cause unnatural amounts of soil loss and water runoff which should be replenishing underground reserves. Destructive technologies would have to be outlawed if the fresh water supplies and the soils of the earth are to be protected and replenished.

Universal participation in enforcing an end to the disposal of sewage, toxic chemicals, heavy metals, oil, poisoned runoff, detergents, cleaning fluids and medicines into both fresh water systems and the oceans is crucial to sustainable management of the planet's water reserves. As the amounts of pollutants grow daily, fresh water is in such short supply that contaminating the remaining reserves can no longer be tolerated. All industries and manufacturers who produce toxic wastes and emissions would have to afford the costs of cleaning up their wastes and recycling them in ways which cannot damage the environment. Many use large amounts of power and other chemicals. If industries cannot meet these restrictions, they should not be allowed to manufacture or sell their products.

Humanity's continued existence now depends on extreme reversals in the manner in which we occupy this planet. To survive we will have to redirect employment, reduce living standards and minimize destructive technologies. An impossible paradox as it entails finding employment for all who need it while bringing an end to traditional manufacturing which underlies our whole way of urban living. It would mean a reduction if not an end to the manufacturing of chemicals, glass, clay, oil and gas, paper, primary metals, wood products and transportation which use any form of energy. Together, these, for example, use 80 to

85 percent of the energy consumed by industry in the United States and release an equivalent share of toxic pollutants, while offering the lowest employment rate.[3]

Unfortunately, most solutions aimed at regenerating the natural environment seem to be predicated on continued resource extraction and depletion. Recycling, for example, requires energy and other materials to reprocess the used commodities. In most cases the recycled product is more expensive than the original. Some items, such as aluminum cans, recycle easily and at a lesser cost than manufacturing new cans, but most items, such as glass, reflect the heightened consumption of energy in their purchase price of collecting and transporting the waste materials to recycling depots, manufacturing them into new products and then redistributing them. Conservation of resources may be gained by recycling used commodities, but the consumption of energy and distribution generally offset the gains. Unless recycling brings a greater profit, manufacturers will continue to use raw materials unless forced by government and scarcity of materials to recycle.

Human consumption of everything on this planet must be vastly reduced and restricted: the burning of gas, oil, and coal, all fossil fuels, an end brought to cutting down forests and destroying arable soils, the removal of natural and wilderness vegetation and a total ban on imported exotic species. No one would be allowed to catch or kill marine life, animals, birds or any of the remaining ecological species still in existence. Moreover, all marginal lands and wetlands must be off limits to humans.

People must be kept from invading wilderness areas. Roads, parks, buildings, tourism in wilderness habitat would be universally discouraged. The false myth that tourism saves species and ecological systems from industrial and urban growth is the product of eco-tourist promoters and wishful-thinking environmentalists. What industry fails to do to the environment, human feet, garbage and desecration of the virgin land accomplishes.

A universal reduction in all forms of travelling is needed, ranging from going to work by car to transporting vast quantities of unnecessary luxury goods and services world wide. Long distance travel vacations are costly in their use of resources ranging from fossil fuels to fresh water to arable land. The number one villain in destroying world climates and environments are cars, trucks and all vehicles which burn fossil fuels. They should be replaced with transportation systems which carry many more people per unit of energy burned and use much less land space. The amount of farm land which could be saved from cement and asphalt roads would be phenomenal.

The overproduction of goods and services is equivalent to the production of "useless things" in that neither contribute to basic survival. Curbing the manufacturing of unnecessary goods would reduce the dissemination of the most polluting products such as paper, plastics, glass, metals, wood, chemicals and chemical derivatives which now contribute vast quantities of garbage and sewage to all landfills. Much proof exists that the use of chemical fertilizers, herbicides and pesticides should be stopped as nature cannot tolerate their presence.

Consumption of all resources would be vastly reduced if homes and workplaces in the industrial world were smaller and filled with fewer possessions, reducing living standards and thereby decreasing consumption. Realistically, however, no nation can will its people to become poorer or disadvantaged so that ecological systems will survive. Even worse, the entire elan behind industrialization is for greater consumption and more widespread access to the "good things" in life.

Maintaining 10 billion people over the next century may surpass human ingenuity to devise technologies of survival which will not poison the human body nor destroy the environment. Meeting the needs of so many will push all societies to the extremes of their physical and mental endurance. Is the magnitude of change needed to save the planet possible when over 10 billion will have to be accommodated? We are already in difficulty trying to provide for 6 billion. The dilemma arises as to which master will we serve? The environment or the human masses. Either way we invite extinction.

PART FIVE

Extinction Or Survival
In The 21st Century?

CHAPTER EIGHTEEN

Extinction Or Survival
In The 21st Century?

The year is 2050 A.D. Earth's human population is approaching its predicted 10 billion. Each of the major cities of the world is inhabited by 20 to 50 million people. Urban congestion, failed and overwhelmed infra-structures, widespread deprivation, environmental pollution, epidemics, industrial diseases, starvation, violent crime and civil wars are the main causes of death.

Much of the ozone layer is depleted and the greenhouse effect is causing extremes of weather patterns world wide. The average temperature of the planet's atmosphere has risen several degrees Celsius. Droughts, floods, tornadoes, heat-waves, hurricanes and disastrous ranges of high and low temperatures are common in former temperate zones. Most arable lands, especially fragile drylands, where once the bulk of the world's grains were grown, are now largely abandoned deserts of salt and dry sand.

Fuel reserves are all but used up. Energy production depends on nuclear power and the sun. Fresh water supplies are so low that more than half the world lives without enough to drink or cook, let alone keep their bodies and homes clean. Children in the millions have not had the luxury of washing their bodies. Crops, animals and humans are dying from chronic drought, fire and flood.

The signs of abject poverty are everywhere. No nation can avoid it. Millions scrounge the garbage dumps and the land for food and water. Many occupy ancient tombs and graveyards because living space and housing are in short supply.

Human illnesses, deformities and mental deterioration are common as malnutrition and industrial contamination reduce resistance to disease. A lack of atmospheric oxygen and an abundance of polluted air restricts the intake of oxygen needed for metabolism and brain cell utilization. Atmospheric oxygen supplies are inhibited by the burning of carbon fuels and the lack of tropical and temperate forests which had been cut down for use as fuel, lumber and paper pulp or cleared for farmland.

Tens of millions die annually from viral and bacterial diseases, most of which are immune to human drugs. Poverty and malnutrition prevent the successful implementation of universal programs to control communicable diseases such as cholera, tuberculosis, dengue fever as well as many other life threatening bacterial illnesses. Total occupation of and intrusion into the earth's wilderness lands have set free dozens of viruses lethal to the human body that take a constant toll in human lives.

Traditional family, community and national structures have broken down. Tribal and ethnic battles are in progress on every continent as civil wars are fought for control of shrinking, overcrowded land bases.

Daily existence is dangerous, always at the mercy of thugs and marauding armies and gangs. Crime provides an overly large proportion of populations with a living, and drugs and alcohol are widely sold and consumed to stem the constant fear and horror that haunt decaying, war-torn societies.

Industrial lands which thrived during the 20th Century are now destitute in mid-21st Century. They are swamped with migrating hordes of economic and environmental refugees, fleeing famine and civil wars. Chaos and anarchy dominate on most continents as democratic authorities lose their capacity to control the hordes. International gangsterism and terrorism have replaced governments and are the main avenue to wealth and power as international crime syndicates and warlords assume political or tribal control in most nations.

People are afraid to travel. The fear of contracting a fatal viral or bacterial disease and the fear of theft, violence, racial hatred and persecution have turned much of the world's population inward to live behind protective walls, guarded with weapons and armies of aggressive young men. The few rich are building their own armies to protect themselves from vandals and thieves. Few dare leave their walled communities for fear of being attacked and killed.

The natural wildlife of the earth has been reduced by hundreds of thousands of its species. Pests, viruses, and plagues are an everyday constant of living. The natural vegetation of every environment is mostly destroyed, much of it lost to overcropping, overgrazing, invasive weeds and desertification, putting it beyond the powers of regeneration or sustainable management programs. Genetically engineered ecologies are plagued by disease and a self-destructive ecological imbalance.

Religious leaders have formed large armies of soldiers, trained as death squads and recruited for vengeance and plunder. Ethnic cleansing is common and it is hinted that cannibalism is on the rise.

A gruesome picture of our future 55 years from now! Or is that future already with us? It certainly describes West Africa today as Robert Kaplan saw it when he toured the area in 1993.[1] It is also a modern replay of the final stages of life among the Easter Islanders four hundred years ago.

To assess humanity's chances of having a viable future existence in the technologically altered environment we are preparing for ourselves is an audacious feat. Predicting the future is always complicated by the unexpected whether it be a scientific invention which improved living standards as did the discovery of electricity; or whether it is the unmanageable industrial production of greenhouse gases and ozone which threaten all life forms. Achieving credibility for one's predictions is even more difficult than assessing what has occurred. Too many unknowns exist in the future.

However, by evaluating the human behaviour which created the present conditions in West Africa or the many vanished civilizations of the past, it is a small step to predicting how we will behave in the future. Recognizing that our evolutionary development gave us the physical and intellectual powers to overcome the limitations of survival within nature also entails admitting these are destructive powers whose effects are ongoing and irreversible. The magnitude of the demands of our populations in the 21st Century which will have doubled five times in just 100 years and the unbridled consumption of resources by our industrial revolutions supports the hypothesis that our populations are both unable and generally unwilling to reverse the present course of industrial expansion and environmental destruction. In this way we have taken our future survival and extinction into our own hands.

Having examined the technological evolution of Homo sapiens and the massive changes so much development has inflicted on the four life giving components of the environment, climate, vegetation, soils, and life forms, it is not difficult to move to the next conclusion, that the physical forces of extinction are piling up against the human species: overpopulation, overconsumption of fresh water resources, diminishing food supplies, deteriorating health and reduced reproductive capacity caused by the rising incidence of industrial poisoning, increasing aggressive violence and self-inflicted warfare and an escalating in the rate of destruction of supportable habitat. The predicted doubling of the human population over the next fifty years and the amount of resource consumption and pollution they will unleash upon the planet makes it very evident that we are programming early extinction into our daily lives by the very activities which embellish our survival.

With each passing year problems of food production and distribution affect the health and stability of more nations; industrial expansion relentlessly forces one nation after another to use up its "environmental capital" to manufacture "industrial capital". Ethnic and racial wars explode wherever poverty, anarchy and overcrowded living conditions reduce humans to a life of deprivation. Well over a hundred million now roam the earth in search of a better life and over one billion live on the verge of famine daily.

No rational person would dispute the fact that our survival beyond the next 50 years will depend on the quality and sustainability of the earth's physical environment. To continue destroying it is to go beyond its ability to regenerate its natural resources and to destroy the critical interdependence of climate, vegetation and life forms.

No human activity is more involved in maintaining this balance than our individual and national economic policies of environmental exploitation. The dilemma is horrendous: Do we save what little remains of the natural eco-systems of this planet and reduce our consumption and contamination of the biosphere; or do we continue to leave it to technologies and faith?

Over thirty years ago Rachel Carson warned us of the inordinate stress our industrial development was putting on the natural environment. She was one of the first to break through the psychological barriers of ignorance and disbelief that dominated our attitudes towards unlimited exploitation of the environment. She did so by relating story after story of the disappearing wildlife and marine species.

But the Western industrial world was intoxicated with the array of scientific inventions and technologies that promised a visionary world where everyone would soon live a life free of poverty and social stress. However, the dreams of luxury, more leisure time and easy access to exotic places of the 1960s failed to materialize; instead, increased production became the major cause of environmental degradation in the 1970s, 1980s and 1990s.

About the same time Miss Carson made us aware of the disappearing ecological world, environmentalists and demographers warned us of the impending threat of exploding populations, as birth rates began to double and redouble within decades, not centuries.

Ever since we have been constantly forewarned by scientists that we are polluting the air, land and oceans at an alarming rate, effecting negative changes in our climates and eradicating ecological systems on which our own lives depend. Yet in over thirty years of awareness, we have done relatively little to protect the natural environment while making huge advances in industrial and agricultural expansion, leaving the planet gasping under the pollution and environmental destruction. Neither have we made a concerted effort to decrease exploding birth rates.

Although our economic and social problems are multiplying worldwide, the human attention span remains very short. Only momentarily are we absorbed by crises and catastrophes around us. We rise to an occasion with great emotion and conviction, then quickly descend to the status quo. As a whole, our societies seem unable to sustain the long term effort and concentration needed to solve the problems of overpopulation, unemployment and a deteriorating environment.

A recent impact of this short term interest is the toll it has taken on environmental organizations. They can no longer solicit enough donations to keep their organizations running. Even some of the most effective groups have had to lay off many of their dedicated workers or close down completely. Public interest has waned and grown increasingly cynical. Overwhelmed by the number of charitable organizations asking for money for human causes, support has turned away from the environment to meet immediate human needs first.

Nations rallied world wide to celebrate Earth Day in 1990 and again for the Rio Summit in June of 1992. The run up to both was a six month period of getting involved through clean up projects, recycling wastes and watching television programs which showed us pictures of the suffering planet. These were followed by emotionally oriented images taken in several countries of the various isolated projects being tested to improve on our methods of exploitation while decreasing the accompanying contamination of development.

To date universal efforts have been few and far between. On paper they are the policies of most nations, but in practice, little has been done to meet agreed upon goals. The amount of carbon dioxide emitted into the air increases annually, despite the agreements to reduce them or maintain them at the 1990 level. But millions of cars are added annually to those already on the roads. Industrial nations are tripping over themselves, hoping to provide one billion Chinese in the near future with cars as the nation industrializes. Ecological systems continue to become extinct as deforestation runs apace in both the Third World and the Western nations. National governments fail to extend regulations, limitations or penalties onto every individual who drives a car, wastes energy and fresh water, travels thousands of unnecessary miles for entertainment and refuses to recycle the bulk of his garbage. Industry expands and populations explode.

The general public is becoming immune to dire warnings of impending environmental and social disaster. Instant communications through television and other media bombard us daily with stories of human crimes, violence, wars, starvation and environmental sabotage. We are no longer shocked by death and destruction. To gain public attention and high credit ratings, news media must present events that are shocking and filled with violent behaviour and death. Movies are seldom successful unless they portray extremes of human depravation and violence. Television continues to demolish human values, dignity and conscience, and replace them with extremes of human cruelty, greed and primitive aggression.

In the Third World and the inner cities of most Western nations change is derailed by poverty, illiteracy, hunger, disease, unemployment and a day to day struggle to stay alive, all conditions which obstruct any universal attempts to collectively enforce the preservation and protection of the planet.

Overpopulation now threatens every nation with environmental and social collapse. The daily survival needs of 6 billion people and the additional 90 million a year are anathema to repairing and conserving what is left of the planet. Aggravated by natural and social forces of reproduction, human populations are further abetted by the only forces which could reduce their fertility rates: governments reluctant to get involved in coercive measures to curb populations, while religious leaders uphold archaic doctrines opposing universal contraception, sterilization and abortion.

If science holds that reproduction of every species is always at a maximum and reduced only by external forces, then our exponential occupation of the earth is a given fact. Without contraceptive measures and sexual education of all women or coercion and imposed penalties for having too many children, the only other controls left to reduce human numbers are the cruel realities of infanticide, starvation, disease, harsh climates and wars.

Permanent changes in the natural balances of the temperate environments in which we evolved as a species are beginning to subject us to extremes of climatic and geological conditions which our physical bodies cannot tolerate: excesses of heat and cold, more violent tornadoes and hurricanes, longer periods of drought and freezing and widespread flooding which devastates major croplands.

Environmental degradation is no longer limited to occupied lands. It is now global and escalating in its destructive powers of the planet's biosphere. Projecting temperature changes over the next 50 years, scientists estimate that if global warming continues at its present pace, a worldwide rise of three degrees Celsius in average temperatures would reduce presently farmed marginal lands to deserts. The ice caps would melt sufficiently to raise the oceans as much as three meters, enough to inundate all low level coastal regions where the bulk of populations now live and from which they would have to be evacuated and relocated. A three degree rise would produce rainfall at the wrong time of the growing seasons for crops and intensify wind storms, drought, cloud cover and flooding. Higher temperatures now felt in the subtropics would be experienced deep within present temperate zones.

We have passed the point at which we can ignore the perilous competitive forces building between employment and the environment. Many tough decisions must be made immediately and not glossed over in determining the future of industrial growth and population expansion. Foremost is the need to decide if universal industrialization and employment really are a feasible solution to reducing population expansion, or is it a myth perpetrated by governments and entrepreneurs, both in search of profits. Although industrial development may offer improved living standards for some in the short term, can national economies sacrifice their environments in the long term to create employment for everyone? And if we don't give employment priority, will rising unemployment end in widespread violence and the loss of political and national stability? Even more so, if the majority of working people cannot be gainfully employed, can the "haves" carry the "have-nots"? Will they and can they be forced to redistribute their wealth without violent revolution?

Overcrowding, measured by the extent to which the carrying capacity of any land base is overwhelmed, is exaggerated by any restrictions we choose to place on our exploitations of the natural environment. Therefore, if we reduce industrial expansion to conserve the remaining environment for future generations, we are limiting employment opportunities, reducing living standards and forcing billions to live in even greater poverty than they do now. Reducing employment opportunities faster than they are already disappearing, will lead to a more violent, unstable world than it already is. And yet, if we do not stop the expanding course of our activities, we will soon be living on a planet whose deteriorating climates and disappearing eco-systems begin to kill, not nurture the human species.

Obviously, we must ask ourselves if we are entering the most dangerously exploitive, economic period of our existence: a new century dominated by global cutthroat capitalism, unlimited industrial development and the invasion of a "greed" culture into the lives of every society in the world. The present global economy, motivated by a desire for immediate profit for the rich and fuelled by slavery and hunger of the poor, is rapidly emerging.

The future portends to be filled with dissatisfaction, avarice, criminality, environmental poverty, slavery, industrial disease, instability, chaos and wars over shrinking supplies of arable land, food, fresh water and forest resources. With the power in our hands to submit the entire planet to drastic change through destruction of all its life-giving forces - climate, vegetation and life forms - the choice of when we will become extinct is now ours alone. Survival on this planet is no longer determined by natural limitations governing the existence of all species; it is now subject to the speed at which the human species destroys the biosphere within which we must live.

CHAPTER NINETEEN

Has Technology Become Our Nemesis?

One cannot deny technology has been the driving force and underlying means behind humanity's evolutionary development and expansion over the last 10,000 years. It is also the mode by which we have reached the present state of disarray. Extreme exploitation of the natural world is now manifest in the depletion of resources, environmental pollution and ecological extinctions. They are the victims of our relentless abuse and mastery over the natural world, demonstrating our willingness to take all we can from the environment through our technologies, while ignoring the effect such self-centred actions are having on the biosphere and the natural ecological systems. Ultimately, such actions affect our very existence, turning those technologies that have ensured our survival in the past into weapons of mass destruction in the future. Human extinction as a species may be intrinsic in this dilemma. E.F. Schumacher stated it clearly as early as 1973 in SMALL IS BEAUTIFUL, "At present, there can be little doubt that the whole of mankind is in mortal danger, not because we are short of scientific and technological know-how, but because we tend to use it destructively, without wisdom."[1]

Humanity's major dilemma is that a technologically determined existence on a planet of finite resources is a paradox which can be sustained for only a short period of time. Our planet is finite in resources and carrying capacity, but human reproduction and industrial development are exponentially expansive. Driven by a need to provide for this exponential growth during the past 200 years, we have devised many ways of increasing agricultural output and resource extraction in an attempt to reach rates comparable with population growth and need.

In the process the successful use of technologies has multiplied the amount of consumption and depletion of resources manyfold. They push people into producing and purchasing the myriad of luxury goods or "useless things" that we buy and collect around us because they raise our standard of living, please our desire for possessions and appeal to our aesthetic and mercenary senses, but are not vital to our survival. Our homes are filled with them. They are the profusion of unnecessary adornments and paraphernalia which we have come to enjoy but have been manufactured at a high cost to the environment in resources and pollutants. It has been estimated that a child growing up in the United States surrounded and indulged by these products of high technology and industry, will consume 90 to 500 times the amount of resources and energy in his or her lifetime that a child in the Third World will use. Rising consumerism, now moving into the developing world, is a major force reducing our long term survival.

In our technological evolution, we have chosen to ignore our ultimate dependency on a healthy natural environment to sustain us. Although we are presently able to produce all the food we need to feed existing populations with machines and chemicals, we still need nature to provide the abundant arable soils, fresh water and sunshine which grow our foods. We can protect our bodies from the elements through the clothes we manufacture and the homes we build, but we are still vulnerable to weather disasters; just as we are able to manufacture the thousands of accoutrements that make our lives more comfortable, but we still require nature to provide the renewable and non-renewable resources to make them and the natural environment to absorb the wastes and pollutants that result. Our technologies have enabled us to keep billions of people alive in the short term, but we must never lose sight of the fact that we are limited by the natural forces of climate, vegetation and life forms which endow this very small, fragile planet. We will learn to conserve and protect them, or we will perish.

With populations growing and industrialization the goal of most nations, ultimately nothing will be permanently withheld from human use. No area of the natural environment is now safe from human exploitation or the wastes and contaminants of industrial and agricultural manufacture. Even the most remote, isolated areas are suffering from industrial pollution carried by the prevailing winds and ocean currents. Eventually, nothing on earth will escape ultra-violet B rays or the effects of catastrophic weather phenomena. Depletion of resources and destruction of the biosphere is only a matter of how long we allow it to take.

The dilemma which will destroy our technologically-determined existence is the contest we have created between consumption and conservation. What can be temporarily protected will give way to population pressures within the next 50 years.

How then do we ensure survival on a planet of finite resources?

Our human ancestors overcame the first of such extreme threats to their continued existence when, as hunter-gatherers, they turned to domesticating crops and animals to meet their food requirements. Over the last 10,000 years, populations survived and civilizations expanded on agrarian economies which natural phenomena nurtured with warm summer temperatures, seasonal rains and fertile soils. During the last three centuries our growing skills even surpassed the limitations nature had placed on the number of domesticated animals and crops we could raise on an acre of land. Modern technologies of irrigation, machinery, pesticides, herbicides, fertilizers, hybrids, genetically engineered crops and various other farming techniques improved both the quantity and quality of food production.

However, advancing industrial technologies also cause as many problems as they yield in solutions to human survival. Chemicals and farm machinery have not only permanently polluted and ruined vast areas of arable lands and fresh water reserves, they have forced millions to leave the land and migrate to the cities. Automation and electronic communications produce wealth for the entrepreneur while making human labour redundant. Transportation systems permit people and goods to overcrowd urban centres, spread poverty and deepen social chaos and crime. Housing developments and industrial parks are allowed to preclude farm land and natural wilderness conservation. Population growth outpaces the ability of all cities to build and maintain adequate social programs, infra-structures, water and sewer systems. Industrial pollution causes untold problems of poor health, disease, epidemics, poisoned eco-systems and polluted land and water bodies. Deadly toxic smog is deteriorating human health and intelligence while lowering the productivity of workforces.

Past experience has shown that it takes a relatively short period before the advantages of technologies are outweighed by the environmental problems. Increasingly, new technologies must be designed to undo the damage of previous technologies or geared to find new ways to make our continued economic expansion possible. The most vital changes include the scramble to produce new chemicals to replace the chlorofluorocarbons which are destroying the ozone layer as well as genetic changes which will provide food crops and animals that can withstand the deteriorating conditions of the soils and the shortage of water. Furthermore, a desperate race is underway to find methods which will control the new viruses emerging and the bacterial infections which have evolved more deadly mutations immune to our antibiotics.

In the 21st Century we face the second major historical threat to our continued existence. Once again, as happened to the hunter-gatherers when they overwhelmed the natural carrying capacity of their land bases and were forced to turn to farming and herding to survive, we, too, are now scrambling to find new ways to save ourselves from extinction.

We prefer to believe we are living in a wondrous age of science where existence is guaranteed through artificially engineered foods, disease and pest free environments, computerized machine labour, man-built biospheres and rocket trips to colonize other planets. Some among us believe our survival will come as we enter a state of empathetic existence within nature that will be achieved through voluntarily lowered living standards, decreased resource consumption, recycled and reused products and an educated, voluntary curbing of fertility rates.

Still many others argue that we have managed to employ and control our technologies in the past, therefore, we will do so in the future. But our record of survival techniques is strewn with many colossal failures as well as unwanted consequences. We now realize that the overall environmental damage we have done through the millennia is universally permanent. The extent of the degradation suggests a point has been reached at which the earth can tolerate no more.

It is possible we are so dependent on the complexity and sophistication of our technologies that they now exceed our ability to control their use and destructive impact. Many dams and river diversions are in the building and planning stages, yet they have proved more socially, economically and environmentally harmful than useful. Climate changes, caused by greenhouse gases warming the atmosphere, are destroying growing areas through flooding and drought. Genetic engineering, now coming into its own, may set lose unknown life forms and vegetations which can destroy evolutionary stamina or have the capability of destroying other life forms. Medications are failing to protect us from fatal diseases while increasing the fatality rates. The Green Revolution sterilized large areas of arable land and poisoned underground water supplies. Weapons, urban development, food production, all have forced ecological systems into extinction. The list goes on and on.

From an optimist's view technological development in bio-technologies and sustainable management programs will solve future shortages of food and water reserves. They prefer to believe that human intelligence will replace, regenerate and conserve the natural environment and produce some remarkable solutions. A few attempts have been successfully carried out on a small scale. A smattering of land areas have been returned to their natural state, a few rivers and lakes have been cleaned up to mitigate public displeasure, some attempts at reforestation have been made, and a minimal number of species have been protected and their numbers rebuilt, often in increasingly fragile, non-sustainable environments. But the successes are still sparse compared with the number of failures and species' extinctions.

Overall, most of us still choose to put our faith in science, and if this doesn't appeal, then we place our continued survival in the hands of our gods.

What we forget in either case is that we cannot replace nature's basic components,- climates, vegetation, life forms and soils,- with manmade substitutes on a scale necessary to ensure human survival. Furthermore, once the balance of temperate climates and bio-diversity of species is lost, the entire composition of the biosphere which makes life possible will be altered. Few living species, including Homo sapiens, will be able to withstand years of drought, insufficient supplies of fresh water, food shortages, extremes of wind and flood, increased heat and cold and the loss of bio-diversity.

The artificial, technologically constructed existence we have created for ourselves is already proving too costly in resources and environmental destruction. The costs are mounting in pollution, sewage and garbage disposal, diminishing water and food supplies, toxic, nuclear wastes and universally poor human health. Those who promote the myth that an end to poverty through artificial technologies would bring an end to universal social problems choose human expansion over environmental conservation. However, evidence of industrial solutions shows that by increasing populations and making the few richer, the multitudes grow poorer and the environment becomes less and less habitable for all.

Homo sapiens have been rushing headlong towards self-destruction for the last several thousand years. Only now is our total destruction so apparent and so close. Each major period of technological progress, the Neolithic Agricultural Revolution, the Industrial Revolution or the Communications' Revolution, stands out as a time of great technological advancement and population expansion. But each has also been a period of environmental abuse as a progression of technologies has allowed us to take bigger and bigger bites out of the earth.

Seldom in the past have we stopped the development and implementation of technologies, even when they benefitted only a few people and destroyed the environmental eco-systems. The adverse use of technologies can be traced back to the hunter-gatherer with the power his bows and arrows gave him to annihilate the grazing herds in Europe and Asia. Today's hunter-gatherers are accelerating their capacity to obliterate all wild species in the oceans as they employ the most advanced technologies of locating and netting them. Bird and animal species which escaped extinction in the past are now disappearing to the powers of agricultural chemicals, urban development and the high powered rifles, deadly traps and poisons of the modern hunter.

The last 10,000 years of human settlement have had an equally ignominious history of deforesting the continents, eroding the arable lands, poisoning the soils with salinization and waterlogging. As explained in an earlier chapter, the history of deforestation and desertification predates the Greeks and culminates in the destruction of Europe and North Africa's forests under the Romans. The process continues today in full force on all seven continents, some suffering worse than others. Africa, Southern Europe, Asia, and Australia can be described as being in the final stages of land and forest degradation.

The trend to urban living and industrialization has brought technologies of even greater destruction affecting the entire planet as they pollute the air, the water and the land, often destroying them permanently or making them unfit for future use.

Each technological leap over the millennia not only accelerated human exploitation of the natural environment, but evolved human behaviours and attitudes which have changed us from creatures with a strong awareness and awe of natural forces, living a primitive existence "within" nature, to a master species which has "stepped outside" nature's limitations to dominate and exploit the natural world with a very heavy hand. With human populations as large as they are and the environmental carrying capacity so diminished, there is no way "back in".

In reviewing historical precedence, several distinct steps in our evolution and extinction occurred. The Neolithic Revolution changed Homo sapiens from a relatively agreeable, cooperative and communal being to a self seeking, aggressive and increasingly violent species as they moved from the status of nomadic hunter-gatherer to property owners. The Industrial Revolution changed modern man from a relatively benign occupier of the planet to a monstrous consumer and destroyer of the total environment. The Communications Revolution of the late 20th Century has put all elements of the biosphere at risk and usurped the privacy and safety of the individual and the community.

Many dangers lie ahead for humanity. To attempt to sustain twice as many people in the next century as are alive now will exploit nature to the benefit of the human species alone. Herein lies our nemesis. If we destroy nature's eco-systems in the process, we destroy the human species. In changing all the interdependent parts that comprise the environment, we destroy the whole needed to support life, particularly our own.

CHAPTER TWENTY

Dilemmas Inherent in Our Solutions

Humanity's survival is now conditional on " sustainable management" activities. But all solutions begin and end with the impossible. For drastic solutions to be universally implemented, peace and co-operation between all peoples in the world must be negotiated, if not "enforced", which, in the beginning, is a non-starter.

The philosophical question arises: Are we capable of universal sacrifice to save the earth's environment if we must relinquish the advantages of technological progress? Civilizations in the past always destroyed their landbases by technological innovations: forests were cut down to make charcoal and build ships, arable lands became deserts through overcropping, irrigation and salinization, and water supplies dried up as desertification spread. Experience is showing us that we are not any different today in our technological destruction of the planet, only that we are more adept in that destruction and can cut great swathes of devastation in much less time.

But if we reduce consumption and pollution by restricting industrialization, poverty in an overcrowded world will increase. This, in turn, causes more overcrowding of a land base on which the individual has less social space or security and poverty becomes entrenched among the majority. On all continents dispossessed farmers either desert the land for the city or become hunter-gatherers, poaching and robbing the land of all its life forms and vegetation just to stay alive.

Subsistent survival only deepens universal poverty and worsens the struggle of humanity as a whole to survive. This is well demonstrated by the poor of Africa and South America where they overcrop and overgraze the land while ravaging the forests and vegetation for fuel. In the process they overuse or contaminate their precious fresh water reserves. Six billion, eight billion, ten billion, fourteen billion people in one century will rapidly slip into abject poverty as their needs deplete the planet.

If productive land continues to disappear at the rate of 10,000 square miles a year, we will be forced to live on even more crowded landbases than we are experiencing now. The loss of habitable land and social space will embroil humankind in violent struggles over land, food and water supplies. The future is already with us in West Africa where wars and social anarchy are killing thousands annually in tribal conflicts over territory. Never in our history has racism been so universal or so vicious as is now reflected in the xenophobic behaviours cropping up on every continent. Ethnic cleansing has become a universal plague.

Perhaps one of the greatest boons to environmental conservation and protection would be an end to the production and sale of military weapons which have the capacity to destroy whole urban areas and eco-systems during civil wars. Bringing an end to nuclear weapons and power plants would alleviate the deadly production of nuclear wastes which threaten the planet with an insidious permeation of radiation materials into the oceans and the air.

Correcting our hubris begins with an end to overcrowding our landbases by enforcing an immediate reduction in world populations, not waiting for natural attrition and higher living standards to build a desire in men and women to have fewer children. If humanity is to survive past the next century, the world's total population must be reduced to two billion within two or three decades. No one should accept that it is preordained our numbers can reach 10 to 14 billions and life will remain viable. The grim reality is we have yet to learn how to cope with the additional 4 billion added to the earth in just the last 50 years. We are even more poorly prepared to manage the additional 4 billion arriving over the next 50 years.

If the environment is to be protected and the costs met to restore its health through sustainable management programs based on reduced consumption, as experts in environmental solutions would have it, then impoverished, overcrowded nations must be given the financial aid and resources to raise their people out of poverty and into self-sustaining production of their basic needs. This would entail wiping out world debts and finding the investment capital to establish a primary industrial base in every nation. Some 10 to 20 trillion dollars in capital might enable us to make a start towards protecting the environments. It would certainly pay off existing world debts, help rebuild economies and provide viable infra-structures to educate and employ the bulk of workers, thereby easing their daily destructive scavenging of the environment.

Of course, the logistics of this solution are totally illogical. Governments are unable to produce enough money just to manage their economies from year to year, much less commit their nations to even deeper debt. And if we could create employment and raise living standards for the majority of the present 6 billion people, let alone 10 billion over the first half of the 21st Century, the planet would be depleted of its fresh water reserves, forests, soils, vegetation and eco-systems within the next two to three decades.

The reality of the 21st Century will be the universal migration of hundreds of millions, even billions, of impoverished, environmental refugees, seeking a chance to survive on overcrowded, despoiled landbases. The growing presence of these migrating hordes puts them in as much danger from human violence as from death by starvation and disease if they stayed put. Obviously environmental conservation demands the impossible: an end to the migrations of economic and environmental refugees. Meanwhile, modern technologies permit present day refugees passage to "invade" other lands, turning illegal immigrants into the bane of every nation, developed and undeveloped. As these waves of refugees swell, the fear of being inundated by them has intensified xenophobia and ethnic conflicts.

This book has set out the problems and inefficacies of popular solutions to the dilemmas which continue to prevent a universal move towards reduced exploitation and expanded rejuvenation of the environment. To attempt universal changes such as those listed above, we would first have to undergo even more difficult changes within our many cultural societies. It would involve a far greater dream of universal coexistence than that proposed by the United Nations whose basic tenet is peace and understanding of all peoples in a world of freedom and equality. This in itself is a paradox. Human freedom must be totally controlled if the environment is to be protected.

Furthermore the UN goals laid out in the agenda for the World Summit on Social Development held in Copenhagen in March of 1995, for the global eradication of extreme poverty only underlines the dilemma of employment versus conservation. Their aim to "commit governments to work toward full employment and to improve access for all citizens to food, water, shelter, health care and education"[1] carries with it all the repercussions of a corresponding rise in populations as a result of food and health care, of rapid and immense exploitation of the environment, of a steady rise in international debts and of a universal ability to migrate. Ending poverty is a magnanimous goal, but its impact would be devastating for all.

Idealistic goals such as the United Nations espouses will remain far from fruition. To begin with, the rich nations will not finance the poor countries into a dependency that even the richest nations cannot afford to undertake. Lessons of the 1970s and 1980s showed the complications of unlimited development aid to the Third World. It failed miserably because we humans are not capable of the necessary altruism. Greed and self-aggrandizement took over and national debts almost destroyed the world's financial systems. Furthermore, too many "rich" nations have accrued huge debts as their large unemployed work forces and infra-structures outrun tax revenues.

Altruism does not motivate the realities of the modern world and the global economy; money, power and greed do. The forces of economic destruction are in themselves an insurmountable roadblock to implementing solutions which would save our dying planet. Neither does the global economy have a conservationist bent that would reduce its exploitation of the environment. Rather the world is experiencing a return to uncontrolled aggressive, greedy behaviours under the management of authorities who measure success in profits, not preservation and human progress. Governments find they must aid and abet the self-seeking corporate structure in the creation of employment to quell civil unrest and promote national stability.

The policies of a global economy encourage crime on an international scale from computer theft to successful smuggling of human cargoes to spreading racial hatred. In every nation global economic polices widen the gap between the rich and poor, while occupying and exploiting every inch of habitable land, destroying eco-systems in the process. They impede national programs and rave against universal efforts to conserve the environment. The forces of human progress are adding to the distrust and greed of all nations at a time in our history when our own needs should be taking second place to those of the physical environment.

Even finding government leadership willing and strong enough to force social and economic changes favouring environmental conservation continues to prove futile. Yet this is the only institutional structure capable of outlawing pollution, restricting permission of industrial growth and spending billions of dollars on pollution control, recycling, environmental cleanup and protection of remaining wilderness from human use. Unfortunately, government is only as good as the people elected to office and the environmental policies they bring with them. Most are elected on the promise of creating jobs, not dismantling them for the sake of endangered species. As our evolutionary timetable ticks closer to midnight, saving the environment continues to take second place to human exploitation.

This attitude is supported by a growing militaristic buildup in defense of our national territories and the right to use and destroy our own lands as we wish. Civil wars are in progress around the globe, and more are in the offing, the majority being fought with the purpose of creating ethnically pure landbases. With populations burgeoning and social space disappearing beneath the seething masses of humanity, racial and ethnic roots motivate us to seek identity and purpose within smaller and smaller tribal enclaves. Ethnic leaders are willing to destroy not only their enemies but their lands and resources to protect ethnicity. It has become more vital to establish our racial identities, tribal rights and religious beliefs than it is to protect the resources and environments of those landbases for our physical survival.

Ethologists would say this is the instinctive course of nature. An animal or a bird will sacrifice everything, even its own life in defense of its territory. For without territory, there is no food supply; without territory there is no assurance of survival for the individual or the group. Without territory there is only extinction of species. Perhaps these ethnic wars are a manifestation of nature's instinctive drives of the gene pool over human reason.

Obviously the human brain is capable of devising solutions that would resolve our destructive exploitation of the environment. But, at the same time the magnitude of the roadblocks to the implementation of any solutions would devastate much of humanity if implemented. For instance, if every nation were to stop expanding industrially and lower their consumption of resources, unemployment would skyrocket and nations would be destabilized. The experience of enforced unemployment, abject poverty and spreading hunger in collapsing environments where resources are beyond preservation and regeneration are with us now. It is there in urban areas where massive unemployment and displacement exists among large sectors throughout much of Africa, South America, Asia and the Middle East. It is there is the inner cities and slums of the industrial world.

The carrying capacity of cities to employ and feed large numbers of internal immigrants is now beyond even the most progressive technologies to sustain them. Their dependency has turned 20th Century technologies into destructive forces. In China, an impoverished, hungry peasantry that exceeds 860 millions is moving by the tens of millions to the cities where over 150 million surplus farm labourers are already seeking jobs. Millions more are being pushed off their farm land to make room for spreading urban development. Homeless, uneducated, unskilled and easily abused, these migrants roam the cities, gathering feelings of disillusionment and unrest. Such conditions have provoked many uprisings in history, including China's Communist revolution.

China's story repeats itself in most nations, rich and poor, if only on a lesser scale. Third World cities, such as Rio de Janeiro, Mexico, New Delhi, and Cairo are overrun with farm labourers whose large families have swamped the urban infra-structures. Consequently, major world cities are short of water supplies and lack sufficient means to dispose of their sewage and garbage which pollutes their rivers and water sources and contaminates the land and air. Poverty, malnutrition, epidemics, high infant mortality rates, crime and total loss of civil order are rampant. The imbalance between the number of jobs and the overabundance of workers is a constant source of irritation and aggressive behaviour among urban inhabitants. Cities can no longer viably absorb the millions of refugees from the land in search of employment, and yet the populations of the major cities around the world will double or triple their present populations within the next 30 to 40 years.

A strong irony in the displacement of the farm communities exists, especially in the Third World. Many peasant farmers and their families wish only to return to the land. They would use natural farming methods which would conserve the landscape, not destroy it. But their numbers are too prolific. Also, First World nations have done much to prevent this happening as they continue to preach that overpopulation can be controlled only through industrialization and working women.

The mounting "poverty" that now haunts so many countries does not bode well for the future. As populations expand, consumption of the earth's resources grows and destruction of the biosphere expands. Finding money supplies to promote conservation of arable soils, old growth forests, diminishing reserves of fresh water and rapidly disappearing eco-systems comes far behind the needs of people. Clean up costs and most recycling programs will come into their own only when all the original resources are so rare and expensive that recycling is more profitable.

In the last half of the 20th Century, governments, entrepreneurs and investors have developed a ravenous appetite for resources and land. It is an appetite that is never sated and expands as populations and technologies expand. The process ignores human projects to work in harmony with nature and to leave sufficient amounts of natural vegetation on the land and fish in the sea to ensure future generations. A growing unwillingness exists to reduce our luxurious lifestyles. At present every society is driven to improve or import technologies of production, create more jobs, use more renewable and non-renewable resources and expand every nation's economy and wealth. There is no such thing as enough of a commercial product if there is money to be made in its sale.

Humanity has mined the seas until entire species of fish are gone. We have irrigated deserts and fragile grasslands until rivers, lakes and aquifers are nearly drained and vast flatlands are contaminated with salts beyond any immediate remediation. We have cut our forests until the lands are barren, eroded hills and plains that can never again support vegetation during our evolutionary existence. We have dammed rivers and drowned millions of acres of arable soils and forests, killing off thousands of other species to produce a few years of hydro power. Our lands, rivers, seas and the air we breathe are polluted, our bodies are contaminated with the chemicals our technologies have torn from the earth and our immunity to disease is lessening every day.

Governments of the 19th and 20th Centuries have been economic engines, fuelling industry and exploitation of the planet to its very limits. The goal has been to improve the lot of everyone under the guise of making the few richer and richer. But all has been done at the expense of the planet and its environmental resources. We have come to see the planet as there for our use alone, to be mastered, occupied, exploited and conquered. We have yet to admit that our modern technological exploitation of it is abusive, immoral and self-destructive.

Two very definitive solutions appear to have any chance of forestalling our disappearance as soon as the next century: universally enforced birth control organized to reduce the earth's populations to at least two billion over the next 100 years; and reduced industrial development and consumption world wide. Contraception, sterilization and abortion, if openly imposed on the women of all societies, could stem the population explosion as well as the immediate consumption of remaining resources. Every society, every ethnic group and every race must come to believe we will all be better off with far fewer children and a lower living standard.

CHAPTER TWENTY ONE

How We View the Human Role in Nature

In our short time on earth, humankind has been responsible for the extinction of tens of thousands of other species and much permanent damage to the planet. Over five million years of evolution these destructive behaviours have become inherent in our evolution and technologies. Perhaps more than any other rationale this leads to the conclusion that we will not stop until the human species is extinct. We moved beyond nature's territorial limitations for human survival by settling the land; we are now moving beyond the carrying capacity of the artificial limitations we gained through technology.

With so many critical problems facing our immediate survival, trying to analyze human motivation and commitment to the future reveals some unpleasant truths about human nature. They begin with one of the earliest influences on our social behaviours, that of private ownership of property. Farming the land strengthened the instinctive drive to hold and protect territory. Ingrained in our concept of civilization, the acquisition of property ensured the individual of his survival and relative safety of person. It also enhanced the desire for physical power to dominate one's own species through the accumulation of land, goods and wealth. This conclusion is justified by the corollary: those who are homeless and landless are viewed as the unfortunate flotsam and jetsam of human society.

Private ownership ended communal sharing and exacerbated human greed. We became self-seeking creatures, driven to exploit the bounties of nature in return for profit. In the process we began to see ourselves as the master species, superior to nature. To date we have not changed that view, nor have we slowed our consumption of the natural world.

No human activity demonstrates the ferocity of this behaviour more clearly than the all-consuming race to fish out the oceans. Poachers in the North Sea, off the Grand Banks of Canada and throughout the Pacific Ocean from the Northern Hemisphere to Australia behave like pirates, using the most advanced technologies available, leaving few fish to reproduce the next generation and killing millions of non-edible creatures with their nets and garbage. Leaders of Asian countries have stated publicly that all life in the sea rightfully belongs to humans to do with as they please. International quotas, fishing bans, whale bans and regulated fishing seasons do not stop such people. Only the total depletion of commercial fish stocks, bankruptcy and open fish wars finally end their pillaging.

Our universal choice between satisfying human needs or conserving the planet is one of selfish expediency. We continue to pollute and degrade the earth's environments while openly admitting to our destructive ways and arguing the problems we are creating for ourselves at international gatherings. Much rhetoric has been forthcoming and many signed but unfulfilled promises have been given by national governments to reduce toxic emissions and pollutants worldwide within a few years. The most recent high level attempt to reform destructive environmental habits was that of the International Conference on Population and Development held in Cairo in September of 1994. No cogent promises were made to stop destroying the planet, no agreement of any value was reached on population control, and little time was given to finding workable solutions.

Some estimates say we have as few as 50 to 100 years left as a viable species on this planet. If we continue to increase our populations by over 90 to 100 million annually for the next fifty years based on present day fertility rates, attempting to meet even the very basic minimum of human needs will initiate nature's most powerful forces of species' extinction: a shortage of social space, insufficient food and fresh water. Like the former inhabitants of Easter Island, we may soon be reduced to populations of thirsty, starving, diseased people at war with each other everywhere over the remnants of arable land, fresh water and natural resources. Shortages of food and fresh water are already contributing to human suffering in many regions of the Third World, the Middle East and Eastern Europe. If there are solutions, we had better find them fast as we are running out of time.

Evolutionary greed, private ownership and ethnicity have not prepared the modern human for the degree of universal co-operation needed to find solutions. Neither have they invested the majority with strong sensitivities towards the environment and other species. The capitalistic nations especially are not bent on self-sacrifice or international co-operation to prevent environmental collapse. These self-fulfilling character traits may prove intransigent when everyday survival becomes everyone's greatest challenge.

Lewis Thomas summed it up when he wrote "So far we have learned how to be useful to each other only when we collect in small groups -- families, circles of friends, once in a while (although still rarely) committees. The drive to be useful is encoded in our genes. But when we gather in very large numbers, as in the modern national state, we seem capable of levels of folly and self destruction to be found nowhere else in all of Nature".[1]

Capitalistic traits of modern civilizations have led us on a universal course propelled by irreversible forces,--overpopulation, overconsumption, overdevelopment, overindustrialization and over-abuse of the environment,-- each in their own immutable way capable of bringing about human extinction. Together they comprise a deadly, omnipresent force of environmental destruction in a very short time frame. The more crowded the territorial base becomes, the more insensitive and destructive the human occupants are to nature.

We seem to have entered an age of cold, objective science and in our mechanical, artificial world we have lost the spirituality and sense of awe that nature can inspire. Instead, a growing self-centredness, aggressive destructiveness and fear of others have emerged. We are on a universal course of xenophobic bigotry as ethnic hatreds and conflicts spread. This insensitive mould into which modern humanity is being poured comes to us through the enticing media of television and electronic gadgetry. Their messages reach into every home, creating dissatisfaction and racial intolerance. They are shaping cultures into one universal culture, patterned on Western values and creating an obsession for manufactured goods and services.

Technologies increase social tensions as they eliminate the need to depend on each other. The isolation that comes with unemployment, loss of purpose and low self-esteem leads the individual away from the family, the community and the social/cultural structures which give one the sense of who we are and where we belong. Instead, we move among strangers and survive without social restraints. Millions now travel or migrate relatively easily, breaking through the cultural and physical barriers of nations, throwing everyone into an overcrowded pot pourri of conflicting attitudes, beliefs, desires, values and customs.

Changing universal behaviours and attitudes which might delay but not prevent our impending extinction comprise an impossible wish list of DO's and DON'Ts of survival. Few nations would agree to the many restrictions such a list of activities would place on their societies, for their implementation would strike at the very substance of modern progress and survival: employment, unlimited industrialization and productivity, high living standards, physical security, political power and wealth. Yet common sense tells us we must make considerable sacrifices now if we are to survive as a species over the next hundred years.

To understand how and why humanity approaches the many problems inherent in our survival the way it does, it is first necessary to understand several major variations in universal perceptions of our existence and our relationship to nature. At present most of these perceptions pose immutable roadblocks to resolving the conflicts and dilemmas now threatening our existence.

One widely held view sees our evolutionary destiny as not within our power to determine. Rather, the course of human progress and expansion over the earth's surface has been "charted in the stars" so that our evolution and our extinction are predetermined by natural laws over which we have little, if any, control. This point of view does not totally disallow our participation in our own evolution and extinction, however. It just assumes our destructive powers play a minor secondary role to the natural forces of climate and physical phenomena. This can then be misconstrued as either the planet has unlimited carrying capacity and regenerative powers to accommodate many more billions of people and ever expanding industrialization, (the stand taken by the Catholic Church in June of 1994 in preparation for a conference in Cairo held to develop a 20-year plan for human survival); or we are at the mercy of natural forces, and therefore, the victims, not the cause of environmental collapse.

Another similar perception of our existence is that humanity is superior to nature, created by God and therefore not subject to natural laws of survival and extinction. This perception is basic to religious doctrines which downplay the human role in its own evolution and extinction. The cold, implacable reality of humanity being at the mercy of nature and, therefore, having no control over our physical and spiritual destinies has never been easy for the human mind to accept. Consequently, through the millennia the natural powers governing our lives and activities, both good and evil, were gradually relegated to divinities and spiritual beings. These deities could be coerced through prayer and sacrifice to protect humans in their struggles to survive. They also offered a way to assuage human fears of natural forces and the unknown. The consecration of one's mind and body to the discretion of the gods led to the belief that our existence is predestined, not left to the vagaries of nature. We came to believe that if we appease our gods, we would flourish and nature would provide for us.

Both the above approaches remove the human species from all blame for overpopulating and degrading the earth, excusing them from a forceful program of universal population control and downsizing technological development. Industrial leaders and sycophant scientists frequently support this view through published results of "studies" paid for by the large corporations. Their aim is to convince the public that industries are not at fault for our collapsing environments and those who predict chaos and extinction through overpopulation and industrial development are falsely exaggerating. Such attitudes are not good for business. Industrialists would prefer we believe the growing number of climatic aberrations of the 1980s and 1990s which caused widespread crop and property damage were natural phenomena such as occurred frequently in the past and have no connection to human activities.

Religions have led us even further afield in denying human responsibility for our survival and our extinction. They stop short of accepting an evolutionary beginning for Homo sapiens;

therefore, they find it unnecessary to consider the possibility of a natural, evolutionary end. This stance avoids the unpleasant realities that human extinction could come through natural causes, the result of our destruction of the environment and its ecological systems. The religious approach takes the position that God created the Earth and all its creatures; therefore, He and He alone will decide when humanity should become extinct.

A third view, the scientific approach, is that nature, on the other hand, does not avoid the inevitability of species' extinction. In nature all species eventually die out. It is only a matter of time and the right physical conditions. Species are generated, they develop and then disappear. The reasons for their disappearance are generally clear cut and consistent in that they are commensurate with the natural carrying capacity of their physical environments.

In approaching our future survival from any of these three positions, we must ask ourselves: Do we have natural evolutionary attitudes and behaviours which have assured our survival at the cost of the environment? Are we being sustained by religious creeds that ignore our role in the evolution and extinction of species on this planet? And if so, are these behaviours and this belief now threatening us with self-destruction? Primary among such attitudes and creeds is the ancient Christian edict of "Go forth and multiply and replenish the Earth, and subdue it, and have dominion over the fowl of the air and over every living thing that moveth upon the Earth". This perception of our role in nature is largely responsible for both humanity having overpopulated the earth as well as the disappearance of so many other species.

An opposing view would suggest that we have been given complete control over our existence by dint of our superior intelligence which will ensure our survival through innovative technologies and "sustainable management" programs. Having overcome the natural carrying capacity of nature in the past through our technological ingenuity, we can do so again in the future. Although we are diminishing the earth's resources at a spiralling rate, this view advances the theory that we have the power necessary to manage the earth and ensure our survival far into the future. This "hubris" is now so ingrained in our social makeup that as resources run short and ecological systems disappear, our economic and political leadership would have us believe we are capable of replacing what we are losing through genetic engineering, artificial chemical nutrients, planted forests, diverted river systems, medical cures, fish farms, irrigated deserts. The list has become very long, but so has the inventory of impossibilities and destructive consequences.

Throughout this book I have chosen a combination of views from which to argue that humanity has and is playing a major role in its own survival and extinction. By accepting the capacity of human intelligence and ingenuity to "manage" the ways in which we occupy the earth, one must assume we CAN stop our destructive ways. More importantly, we should be able to recognize the consequences of our actions before we do them which would then make it possible for us to implement solutions to our dilemmas and make changes in our living standards. Preparedness would put us more in balance with environmental regeneration and conservation.

Unfortunately, the many cultural and social dilemmas our technologically-determined existence has brought us, as well as the human characteristics of greed and hubris, WILL NOT let us stop our destructive rampage. The major roadblock to reversing our present course of self-destruction lies within our disparate societies which are more deeply influenced by cultural, economic and religious forces in their relationship to the environment than by natural territorial laws of carrying capacity. As a result societies prefer to downplay the human role in environmental destruction. Instead they choose to view human development as a progression towards a higher plane of universal cooperation and peace, managed by divine powers. Unfortunately, all the prayers and obeyance in the world will not help us if we do not accept full responsibility for our relentless destruction of this fragile planet.

We must ask ourselves whether we have become an aberration of nature that is out of control. Our powers of self-determination have grown with the genius of our technologies. And yet the swelling awareness that the environment may soon collapse under our abuse of it has not curbed our consumption of resources or our contamination of the biosphere to satisfy our technological obsessions.

Throughout our evolution human attitudes and behaviours have remained arrogant and self-fulfilling as living standards improved. Neither have they softened our awareness of nature, nor reduced our aggressive, self-centred exploitation of our surroundings. Historical events and records reveal the same thirst for warfare, destruction and cruelty in Roman times as African tribes exhibit today. The same racial/religious conflicts that wiped out whole tribes 5000 years ago seek to obliterate human and natural landscapes in the 1990s. Natural resources that were not consumed in the past through human occupation, technological exploitation, pollution and internecine wars are now being utilized and will continue to be consumed at an accelerating pace in the 21st Century.

Consequently, we are more likely to defend with violent force the right to continue as we are within traditional cultures. Designing and imposing new social and economic values on the various societies on earth seem less and less possible as failed experiments of socialism and capitalism have shown. Social and cultural structures in the modern world are proving to be more the products of their technological progress and the resources of their land bases, than of the rational mind trying to devise the utopian society. Change, whether for better or worse, is now coming only with the standard of living we attain for ourselves through exploiting the earth. Goals to provide an equitable life for all while preserving the environment have little moral authority in the global economy. Nor has any social or political system been devised to date which would unite our multicultural world ethnically, racially or religiously to find solutions.

In fact, in this overpopulated, over-industrialized world the elements of international unity and co-operation are becoming more polarized than at any other time. Rational solutions to environmental conservation have little influence in ethnically driven conflicts or multinational profiteering. Our continued existence is universally in conflict with the pursuit of higher living standards for the rich and the destruction of the natural environment to sustain the increasing number of poor.

Granted there are as many proposed solutions for localized environmental problems as there are unsolvable dilemmas in this contest between ourselves and the planet's biosphere. Coming up with solutions is not the problem. Putting them into effect and following through with them on a world scale is.

Some environmental activist groups have managed to save small areas of the planet and its endangered species by convincing governments and the courts of the advantages gained in reducing or controlling industrial exploitation. Still other government legislation and court decisions uphold the exploiter and persecute the defender of ecological systems.

Governments to date continue to ignore United Nations' prediction and conservation suggestions and give in to the pressures of labour, big business, industrial expansion and commercial development, disguising their capitulation as "study projects" to be carried out in given time periods or as scientific research programs which they claim are necessary to evaluate the extent of environmental impact. Japan, for instance, continues to use its drift net fishing fleet in the Pacific and also kill whales for food, obfuscating their actions as scientific studies aimed at saving the environment.

Can we honestly believe such wanton killing of species is helping save the planet? Furthermore, few nations are willingly following the United Nations' guidelines. Can we ever be sure that good changes and environmental protectionist policies put in place by one set of politicians will not be overturned by those next to hold office? Will those in power 30 to 40 years into the future ignore the concerns of the past and undo endangered species' laws which saved the wetlands and the mountain forests in the 1980s?

Destruction of the planet and the human race are now at hand. Physically we have exploited the earth to its limits and emotionally we are destroying the human psyche, its spirituality and the fabric of the physical world which sustains us. The machines of industry and electronic communications have taken over our daily lives and therefore our humanity. Everything we do and have is dependent on and programmed by machines, computer models, learning programs, scientific data, instant communications, unlimited media analysis and propaganda, and the inability of leaders to lead in a world without borders.

Human life is geared to making money, to scratch out an existence, to retain one's sanity and survive physically in an over crowded world. Machines have taken our morality, our spirituality, our humanity and our essence of self. The Information Revolution has made us hostages to media manipulation. We are alienated amidst plenty, hidden behind concrete walls, clinging to life through electronic media. Most of us are totally removed from nature and the powers of the natural world which are needed to sustain us emotionally and spiritually. We live in monstrous cities of concrete and glass.

There is little expanse of philosophical thought anymore. The visionaries of the 18th and 19th Centuries have no equals in the late 20th Century. The human role in the universe is seldom defined or examined in depth by philosophers because the overwhelming amount of physical knowledge and social changes we are undergoing are happening so fast no one has time to collate, digest, evaluate and theorize where we might or should be going. Within two years information is outdated, political and economic trends have changed, and the visionary is made a fool.

The greatest challenge of the 21st Century will be to employ the billions alive and the billions yet to be born who will be in search of paying jobs. The irony of this feat lies in having to maximize labour through technologies, rather than reduce human labour through automation and robots, at a time when all industrialization is driven by reducing costs and improving market share through lower labour costs. Whatever methods are used, they must be accomplished while not destroying the environment any further nor reducing its carrying capacity. But with human nature being what it is, will we be able to afford the excessive costs of increased labour in our purchases; or will we widen the practice of using "slave" labour so that we can trade our products on a world market that now flourishes only at the most competitive level by selling the highest quality product at the lowest price?

The priority given profit at the expense of the environment has been the human way since the notion of property began controlling our psyche 10,000 years ago. It gave impetus to our individual and social greed and aggression. The unbridled drive for wealth widened the gap between rich and poor from our early settled beginnings, exaggerating the inequality, repression and poverty that affects over 80 percent of the world's people today. Our experience with present climatic changes, declining supplies of fresh water and arable soils, all deteriorating under our increasing demands, tells us we must resolve our dilemma of carrying capacity immediately; or, like the ancient hunter-gatherers who were forced to settle the land or perish, we face extinction in the immediate future. If, through the miracles of science, we can find solutions to repair the environmental destruction we have brought about and continue to meet our food needs, can we live cooperatively and successfully within the unnatural conditions and stresses that overcrowded social spaces and ethnic differences will cause? Do we then face extinction at our own hands as we employ nuclear arsenals to defend our shrinking land bases against the ethnic or racial "outsider"?

The unequal distribution of wealth, land and resources has historically promoted xenophobia, racism, terrorism, civil and international wars. To indulge these aggressive behaviours and attitudes we have developed weapons capable of destroying entire populations, if not the whole planet in an accidental or intentional nuclear attack. Our military weapons are now so destructive of environments, as they are of people, that our problem of continued survival may not be just a lack of food and water in the near future, but the physical destruction of our national land bases and the loss of individual security, freedom and social space through warfare.

Evolutionary instincts developed over five million years of scrambling to survive in a harsh world have made us angry, hate filled creatures when we lose our land and living space to another race or group of people. Present internecine wars between racial and ethnic social groups in so many nations should be experience enough for us to realize that we are now in mortal combat over living space and that it is in our nature to fight willingly until one group or the other is removed from our presence and totally decimated. Such hatreds run long and deep; some have a history that predates Biblical times.

Expand this instinctive attitude to the earth's overcrowded nations everywhere, from the cities with their criminal gangs, to the states and provinces with their struggles to secede, to entire nations willing to perish in battle over sovereignty for their own ethnic enclaves. Add the xenophobia and racial hatreds that arise out of the loss of social space which tend to flare up into violent conflicts that trace their "killer" instincts back millions of years to our jungle origins and you have all the ingredients for human self-destruction. It eventually devolves to nature's law of "survival of the fittest."

The most devastating aspect of this self-destructive tendency is the conviction held by the majority of people that it is a human right to possess the earth and all its bounty. Religions have promoted our mastery over the earth and have taught their followers that what ever happens is "God's will"; that only He has the power to decide when the human species will disappear from this earth. Our long history as the dominant species of the planet has ingrained such hubris into our social and religious attitudes of rights and privileges that they now threaten to destroy us.

This human arrogance and self-centredness was clearly expressed by a Brazilian farmer I heard interviewed on a television documentary in 1989. He expressed what seems to me to be the majority attitude in many such documentaries and books I have encountered. When asked how he felt about the destruction of the Amazon rainforest so that a few poor farmers might till the infertile lands for two or three years, while ignoring all other reasons for retaining those jungles as they are, he answered, "Man was put on earth to use all things. Everything else must die first, man last." I heard echoes of the same attitudes from the American President, George Bush, in June of 1992 during the Rio Earth Summit when he refused to sign the world treaties that would reduce carbon dioxide emissions to the 1990 level by the year 2000 and a treaty to preserve the earth's bio-diversity. His reason: He would not put American jobs at stake by agreeing to either treaty.

In the final analysis our looming crisis in survival would not have happened without our evolutionary development of technologies. Without our tools, our weapons and our trappings of civilization, we may have remained just another species in nature. Chances are Australopithecine would have perished had he not had the primitive intelligence and simple technologies that helped him to evolve from a bipedal ape into Homo erectus.

Only our intelligence and our technologies have allowed us to evolve into the master species we have become over the past five million years. But in our hubris, we may have gone too far and now behave like tyrants, certainly not appreciative guests on this planet. We are destroying our host and in return, assuring our nemesis.

Can We Reverse Our Present Course?   Those who choose to envision a better future ahead based on technological solutions fail to recognize the truths of humanity's evolutionary nature. They see the physical and economic problems, but overlook the realities of social/economic logistics and dilemmas which drive human nature. Human evolution has included several problematic traits: an instinctual aggressiveness, an overweening self-esteem expressed through our ability to procreate and racial and xenophobic fears of the gene pool.

The attitude that we can resolve all our differences and find ways to overcome our environmental problems suggests we can be co-operative, willing creatures, not the greedy gluttonous species we really are. It presupposes our continuing, successful superiority over all other living species and our innate cruelty to our own kind are not detrimental traits in finding environmental solutions. But does it recognize the ignorance and desperation of the majority of the world's people who live in poverty and ignorance as well as the greed and aggrandizement that drives the need to expand and occupy every inch of this planet without mercy. These are not traits which will promote self-sacrifice and universal cooperation to save an ailing planet.

With our great gift of intelligence, undoubtedly species Homo sapiens has accomplished incredible feats. We have gained god-like knowledge of ourselves, of this planet and of the universe. We have lifted ourselves far above all living things and looked into the smallest microcosm; we have all but discovered the secret of life.

Yet here we are on the threshold of full understanding of the universe and devising the means to travel out into it, only to be cut short of full discovery by the very fruits of our genius and innovation that have made our existence so remarkable, but now threaten our survival. Since that mutant ape, the ancestor of Homo Sapiens first walked out onto the savanna, picked up a large bone and realized he could kill his prey with it, all the rational, intellectual capacity we have gained is still subservient to the forces of nature which dictate survival through unlimited propagation of species and by defense of territory to protect food supply. In our struggle to remove ourselves from the controls of nature and determine our own rules of survival, we have lost the powers of attrition over our numbers which nature exerts over all other species and we have ignored the limitations of territory and natural food supply.

The evolutionary natural instincts and social behaviours remain stronger forces in our natures than the scientific understandings, rational responses and civilized controls which we place on our actions so as to enable us to live more efficiently, peacefully, fully and wisely. Ironically, all the wondrous innovations of our large brain that have raised our survival expectations and capabilities to where they are today have now become the unintentional weapons threatening us with extinction. They have given us the power to increase our populations far beyond the carrying capacity of our planet and have imbedded instinctual and social desires in us that allow us to ignore the natural balance of the forces of nature at our peril.

By overwhelming the planet with our numbers and our relentless destruction of the earth's environment, we have set in motion our evolutionary destiny of self-destruction. There can be little doubt that our aggressive attitudes and behaviours will eventually bring about our extinction, whether it happens in the next 50 years or in the next two or three centuries.

Humanity seems frozen in an historical mould of persistent exploitation and destruction of the earth's total environment. Our evolutionary course has been driven and warped by aggressive hubris and behaviours of self-preservation in our exploitation of the bounties of nature. For the last 5 million years the planet has been able to withstand our wanton ways and still sustain the human species with all its destructive habits. But we may now have passed the sustainable limits of cushioning which the earth has allotted us. Our self-destruction, abetted by increasingly destructive technologies, has brought us face to face with the extremes of our hubris and clearly delineates our nemesis: self-imposed extinction.

Author's Footnote

We have exploited the environment and ecological systems on which we must ultimately depend for survival to the exclusion of our own biological interests. Nothing we have done to date indicates to me that humanity as a whole is capable of finding solutions which would save the remnants of the deteriorating biosphere and put them in place before nature and necessity reduce us to violent, bestial creatures struggling to survive on an overcrowded, devastated planet.

Twenty five years ago I was still optimistic about humanity's chances of solving its many environmental problems. I believed we are intelligent beings who had solved our problems of survival in the past through technological advances, therefore we are quite capable of curbing our profligate consumption and finding new solutions in the future. Environmental organizations had begun petitioning the world to control our devastating actions. The threat to human life was being felt by people everywhere who had to drink contaminated water and breathe poisoned air. Children and adults were suffering new illnesses caused by a new enemy-industrial pollution. I chose to believe humanity could make no other decision but to stop this dangerous course immediately and ensure human survival.

Now, twenty five years later, populations are growing faster than ever, industrialization is the goal of every nation, resources of fresh water and continental forests are facing depletion within the next 30 to 50 years, species continue to be hunted or fished to extinction, weather patterns are harbingers of massive destruction and the environment continues to lose out to human exploitation and pollution in more and more nations as they industrialize.

If we continue at the present rate of overpopulation, overconsumption, over industrialization, over development and overuse and abuse of the environment, I believe that end will come within the 21st Century.

I admit to extreme pessimism after so many years of steeping myself in researching and protesting human destruction of the planet. My anger arises from witnessing the ignorant behaviour of teenagers throwing boulders on spawning salmon in a British Columbia river to city managers in Ontario who handed out permits to U.S. Mafia to sell gasoline in Canada as legal fuel into which PCB wastes had been dumped.

As the immutable forces of human occupation continue to take precedence over conservation and regeneration, keeping faith in our ability to change course and repair the damage seems little more than wishful thinking. Instead, several distressing questions have taken shape in my mind: Will future technological advances be aimed largely at undoing the damage previous technologies have done? Or have we reached the limit of technological solutions which can be implemented without doing more irreparable damage to the environment? How long can we survive in a fully artificial world, created by our technologies?

We know our technologies can exploit and manipulate the natural environment to satisfy our needs at the present time. But in a show down, are our technologies able to stand up to the destructive forces of altered climates, vegetation and life forms? Can we, as a species, move totally outside natural forces to survive? For instance, could we live successfully and continue to reproduce and evolve under artificial domes built to protect us from the earth's polluted biosphere? If so, will such an existence be as "deadly" and sterile as life in a zoo cage or confinement within cement pools?

Or is it possible that Homo sapiens has proven to be such a destructive species that our annihilation has become a biological necessity to nature? Have we reached that point in our evolution where our interference with the natural forces of the planet are not only destroying themselves, but they are turning against us? Is ours a cruel destiny of being only another biological species unique to this planet that has no other meaning beyond our chance existence? Are we perhaps an evolutionary aberration of Nature accidentally given the power (misused intelligence) to destroy the balance of this exceptional planet. As a self-fulfilling species, have we earned our nemesis of extinction?.

Such thoughts are not comforting to the human soul, but challenging to the rational mind.

CHAPTER NOTES

INTRODUCTION NOTES

1.   Louise B. Young, "Easter Island: Scary Parable", WORLD MONITOR, Christian Science Monitor, August, 1991, pp40-45.
2.   Ibid., p.42.
3.   Ibid., p.43.

CHAPTER 1 - NOTES

1.   David Suzuki, "Man's Fate Will Be Known in Our Children's Lifetime, Vancouver Sun, Saturday, July 27, 1991.
2.   United Nations' statistics as quoted in the Christian Science Monitor, July 10-16, 1992 " World Population", P.9.
3.   Steven M. Stanley, John Hopkins University, quoted in article by R. Roylance, Baltimore Evening Sun, reprinted in the Victoria Times-Colonist, Victoria, B.C., Canada, Sunday, October, 1989, "Humanity May Owe Big Brain to the Ice Age Trek."
4.   Ibid., Stanley.
5.   Paul Tisdale, IN SEARCH OF HUMAN ORIGINS, Toronto, Canadian Broadcasting Corporation, c1981.
6.   Richard Foster Flint, THE EARTH AND ITS HISTORY, New York, W.W. Norton, c.1973.
7.   Ibid.
8.   John A. J. Gowlett, ASCENT TO CIVILIZATION: THE ARCHAEOLOGY OF EARLY MAN, London, Roxby Archaeology Limited, Roxby & Lindsey Press, c1984, P.63.
9.   Ibid., P.56.
10.   Ibid., P.64
11.   Richard E. Leakey, THE MAKING OF MANKIND, New York, E.P. Dutton, c1981, P.99.
12.   Ibid., P.97.
13.   Ibid., Flint, P.381.
14.   Ibid., P.389.
15.   Clive Ponting, A GREEN HISTORY OF THE WORLD, New York, Penguin Books, 1993.
16.   Ibid., Gowlett, P. 156.
17.   TV documentary
18.   Colin McEvedy, THE MACMILLAN WORLD HISTORY FACT FINDER, New York, MacMillan Publishing Company, 1985, P. 11.
19.   Ibid., Gowlett, P.153.
20.   David Attenborough, THE FIRST EDEN: THE MEDITERRANEAN WORLD AND MAN, London, Collins, c1987. P. 68.
21.   Ibid., Gowlett, P.158.
22.   Ibid., P.158.
23.   Colin Tudge, THE ENVIRONMENT OF LIFE, New York, Oxford University Press, c1988, P.132.
24.   Ibid., Leakey, P.122.
25.   Ibid., Gowlett.
26.   Joseph Campbell, MYTHS TO LIVE BY, New York, Bantam Books, 1973, P.63.
27.   Ibid., Gowlett, P. 160,
28.   Ibid., P.182.
29.   Ibid., P.183.
30.   Ibid., Campbell, P.179.
31.   Ibid., Leakey, P.266.
32.   Ibid., P.107.
33.   Ibid., P. 229.
34.   Ibid., Gowlett, P. 153.
35.   James Dale Davidson and Lord William Ress-Mogg, THE GREAT RECKONING: HOW THE WORLD WILL CHANGE IN THE DEPRESSION OF THE 1990s, New York, Summit Books, c1991. P.50.

36. Homer-Dixon, "China's Challenge", Maclean's Magazine, September 4, 1995, Pp.25-29.

CHAPTER 2 - NOTES

1. Joseph Campbell, MYTHS TO LIVE BY, New York, Bantam Books, June, 1973, P.63.
2. Ibid., P.65.
3. John Gowlett, ASCENT TO CIVILIZATION: THE ARCHAEOLOGY OF EARLY MAN, London, Roxby Archaeology Ltd. Roxby and Lindsey Press, c1984, P.182.
4. Colin McEvedy, THE MACMILLAN WORLD HISTORY FACTFINDER, New York, Macmillan Publishing Co., 1985, P.183.
5. John B. Theberge, "We Can't Go Home Again", Field Notes, EQUINOX, Camden, Ontario, Equinox Publishing, No. 69, June, 1993, P.21-22.
6. New York Times, quoted in Environment, restated in the Times-Colonist, Tues, September 5, 1995, B6.

CHAPTER 3 - NOTES

1. Gywnne Dyer, HUMAN RACE, Canadian Broadcasting Company, Chn.2, Sunday, Sept. 18, 1994.
2. Ibid., Davidson, Rees-Mogg.
3. Peter Lane, THE INDUSTRIAL REVOLUTION: THE BIRTH OF THE MODERN AGE, London, Werdenfeld and Nicolson, c.1979, P.14.
4. Ibid., P.40.
5. Ibid., P.59.
6. Ibid., P.15.
7. Ibid., The Universal Almanac, P.326.
8. Ibid., P.325.
9. Sylvia Ann Hewlitt, THE CRUEL DILEMMAS OF DEVELOPMENT, c.1980.
10. Ibid., Universal Almanac, P.329.

CHAPTER 4 - NOTES

1. "Stats Quo" INSIGHT, Weekend Vancouver Sun, September 17, 1994, B2.
2. Paul R. Ehrlich & Anne H. Ehrlich, THE POPULATION EXPLOSION, New York, Simon and Schuster, c1990, P.47.
3. Suzuki, "Man's Fate Will Be Known in Our Children's Lifetime", Vancouver Sun, Vancouver, B.C., Canada, Sat. July 27, 1991.
4. THE UNIVERSAL ALMANAC, 1993, ed. John W. Wright, Kansas City, Andrews and McMeel, c1992. P.352.
5. Ibid., P.354.
6. Ibid., P.326.
7. Brad Knickerbocker, "Rio Reminder: Population Is Not an Isolated Issue", Christian Science Monitor, July 10-16, 1992, P.15.
8. George D. Moffett III, "Fertility Rates Decline in Third-World Nations", Christian Science Monitor, July 10-16, 1992, P.10.
9. Ibid.
10. 1992 WORLD POPULATION, Graph display, Christian Science Monitor, July 10-16, P.9.
11. Ibid., information gleaned from the graph.
12. Paul R. Ehrlich & Anne H. Ehrlich, THE POPULATION EXPLOSION, New York, Simon and Schuster, c1990. P.41.
13. Sandra Postel, "Carrying Capacity: Earth's Bottom Line," STATE OF THE WORLD, 1994, ed. Lester R. Brown et al., New York, W.W Norton, c1994, P.6.
14. George D. Moffett III, "World Population", Christian Science Monitor, July 10-16, 1992, P.9.
15. Martin Walker, "A hungry China may soon need to eat more food than exists", Weekend Sun, Saturday, September 23, 1995.
16. Derek Llwewellyn-Jones, PEOPLE POPULATING, London, Faber & Faber, c1975, P.23.
17. PHILIP'S INTERNATIONAL WORLD ATLAS, London, George Philip Ltd, c1991. P.18.
18. Ibid., Ehrlich, POPULATION EXPLOSION, P. 39.

19. Ibid., P.39.

20. Ibid., P.39.

21. Associated Press, "World's city growth swamps services", Times-Colonist, Victoria, B.C., Canada, September 20, 1994. P. A1.

CHAPTER 5 - NOTES

1. George Moffett, "Consensus emerges on need to slow population growth", Christian Science Monitor, September 2-8, 1994, P.10.

2. Ibid.

3. Robin Wright, "Population time bomb", Los Angles Times, The Weekend Sun, Saturday, September 3, 1994, B3.

4. Sandra Mackey, THE SAUDIS: INSIDE THE DESERT KINGDOM, Boston, Houghton, Mifflin Co., c1987.

5. "Facts vital to minimize teen births, says report", London, Reuters, quoted in the Times-Colonist, June 28, 1993.

6. George Moffett, "Needs of Adolescents Become Crucial Challenge at Cairo Meeting", Christian Science Monitor, September 9th-15th, 1994, P.1.

7. Ibid. Moffett.

8. "Youngsters' lungs don't develop well in polluted areas," The Canadian Press, Times Colonist, Victoria, Wednesday, May 1, 1996, P D11.

9. World Report on Women's Health, Associated Press, Gale Book of Averages, "Stats Quo", Vancouver Weekend Sun, Canada, Saturday, October 1, 1994.

CHAPTER 6 - NOTES

1. Christian Science Monitor, July 12-16, 1992, P.9, Graphs illustrating population projections to 2150.

2. Ibid., Llwellyen, PEOPLE POPULATING, P.23.

3. Paul Ehrlich- speaking on radio about the Cairo Conference and David Pimentel, agricultural scientist at Cornell University, quoted by Derek Nelson, "What is Earth's Capacity?" Victoria Times-colonist, Sunday, March 13, 1994, A5.

4. Ibid.

5. Norma Greenaway, Southam Press, "Vatican bows, but won't bless entire strategy", Vancouver Sun, Wednesday, September 14, 1994.

6. Ibid.

7. "South Korea" television documentary, based on Frank Gibney's PACIFIC CENTURY, Channel 4, Monday, October 31, 1994, 7:00 P.M.

8. Gywnne Dyer, HUMAN RACE, Part III, Sunday, September 18, 1994, Channel 2, 9:00 P.M.

9. Ibid., PACIFIC CENTURY.

10. George Moffett, "Needs of Adolescents Become Crucial Challenge at Cairo Meeting", Christian Science Monitor, September 9th-15th, 1994, P.1 and 6.

11. "Sterile Arguments", The Economist, March 19th-25th, 1994, P.99.

12. "Around the World", Pro-Choice News, Spring 1996, p. 10.

13. Dianne Rinehart, "Why China doesn't get it", Times-Colonist, August 25, 1995, A5.

14. "Everywhere you turn, women face a backlash against change", Associate Press, quoted in the Times-Colonist, August 25, 1995.

15. "Pope enlists youth to spread life gospel", Canadian Press, Vatican City, Victoria Times-colonist, Canada, Monday, April 10th, 1995, P 12.

16. Herbert N. Woodward, HUMAN SURVIVAL IN THE CROWDED WORLD, McFarland, North Carolina, c.1983, P.76.

CHAPTER 7 - NOTES

1. Universal Almanac, 1993, John W. Wright, ed., Andrews and McMeel, Kansas City, c1992, P.328.

2. Ibid., Universal Almanac, P.326.

3. Eugene Linden, "Population: The Awkward Truth", TIME Magazine, June 20, 1994. P.63.

4. Ibid., Linden.

5. Robin Wright, "Population time bomb", Vancouver Weekend Sun, Canada, Saturday, September 3, 1994, P.B1.

6. "Earthwatch", UN Population Fund.

7.   Ashish Bose, UN population consultant, New Delhi, quoted by Reuters, "Despite successes, India fails to stem population explosion," Times-Colonist, Victoria, Canada, Saturday, September 3, 1994, P.C16.

8.   Rajeev Malik, "India Seeks Harmony Amid Diversity," Christian Science Monitor, Feb 9-16, 1993. P.19.

9.   Ibid., Universal Almanac, P.288.

10.   Statistics Canada, published by Canadian government, Ottawa, 1994.

11.   "Witness", CBC Television documentary, Channel 25, Saturday, November 5, 1994.

CHAPTER 8 - NOTES

1.   Papaeke, EVOLUTION OF PROGRESS, Random House, New York, c.1993, P.92.

2.   Ibid., Papaeke.

3.   Rob Varrick, Canadian Press, "Study links jobless rate to illiteracy", Times-colonist, Thursday, June 6, 1966.

4.   Mark Kurlansky, "On Haitian Soil", AUDUBON Magazine, January-February, 1995, P.52.

5.   Donella Meadows, BEYOND THE LIMITS, quoted in Victoria Times-Colonist, Canada, Friday, May 7, 1993.

CHAPTER 9 - NOTES

1.   Michael Renner, "Creating Sustainable Jobs in Industrial Countries", STATE OF THE WORLD: 1992, W.W. Norton & Company, New York, c1992. Pp 138-154.

2.   Rosemary Speirs, "Copps goes hunting for ban on lead", Victoria Times-Colonist, Friday, July 7, 1995, P.A5.

CHAPTER 10 - NOTES

1.   Richard O'Mara, "Somalia's Apocalypse" Victoria Times-Colonist, August 26, 1992, A5.

2.   Ibid.

3.   "Earthweek", Vancouver Weekend Sun, Canada, Saturday, March 26, 1995.

4.   Robert D. Kaplan, "The Coming Anarchy", ATLANTIC MONTHLY, February, 1994, Pp.44-76.

5.   "Nowhere to Run", John Darnton, New York Times Service, London, for the Toronto Globe and Mail, Saturday, Aug 14, 1993.

6.   "Stats Quo" Vancouver Sun, Saturday, July 10, 1993.

7.   Ibid.

8.   Paul Kaihla, "The People Smugglers", Maclean's Magazine, April 29, 1996, p.17.

9.   Vancouver Sun, August 9, 1991.

10.   Paul Mably, "Lima poverty-support groups lead cholera fight" Times-Colonist, February 11, 1992, P A5.

11.   Andrew Nikiforuk, "A good time for viruses", Toronto Globe and Mail, Saturday, February 11, 1995, P.D8.

12.   Ibid., Nikiforuk quotes Richard Preston in THE HOT ZONE, an account of Ebola

13.   Ibid.

14.   Peter Jaret, "Viruses, On the Edge of LIfe, On the Edge of Death", NATIONAL GEOGRPAHIC, Vol. 186, No.1, July 1994, P. 67.

15.   Ibid., Nikiforuk, Globe and Mail article.

16.   "Philoviruses", WITNESS, Channel 25, Sat. November 5, 1994.

17.   Ibid., Nikiforuk.

CHAPTER 11 - NOTES

1.   Quotation from Kun Wang, working in the Williston Lake area of Northern British Columbia, published in U.S. research journal "Geology". Discovery made by geologists Kun Wang of Ottawa, federal geologist Helmut Geldsetzer and University of Calgary chemist Roy Krouse in 1994. Margaret Munro, "Evidence of ancient disaster found in northern B.C. rocks", Vancouver Sun, Vancouver, Friday, August 5, 1994, P.A2.

2.   Verne Grant, THE EVOLUTIONARY PROCESS: A CRITICAL REVIEW OF EVOLUTIONARY THEORY, Columbia Press, New York, c1985.

3.   Hoimar V. Ditfurth, THE ORIGINS OF LIFE: EVOLUTION AS CREATION, San Francisco, Harper and Row, c1982, P.75.

4.   Ibid., Grant.

5.	Ibid., Grant.
6.	Ibid., Grant.
7.	Ibid., Ditfurth, P. 75.
8.	Ibid., Grant, P.413.
9.	Ibid., Grant, P.413.
10.	Ibid., Ditfurth, P.77

CHAPTER 12 NOTES

1. James E. Lovelock, GAIA: A NEW LOOK AT LIFE ON EARTH, Oxford University Press, Oxford, c1979, P.11.

2. THE EARTH REPORT: THE ESSENTIAL GUIDE TO GLOBAL ECOLOGICAL ISSUES, E. Goldsmith and Nicholas Hilyard, eds., Mitchell Beazley Publishing, London, c1988, P.53.

3. The Miracle Planet, Television documentary series. No. 2. A Japanese series produced by NHK Japan and TV Ontario. Channel 9, 1991.

4. Isaac Asimov and Frederik Pohl, OUR ANGRY EARTH, Tom Doherty Associates, New York, c1991, P.415. Excerpt quoted from Jeremy Leggett in "The Bulletin of the Atomic Scientists", June, 1992

5. Ibid. Miracle Planet, Tape No. 2.

6. Ibid.

7. Ibid.

8. Ibid., Lovelock, p.57.

9. Victoria Times Colonist, July 11, 1992

10. Ibid., Asimov, Pohl P.406.

11. Robert Cooke, "Weather experts report El Nino has new found sister", Times-Colonist, Friday, Jan 28, 1994. P.C5.

12. Ibid.

13. Associated Press, Washington, "El Nino turns tide on weather to create havoc", Victoria Times-Colonist, Wednesday, March 31, 1993, D.14.

14. Robert C. Cowen, "Scientists question global warming theory", Christian Science Monitor, September 16-22, 1994, P.8.

15. Ed Struzik, "Arctic Nesting Chilled Out", Habitat, EQUINOX, No. 68, April, 1993, P.99.

16. "Ice age follows hot on heels of global warming, say scientists," Ecology Briefs, Victoria Times-Colonist Feb.16, 1994.

17. "Warmer Nights" Popular Science Magazine, Feb. 1994. P.19. Scientists: George Kukla of Columbia University's Lamont-Doherty Earth Observatory and Thomas Karl at the National Oceanographic and Atmospheric Administration's National Climatic Data Centre in Asheville, North Carolina.

18. "Heating the Planet", Maclean's Magazine, February 6th, 1995, P. 37.

19. Larry Ephron, THE END: THE IMMINENT ICE AGE AND HOW WE CAN STOP IT, Celestial Arts, Berkeley, California, c. 1988. P.4.

20. Victoria Times-Colonist, Saturday, July 30, 1994, Associated Press, Bonn, P.A2.

21. Ibid.

22. "Earthweek", Vancouver Weekend Sun, Saturday, July 23, 1994.

23. "Winter shows no mercy", USA TODAY, Graph. P.1.

24. John Ritter, "Season will be recalled in superlatives," USA TODAY, Cover Story, Thursday, February 10, 1994.

25. Catherine Foster, Australian Bush Fires Devastate Wildlife, National Park Habitat", Christian Science Monitor, Jan 21-27, 1994.

26. Michael D. Lemonick, "The Ozone Vanishes", Time Magazine, February 17, 1992, P. 63.

27. Bruce Wallace, "Deluge" London, for Maclean's Magazine, February 13, 1995.

CHAPTER 13 - NOTES

1. "World Notes", Maclean's, Nov 21, 1994, P.33.

2. James Lovelock, "Man and Gaia", THE EARTH REPORT, Goldsmith and Hildyard, eds., London, Mitchell Beaszley, c1988, P. 52.

3. David Attenborough, THE FIRST EDEN: THE MEDITERRANEAN WORLD AND MAN, London, Collins/BBC Books, c1987, P.117.

4. Ibid., P.173.

5. UN Environment Programme (UNEP) study. Quoted on P.14 of the Christian Science Monitor, Scott Baldauf, "Farmers and scientists work to save the earth, one acre at a time." August 12-18, 1994.

6. STATE OF THE WORLD, 1988, Lester R. Brown, et al., W.W. Norton, New York, 1988.

7. "Earth's fertile soil supply dwindling, UN study warns", Saturday, Vancouver Sun, April 11, 1992, P.B7.

8. Scott Baldauf, "Farmers and scientists work to save the earth one acre at a time", Christian Science Monitor, August 12-18, 1994, P.14.

9. Tom Mitchell, "Canada's Farmland Vanishing," Sidney Review, Sidney, B.C., Canada, Wed. Dec. 7, 1988.

10. Johannes Overbeek, EROSION AND DESTRUCTIVE UTILIZATION OF LAND, Westport, Connecticut, Greenwood Press, c1976.

11. "As human pressure increases Europe's Alps suffer damage" New York Times News Service, as quoted in "Enviro-Watch", Vancouver Sun, November, 1992.

12. Steve Norman, "Landslide", Earthweek: Diary of the Planet, Times-Colonist, Victoria, Sunday, April 14, 1996, P.F7.

CHAPTER 14 - NOTES

1. Jean Margat, "A hidden asset" WATER AND DESERTS, Unesco Courier, May 1993, P.15-16.

2. L. Sprague De Camp. THE ANCIENT ENGINEERS, New York, Dorset Press, 1963, P.201.

3. Ibid., P.202.

4. Sandra Postel quoted by Bronwen Maddox "World's fresh water tap in peril", Financial Post, Friday, March 9, 1993.

5. Sandra Postel, "Running Dry", UNESCO Courier, May 1993, P.20.

6. Associated Press. "Water waste threatens to create crisis in 90s". Excerpt from Sandra Postel, "Last Oasis: Facing Water Scarcity", News item in Times-Colonist, Victoria, Canada, Sunday, November 15, 1992, P.C2.

7. Ibid., Postel, "Running Dry," UNESCO Courier, P.20.

8. Ibid., P. 19-20.

9. The Universal Almanac, 1993, ed. John W. Wright, Andrews and McMeel, Kansas City, A Universal Press Syndicate, P.350.

10. "Water", National Geographic Special Edition, November, 1993.

11. Ibid.

12. Patrick E. Tyler, "Water problems pose big threat to future China", New York Times, quoted in Times-Colonist, Victoria, Wednesday, November 17, 1993.

13. Ibid.

14. Ibid.

15. Paul Therroux, "RIDING THE IRON ROOSTER: BY TRAIN THROUGH CHINA", New York, Ivy Books, c1988.

16. Marc Lerner, "To Save a Sacred River" Reader's Digest, June, 1994, P.98.

17. Ibid., National Geographic, P.14.

18. Ibid., Postel, "Running dry," May, 1993, P.21.

19. Cheri Thiessen, "Zimbabwe blind to drought's reality," Letter from Africa, Victoria Times-Colonist, Friday, July 24, 1992.

20. Jon Mitchell, "Open Ship Registries: Lax on Safety, Worker Rights", Christian Science Monitor, April 26-May 2, 1996.

21. George D. Moffett III, "Middle East's Cup Runneth Dry" Christian Science Monitor, Thursday, March 8, 1990. pp10-11.

22. George D. Moffett III, "Competition for Water Heightens Tensions", Christian Science Monitor, March 16-22, 1990.

23. Ibid., Moffett "Middle East's Cup Runneth Dry," P.8.

24. Ibid., Moffett, "Competition for Water Heightens Tensions, P.11,

25. Francoise Chipaux, "Time is running out for water", Le Monde, Guardian Weekly, February 16, 1992, P.16.

26. William H. MacLeish, "Water, Water, Everywhere, How Many Drops to Drink?", World Monitor, Published by Christian Science Monitor, Dec. 1990, P.58.

27.   Norman Myers, "Danger Signals", Vancouver Sun, Saturday, May 7, 1994.

28.   William K. Stevens, "A subtle silent spring", New York Times Service, Toronto Globe & Mail, Saturday, August 27, 1994.

29.   Kate Bouey, "Europe Starting to Move on Waste-deep North Sea." Canadian Press, Victoria Times-colonist, Sunday, Dec. 4, 1988.

30.   Jon Bowermaster, " A Town Called Morrisonville", Audubon, July-August, 1993. P.44.

31.   Ibid.

32.   Ibid.

33.   Terence Monmaney, "Born after Chernobyl, kids have mutated genes", Los Angeles Times, quoted in Times Colonist, Victoria, B.C. Page A8

34.   "Witness", CBC News, Channel 2, Saturday, December, 1994.

CHAPTER 15 - NOTES

1.   Charles R. Frink & James G. Horsfall, "The Farm Problem", THE FARM AND THE CITY: RIVALS OR ALLIES? Englewood Cliffs, New Jersey, Prentice Hall, c1980, P.73.

2.   Lester R. Brown,"Facing Food Insecurity", STATE OF THE WORLD: 1994, W.W. Norton, New York, c1994, P.178.

3.   Ibid, pp.177-186.

4.   Associated Press, Washington, "Lack of nutrients harming millions, World Bank says", Toronto Globe and Mail, Friday, December 16, 1994, A11.

5.   Michael S. Serrill, "Feeding Twice As Many", TIME MAGAZINE, November 7, 1994.

6.   Vicki Allen, "UN sounds urgent warning on loss of productive soil", Toronto Financial Post, Wednesday, July 14, 1993.

7.   Ibid., Brown.

8.   Christian Science Monitor, quoted by Robert C. Cowen, in "The beginning of the food crunch", Victoria Times-colonist, Wednesday, March 15, 1995.

9.   Ibid.

10.   Andrew Nikiforuk, "Soil Loss: A Dirty Secret", Equinox, November/December, 1992, P. 111.

11.   Ibid.

12.   Ibid., Allen.

13.   Ibid, Lester Brown, "The Resource Base", P.9.

14.   "Living in South Africa", THE WORLD'S BEST, CBC production, Channel 20, Saturday, January 7, 1995. 6:00PM

15.   Ibid., Frink and Horsfall, P. 85.

16.   Reuters, "Cholera Spread from Peru", Victoria Times/Colonist, December 2, 1991.

17.   Graham Hancock, LORDS OF POVERTY; THE POWER, PRESTIGE AND CORRUPTION OF THE INTERNATIONAL AID BUSINESS, New York, Atlantic Monthly Press, c1989.

CHAPTER 16 - NOTES

1.   Paul and Anne Erhlich, EXTINCTION: THE CAUSES AND CONSEQUENCES OF THE DISAPPEARANCE OF SPECIES, New York, Random House, c1981, from the Preface.

2.   David Suzuki, TIME FOR CHANGE, Toronto, Stoddart, c1994, P.18.

3.   John B. Theberge, "Lonely in Their Millions", Equinox, No. 70, August, 1993.

4.   Extracted from an article on the works of Jane Robertson, a UNESCO specialist and Nancy Mathews, a journalist specializing in environmental questions, UNESCO-Office of Public Information. The quotation used here is from "Of Cockroaches and Roses", UNESCO COURIER, July-August, 1992. P.43.

5.   Victoria Times/Colonist, June 3, 1990.

6.   "Earthweek A Diary of the Planet", Weekend Van Sun, Saturday, June 24, 1995, B2.

7.   Ibid., Ditfurth, P.80.

8.   Mark Trumbull, "Fisheries crisis stretches across the globe", Christian Science Monitor, July 8-14, 1994 P.8.

9.   Ibid., "Of cockroaches and roses"

10.   Ibid.

11. David Rohde, "Worldwide fish depletion sparks gunboat diplomacy over share of the catch", from his book WHAT IN THE WORLD. Christian Science Monitor, August 26-September 1, 1994.

12. "Fishing for Stamps", W5, Eric Malling, Channel 6, CBC, 9:00PM Thursday, September 1, 1994.

13. Ibid., Trumball.

14. Ibid.

15. Ibid., Rohde,

16. Ibid.

17. Ibid

18. Greenpeace Letter: Marc Beaucheasne from the Rainbow Warrior at Sea in the Pacific to Michael Monolson, Greenpeace, Canada, 1991.

19. Ben Barber, "Warming waters cited in coral crisis", Toronto Globe and Mail, Friday, October 26, 1991.

20. Isabel Butler of Maritimes Fisherman's Union citing figures from studies at the Centre for Marine Conservation in Washington, as cited in the Toronto Globe and Mail, Saturday, September 29, 1990, P.2, Section D.

21. Viorel Urma, Associated Press, Constanta, Romania, "Pollution creating cesspool: Scientists fear Black Sea's fate", Victoria Times-Colonist, Wednesday, October 27, 1993, P.B6.

22. "Sowing for Need or Sowing for Greed", Norman Borlang, Channel 4, Tuesday, June 27, 1994.

23. Ibid.

24. Wilber Smith, ELEPHANT SONG, London, Macmillan London Ltd., c1991, P.22,

25. Robert McCauley, "Of Zebra Mussels and Humans: Rogue Species Out of Control" Toronto Globe and Mail, Saturday, June 4, 1994, P.18.

26. Robert Devine, "Botanical Barbarians", Sierra Magazine, January-February, 1994. P.53.

27. "Earthweek", Weekend Sun, Sat. Aug 6, 1994.

28. Letter from the World Wildlife Fund, written by Monte Hummel, President of World Wildlife Canada, Sept 16, 1994,P.4.

29. Dr. Rick Page, Victoria Times-Colonist, Thurs. Feb. 26, 1991, P. A11.

CHAPTER 17 - NOTES

1. Peter Grier, "Hardier corn can feed more hungry People", Christian Science Monitor, July 15-21, 1994, p.8.

2. Ibid., Grier

3. Ibid., Renner, P. 141

CHAPTER 18 - NOTES

1. Robert D. Kaplan, "The Coming Anarchy", Atlantic Monthly, February 1994.pp. 44-76.

CHAPTER 19 - NOTES

1. E.F. Schumacher, SMALL IS BEAUTIFUL: ECONOMICS AS IF PEOPLE MATTERED, New York, Harper & Row, c1973, P. 82.

CHAPTER 20 - NOTES

1. Lucia Mouat, "A World Summit Aims for a New Deal in world Poverty", Christian Science Monitor, February 10-16, 1995, P.1

CHAPTER 21 - NOTES

1. Lewis Thomas, "Seven Wonders", LATE NIGHT THOUGHTS ON LISTENING TO MAHLER'S NINTH SYMPHONE, Boston, G.K. Hall, 1984, P.85.

INDEX

~6~